891.668.

PRESENTING
SAUNDERS LEWIS

PRESENTING
SAUNDERS LEWIS

edited by
ALUN R. JONES
and
GWYN THOMAS

CARDIFF
UNIVERSITY OF WALES PRESS
1983

© *University of Wales*

First edition, 1973
Second edition, 1983
Reprinted, 1991

British Library Cataloguing in Publication Data

Presenting Saunders Lewis.
1. Lewis, Saunders—Criticism and interpretation
2. Authors, Welsh—20th century—Criticism and
interpretation
I. Jones, Alun R. II. Thomas, Gwyn, *1936-*
891.6'68209 PB2298.L49
ISBN 0-7083-0852-X

PRINTED IN WALES
BY DYNEVOR PRINTING COMPANY, LLANDYBÏE

I'r rhai nad ydynt yn gwybod.

ACKNOWLEDGEMENTS

In September 1968 the North Wales Association for the Arts organized a most successful weekend conference at Gregynog on the work of Saunders Lewis. His achievement as dramatist, poet, critic and political essayist was extensively reviewed and discussed. All those who attended the conference were impressed by the fact that although Saunders Lewis has been at the centre of continuing controversy in Wales for more than thirty years, no one doubted his artistic stature or viewed his work with indifference. There are those who admire him with passionate partiality and those who regard him with hostility, but no one familiar with Welsh life and literature could deny his influence or neglect his achievement. His concept of Welsh Culture is rooted firmly in the Welsh language to which artistically he has contributed so heavily and for which politically he has fought with such uncompromising vigour. He has not hesitated to defy existing institutions or the established hierarchies in pursuit of his ideal of Welsh Wales, drawing on the long tradition of the living past to confront the heterodoxies of the present. Even those who reject his ideas of Welsh Nationalism assent to the unity of the unbroken tradition from which, as a writer, he draws his strength. In Welsh-speaking Wales he has influenced the thoughts and feelings of three generations, although in the English-speaking world he is little known. The original impetus of this book emerged from the Gregynog weekend conference. Our hope is that by presenting a selection of his work to the English-speaking world we may gain proper recognition for this remarkable man who has contributed so much to the long tradition of his own language.

The book is divided into three sections: the first contains an assessment of his personal influence on three Welshmen, representing three generations, all of whom are sympathetic to his views and have been profoundly indebted to him; the second consists of four introductory essays on aspects of his achievement; and the third is a selection from his work as a literary and political essayist, as a poet and as a dramatist. Saunders Lewis has done more than most Welsh writers to introduce the life and culture of Wales to the English-speaking world, and all these essays, except that on *The Fate of the Language*, were written in English by him. The poems and the plays are translated from their Welsh originals. In the volume as a whole we have tried to give a balanced view of his work, at the same time bearing in mind the fact that we could not reasonably expect the English reader to have any special knowledge of Welsh culture. *The Fate of the Language*, the poems and the play *Blodeuwedd* have been specially translated for this book. *Siwan*, translated by Emyr Humphreys, has already been successfully presented on the English stage, and Elwyn Jones's adaptation of *Treason* presented as a television play.

In assembling this volume we are very conscious of the help we have received. We are indebted in the first place to the North Wales Association for the Arts who commissioned us to edit the book in the first instance; in particular we would mention our debt to the Literary Panel whose members helped and encouraged us, to Sir Ben Bowen Thomas, the Association's Chairman, and to Mr. J. O. Jones, the Secretary. We are grateful to our contributors for their generosity, in particular to Emyr Humphreys and Elwyn Jones, and to Bedwyr Lewis Jones and D. Tecwyn Lloyd for their advice. We would also like to express our thanks to Miss Marian Elias for her help, encouragement, typing and all the chores she happily undertook on our behalf. We are particularly grateful to David Jones for his generosity in agreeing to edit what was originally a private letter and allowing us to use it as the *Introduction* to the book.

Finally, we are very aware of our indebtedness to Saunders Lewis himself. He is in no way responsible for the selection of the material or, of course, the quality of the translations. He considered it improper that he should see the book before publication. Yet he is not only the subject of the book—which we offer to him as a token of our gratitude—but at all times made it possible for the book to be produced. We only hope we have done him some justice.

Acknowledgements are due to: R. S. Thomas, *Poetry Wales*, and Christopher Davies, the *Western Mail*, Keidrych Rhys, *Blackfriars*, the British Broadcasting Corporation, John M. Todd and Longmans, Green and Co. Ltd., *Y Ddraig Goch*, *Y Traethodydd*, Gwasg Gee, Gwasg Aberystwyth, Elek Books, John Farquharson, the University College of Cardiff (for the photograph by Hylton Warner of the bust by Kostek Wojnarowski).

ALUN R. JONES
GWYN THOMAS

University College of North Wales, Bangor

March 1972

BIOGRAPHICAL DETAILS

1893   October. Born in Wallasey, the son of the Rev. Lodwig Lewis and Mary Margaret Lewis (*née* Thomas).
Privately educated at the Liscard High School for Boys, Wallasey.

1911–14   Student at Liverpool University.

1914–18   Volunteered for military service. Served as an officer with the South Wales Borderers, mainly in France.

1918–20   Returned to Liverpool University. Graduated with first-class honours in English. Did postgraduate research; a version of this research was eventually published under the title *A School of Welsh Augustans*.

1922–36   Lecturer in the Welsh Department, University College of Wales, Swansea.

1924   31st July. Married Margaret Gilcriest, the daughter of William and Grace Gilcriest, who had come to Liverpool from Wicklow in Ireland. The family were Irish Wesleyans. Mrs. Saunders Lewis is the first Catholic in her family since the time of John Wesley. Mr. and Mrs. Lewis have one daughter, Mair.

1926–39   President of the newly-formed Welsh Nationalist Party (subsequently known as Plaid Cymru).

1932   16th February. Received into the Roman Catholic Church.

1936   With D. J. Williams and the Rev. Lewis Valentine he set fire to an R.A.F. Bombing School at Penyberth in the Llŷn Peninsula, Caernarfonshire. The three were tried at Caernarfon Assizes; the jury failed to reach a decision. The trial was removed to London. The three were sentenced to nine months' imprisonment.
Saunders Lewis was dismissed from his post as Lecturer at the University College, Swansea.

1937–52   Lived at Llanfarian, near Aberystwyth, Cardiganshire. Did some journalistic work (from 1939–51 he contributed articles to a column, 'Cwrs y Byd' ('World Affairs') to *Baner ac Amserau Cymru* (*The Banner and Times of Wales*).

1952   Appointed Lecturer in the Welsh Department, University College of South Wales and Monmouthshire, Cardiff.

1957   Retired from his post at the University College, Cardiff.

1963   Honorary President of Cymdeithas yr Iaith Gymraeg (The Welsh Language Society).
Now lives, and has lived for some time, in Penarth, near Cardiff.

CONTENTS

SAUNDERS LEWIS

And he dared them;
Dared them to grow old and bitter
As he. He kept his pen clean
By burying it in their fat
Flesh. He was ascetic and Wales
His diet. He lived off the harsh fare
Of her troubles, worn yet heady
At moments with the poets' wine.

A recluse, then; himself
His hermitage? Unhabited
He moved among us; would have led
To rebellion. Small as he was
He towered, the trigger of his mind
Cocked, ready to let fly with his scorn.

R. S. THOMAS

INTRODUCTION
by
DAVID JONES

We all find it very difficult to say in written words what we feel about a personal friend, all the more so when that friend is a very remarkable man indeed—the width and range of his abilities is astonishing, his ruthless expression of what he perceives to be true, or what he believes to be true, with regard to any given matter, seems to me one of his exhilarating qualities—and, in my experience, such as it is, he is just as straight-forward in some personal assessment of a friend's work as he is in public matters. I think it is this undeviating 'honesty'—though that's not the word I want—and his inability to say other than he thinks, however painful it may chance to be, is what makes one respect him and hold him in affection. But while one can indicate what one feels in a private letter it is a different matter to find the form of words appropriate to a printed publication. I would dearly wish to be represented among those who pay tribute to him, even if only with half a line. But, for me, the ideal way, owing to what our friends in the States call 'hospitalization', it is not, for reasons indicated above, for the time being possible. I have been trying to think of some alternative way, but have not so far found one.

However, the thing *that matters* is your 'introducing', as they say, this remarkable Venedotian Welshman to English readers, or, at least, to some, and although I suppose but few of those will say what the author of the Epistle to the Hebrews wrote of Melchisedek 'consider how great this man was.' Yet at least your publication can hardly fail to indicate to its readers, Welsh or English, something of the wide-ranged ability, clarity of mind, direct appreciation and undeviating expression (however it shocked the susceptibility of many) of what he saw and sees to be the hard truths—or what, at least, he *believes* to be those truths concerning his ardently beloved *patria*.

Your publication should also not fail to indicate his width of appreciation of the arts of man, especially of Western man and the whole tradition of Europe. A matter which, for historical reasons, is not all that common to most Welshmen.

The intense preoccupation with the oral and aural arts, so that *cerdd dafod* and *cerdd dant* appear to have been quasi-tribal, quasi-feudal Welsh, along, of course, with the necessary and continuous practice in the arts of warfare as noted by Giraldus Cambrensis in the twelfth century, remained characteristic as noted by others; Borrow, for instance, in the nineteenth century—except, of course, there was no interest at that time in the arts of war.

But here again—though Welsh scholars, especially those whose studies have been especially concerned with the history of the Welsh 'bardic' tradition, and who have been or are fully aware of the beauty of that complex metric, have tried to convey to English readers the nature and intentions of Welsh poetry and its particular felicities—no one, as far as I am aware, other than Saunders, has stated quite simply that the corpus of medieval Welsh metric at its height is worthy of comparison with that miracle in stone, seen at its best at Chartres. In fact, *I think* he has said that the edifice of Welsh versification is *the* Welsh contribution to the Western European culture.

So his width of apperception, his love of France and Italy, his ability to read Dante, his sense of the splendour of Santa Sophia and all his visual perceptions have in no sense dimmed his intense, critical, informed, scholarly love and understanding of the *cerdd dafod* and *cerdd dant* of his native 'Kymry Vawr'* (as Bleddyn Fardd, in that terrible and hopeless winter of 1282 had the audacious faith to call his stricken country).

Your publication should, among other things, help to dissipate the idea that Welshmen who show a concern for the things of Wales are necessarily of narrow outlook and the more that image of them is one of restriction in some form of 'nationalism', so much the more are they imaged as unrealistic, fanatical and removed from the actual in our twentieth-century world—perhaps a reading of a translation of *Brad*† may do something to modify these views in such as hold them. And certainly in general his wide interests and attitudes must, except among those of invincible prejudice, make it plain that he is a man of particular *pietas* towards his Welsh heritage

---

* I hope that's the right thirteenth-century spelling for our Cymru Fawr, but I've seen the original only once and have no possible means of checking up anything here. [*It is, of course, correct.—Ed.*]

† I was interested in how the Welsh translation of those German military commanders' ranks and titles, etc., went so convincingly into Welsh, by Saunders choosing forms that took one back to the forms used in sub- or post-Roman Britain. They worked much better than corresponding English terms do. (See p. 301 *et seq.*)

and who is known for his passionate but reasoned love toward and defence of the language and who, as mentioned above, has referred to Welsh versification at its peak as the greatest single contribution of the Welsh genius to Welsh culture and comparable to what was achieved in stone and glass at Chartres, can hardly be regarded as narrow in his assessments or uninformed or liable to make absurd comparisons because of his ignorance of the splendour of forms of a vastly wider culture-complex. There is nothing 'small' or 'parochial' about his fierce and unbreakable devotion to the things of his own land.

I remember that some four or five years back he delivered an address on Ann Griffiths at the National Eisteddfod of Wales, Newtown, and in the intervening years from then until now I have chanced to meet various Welsh-speaking people who were present, and without exception, though each of them was of widely differing professions and views and temperaments, they all confessed to being thankful they had not missed the occasion, and one, if not two, who had previously held Saunders in respect, said what amounted to: 'Well, I have always held Saunders in esteem even while not holding to his view, but I had not previously gauged the intense and very deep religious nature of his mind and how, without the remotest sense of conscious effort, his splendid command of the language at its best, free of all rhetorical padding, held his very mixed audience throughout—it certainly held me—and if only you could follow spoken Welsh I'm sure you would have felt the same.' My only reason for mentioning this particular occasion is that the five or six Welshmen well known to me who were present, all of *very* differing temperaments and professions, were clearly much impressed, and two, one in particular, had still, some years later, a remembrance of the *gravitas* and *pietas* of Saunders. Since then I have read the English translation, and though it gave the sense, restraint and (knowing Saunders) some of his amusing digs, for that's another pronounced characteristic of his, his irresistible sense of humour, it made me still more grieved that I have no Welsh, but merely know a bit *about* it, its behaviour and the beauty of its sounds and correspondences of sound.

Saunders Lewis the Man

Personal Views

Saunders Lewis—A Man of Destiny

London has attracted Welshmen since Tudor days, particularly South Walians; while, since the Industrial Revolution, Liverpool has been the main attraction for North Walians. As stressed in his own writings, Saunders Lewis' home, the manse in Liverpool, and the church in his father's charge, were practically as Welsh in speech and atmosphere as when their members were still at their old homes in some Welsh countryside where most of them had come from. Yet, in his younger days, he does not seem to have indicated any marked attachment to his own country and nation, apart from the real enjoyment of holidays in the native haunts of his family in Anglesey. Indeed, one gathers from his later writings that his attitude was a somewhat superior one, even a snobbish one towards these things, because of their relative insignificance in the wider world he had now entered. Nor was this to be wondered at, perhaps, in a bright young intellectual, who was attracted by the cult of experience for its own sake, and towards a certain group of French authors. Never a pacifist at heart, it is possible that his great love for France and French literature may have prompted his early enlistment in the army.

Even to mention the main events in Saunders Lewis' wonderful career would be like emptying a bucket into an egg-cup. The story of his conversion to Welsh Nationalism, as told by him in a remarkable article in *Y Faner* (*The Banner*), 24th January 1924, is absorbing; at the height of the First World War, in the wet summer of 1916, Saunders Lewis was in the trenches at Loos, in Belgium, flicking aside the buzzing German shells with his one hand, and with the other holding a book by his favourite French author, Maurice Barrès. One of these books by Barrès relates the story of a brilliant, sophisticated artist, completely surfeited by the shallow pretentiousness of the world around him. One day he revisits his old home in Alsace-Lorraine where, for the first time in his life, his eyes are opened to the quiet dignity and the modest, natural, self-assured ways of his fellow-countrymen. This insight so surprises and overwhelms him that his whole philosophy of life and of human existence is changed. Here are two statements of his new convictions: 'It is by throwing himself into the life of his country and his people that a man can come to know himself and cultivate his soul fully and

3

richly and to live as an artist to the limits of his consciousness.
. . . He who cuts himself off from his own past, his own land, is
starving his soul and frustrating his whole being.'

Saunders Lewis sums up Barrès' great influence upon him in this
way: 'It was through him that I discovered Wales, and the
hedonism of my youth was completely transformed. My play
Noble Blood is an unsuccessful attempt to transpose *Colette Baudoche*
into Welsh. And of all my books the one I value most dearly is one
of Barrès' works which he gave me with the words "À Monsieur
Saunders Lewis, sympathique hommage, de Maurice Barrès"
inscribed on the fly-leaf.'

Saunders Lewis does nothing worth doing by half. That is the
secret of his terrific impact. His conversion to Roman Catholicism
and to Welsh Nationalism seem to have taken place simultaneously
within him, the ideal and the practical aspect of his being, each as
it were a complement to the other.

On his conversion to Welsh Nationalism, Saunders Lewis, with
the insight of a true prophet, saw from the beginning that the only
way of preserving the life and integrity of the Welsh nation was by
the establishment of Self Government and a Parliament on Welsh
soil, responsible to the people of Wales. A nation without a past
was a nation without a future. So the primary objective was to
restore to Wales a fair picture of her own past. His book, *An Outline
of the History of Welsh Literature*, may be regarded as a kind of blue-
print for his creation of a new nation in Wales, based on her worthy
past.

A mere mention of one other event in the marvellous career of
Saunders Lewis must suffice. His trial and condemnation by a
foreign jury at the Old Bailey, after the failure of a Welsh jury to
convict at the Caernarfon Assizes in the Penrhos Aerodrome case,
and his subsequent shameful dismissal as a lecturer by his own college
at Swansea—whilst his fellow 'criminals' on the same charge,
a well-known Baptist minister and a secondary school teacher,
without any English, were immediately reinstated in their offices on
their release from prison—all these, at the time, received wide
publicity.

He was for many years a political and literary critic and sustained
the mind and spirit of the Welsh nation during the arid and dangerous period of the Second World War. And at the end of fifteen years
he, the most brilliant son of Wales, was reinstated as a lecturer at

the University College, Cardiff, under his old friend, Professor G. J. Williams.

What kind of man is this Saunders Lewis in ordinary, everyday life? Well, quite a fair question. But the answer lies mainly with the person asking. Many people who only know him at a distance seem to regard him as a snob, a little aristocrat, stand-offish, a hyper-highbrow who would freeze you stiff with one glance of that pair of large and wonderful blue eyes of his. Naturally, you cannot expect a man of his type to suffer fools gladly. But should he, by any chance, strike upon a quaint or an odd one, he can be very tolerant and amusing with him. But to know him well, to know him as he really is, you must go on a holiday with him, a long, long holiday— with all expenses paid, all the better. (Ask Val, then.)* There you will find him delightful, charming, loyal, and as warmly affectionate as a schoolboy without homework. He can also be, mind you, as deadly serious as a committed saint, with all the sins of his generation on his soul.

Saunders Lewis, in some respects, may be compared with the late Charles de Gaulle. And the long and short of it is—that Saunders is rather fond of European comparisons. Both gentlemen, to start with, are about the same age, and have apparently been in the wars from birth. Both have long noses and have long memories; and both have become profoundly involved in the destinies of their own respective countries. And as de Gaulle helped to lift France out of the ditch of her own temporary political ineptitude, so has Saunders Lewis helped to jerk Wales to a considerable extent out of the *swamp of her own political ineptitude, centuries deep.*

The main difference between the two champions appears to be that de Gaulle on his part entered the lists with the mass of his people shouting lustily for him, whereas Saunders Lewis entered his lists with the vast majority of his own fellow countrymen howling him down. In that respect, then, the personal triumph of the latter seems, potentially, the greater of the two.

D. J. WILLIAMS

---

* 'Val', i.e. the Rev. Lewis Valentine, who, together with D. J. Williams and Saunders Lewis, was responsible for burning the bombing school at Penyberth. (See p. 115 *et seq.*)

The 'holiday' is, of course, a reference to their subsequent imprisonment.

D. J. Williams was a most respected Welsh nationalist and writer who died on 4th January 1970. This tribute to his friend was one of the last things he wrote.

Outline of a Necessary Figure

i

A narrow white face above a large steering wheel. Recognizable even in a squat car hurtling down an Aberystwyth street. There is a schoolgirl in the back enjoying the ride. And there he is. The necessary figure. The author of books that evoke a more exciting country slaps the steering wheel with his gloved hand. By force of personality he has made the old language a mystery you must struggle to decipher. If there is more to history than a catalogue of classroom defeats he is the one who offers an honourable future. And Welsh is the only true key to open the locked caves where the heroes sleep. The University of Wales doesn't believe this. But he does. That is why they turned him out. But he still exists. And always will. A narrow white face above a large steering wheel.

ii

You have been struggling to read *Canlyn Arthur* (*In the Steps of Arthur*) using a dictionary. It has made you attend meetings and it has made history less confusing. Here at last is a picture of a possible Wales. A viable unit. Written as vigorously as a little Lenin but concerned not with power but with the vital life stream that it is the purpose of power to preserve or destroy. Fundamental stuff but not appreciated by left-wing friends. He's right and they are wrong but you are still slightly torn. You wander into a mass meeting by the back entrance and there he is, waiting in an ante-room, his arms folded, his head lowered and chin extended grimly. He has just been vomiting. He says so. He can't bear public meetings. You see at once he is doing it against his will. Duty. Conscience. Integrity. They exist. He has them. That is what makes him fold his arms so tightly. To prevent himself running away. Or keep down the revulsion. Does that mean he hates or merely dislikes the masses? The Welsh mass in particular singing hymns in an orgy of sentimentality, pointlessly and windily ardent; crafty and cowardly after cooling down.

You decided it is perhaps love after all and that this accounts for the stern measured words when he speaks, a diminutive figure on a distant platform. He is teaching not wooing. Are politicians meant to teach or to woo? No wooing here certainly and no purple patches. Extended reasoning. Flashes of caustic wit. The mass admires but only a small minority adores. He is a leader giving a lead but the path to follow looks ominously like the edge of a razor. Now you say wisely to yourself if only he made a few concessions. Especially to fashionable left-wing sentiment. A friendly reference to such popular figures as Joseph Stalin or Harold Laski. Then your friends might stop making those hurtful gibes about putting the clock back. A few concessions. He is startlingly intelligent but he doesn't know how to make them.

iii

A war has been arranged. But it hasn't started. There are black-berries still on the brambles but the devil has spat on them and they are no longer fit to eat. The west is getting ready for winter. All afternoon in the damp wood he stalks game. Shots are fired but nothing gets killed. Then there is a farm house tea before a wood fire. The wind turns and the room fills with smoke. The news on the wireless is minimal and fatalistic. Rain falls at nightfall. Some-where on the road home the car breaks down. It isn't far from Cwm Cuch and the thick woods that hid the mouth of Hell. This is the moment for the Prince from the Underworld to appear with a crying pack of trained white hounds with red tipped ears! They could change places for a year or for the duration. The Prince of the Underworld could take over or cast a spell and preserve Wales from extinction during the coming Armageddon. There is nothing unrealistic about this. The Ministry of Information, Thomas Jones, C.H., Ll.G., University Principals, Archbishops, Miners' Leaders, Mr. Chamberlain and Mr. Churchill have all in their different ways made it clear that Wales and Welshness are a bit of fancy-dress to be put away in a bottom drawer until the serious business is over: along with Welsh Broadcasting, the Eisteddfod, sweets, bananas, Sunday School trips, silk stockings and other non-essentials. Couldn't we all hibernate in a Hobbit-like under-world and reappear as fresh as paint when the war was all over? There isn't much point in passing on the bright suggestion. He is concerned with getting the car repaired. He is concerned with his wife at home worrying, and an article he has to write that night. And he knows what's coming. He knows all about war.

iv

Late morning in the intense heat of an Italian army barracks serving as an overcrowded refugee camp. Everywhere there is a stink of displaced persons and stale soup. The man in the corridor still has a kid lying in a broken suitcase lined with filthy straw. The goat died. The mail has arrived. Several copies of *Y Faner* and a copy of Thomas Parry's *Hanes Llenyddiaeth Gymraeg* (*A History of Welsh Literature*). Outside the camp there are the marvels of the renaissance city. What does it matter whether or not you are Welsh in a place like this? You only need to see his name and you are fascinated by the same old nagging question. Is he seriously suggesting that no good will come of Welshmen unless they have their roots in Wales? All this business about roots is peasant language. Like these men from the Abruzzi impatient for their own soil, land mines or no land mines. Not everyone wants to go back. Not all places are worth going back to. In the long barrack room a party of one hundred Jews, who have somehow spirited themselves down the peninsula, have to be locked up for the night. They are determined to get to Palestine but the authorities don't want them to go. (Who are the Authorities? The Armies of the Occupying Powers. Words for a Cantata.) While you are privileged with a little solitude in your sweaty sleeping quarters in the Administration block, you read successive numbers of *Cwrs y Byd* (*World Affairs*) far into the hot night and the Jews steal away through the high windows. They pass two Caribiniere fast asleep and bribe their way through the locked gates. They have accomplices in the occupying armies and they are quickly poured towards Brindisi and into the Palestine pipeline. A white-haired Indian Army colonel is very cross, but nobody really seems to mind. There is too much else to worry about. They are off to reoccupy a land they lost more than a thousand years ago. Does he want to turn the Welsh into troublesome Jews? His sermons are always uncomfortable.

v

Why do so many exiles seem to end up in London? You are housed in the wrong end of Chelsea and you have given up sugar because of the Mister Cube campaign: rampant capitalism is trying to prise the dying labour limpets out of the stone seats of power. The old order is flooding back on a tide of public appetite and the nonconformity into which you have married would prefer rationing and fair shares for all. Somewhere an English vision has faded and it brings you as near as you will ever come to supporting socialism. All this has to be said to explain the odd fragments of lengthy letters, ungainly and fortunately unposted, unpublished, polemics against his 'Catholic' social and economic policies. As a bizarre intellectual exercise you try to reconcile left-wing reformism and practical nonconformity and keep in touch with Bohemia as well. Not a bad world when the sun sets behind the black chimneys of the power station and the tugs hoot as they fuss up and down the broad river. Painters live here and work in a bizarre poverty undreamt of in bourgeois or peasant Wales: rooms without carpets, cups without saucers, men without please and thank you and women without inhibitions. Here comes a philosopher, heavy beads about his neck, hand in hand with a piano-playing Pole engaged in a life-long search for the first Chinese Pope. But traffic jams are slowly assembling in the streets again. Armies of cars advancing. The journey to a consumer's heaven has begun. Ration cards, those noble symbols of equality, are being burnt and the long shop windows are gasping with the first pyramids of mass production. The light of austerity is going out and in any case as the person who is wiser than yourself assures you, London is no longer a place to bring up children. Not Welsh children anyway. All good roads lead back to Wales.

vi

With the excuse that all writers are communicators you find yourself working with the BBC. One of the charms of the position is that you are obliged not to interest yourself actively in politics. Henceforward all struggles must take place on the cultural front. You have a simple policy and it gets blessings all round: get new work out of Welsh writers in both languages: put European drama into Welsh: put the best Welsh dramatists into English and have nothing at all to do with Shakespeare. You guide your uncertain steps across the road to the University. In the library there is a fierce-looking bronze bust of our necessary figure and there he is not far away browsing among the foreign periodicals. Now he is not so much necessary as unavoidable. No programme for Welsh drama could avoid having this figure firmly in the centre. It is all so clear but should you conduct business in a series of flashes of intuition? Hardly. He has no idea who you are. The whole library ticks like an unexploded bomb. Any necessary figure is experienced in saying no. You belong to an organization now and perhaps he believes that alien organizations are the devil? You mumble ineffectively but outside the silent library he gives you a fair hearing. He folds his arms and lowers his head. He approves of your purpose and the job immediately becomes lighter and much more enjoyable.

vii

A canteen full of anecdotes . . . Images of actors. Hugh Griffith, in the most inconvenient studio in London, plays the leader of an Eastern European underground movement lying on a sofa the microphone a few inches from his mouth, because he is recovering from a motor accident. The necessary author is present and he happily writes and plays the brief part of a messenger. Hugh is making a spectacular appearance in *The Waltz of the Toreadors*. He amazes us one evening by limping across the stage with a grown woman on his back and then he takes us out to a late supper where we are surrounded by glamour. Hugh bewilders the wine waiter and the necessary figure smokes the largest cigar you have ever seen. He has an electric effect on actors. They all want him to write plays for them—preferably in English. He is tempted. You are sure he is tempted. Late at night in the West End the Theatres stand like the kingdoms of the earth and the stars glitter in their expensive suits . . . Images of food. *Sole bonne femme* and *Muscadet*. An oasis of France in the Cardiff docks. Seagulls circle around rusting derricks. Elderly Welsh waitresses march in and out of the kitchen with varicose gaiety. They are anxious to please. So are the stockbrokers and the merchant adventurers inside their stiff collars and dark suits bulging into plans for profits and expansion. They want to pay him court over the brandy. What do they see in him? Daring of course. A potential pirate. Like Gwilym Breos he would climb to the top of the ladder and jump without giving a damn . . . Russians. Images of Russians. A delegation on tour under the auspices of the British–Soviet Friendship League. Squat confident men in the Angel Hotel, Cardiff. More earnest than the business men. A very agreeable dinner. They are chiefly interested in heavy industry and peasant poetry. They are led by the secretary of the U.S.S.R. Writers' Union who looks like Kruschev masquerading as a *bardd gwlad* (people's poet). Your necessary figure is in merry mood. He mentions Pasternak. There is an awkward silence followed by lengthy explanations. It turns out that Pasternak may be quite a lot better off than your necessary figure was when he was sacked from the Welsh University. You mention this to him and he is greatly amused. The Russians look suspicious. You decide not to explain. The meal progresses. The secretary of the U.S.S.R. Writers' Union announces he is about to recite Pushkin. He does so with great vigour, thumping the table and flinging his arms about. Your necessary figure pushes back his chair and announces he is about to recite Dafydd ap Gwilym. Respect all round. On the way home he is overtaken by a laughing fit. He recited the middle part of the poem twice over and nobody noticed.

viii

It becomes acceptable to say that his plays lend themselves beautifully to television. There are many two-handed scenes, many passionate arguments finely constructed and the plots are compelling to the point of being melodramatic. They translate well and for a time they enjoy a vogue and they are televised in Germany, Belgium, Spain, Scandinavia. *Treason* goes particularly well in Germany. But there are legal difficulties. Names of living generals have to be changed. He admits to enjoying it all. With a sudden burst of patriotic zeal a muster of internationally famous Welsh actors agree to take part in a dual production, one in Welsh, one in English. But they are filming all over the place. One has to be in America, another can only work in the evenings. The dual production is transferred to radio. Everyone is marvellous and altruism triumphs. Over a fortnight in a dozen different studios at all hours of the day and night *Brad* and *Treason* go piecemeal on tape. One lunch hour Emlyn Williams and Richard Burton propose we send a telegram which reads like a loyal address composed in basic Welsh. A further word will be sent inviting him up to a special performance. (It will be a preview of what a national theatre could do.) This goes astray. The special performance never materializes. You return with innumerable cans of tape. He is disappointed but wholly forgiving.

ix

It becomes acceptable to say that a failed politician has been transformed into a triumphant playwright or that the idealist who failed to change the course of Welsh history is finding completeness and fulfilment in Welsh literature. A comfortable doctrine. It fits with the image of a mellow ageing, a man in his late sixties enjoying his due mead and fair measure of success. The bomb has been defused. Moguls of the corporations smile expansively, nod and tell each other how wise they were to tell each other so. He looks forward to accepting an honour in the near future from a University college fully Welsh in language and spirit. There are other offers. In the land of fixers everything and everybody can be fixed. And it's not just the honours system. But the phase is temporary. A very intelligent Irish actor-producer soon to become a millionaire goes pale one day at rehearsal and says 'so much violent integrity in one bloody little man'.

x

He is a very private man. In a land where back-slapping and badinage are tokens of manly cameraderie his dignity is often mistaken for aloofness. And he doesn't suffer from that common Welsh weakness: the overwhelming desire to be agreeable. He is perfectly aware that the Welsh nation has rejected his leadership. Even the party he founded would prefer him to become a silent icon that it could bear up aloft as it softly circumvents the narrow and dangerous path he would have it travel. You remember his striking humility. Not the best qualification for a national leader. A definite lack of Hitlerian hysteria or Lloyd George capacity for rhetorical deception or even the common egomania of the romantic artist. You are rehearsing *Esther* in the Temple of Peace. The acoustics are awful but the sun is shining through the long windows. Clifford, playing Mordecai, is wearing the first rose of the season in his buttonhole and the national theatre in his heart. An English actor plays Haman and wants to cut a speech he can't understand. In the second act he is talking to Jewish Esther not knowing of course that she is Jewish. '*It is clear, my lady, that you know nothing of subject races. A defeated people is paralysed with fear. They will go to their destruction like sheep. You can drown their homeland under water and like beggars in a gutter they'll whine their thanks for the trouble you are taking.*' 'What's all this about drowning homelands?' He has a rich actorish voice and gestures like aquatints of Edmund Kean. Your author is leaning against a substantial pillar of the Temple. He gives a grim smile. 'You are lucky enough to be English', he says. 'Leave it out if you don't understand it.'

xi

He moves with unobtrusive skill out of all the niches and down from all the pedestals that are prepared for him. This is very necessary.

To a people with overheated imaginations and low thresholds of pain it is always necessary to emphasise that art is not illusion. In an age manipulated by mass communicators truth often belongs to the single voice. Increasingly our intelligentsia is composed of servants in the pay of an alien state. It is not a situation which allows for great clarity of thought. In fact after so many years you have become convinced that every responsible office in Wales is held by a common type of native whose capacity for self-deception, whose delusions of grandeur are only just contained by his even more powerful instincts of self preservation. Imagine a collier and a socialist riding in a golden coach with the heir to the British throne, deluding himself into the belief that the staged event is his own napoleonic coronation, his hour of glory the ultimate revelation of his life's purpose. In the Welsh atmosphere of sulky and shamefaced inertia such men select each other. Their careers often begin in a burst of undergraduate patriotic fervour but before they reach forty their tongues wag their mother tongue for wangling purposes only and their nationalism has shrunk to an after-dinner joke. They are professional embalmers surrounded by their supine monuments. There seems very little that they cannot prevent happening. For the third or fourth time in ten years they have managed to prevent the idea of a National Theatre becoming a reality that could threaten their complacency. They have every possible source of finance and every large-scale organization firmly under their control. Their masterly inactivities win for them in London golden opinions and honours. Such nice men. And yet you hope they still tremble when one small foot stamps in Westbourne Road. A very necessary figure.

EMYR HUMPHREYS

A Personal View

When I was about seven or eight years old, I happened to hear some people much older than me discussing preachers and related topics in a neighbour's house.

'Who have you got next Sunday?' said one of them.

'Mr. Valentine,' answered another.

Until then my interest in the conversation had been minimal, but my curiosity was aroused by the strange melodiousness of the name. 'Who is Mr. Valentine?' I asked.

'The man who set fire to the aerodrome with Saunders Lewis and that other fellow.'

The answer to my question was spoken quite casually, but I was almost thrown into a trance. 'Setting an aerodrome on fire!' I said to myself. 'If Owain Glyn Dŵr were alive today, that's what he would do!' I delighted as much in the modernity of the deed as in the daring and the undeniable patriotism of the men who had done it.

About twelve years later I had a similar visionary experience when I came across the pamphlet *Why We Burnt the Bombing School* when looking through some books which belonged to an aunt of mine. I had joined the Plaid some two or three years earlier, and as I read the statements of the lecturer and the minister I was thrilled not only by their fearlessness and their sincerity but also by a deep conviction that the current leaders of the National Movement would follow their example by committing an act at Tryweryn which would initiate the National Revolution which would bring our country's freedom.

I was disappointed. Shortly before the demolition and the digging began at Capel Celyn, Plaid Cymru's Executive Committee tried to compromise with the Liverpool authorities. The Scouse imperialists gave their plan a patronizing welcome, the task of building the dam was begun without delay, and eventually the valley was drowned.

The Plaid continued to hope that its prudent diplomacy would be rewarded with sweeping and justified success in the 1959 General Election. But it fared very badly, and many nationalists began to search for more effective and honourable means of defending the interests of the Welsh nation and of ensuring its continued existence.

In 1960, after graduating and before embarking on the inevitable teacher's training course, I went to Bordeaux as an *assistant de langue anglaise*. Influenced by the writings of Saunders Lewis and of Emrys ap Iwan—of whom the former was a disciple—and by friendship with a group of intelligent, cultured and patriotic Catholics, I had come to believe that Wales would be saved only if she re-embraced her European and Catholic inheritance. Therefore, I wanted my stay in France to give me a deep and lasting acquaintance with European Civilization, together with a second language which would be more congenial than English.

I already accepted almost all the customs, liturgies, creeds and dogmas of the Church, reacting cheerfully against the narrowness, philistinism, stupidity and cowardice of the Nonconformity that I knew. To tell the truth, it was one thing only which had held me back from long since becoming a convert, namely the fact that I did not believe in the existence of God. I had asked a Catholic friend how this difficulty might be overcome, and he told me that God was certain to respond to everyone who was truly eager to hear His voice. I believed in all conscience that I was such a person, and I concluded that my unbelief was one of the innumerable disadvantageous consequences of living in Wales. 'He must find it very difficult to communicate with the people of a country which has wandered so far from His paths,' I told myself. 'The position must be very different in France. Is it not his favourite country? Is it not the country most blessed by Him of all the countries of Christendom?' I had anticipated that it would not be very long before I was converted once I had arrived there.

More's the pity, however, I had not lived in France for long before I was forced to acknowledge that it was not the Land of Promise for a Welsh Nationalist, and forced also to change my mind concerning the benefit that Wales would derive from re-embracing the Old Faith. I observed how different the troubled, dirty, industrial France of the time was from the rural civilized France of which our intellectuals of all political shades were enamoured in the thirties. I observed, too, how much more like the conformist Nonconformists of Wales than its fervent Catholics were the Catholics of France. However, it is possible that I should have succeeded in ignoring these blemishes were it not for the attitude of the Church towards the war in Algeria.

At twenty-two I could not confidently declare an incontrovertible belief in the reality of any phenomenon or principle apart from the right of every nation to govern itself and the immorality of everyone and everything that denied that right in any way. I was forced to acknowledge fairly soon after settling in Bordeaux that the vast majority of Catholics whom I knew were not convinced of these truths. I had to conclude, therefore, that either God had neglected the all-important task of enlightening them on the subject, or that His means of communicating with His creatures was abysmally and unpardonably at fault, even in France. Gradually I stopped caring whether He would speak to me or not.

If Catholics were scarce at the meetings and rallies held to protest against the abominable crimes of the French Army in North Africa, Communists were not. And although many were suspicious of their motives and would even deny that they had a right to protest, they *did* at least protest, and were ready also—this could not be denied at all—to fight to the death against the Fascism which the men of the Church were so reluctant to condemn or so anxious, some of them, to defend. I decided at that time that henceforth I would dwell on the Left politically.

In February 1962 Saunders Lewis delivered his radio lecture, *Tynged yr Iaith* (*The Fate of the Language*). At the same time I was a student at the University College of Wales, Aberystwyth. It is likely that the lecture was aimed at the Plaid, but the Plaid did not realize this. Neither was it realized by the nationalists of Aberystwyth. We supposed that the only Welsh nationalist leader whom we respected was calling on us, and on Welshmen of similar inclinations, to form a new movement to fight for the rights of Language. We obeyed, and in August 1962 *Cymdeithas yr Iaith Gymraeg* (*The Welsh Language Society*) was established. By now even the English readers of this volume may be fairly well acquainted with the aims of that movement and with the part it has played in the nationalist struggle during the last eight years. Without doubt, they will become even better acquainted with its activities and methods in the future.

*   *   *   *   *

Saunders Lewis was born in Liverpool. In an interview with Aneirin Talfan, which was televised in May 1960 and published later in the journal *Taliesin*, he claimed that this was not the same as saying that he had been exiled from Wales during his formative years. 'I don't know what the statistics are,' he said, 'but I am fairly certain that there was somewhere in the region of a hundred thousand Welsh-speaking Welshmen in Liverpool throughout my boyhood period. And I should say that at least half of these were monoglot Welsh-speakers who had hardly any English. For example, girls would come to our house—and to my aunt's house in Liverpool —as maids from Anglesey and Caernarfonshire, and they would be monoglot Welsh-speakers. They would attend chapel with us for a few years, then get married, and return to Wales with as little English as they had had when they came to England. There was a monoglot Welsh-speaking community in Liverpool in my time, just as in a village somewhere in Anglesey. Thus it was not in English England that I was born at all, but in a completely Welsh and Welsh-speaking community.'

So be it. But however Welsh his upbringing may have been, it was not the same as that which he would have got had his father been a minister 'in a village somewhere in Anglesey' rather than in Wallasey. The foundations and structure of the Society where Saunders Lewis spent his youth were very different from those of the village and urban communities of Wales in the same period. The secular and religious leaders of Wales during the second half of the last century and the beginning of the present one were cultured shopkeepers, farmers, artisans and common folk. The leaders of the Welsh community in Liverpool were merchants, financiers, and wealthy industrialists.

Saunders Lewis is one of the most brilliant sons of this bourgeoisie —the only strong, self-conscious bourgeoisie which the Welsh nation has ever had. It was from this community that he inherited the thoroughly bourgeois characteristics which make him such a different creature from any of his contemporaries—his energy, his fearlessness, his self-confidence, his arrogance, his uncompromising individuality, his wide culture and his occasional animosity.

He has never disowned the class from which he came. He has praised it more than once. 'The bourgeois is a satirical butt for two classes,' he said in 1923 in a preface to his own translation of *Le Médecin malgré lui*. 'He is ridiculed by the artist because his unadventurous life, his prudence and his respectability appear at a glance to be opposed to the audacity and the freedom which are demanded by those who serve art. In that respect the artist is mistaken. Firstly because it is on the safe foundation of bourgeois society that the artist's life can most easily be maintained; wealthy shopkeepers have often been patrons of art. It happens also that a number of the most brilliant disciples of art have been children of the bourgeoisie. The middle class of society is a good nursery for an artist, for it can give him a good education, the luxuries of civilized life, and money—things which are essential—and can keep him, nevertheless, within the bounds of diligence which will be to his advantage.

The anarchist is the bourgeois' other enemy. For in his view the bourgeois is the great conservative, the man who is satisfied with things as they are, who loathes revolution and who likes to move slowly. And the anarchist's view is a just one, for that is what the bourgeois has usually been.'

It was because he was brought up in Liverpool and not in Wales that Saunders Lewis could praise bourgeois virtues with such passion. It was because he was a Welshman, not an Englishman or a Frenchman, that he chose to do so, or that he was obliged to do so. He was a one-man national bourgeoisie for Wales in the period between the two wars. As a politician, his aim was to endow Wales with statehood, together with all the other national institutions which are the boast of bourgeois democracy. As a writer and critic he strove unsparingly to present Wales with works and standards which could be unblushingly compared with the bourgeois literatures of France, England and Italy. He demonstrated in an unambiguous manner in the television interview with Aneirin Talfan that his original ambition was to accomplish those historical tasks which the middle-class undertakes in its heroic, patriotic and revolutionary phase in more developed countries: 'I had a desire, not a small desire but a great desire, to change the history of Wales. To change the whole course of Wales, and to make Welsh-speaking Wales something vital, strong and powerful, belonging to the modern world. And I failed completely.'

Yes, he failed—in his own view and according to his own standards—because it is impossible either to persuade or to force a nation to accept political doctrines which the fabric of its economic and social life cannot sustain. It was not because he was a Catholic, nor because his nationalism was too extreme for its taste that Wales 'rejected' Saunders Lewis, but rather because it was a nation of common folk and *petits-bourgeois*, whilst he offered it ideals which were better suited to a wealthy bourgeoisie.

But if success comes to those who are fighting for the continued existence of the nation—and that is not impossible—it will be seen that this 'failure' was one of the chief moral and spiritual sources of their victory. Although Saunders Lewis did not succeed in his intention of making Wales a power in the world, his political career and his literary output have been effective means in making nationalism a power in Wales's own life, and, according to every indication, that power is on the increase.

In a way, the young, long-haired, budding revolutionaries of the Language Society and their Honorary President appear to be members of two different races. Nevertheless, there is no doubt about their political paternity: they are his children. It is he who has taught them that it is impossible to serve Wales whilst at the same time battening on the bribes of Britishness. It is he who has taught them too that the Welshman who wants to liberate his own mind, and the minds of his compatriots, from the grip of Englishness must break the law of England.

Unfortunately, they have not yet discovered one truth which he grasped at a very early stage, that is, that there is no hope of solving the problems of Wales unless they are considered in an international context, and that Welsh nationalism will never become a truly revolutionary creed unless it is placed within the framework of a wider ideology. When that happens, there will be room to believe that the Welsh language and the Welsh nation will survive as long as the other languages and nations of mankind.

GARETH MILES
(*translated by* G. ALED WILLIAMS)

Aspects of his work

His Politics

Saunders Lewis is that kind of classicist who takes a particular delight in acknowledging the sources of his inspiration and in announcing his artistic and intellectual debts. So it is with the origins of his political thought. In an interview published in 1961 he tells us that it was through Yeats, Synge, Colum and other writers belonging to the Irish literary revival that he first came to understand the meaning of nationhood and the experience of patriotism.[1] This was the first beginning. A second discovery was made during the Great War, when he was a soldier in France. It was there that he discovered Maurice Barrès, and read the trilogy of novels entitled *Le Culte du Moi*. 'I believe,' he says, 'that it was Barrès, after Yeats and the Irishmen, who made me a Welsh nationalist by conviction.' It was after this that he resolved to acquire a mastery of the Welsh language and to read extensively in its literature. Home on leave, in or around 1916, he turned into a bookshop in Swansea and picked up the biography of Emrys ap Iwan, by Thomas Gwynn Jones,* published some four years earlier. Reading this book clinched everything that Barrès had begun, and in another place Mr. Lewis writes of it: 'It is one of those infrequent books which change history and influence a whole generation, inspiring it and giving a direction to its thought.'

Of Emrys ap Iwan we shall have more to say later. What of Barrès? The reputation of Maurice Barrès was a late casualty of the 1914–18 war, and it came down with an appropriately loud noise. A year and a half before his death, the Dadaists had put him on trial (*in absentia*) on a charge of 'making an attempt against the security of the spirit;' Tristan Tzara, giving evidence for the prosecution, called him '*la plus grande canaille qui s'est produite en Europe depuis Napoléon.*' Since then, both in France and elsewhere, we have had an even more impressive selection of *canaille* to offer for comparison, but the general verdict of the French intelligentsia over the past fifty years would still place Barrès high in the charts. Gide, graciously abjuring a title which he himself had more than

---

1. The interview was originally televised by the BBC, and the text later printed in *Taliesin*, Vol. 2. The interviewer is Aneirin Talfan Davies.

* Thomas Gwynn Jones, *Cofiant Emrys ap Iwan*, Caernarfon, 1912.

once been offered, declares Barrès the most disastrous teacher in the whole of history, and dismisses everything touched by his influence as 'already moribund, already dead.' This latter claim, at least, has been questioned by more recent commentators, who point out that the group of French writers who owe a debt to Barrès is a large and not undistinguished one. Along with a handful of men of action, it includes Bernanos, Montherlant, Mauriac, Saint-Exupéry, Vercors, Sartre, Malraux, Camus and probably many more. But the number of those who saw fit to acknowledge their debt openly is very small indeed. And among this number we come across a trio which, if only for its incongruity, would deserve mention: one is Maurras, writing from his prison in 1949; another is the French socialist leader Léon Blum; and the third is Saunders Lewis. In 1924, with the crash of Barrès's renown already resounding through the intellectual world, Mr. Lewis felt bound to write, in a memorial tribute: 'I cannot hear of this man's death without openly acknowledging my debt to him. Discovering his work had the effect of changing the course of my life . . . It was through him that I discovered Wales, and that the hedonism of my youth was transformed into something else. My play, *Noble Blood*, is no more than an attempt at turning *Colette Baudoche* into Welsh and into a Welsh setting.'

When we come to practical politics there are differences a-plenty between Barrès and Saunders Lewis, both in the situations in which they found themselves and in the results which they obtained. Barrès was the mouthpiece of a populistic nationalism, much as Mr. Enoch Powell is in England today. At the lowest ebb of his fortunes, he had a good half of the country behind him. Though, around the turn of the century, the French right wing suffered three technical defeats—over Boulanger, over the great Panama Scandal and over Dreyfus—their faith and diligence were gloriously rewarded in the *Union Sacrée* of 1914. In carnage upon carnage, from the first weeks on the Marne to the final convulsions of the Hindenburg offensive, Barrès saw the achievement of all he had worked for, and the war years brought him a rich harvest of that which, as a thin sickly schoolboy who could not eat his school dinner and who lived in terror of his fellows, he had set out to achieve— popularity, acclaim and as many decorations as he could find room for on the front of his frock-coat.

Saunders Lewis, by contrast, set out to sell nationalism to a people who were shy of practising it, and a brand of nationalism which he must have known was too sophisticated for most people to understand. When his party came to fight its first parliamentary election, it was supported by 1.5 per cent of the electorate. This was in 1929. Seven years later, his commitment to Wales was to cost him his job and earn him a term of imprisonment. Barrès, we can be quite certain, would have burnt no bombing schools. True, like several other French writers of a Catholic or conservative persuasion, he argued strongly for decentralization of power within France, and sought to strengthen and invigorate the life of the provinces. But this was, first and last, regionalism. Lorraine, Savoy, Normandy, Provence were to be defended as parts of one strong, indivisible, authoritarian, expansionist, colonialist and anti-German France.

But again there is a difference between the Barrès of *Colette Baudoche* or *Les Déracinés* and the Barrès of *La Politique Rhénane* or the atrocious *Chroniques de la Grande Guerre*. As several commentators have noted, the life and writings of Barrès are not without their share of complexities and contradictions. He could be subtle and he could be crude. In him, vicious prejudices were combined with sound instincts; doctrinaire intransigence with an intuitive understanding of how the ordinary man thought; rhetorical posturing, which turned his career into a travesty of *gloire*, with an honesty which, increasingly as he advanced in years, made him question and revise his own beliefs; a total unwillingness to grant that there might be an ounce of justice in the opponent's case, with a generous admiration for men of spirit and courage, on whichever side of the barricade they might be found. Barrès's political creed embodies more than one kind of nationalism, with much else besides. Amidst a great deal of militaristic rubbish and Jew-baiting demagoguery, there stand one or two lasting truths which Barrès had grasped and which often evade both supporters and opponents of nationalism. Hegelian and *étatiste* though he was, Barrès understood that there is a dimension to nationhood other than the complete submission of the individual will to the claims of state: it is what we might call belonging or, alternately, remembering; to share in the experience of a historical and spiritual community, to assume responsibility for its continued existence, to stand by it in defeat as in triumph. He did in a crude way what Simone Weil was to do, half a century and two world wars later, with greater humanity and more depth. Saunders Lewis's writing belongs to the same current of thought as that which produced *L'Enracinement*, and his debt to Barrès is not irrelevant in that respect. It is a debt not so much in respect of a political programme as of a personal awakening, a dimension added to his own life. Barrès made him a nationalist, but to explain the content of his nationalism, its philosophy and its practical objectives, we have to look elsewhere.

*   *   *   *   *

For some ten years, roughly 1925 to 1935, Saunders Lewis was engaged in constructing a philosophy and a programme for the Welsh Nationalist Party. During those years he was the party's president and editor of its Welsh monthly paper, *Y Ddraig Goch* (*The Red Dragon*). A selection of articles originally written for that paper appears in the book *Canlyn Arthur* (*In the Steps of Arthur*), published in 1938; we shall be referring to this book and also to two, in particular, from among the several pamphlets which he wrote in the same period.

Let me note one omission. Saunders Lewis was not alone in this task, and a full account of Plaid Cymru's early development would have to include the names, for example, of Ambrose Bebb, who provided the interpretation of history so essential to a new and revolutionary political movement; D. J. Davies, an economist who made a life-long study of co-operative practices, particularly in the Scandinavian countries; and John Arthur Price, a veteran of the late nineteenth-century *Cymru Fydd* (Young Wales movement), who, reflecting on the failure of *Cymru Fydd*, put forward, in an important but largely forgotten series of articles, new lines on which Welsh nationalism might develop. Price has never received his due share of credit for his contribution to twentieth-century Welsh nationalism, and many of the themes later articulated by Saunders Lewis are foreshadowed in his writings. I have not made the detailed study which would enable us to place Saunders Lewis in his relation to these other pioneers, or adequately to explain why it should be he, rather than one of the others, who became chiefly responsible for synthesizing the thought of the new party and—to use a phrase happily not invented in 1925—'projecting its image'. All his colleagues would gladly grant that he was the ablest man among them. He was also the least typical.

Saunders Lewis is neither a philosopher nor a politician. He is an intermediary between philosophy and politics. And before anything else he is an artist and a critic, a man impatient of imperfections.

*   *   *   *   *

To the Welshman, unlike his nearest neighbour, nationalism does not come naturally. It is something that must be discovered, debated and defined. Most appropriately, it is with a definition that Saunders Lewis begins, and the word applies here in two of its meanings: the more usual sense, of saying what a thing is, ideally as well as actually; and also the less common but more literal sense, of placing limits upon it. Thus Mr. Lewis writes, in the first paragraph of his first political pamphlet:

> Now let us remember this: excess, in all movements, is an ever-present threat. I have no hesitation in saying that hot-headed and limitless nationalism is a highly dangerous thing. To know the limits; to fight only for those things that are indispensable and essential . . .; and then to restrain oneself, and not to go to extremes, this is the soul of wisdom and of justice.

The pamphlet from which these words are taken, *Egwyddorion Cenedlaetholdeb* (*The Principles of Nationalism*) is the first in a line of some 200 published by the Welsh Nationalist Party between 1926 and the present day. Its substance was first given as a lecture to the party's first Summer School and Conference, held at Machynlleth in the summer of that year. I make no apology for quoting liberally from it and summarizing part of its argument. Though its message may have become somewhat obscured by accretions of policy, over a period of forty-five years, and by some inevitable changes of emphasis, it remains the cornerstone of Welsh nationalist thinking, and if reprinted today it would have a value above and beyond its historical interest.

Its logic is calculated to perplex, and to dislodge some familiar and cherished notions. We read, for example, following a quick resumé of Welsh history:

> When, in the Middle Ages, Wales was subjugated by England, it suffered no irreparable harm. When Wales was made free and a part of England under the Tudors, it received a death-blow.

There are listed several of the explanations which have from time to time been offered as to why this should be so—the betrayal of Welsh hopes by the Tudor kings; the decline of the native aristocracy and, with them, the professional poets; the emergence of a new middle class which cared little for the country's traditional culture; the banning of the Welsh language from administration and law and the imposition of an all-English system of education. All these, Saunders Lewis concludes, are but secondary causes.

There was a deeper cause; that which destroyed the civilization of Wales and wrought havoc on Wales's culture and brought into being the critical condition in which Wales finds herself today—it was *nationalism.*

This, he realizes, requires a word of explanation:

Have you noticed? We are so familiar today with hearing such sentiments as: every nation ought to be free; no nation has the right to rule another nation; a nation must be independent; and sentences of like kind—that we but rarely dispute them or inquire as to what they mean. What do we mean by the terms 'free', 'to rule', 'independence'? Assuredly, meanings could be assigned to each of them which would justify each one of the sentences I have quoted. But they could just as easily be understood in such a way that we could in all sincerity say: no nation ought to be free; no nation is entitled to independence or to rule itself. And these are the truths which most need to be stressed today.

The nations of Europe in the Middle Ages, he continues, were not 'free' in the sense generally assigned to the word at the time of writing. They all recognized a supra-national authority in the form of the Church. 'The whole of Europe shared one law and one civilization; but that law and that civilization had varied forms and many different hues.' Under such a system, one form of civilization was not thought of as a danger to any other forms, nor did a variety of languages militate against the unity based on moral law and a common belief.

In the sixteenth century—the age of Luther in Germany, of Macchiavelli in Italy, of the Tudors in Britain—this was undone, and replaced by another kind of nationalism, the one still current in Europe, that which set up the state as the supreme arbiter of morality and the sole object of loyalty. It placed the power of the state, its rights, its freedom, beyond restraint and conditions. Each authority came to be thought of as a threat to its neighbour, one civilization as the enemy of another. Diversity could not be conceived of except as a divisiveness. One state became the enemy not only of other states, but also of all differences in tradition, culture and language within its own domain. As authority came to be based exclusively on material force, uniformity within the state was insisted upon, under the tyranny of one law and one language. It is in this context that the relationship of Wales and England within Britain is to be seen:

These, grossly simplified, were the principles of the nationalism conceived in the sixteenth century. Such were the ideas of the Tudors in Britain. These were the very principles which destroyed the civilization of Wales . . . The two countries were given one government, one civil law, one culture, one system of education, one religion—being the state's religion, the state's language, the state's education, the state's culture. Sixteenth-century nationalism represented nothing less than a victory for the material over the spiritual, for paganism over Christianity. It was this pagan and materialist victory which destroyed our Wales.

The task of the new political party was to reverse this change, to dislodge one kind of nationalism, that is the one most commonly practised among the nation-states of Europe in the modern world, and substitute for it another, comparable in kind to that which existed under mediaeval Christendom:

What then is our nationalism? It is this: to return to the principle accepted in the Middle Ages; to repudiate the idea of political uniformity, and to expose its ill-effects; to plead therefore for the principle of unity and diversity. To fight not for Welsh independence, but for the civilization of Wales. To claim for Wales not independence but freedom. And to claim for her a place in the League of Nations and in the community of Europe, by virtue of her civilization and its values.

Several times before we reach the end of the pamphlet, the difference between the idea of 'freedom' and the idea of 'sovereign independence' is clearly reiterated:

We do, therefore, need a government of our own. Not independence. Not even an unconditional freedom. But exactly that degree of freedom which is necessary in order to make civilization secure in Wales; that freedom will not only benefit Wales but will also contribute to the welfare and security of England and all other neighbouring countries.

Saunders Lewis begins, then, with the recognition that nationalism has several forms, some of which have quite plainly to be rejected; and that it should at all times be exercised with moderation and subjected to strict conditions. He is merely offering one model, while all the time, of course, urging the Welsh people to secure the political means of determining their own future.

It was not until 1930, that is five years after its inception, that the nationalist party officially adopted Dominion or Commonwealth status as its constitutional goal. An English pamphlet by Saunders

Lewis, entitled *The Banned Wireless Talk on Welsh Nationalism*, marks
the point at which the new movement became finally committed
to the creation of a Welsh state, in no way subject to Westminster,
but recognizing the Crown, and free to co-operate, as the need
arose, with Westminster as with other governments. The story
behind the title is that the BBC had invited Saunders Lewis to
deliver a radio talk of some fifteen minutes on 'the new nationalism
in Wales,' and had fixed the date of the broadcast. Two days before
it was due to go out, the author was informed that the Headquarters
of the Corporation did not approve of the content of the talk, and
had cancelled the broadcast, and the reason given was that it was
'calculated to inflame Welsh national sympathies.' A prefatory
note to the pamphlet remarks: 'The author fervently hopes that its
publication now as a pamphlet may have that effect.' It is fun to
try and conjecture what Sir John Reith and his friends in London
had anticipated when they commissioned the talk in the first place.
No doubt some jolly piece of *hwyl*-mongering in which the original
Cambro-Britons would be urged to cling to their old hymns and
ever-so-charming folk verse, while making the most of their membership of Mr. Baldwin's dynamic British nation and empire. Saunders
Lewis's script was not quite what they had bargained for. It has, as
its main theme, the rejection of a nationalism that is merely cultural.
Such a concept, it argues, is based on the premise that a nation
'can divide its life and activities into separate compartments with
no communication between them.' This, Saunders Lewis holds, is
no more possible for a nation than it is for an individual person:

> . . . if a nation that has lost its political machinery becomes content
> to express its nationality thenceforward only in the sphere of
> literature and the arts, then that literature and those arts will
> very quickly become provincial and unimportant, mere echoes of
> the ideas and artistic movements of the neighbouring and dominant
> nation. If they [the Welsh people] decide that the literary revival
> shall not broaden out into political and economic life and the
> whole of Welsh life, then inevitably Welsh literature in our
> generation will cease to be living and valuable.

In the second part of the pamphlet attention is turned to an
immediate problem—unemployment, and the depression whose
effects were by now acutely felt in the South Wales mining communities. One of the saddest features of the crisis is 'the apathy, the
uninventive patience of South Wales itself, the fact that we who
live here wait and wait hoping for some god outside the machine
to step down and lift us away from our troubles.' It is in this impasse

that nationalism can provide a service. What Saunders Lewis is saying is not that his party has a plan to conquer unemployment (though, at the right place and time, it was to put forward such plans): the message here is that the fact of nationhood is a spiritual force which, properly channelled, can help men overcome their material difficulties. The past is there to be used as an inspiration in the present:

> There is nothing like the sense of belonging to a noble country and to courageous ancestors for inspiring youth to heroism. Nationalism is above all a fountain head of heroism and of brave resolve. It gives a beaten people hope. It gives them resourcefulness and drives away apathy and cynicism and selfishness. It rouses them to co-operation and it kills obstruction and the spirit that says 'No'. In the present economic and social distress of Wales this inspiration is just what we lack.

One thing which 'The Banned Talk' makes amply clear, and I believe that enough has been quoted to illustrate it, is that nationalism, for Saunders Lewis, is not an end in itself. What then is the end in view? Starting, as he does, with the fact of a Welsh cultural identity, without which political nationalism could not exist, and arguing as he does, that this identity of itself demands an extension of nationalism into the political field, Saunders Lewis might quite easily have fallen, as did Eliot, Pound, Wyndham Lewis and others with whom he shares certain ideals, into the trap of making the defence of cultural standards the ultimate aim of political endeavour. This he does not do. As we have seen, he does expect political nationalism to benefit culture in Wales: he sees it as the only answer to provincialism in literature and the arts. But the process is, in his mind, reciprocal. The cultural endeavour which he advocates is in its turn regarded as part of the defence of certain political freedoms. Regarding the Welsh language, he had a strong and clear policy (which was even then thought drastic by some of his fellow-nationalists and has itself, for good or ill, been abandoned by Plaid Cymru). It is the gradual abandonment of English in Wales as the language of daily intercourse and of government, and its replacement by Welsh. That minority of people who do normally learn languages, for reasons cultural and professional, would of course be given all encouragement to learn as many as they liked. But, in contrast to the present policy of Plaid Cymru, and in conformity with the traditional assumption of European culture, he refuses to accept that bilingualism is a normal condition for a majority of a country's citizens to be in. The defence and extension of the Welsh language is, for him, bound up in a direct and literal way with the freedom of the ordinary Welshman. He sees the language as the one surviving, unbroken tradition which belongs to the whole of Wales. It is the key to that 'deep unity of tradition and awareness of the past,' which is the prerequisite for the restoration in our country of a vital, forward-looking, creative community. It is the secret weapon in the fight for personal freedom and social justice:

> To create a Welsh-speaking Wales is the surest way of building up a country within which the oppression of international capitalism cannot dwell. Of course, our socialist friends are quite unable to grasp this. So enmeshed are they in the coils of nineteenth-century materialism that they do not see that economic oppression will ultimately be defeated by spiritual forces.

Canlyn Arthur assumes throughout that the nation is the normal form of society in Europe and the basis of Western civilization. 'The experience of generations has found it small enough to cherish and large enough to afford men a fullness of life within itself.' Professional students of politics, almost to a man, would question the validity of this premise; valid or not, it is accepted in practice by nearly everyone else. It is not the assumption itself that is new or unusual, but its application to Wales. To be, to exist, and to be recognized by other national communities as existing, this, Saunders Lewis maintained, is the only way to extraversion and normality, the only way in which Wales can fully and creatively participate in a wider community.

That participation, moreover, is indispensable if self-government is to have any meaning. And it must be direct and first-hand. A Welsh parliament is necessary not in order that Wales may retire into self-sufficiency, but so that she may recover her contact with Europe. Possibly the most radical feature of *Y Ddraig Goch*'s policy in the twenties and thirties was its advocacy of a European union of interdependent states. True, the idea had been broached by a handful of philosophers and historians of culture, including some of the very greatest, but to include it in the practical programme of a party competing for seats in the Westminster parliament, when the British Empire still had another twenty years to run, was moonshine, and further proof of the Welsh Nationalists' extreme lack of common sense. 'Europe is the world's leader and its centre,' Saunders Lewis writes in 1927. 'To bring political and economic unity to Europe should be one of the first priorities of our century.'

And a basic condition for the success of that union was that the countries of Britain be part of it. In all this, Wales is assigned a grand rôle, supported by a grand thesis:

> But is there a European tradition to be found within Britain? Is there here a nation which was, in its origins, part of Western Civilization, which thinks in the western way, and which is able to understand Europe and sympathize with her? The answer is: Wales. The Welsh are the only nation in Britain who have been part of the Roman Empire, who, in childhood, were weaned on the milk of the West, and who have the blood of the West in their veins. Wales can understand Europe, for she is one of the family. If a choice must be made, as Chamberlain insists, between the Empire and the League of Nations, there can be no doubt as to which way Wales will tend. To her, always, and to the greatest of her sons in thought and learning, contact with Europe has meant a renaissance and an inspiration. To her, the Empire was never anything but a name and an empty noise. . . . This, then, is the reason why she must demand a seat in the League of Nations, so that she may act as Europe's interpreter in Britain, and as a link to bind England and the Empire to Christendom and to the League itself.

It is a thesis which invites a good deal of qualification, but can stand it. Oversimplified it may be, both in its idea of Wales and in its idea of Europe, but a study of modern Welsh literature, for one thing, would bear out that there is truth in it. It will be seen to concur with that interpretation of the beginnings of the Welsh people which was evolved, and defended in the face of much indifference, by the Rev. A. W. Wade-Evans. He chose to regard the Welsh, in their origin, not as a people driven headlong to the West and the mountains before a swift and irreversible Anglo-Saxon onslaught, but as that section of the *Britanni* who, during and after the Roman withdrawal, opted to identify themselves with the cultural and spiritual ideal of *Romanitas*, which by then included the Christian religion. Ignored and rejected by the University of Wales, as by his own university, Oxford, Wade-Evans seems to have been unofficially adopted by Plaid Cymru as the authority on the beginnings of Wales and the Welsh. A lecture by him opens the symposium entitled *Seiliau Hanesyddol Cenedlaetholdeb Cymru* (*The Historical Bases of Welsh Nationalism*), published by the party in 1950, and his theory is accepted unquestioningly in Mr. Gwynfor Evans's recent book *Aros Mae* (*It Still Remains*). A chapter in the conflict between *Romanitas* and *Barbaritas* in fifth-century Britain is dramatized by Saunders Lewis in his play *Buchedd Garmon* (*The Life of St. Germanus*).

Even if Saunders Lewis's thesis of the European character of Welsh civilization, of Wales's need for Europe and Europe's need for Wales, is completely wrong and false, its fault does not lie in any of the common sins which are laid, today more than ever, at the door of the Welsh nationalists—intraversion, isolationism and a lack of concern for the fate of other peoples. That it was not, in fact, sufficiently inward-looking, that it did not take due account of conditions peculiar to Wales, that it was not properly attuned to Welsh feeling and thought, were points of criticism often put by intelligent critics of the Nationalist Party in its early years. R. T. Jenkins, himself no stranger to European culture, used to treat the Nationalists' studied Continentalism as the greatest joke on earth. When in Rome, he suggests, you may well have to eat macaroni, because it is the food most readily available in most eating-places, but there is no sense at all in *making a show* of eating it. For some ten years a debate was conducted, intermittently, between Saunders Lewis and W. J. Gruffydd, on the question 'Can a man be as parochial in Paris as in Mold?': it consisted mainly in Gruffydd saying 'Yes, he can' and in Saunders Lewis saying 'No, he can not.'

Turning now from a country's external relationships to her internal social order, we see that the same principles apply here—inter-dependence, co-operation and the free association of organic or functional groups. *Canlyn Arthur* conceives of the nation as a 'community of communities,' in which a multiplicity of lesser associations such as the family, a church, a professional or trade union, come between the individual and the state and thereby protect the individual person's freedom of thought and action:

> Family and tribe existed prior to the state, and voluntary organizations existed prior to the authority of sovereign government. . . . A nation's civilization is rich and complex simply because it is a community of communities, and for that reason also the freedom of the individual is a feasible proposition. . . . His liberty depends on his being a member not of one association but of many.

The main aim of social policy, therefore, should be to strengthen the lesser associations, both organic and functional, and in particular the family.

One of the most effective items of polemic in *Canlyn Arthur* is an attack on those tendencies in modern society which, under the guise of humanitarianism, loosen the bonds of the family and undermine its freedom and responsibility. It is mainly through the agency of the schools, we are warned, that the state has taken on

itself those responsibilities towards children which parents have for
centuries accepted as part of their life and duty. The school 'welfare'
services are attacked as being un-Christian and inimical to a free
society; they represent 'the awful humanitarianism which kills
humanity, the very plague of our day and age.' It is a topsy-turvy
logic, Saunders Lewis argues, by which government appropriates
to itself obligations traditionally regarded as those of parents to
their children, and at the same time encourages educational institutions to abdicate their traditional and legitimate function of
ensuring that the children know something of their country's
history and culture, and are trained in the competent use of their
own language. Leaders of religious bodies are accused, with some
regret, of actively furthering these trends:

> In their eagerness to be 'progressive', they chase after scientistic
> notions and tendencies which destroy the bases of their own
> community and of their country's traditions. It is an inability to
> think that is destroying Wales today. It is for this reason that she
> is unable to face the tendencies of her age, to comprehend them,
> and either to accept them boldly with their anti-Christian,
> Marxist premises, or else firmly to reject them and cast her lot,
> whether that be right or no, with the traditions of the Welsh
> fathers.

Although the element of patriotism in Welsh nationalist thinking
is accompanied all the way, and in some respects preceded, by a
sociological ideal (and one which is in no way peculiar to Wales),
the Nationalist Party took its time in defining the principles of its
social policy. It was well into the thirties before they were finally
declared. A summary of them is found in the 'Ten Points of Policy,'
published in *Y Ddraig Goch* in 1933 and reprinted in *Canlyn Arthur*.
The brevity of the summary—it takes up less than three pages of
the book—says much about the nature of the ideal. Certain fundamental human rights are reiterated, so briefly as to suggest that
they ought to be self-evident, and not many words are wasted on
the function of the state. The first point reads:

> It is not the function of a country's government to create an
> integrated system and an economic machinery for the people to
> accept and conform to. The task of government is actively to
> create and sustain the conditions which will provide an oppor-
> tunity, a lead and an encouragement for the nation itself to
> develop that system which is consistent with its ideals and tradi-
> tions, and which will be a means of securing the welfare of society
> and the happiness of individuals.

Thus the state, which is a machine or an agency, is made clearly subservient to the nation, an organic being conceived of on the model of a human person. The great confusion between the nation and the state, which for close on two hundred years has confounded nationalists, nationalisms and (perhaps especially) interpreters of nationalism and critics of it, is thrown out at the start. Once this has been done, it is safe to move on to the second point, which declares that 'the economic unit, so far as is possible, should coincide with the political and social unit, because only in that way can a people be protected against pressures from outside.' The third point is a rejection of *laissez-faire* capitalism and free competition, from which we proceed to an alternative model of the social order, outlined in the fifth, sixth, ninth and tenth points. These are content, for the main part, with defining certain spheres of activity and declaring certain freedoms and rights.

Not least among these is the right to property, in the form of land or credit. Government should ensure through fiscal measures that capital never becomes concentrated in the hands of a few people, but is distributed as widely as possible. One means of ensuring this is to encourage the co-ownership of industry by the workers within it. In several other articles, Saunders Lewis was to expound on the same theme, and more detailed work on it was being done concurrently by D. J. Davies, in articles and books.[2] Plaid Cymru belongs among several movements—and they are to be found on the left, on the right and at the centre—which have advocated the wide distribution of credit, coupled usually with direct participation by the workers in management, as alternatives to both capitalism and state socialism. It says much for the resilience of capitalism, and for the staunch support it has been given by parliamentary socialist parties in the major Western democracies, that these ideas have so rarely come anywhere near to being realized. Guild Socialism we no longer hear of; a thin residue of Belloc's distributism can be found, if one looks diligently, in the present-day policy of the Liberal party, but that party's annual conference in 1969 was greatly shaken when it found that the Young Liberals actually took the policy seriously; Major Douglas's brief reign in Canada is an exception which proves the

---

2. D. J. Davies was also the man entrusted with presenting the economic case for home-rule. The 'Wales can pay its way' theme is now so prominent in Plaid Cymru's propaganda that we do not always realize how little a place it has in Saunders Lewis's writings. Not one chapter of *Canlyn Arthur* is dedicated to this subject.

rule. For working examples of a co-operative democracy it is to the Scandinavian countries that Plaid Cymru usually turns.

'Let it be said here, immediately and emphatically,' writes Saunders Lewis in his first article as editor of *Y Ddraig Goch*, 'that capitalism is one of the prime enemies of nationalism.' Nor can 'socialism' be admitted, for all its elasticity, as a name for the alternative. Capitalism and socialism (the latter being understood exclusively as Marxist state socialism), are regarded not as antithetical but as complementary, and the 'class war' as a symptom of a malaise which a healthy community ought to be able to eradicate. Political power being appropriated increasingly by a new proletariat which knows no tradition and no feeling of debt, and economic power being concentrated more and more in the hands of new capitalists, equally without tradition or obligation, the result will be an unholy alliance in the attack on culture and personal freedom. 'These two classes between them will formulate a country's education and its laws, and between them will be lost that link with the past and that love for the nation which are indispensable if civilization is to continue.' Education ceases to become a vehicle of culture and becomes, instead, a weapon in an economic war.

The ending of capitalism in Wales would also mean the end of industrialism, in the form which we have known for the past two centuries. The social and economic policies of the early Welsh Nationalist Party were designed to hasten, in our corner of the world, what Peter Drucker was to call 'The End of Economic Man'.[3] One of the Ten Points, the eighth, puts it quite bluntly: 'For the moral well-being of Wales, and for the health, moral and physical, of its people, there must be a de-industrialization of South Wales.' Other writings of Saunders Lewis suggest that this is not, in fact, quite so drastic as it sounds, and that what it means is a general re-distribution of industrial activity throughout the country. To encourage the establishment of light industry, widely distributed, and generally to avoid the creation of large industrial conurbations, is an aim still accepted by Plaid Cymru. But it is no longer a hard-and-fast doctrine of the party that (to quote the seventh of the Ten Points) 'Agriculture should be the main industry of Wales and the basis of its civilization.'

---

3. Drucker's book under this title, which appeared in 1939, is quoted approvingly in some of the later writings of D. J. Davies.

Enough has been said, I believe, to suggest that the political doctrine of Saunders Lewis is no longer the sum-total of Welsh Nationalist thought. Forty years have gone by since this philosophy was put together, and many of the documents in which it is set out are unobtainable. Only a small minority, even of nationalists and of Plaid Cymru members, know what it was in its original form. Some small ironies come to mind immediately; a party which was once forthright in its attack on the interference of bureaucratic paternalism in education is today found supporting the councillors of Merthyr Tydfil when, in defiance of a Conservative government's order, they continue to provide schoolchildren with free milk; the party which was the first in Britain to broach the idea of European unity, is now forced, quite understandably, into a position of opposing British entry into the Common Market; the party which, after the arrival of organized Labour as a political force, was the first to confront the electors with a non-capitalist alternative to socialism, now applies the adjective 'socialist' to aspects of its policy, and probably has socialists as a majority of its members. One need not assume that there has been a great act of betrayal. This is simply the way things evolve as time goes on. What Plaid Cymru has done, it appears to me, is to abandon all economic doctrine as such. It has abandoned economic nationalism, abandoned the attack on *laissez-faire*, abandoned the systematic critique of both socialism and capitalism. Accepting the economic framework as at present we find it, it has, in effect, concentrated increasingly on the issue of self-government. This has been the work of gradual consensus, and Welsh Nationalist policy today, taken all-in-all, represents a veritable triumph of compromise. At no point at all, as far as I can gather, have the policies of Saunders Lewis been consciously rejected by the party. Some of them have been integrated with policies which have roots in other traditions, and others have been left in cold storage. Together with the compromise, a certain amount of untidiness has had to be accepted. It is the coherence of Saunders Lewis's system which has been lost.

The very first paragraph which Mr. Lewis wrote as editor of *Y Ddraig Goch* insists on the necessity of a general theory of social life which is whole and consistent—a philosophy. Pragmatism as the basis of political thought he rejects, but once a coherent system of political philosophy has been defined, he is prepared to allow a large degree of eclecticism. Nationalism, we find, is essential as part of the philosophy, but is not the whole of it. It is not the starting-point, nor the end, nor the justification. What Saunders Lewis has done is to take nationalism and fit it into a broad concept of Christian humanism, where it finds a rôle and a function. Some confusion is occasioned by the fact that often in his writings the word 'nationalism' is used as a code-word for the whole of which it is part.

This brings us back to the question of origins and of the immediate intellectual context in which the philosophy was assembled.

*   *   *   *   *

It is natural to expect that a Welsh Nationalist Party formed in 1925, and an amalgam of several small groups which had existed since the early twenties, should draw some inspiration from the Irish home-rule struggle which reached the end of a phase in 1922, with the establishment of what was then known as the Irish Free State. Some of the early founders, notably that group which had been connected with a small and outspoken magazine called *Y Wawr* (*The Dawn*), published in the University College of Wales at Aberystwyth, had been supporters of the Irish cause during all the 'troubles' from 1916 onwards. It was to be expected that some of the early contributors to *Y Ddraig Goch* should speak with enthusiasm of the Irish struggle. When Saunders Lewis speaks of it, it is with some caution. It is to the Irish dramatists and literary men, we notice, that he acknowledges a debt, not to the political leaders or the men of 1916. Commenting on the cultural programme of Arthur Griffith, he ventures to criticize it for not being sufficiently European in outlook. Celticism has no place at all in his teaching. It is always Europe.

Protestant Europe is not entirely excluded. It is from two Protestant countries that he takes his favourite examples of a national revolution both humane and successful. The achievement of Grundtvig in Denmark, and that of Thomas Masaryk in Czechoslovakia, these are the examples he seizes upon to analyse and to underline their lessons for Wales. His biographical sketch of Masaryk, in *Canlyn Arthur*, is a *tour de force* in the Plutarchian mould, not without some element of wish-fulfilment to give it passion. Here was a scholar of vast and profound learning, called in an hour of stress to lead his people to freedom and to found a new state, a man of unimpeachable integrity who also encountered a great deal of good luck, and who had the courage to strike when the hour had come. Here was proof that the age of philosopher-kings is not past. We might yet have one in Wales.

But in order to understand the essence of Saunders Lewis's social philosophy, and all its implications, it is to Catholic Europe, and to France in particular, that we must return. The doctrine, as I have suggested, is not that of Barrès, but it represents one development of the broad movement to which Barrès belonged.

By the turn of the century, a sizeable majority of France's scholars and men of letters aligned themselves with the 'Catholic Revival', or, as some would prefer to call it, 'Reaction', which had begun to gather force immediately after the defeat of France by Prussia in 1870. Whichever of the two terms we may select as being the more apt, it is bound to be something of a misnomer for a movement of radical, aggressive conservatism in which Catholicism is but one element among several. All of its members gave support to the Catholic Church, but not all for the same reasons. Some, possibly even a majority, did so because they accepted the Christan revelation; others, like Barrès, who was an agnostic, and his younger contemporary, Maurras, who was an out-and-out atheist, saw in Catholicism a force which represented tradition and authority and which made for social cohesion. Of the believers, many were converts, who exemplified in full degree the convert's proverbial zeal, and sometimes, in their passion for orthodoxy, uttered wild heresies which quickly earned their works a place on the Index. Of the non-believers, there were some, including Barrès, who had fashioned for their own use a private religion fusing Catholic and pagan elements. From whichever direction we may approach this school of writers, politicians and prophets, we meet with contradictions and paradoxes which, when we look further afield, are found to be the common ones of the same period and milieu. Like the symbolist movement, to which it is related at several points, it combines in a fine balance the prophetic and the pathological. Seeing themselves as exiles in their society and their age, these men were at the same time fiercely establishmentarian; railing against bourgeois respectability, they worshipped the symbols of order; groaning under the tyranny of democratic government (and, admittedly, there were periods under the Third Republic when true Catholics had reason to feel themselves an oppressed minority), they still craved for the compulsion, the discipline, the dictatorial leadership which would restore France's greatness and would crush all, but especially Jews, who impaired her political and spiritual solidarity; calling for a holy crusade against Germany, the home of Protestantism and the embodiment of *la barbarie*, they themselves exhibited a veneration of armies and brute force which at least equalled the Prussians' own; attacking the materialism which supposedly came into the world with the Reformation, and increased in the wake of the Enlightenment, they fell victim to one of its worst side-effects, the worship of the nation-state; protesting loyalty to the family, the regions and the land, by their militarism they did as much as anybody in their country to strengthen the hand of the centralized, industrial bureaucracy; proclaiming an apocalypse, they did their share, and perhaps a little bit more, to bring it about. And when it came, they were enraptured with a rapture which the ensuing four years of slaughter and waste did nothing to abate. In that, at least, they were consistent.

With the Great War the 'Catholic Revival' reached the end of a stage in its development. It now divided itself into two clearly distinguishable camps. One strand, continuing, without basic alteration, the themes of the pre-war movement, runs through the *Action Française* to the fascist leagues of the thirties, to the *débâcle* of 1940 and to Vichy. A new and very different emphasis is developed by the handful of Catholic scholars, led by Jacques Maritain, who undertook to interpret the modern crisis in the light of Thomistic teaching. In the changed climate of the post-war period the Neo-Thomism of Maritain becomes an influential force not only in the sphere of religion and theology, but also of literary, aesthetic and social criticism. In the latter field, which primarily concerns us, it is to be seen as a major rescue-operation. Therein lies its remarkable achievement.

Maritain retains much of what had been genuinely prophetic in the thought of the earlier generation of Catholic thinkers—the many-fronted attack upon complacency, the critique of rationalistic materialism, the rejection of a naïve evolutionist philosophy—but shook these themes free of the viciousness, the exaggeration, the intransigence and the childish anti-intellectualism which had once accompanied them. Simultaneously, the modern aspiration, which includes democracy and science, is subjected to a similar weeding-out process. The modern democratic movement, Maritain is never tired of reminding us, has produced its share of calamities. It has led to collectivization and slavery, to the deification of both the individual and the state. But it can still be redeemed by the correction of certain emphases, because its fundamental objective was sound. What must therefore be sought is a theocentric humanism in which the lessons dearly learnt in the last two centuries would be integrated with some of the fundamental truths which the post-Reformation world has tended to lose sight of. On the level of metaphysics and epistemology, this involves awarding to science a rôle in the quest for truth, while guarding against the heresy of making knowledge scientifically perceived into the whole of wisdom. In politics and moral philosophy, it involves the ideal of individual freedom and the ideal of an ordered society being reconciled in a new pluralism, which avoids both totalitarianism and *laissez-faire*, and ensures that responsibility is distributed over a wide field.

Like much of the sanest thought of our century—like that of Berdyaev and Buber, of Camus and Erich Fromm, to name representatives of but four highly diverse traditions—the political philosophy of Maritain represents an effort, no less bold for being couched in such restrained and unemotional terms, at rescuing and rehabilitating the idea of selfhood, which, by Hobbes and Rousseau, by Hegel and Nietzsche, and most of all by Freud, had been treated as inseparable from the idea of aggression. In arguing that self-fulfilment does not necessarily mean war upon other selves, Maritain relies heavily on the distinction between the two concepts of 'individual' and 'person'. The definitions of the two terms, he insists, are not new, and not his own, but classical ones, belonging to the intellectual heritage of mankind. 'Individuality', according to this distinction, implies separation from others, and confrontation with the Other. It is that part of a man's totality which is rooted in matter. 'Personality' has its roots in spirit; it is that part of our substance which bears the imprint of the spiritual; its inclination is necessarily towards perfection or fulfilment. It implies participation in a spiritual community, and requires communication and love. For that end—and not merely for the sake of security—it freely accepts conditions on its freedom. Its fulfilment is in the giving of itself, but in order to give itself, it must first of all exist. Self-assertion is the necessary passport to enter any community. Camus was concerned with the selfsame truth when he offered his parody of Descartes—'I rebel, therefore we exist.'

Maritain's theory of personality is one which applies in full not only to the single human being but to all and any of the natural, organic entities which are extensions of the single human being. It applies to the family and to the nation. These, too, if they are to achieve justification and fulfilment, must give, share and participate with others in a larger entity. But, conversely, if they do not first of all exist, and if they do not accept and assert their own existence, it is nonsense to speak of their participating in anything. Thus, the claims of the nation and of the smaller communities which make it up, can be upheld as complementary the one to the other; so can the claims of the single nation and those of the international community. We may, says Maritain, legitimately speak of 'a nation's mission,' but it must always be seen as a particularization of the whole mission of the human family, namely to develop and display its own potentialities. 'National rights' are defined, admirably, as being the rights of the human person to participate in the human values of a particular national heritage. The rights and the obligations both of the human person and of the organic communities, it is held, are grounded in Natural Law, which, for man, is also a moral law, existing by virtue of man's especial and exceptional nature.

Even the most cursory glance at the pages of *Canlyn Arthur* would show the extent of Saunders Lewis's debt to the social philosophy of Maritain, and his affinity with Gabriel Marcel, Emmanuel Mounier, Denis de Rougemont and others of Maritain's disciples. In his writings the distinction between 'person' and 'individual' is not always strictly observed, but all its implications are there. Whether it was the initial impetus for his social ideals, or merely confirmation and amplification of principles which already attracted him, that Mr. Lewis received from Maritain, it is difficult to say. More probably the latter. The quarrel with Hegelian concepts of person, country and state is already present in Welsh nationalism at a time when Maritain's social philosophy is still at a rudimentary stage. This quarrel is forcefully expressed by John Arthur Price in a series of articles published during the First World War—the earliest of them antedate Saunders Lewis's conversion to nationalism. All we can safely say is that there were other possible influences— Arthur Price may have been one, Belloc another—through which Mr. Lewis may have become initially introduced to those ideas of which Maritain, in the nineteen-twenties, was to become the leading exponent.

That a synthesis as broad and as inclusive as that of Maritain, and one set forth in such moderate and constructive terms, should have been made by a disciple of Léon Bloy, is one of the miracles of modern intellectual history. Even more of a miracle is that Maritain's statement of the democratic ideal, possibly the best offered in this century, should come from a one-time supporter of the *Action Française*. One of the mysteries of Maritain's career, not wholly explained in any of his own writings or in any study of him that I know of, is why he took so long to part company with Maurras. It was not until 1926, when Pius XI condemned the *Action*, that the final break came. *Primauté du Spirituel*, the first of Maritain's major works on the Christian social order, arises from this disagreement and is a systematic repudiation of Maurras's gospel of '*La Politique d'Abord*'. It was published the following year. In that year, too, in the Welsh literary quarterly, *Y Llenor* (*The Writer*), there appeared an item which is of the first importance in understanding Saunders Lewis's thought. It is entitled 'Llythyr Ynghylch Catholigiaeth' (A Letter Concerning Catholicism).

The Letter is addressed to W. J. Gruffydd, the editor of *Y Llenor*. Its intention is, first, to counter certain misconceptions which Gruffydd had been putting about, concerning the 'Neo-Catholic Movement' in Wales. This term, as used by Gruffydd, referred to two men in particular, one of whom was to wait another six years before finally joining the Church of Rome, while the other was to remain a Welsh Presbyterian all his life. One is Saunders Lewis and the other is Ambrose Bebb. Mr. Lewis points out that Gruffydd is not quite accurate in his facts, and he goes to some trouble to repudiate certain ideas which Gruffydd had attributed to him, but which in reality belong to Bebb, alone among Welsh nationalists. Among these is admiration for Maurras. Among Welsh nationalists today, not one out of every hundred has heard of either Barrès or Maurras. But if, for the small minority who have heard of them, there is one thing more difficult to accept than Saunders Lewis's affection for Barrès, it is Bebb's uncritical championship of the man who became Barrès's successor as France's leading right-wing rabble-rouser. Bebb, from what one can gather by reading his works, had no similarity at all to Maurras, but up to the outbreak of the Second World War he continued to speak of the daily paper, *L'Action Française*, as 'my daily bread' and to recommend its editor to the Welsh public as the man who held the key to Europe's future. Saunders Lewis will have none of this, though he grants to Maurras his importance as a literary critic. He can only say that his own ideas about a country's internal order, and the relations of countries the one with the other, are essentially and necessarily opposed to those of Maurras. Nothing, he suggests, could be less acceptable to the *Action Française* than the Welsh Nationalist Party's stress on European unity, and its rejection of *étatisme*. 'For the *Action Française*, France exists in opposition to Europe. For *Y Ddraig Goch*,

Wales exists only as part of Europe.' Four Catholic thinkers are named here by Saunders Lewis as the ones whom he particularly reveres and follows: the poet and dramatist, Claudel; the novelist, Mauriac; the historian of philosophy, Etienne Gilson; and the literary critic, Jacques Rivière. Gruffydd is urged to start reading these authors, and it is suggested that after doing so he will be in a better position to understand why Saunders Lewis feels 'no sympathy with the trends of Nonconformist Modernism in Wales today, or with the sentimental Christianity of books like *The Life of Jesus* by Middleton Murry.' Whether *Primauté du Spirituel* had been published I do not know. There is no reference to it or to its author's name. But it is clear that, in its political and social aspects, the argument of Saunders Lewis in the 'Letter' concurs closely with that of Maritain.

Having established to what camps of Catholic and traditionalist thought he adheres, Mr. Lewis goes on to justify his alignment with them, against 'Modernism' in theology and against that literature which fails to take account of Original Sin. The second half of the letter is a strong onslaught on what is termed 'the religion of the Prophet,' and the idea of Christ as a humanitarian visionary, symbolizing the perennial revolt of youth against the old and the moribund. The letter, as a whole, underlines one of the interesting paradoxes of Saunders Lewis's thought. It shows that as a Christian believer, he is of that school of Catholics which stresses the hard and drastic aspects of Christianity and sees the faith as something inherently offensive to human logic; the plays which he was later to write—*Amlyn ac Amig, Gymerwch Chi Sigaret?, Cymru Fydd*—confirm this, and place him squarely, with Claudel and Bernanos, in the tradition of Léon Bloy, and in line with the 'Condemnation of Modernism' issued by Pius X in 1906. His social and political ideas, however, place him among the more liberal Catholics, and in the tradition of Leo XIII (against whose policies the earlier phase of the French Catholic revival was in part a reaction).

Saunders Lewis's letter is followed by W. J. Gruffydd's reply, an eloquent statement of that radical liberal individualism which had been Wales's main political tradition in the second half of the nineteenth century. It is easy to over-simplify the difference in standpoint between the 'Letter' and 'The Editor's Reply.' It is not a simple clash between a conservative and a modernist, or, as Gruffydd would put it, between Reaction and Revolt. Two kinds of traditionalism, and two kinds of radicalism, are involved. The conflict of the two philosophies is one of the chief factors in the vitality of Welsh intellectual life in the nineteen-twenties, and in the excitement to be felt on the pages of *Y Llenor*. We are involved in a European debate, echoes of which are heard also in the English writing of the period. The year 1927, in Wales as in other countries, seems in many ways to mark a climax in the intellectual ferment of the twenties, a decade to which writers on English and French culture look back, from our own quieter days, with some nostalgia. Mr. Alun Llywelyn-Williams, in a most useful essay entitled 'Meddwl y Dau Ddegau' (The Thought of the Twenties), has recently reminded us, with a wealth of examples, how creative a period it was for Welsh scholarship and criticism, and how the interest sprung in large part from the lively clash of views on a select number of central questions, forced upon all thinking people by the upheaval of the First World War.[4] In Saunders Lewis's letter, and the answer to it, what we see is one climax in a debate which had been running ever since *Y Llenor* began, in 1922, and which was to continue well into the thirties. It can be traced through two remarkable series of articles and reviews by the two authors, and is paralleled by a debate between R. T. Jenkins and Ambrose Bebb.[5] The 'Letter' and 'The Editor's Reply' stand today as examples of fair but trenchant disputation in which rule and courtesy are observed to the point of ceremoniousness. Reading them is like reading a tiny extract from one of the vast correspondences of French literary men in the first quarter of this century.

* * * * *

Although it is to France that he acknowledges most of his conscious debts, and it is to the world of the *Nouvelle Revue Française* that he is naturally drawn, we must not forget that Saunders Lewis has plenty of intellectual cousins also in the English-speaking world. He is the representative in Wales of that broad international movement which, rather oddly, straddles the First World War, and which includes, among its leading figures, Ezra Pound, T. E. Hulme, W. B. Yeats, Wyndham Lewis, T. S. Eliot, G. K. Chesterton, H. Belloc, Irving Babbitt and even (in some respects) D. H.

---

4. *Nes Na'r Hanesydd?* (*Nearer than the Historian?*) Gee, (1969), pp. 31–69.

5. Why we do not refer to Saunders Lewis as 'Lewis', when we regularly refer to W. J. Gruffydd as 'Gruffydd' is something which may strike the newcomer as a bit odd. It is impossible to rationalize, but this is the way we always do it. There is another unwritten law which allows 'Bebb' for Ambrose Bebb, but never 'Jenkins' for R. T. Jenkins.

Lawrence. It must be a large umbrella indeed that can cover both Lawrence and Paul Claudel, but there is a definite sense in which this movement of English writers and the Catholic movement in France (in its pre-war and post-war stages) can both be seen as aspects of the same realization and the same protest. In the secular sphere at least, they have plenty of themes in common. In criticism and aesthetic theory we have the attack on romanticism, and the desire for rule and discipline, coupled with the acceptance of tradition. And from aesthetics to ethics it is but a small step. Order, hierarchy, authority—these were the things to be aimed at, in society as in art, and these were felt to be the things most lacking in modern, democratic, capitalist, industrial society.

All these writers—French, English and Welsh—took it upon themselves, at one time or another, to attack the middle class, which is as good an indication as any that they belonged to it (Lawrence seems to be the only important exception to this rule). Educated members of the *bourgeoisie* have always wanted to be either workers or aristocrats. In the nineteen-thirties, they are mainly workers, but for the generation of artist-heroes who achieved maturity between 1910 and 1930, an aristocratic society is the desired ideal. Coupled with it is the Arcadian dream. However much they may differ among one another, in conviction and in caprice (and, to be sure, they are a sufficiently diverse company to make any generalization about them a risky exercise), they are all absolutely agreed on one thing: that something, somewhere has gone wrong with civilization, and that it is the task of their generation to restore the proper order of things. When they come to locating the fault and apportioning the blame, they may differ widely, and I can do no better than quote what Stephen Spender says in his interesting book *The Struggle of the Modern:*

> Twentieth-century criticism is full of sophisticated attempts to explain what has been lost—the once associated forms of a sensibility now become dissociated, the pattern of living of the 'organic community.' But there is the possibility that the sophistication hides a nostalgia just as heavily romanticized as that of Thomas Carlyle for monastic life in the eleventh century, or William Morris for Merrie England. Eliot looks back to the Elizabethan age as 'a period when the intellect was immediately at the tips of the senses. Sensation became word and word sensation.'

From Carlyle, Ruskin, Morris and Arnold, to T. E. Hulme, Ezra Pound, Yeats, Eliot, Lawrence and Leavis, there is the search for a nameable boojum or snark that can be held responsible for splitting wide apart the once fused being-creating consciousness. The Renaissance, the puritan revolution, the French Revolution, the industrial revolution, have all been named as villains. There runs through modern criticism the fantasy of a Second Fall of Man. The First Fall, it will be remembered, had the result of introducing Original Sin into the world of Man, exiled from the Garden of Eden, and knowing good and evil. The Second Fall seems to result from the introduction of scientific utilitarian values and modes of thinking into the world of personal choice between good and evil, with the result that values cease to be personal and become identified with the usefulness or destructiveness of social systems and material things.

For Saunders Lewis, the boojum is the Tudor revolution in Britain. As we have seen, to damage the civilization of Wales was only one of its crimes, but the one most immediately relevant to us. On the threshold of the Tudor revolution—the timing is an essential part of the myth—the old civilization of Wales was to be seen in its fullness and its perfection. A portrayal of it, lovingly drawn, is to be found in his many critical writings: his epoch-making study of William Williams, Pantycelyn, his *Braslun o Hanes Llenyddiaeth Gymraeg (An Outline of the History of Welsh Literature)*, and the splendid series of essays which begins with the study of Dafydd Nanmor, published in *Y Llenor* in 1925.

Throughout his study of the Welsh aesthetic and the ideals of Welsh civilization, three consistent emphases are maintained. First, that the poets, from Taliesin in the sixth century to Gruffydd Hiraethog in the sixteenth, had, as a necessary foundation for their work, a philosophy, a clearly defined interpretation of life, an ideal of man and of society. Secondly, the philosophy and the ideal are in no way exceptional or peculiar to Wales. As a critic, Saunders Lewis is totally uninterested in demonstrating the independence of any Welsh tradition. Only a nation that has lost its self-respect, he suggests, will console itself by claiming to possess some arcane heritage, peculiar to itself. It is the shared heritage which should be an object of pride. The third emphasis is that the literature of past centuries should be seen as a force which can influence the present, by helping us to understand, criticize and change it. 'His work comes to us today as a contemporary message,' he says of Dafydd Nanmor, 'for we shall not see again a fine flowering of civilization in Wales unless the vision of this poet is given its proper place in our lives.' It is in our old literature that we shall find that thought which can guide us, in the spheres of religion, politics, philosophy, even economics, on those lines which are natural to our people and therefore in their interests.

He goes further: 'Without a profound appreciation of these things, tradition in thought and art, Catholic Christianity, an aristocratic society, and more besides, we cannot appreciate the Welsh literature of the Welsh centuries fully enough to thrive on it, to accept it as our heritage and spiritual sustenance.' To left-wing Wales, now in the process of abandoning its Liberalism and going over *en masse* to the Labour Party, he declares that the principle of conservatism and nobility, and the communion of the generations, constitutes the greatest achievement of all human life. In an unbroken tradition lasting a thousand years, the Welsh poets, in their praise for princes and gentlefolk, have celebrated this principle. To do so was to celebrate the ideal towards which life itself aspires, to bear witness to a faith in life and in the underlying harmony of the cosmos. Courtly panegyric, far from being a matter of mere formalized sycophancy, should be understood as a *genre* of philosophic poetry, which transmutes the individual instance into a symbol of real, ideal, unconditional and objective perfection. All this achieved its finest flowering in the century between 1435 and 1535, the age of Gutun Owain and Guto'r Glyn, Dafydd Nanmor and Lewis Glyn Cothi, Dafydd ab Edmwnd and Tudur Aled. Here, for Saunders Lewis, is the *grand siècle* of Welsh literature, an age of connoisseurship and high humanism, delighting in the plenitude of God's gifts and in the work of man's hand; an age also of master poets who praised, inspired and celebrated a joyful, integrated community centred on the hearths and homes of a generous minor aristocracy.

But all this was to end. 'Such an understanding of the nature and purpose of poetry could only exist in a stable and well-ordered society, its solidarity guaranteed by consensus of thought on the important things of life—God's authority in the world and men's obligations towards one another. . . . For during the sixteenth century and the seventeenth, the order of the old Welsh life was destroyed, and the old religion of the Welsh people was supplanted also, and instead of order and civilization there came upon Wales darkness and anarchy.' It was at this juncture (I am still summarizing Mr. Lewis's argument) that Wales became a country of lonely people, and that solitude became the strongest note in her poetry; it is to this point, he suggests, that we can trace the origin of 'that plaintive singing which critics of an earlier generation used to think of as something so very Celtic.'

And now we must go back. If Wales is to have a future at all she must somehow re-possess some of the virtues of this old civilization. The manner of the possible return shows as clearly as anything the influence of Neo-Thomist dialectic. As Maritain repeatedly makes clear, the aim should be to re-create, not a society which will correspond in all its details to the mediaeval model, but one which will be analogous to it, and which will somehow embody the human values which sustained society in the ages of faith. The social and economic programme of the early Welsh Nationalist Party was aimed at exactly this, the restoration of *perchentyaeth* (literally, 'house-holding') as a dynamic principle of social life. As in art and literature, so again in the social sphere, we are not concerned with recovering the exact outward forms which were to be had in the fifteenth century, but we are concerned with re-possessing the ideals which underlay those forms. In the important last chapter of *Williams Pantycelyn* we read:

> We can no longer return to the literary theory of the Middle Ages and base our work on that. Nor can we, in our lifetime, hope to see an integrated society which will provide the foundation for a coherent and social art. Poetry can no longer 'entertain' us as it did in the classical period. But the ideal of the classical poets must remain our ideal as well. We too must endeavour towards order, wholeness and synthesis in life.

This, at least, the striving for the re-possession of an old ideal, is possible because the ideal itself has reality and substance; because Natural Law, being grounded in the nature of man, overrides any economic law; because man is free and history is as much the product of choice and will as of economic forces. The ideal belongs not to any set of economic circumstances, but to mankind. It is there, waiting to be brought out again.

The meaning of a country's history and tradition, and the uses which might legitimately be made of them in the present, are among the major points at issue in the intellectual debate of the nineteen-twenties. R. T. Jenkins, in a masterly critique of the way in which the mediaevalists utilized history and appealed to the authority of the past to sustain an ideal of society which they found attractive, had written thus:

> . . . my quarrel with them is that they suppose that they can revive those things from the past which please them, without reviving the *whole* of the social complex of which those facts were part. I have tried to show how wretched would be the condition

of most of us if it were possible to bring back the past. I can now add that it cannot be done at all, and remind the reader of that nursery rhyme about the gentleman who fell off the wall.

Saunders Lewis, reviewing the book in which this article was reprinted, and to which it gives its title—*Yr Apêl at Hanes* (*The Appeal to History*)—remains unconvinced. He replies:

> There does not appear to be any definite philosophic proof that such a selection cannot be made, and that some things from the past cannot be recalled, if a good number of people find them pleasing. For instance, is it not possible to revive the philosophic realism of the thirteenth century? At least, Jacques Maritain has made it a force in Europe today, and it is not without its influence on philosopher-critics far removed from Thomas Aquinas.

The myth of the Golden Age, related as always to the myth of the Fall and the Great Return, is one which nationalism tends frequently and naturally, though not of strict necessity, to employ. Saunders Lewis, through his work as a literary critic, quite as much as through his political writings, provided Welsh nationalism with an inspiring version of it. It is a version for which several parallels can be cited in the inter-war years: from Cambridge to California, and from Dublin to Dixieland, a cherished version of *Gemeinschaft* was part of the stock-in-trade of the artist-hero. So often, it is a vision of a kind of yeomanry, placed, of necessity, in a rural setting, and connected, if not with nationalism, at least with a regional loyalty. It belongs to a province or to a part of a country which has resisted the fatal touch of industrialism and the financiers, and can still provide a vital contrast to the Unreal City. To strengthen or restore this old glory, provincial life must be re-invigorated; there must be a return to the land; society must be rebuilt on economic principles similar to those rightly or wrongly attributed to the society of the vision: sometimes the answer is the wide distribution of power and capital; in other cases its concentration in the hands of an élite who can be trusted to use it for the common good; and occasionally both methods are combined.

*   *   *   *   *

This, however, must be added: the idea of the Fall and the Return was part of Welsh political nationalism long before it became constituted as a separate party. It is part of the legacy of Emrys ap Iwan.

Robert Ambrose Jones, or Emrys ap Iwan (1851–1906), was a Methodist minister in the Vale of Clwyd. He is one of the two men directly responsible for the way in which every Welsh-speaking person who has any culture at all thinks and feels today. The other is Owen Morgan Edwards. These two men established two traditions in nationalism, the one primarily political, the other primarily cultural, which have functioned side-by-side to the present day. Both of them saw the nation's life as a totality, conceived of it as an organic being, and restored into currency the metaphor of the nation as person. When O. M. Edwards speaks of 'the soul of the nation,' and when Emrys declares the nation to be 'a moral person,' responsible for its life and actions in the same way as an individual person, what we have is a serious use of the metaphor, which is not to be confused with popular visual personifications of the national being, nor yet with the ancient parallel between the body politic and the human body. But in the view they take of this person, their mode of addressing it, and the kind of action they demand from it, they differ greatly. O. M. Edwards saw the ordinary Welshman as literate, diligent and earnest, faithful to true religion, faithful also to the highest values of his own past tradition, while committed at the same time to the idea of advancement, material and spiritual. He saw him in fact as not ordinary but extraordinary, possessed of a great and ennobling aspiration. Emrys ap Iwan saw him as a hypocrite and a philistine, parochial and un-European, being led astray by an ignorant *bourgeoisie*. According to Emrys, the besetting sin of the Welsh in the year 1891 was *cysêt*. The word is derived from the English 'conceit', and as well as the meaning of the original it includes several other things beside. A man who is characterized by *cysêt* is squeamish, sedate, censorious and sanctimonious, fussy over trivialities, blinkered in vision and mean in spirit. He has, in fact, those very traits of character that are ascribed to the Welsh by Caradoc Evans or, more recently, by Goronwy Rees. There are times when the renegade Welshman and the political nationalist would seem to be standing together against O. M. Edwards and those popular writers, from Crwys to T. Rowland Hughes, who are influenced by his vision.

The essential thing, for our present purpose, is that Owen Edwards saw the nonconformist culture of his own day, the civilization of Llanuwchllyn, as being a natural, unbroken continuation of the history of Wales. All the centuries of the past had been a preparation for this democratic fulfilment. Alun Llywelyn-Williams puts it well, discussing Owen Edwards's use of Owain Glyn Dŵr:

> And looking at the centuries of Wales's past, he looked, probably without being conscious of it, for worthy precursors and interpreters for the awakening of the ordinary man in the nineteenth century. . . .
>
> He found them, of course, and often in characters who may strike us today as highly unlikely. One of the best examples of this is his treatment of the character of Owain Glyn Dŵr. . . . Owen Edwards created a new Glyn Dŵr, a hero formed on the model of the democratic and liberal image. . . . Thus was Glyn Dŵr metamorphosed into the defender of the ordinary man against the oppression of the landowners, into a kind of fifteenth-century Tom Ellis, into a politician who tried to set up in Wales a university and an independent Church, in fine, into the upholder of those very ideals which the common people in the nineteenth century fought so tenaciously to realize. This Glyn Dŵr could most fittingly fill the post of the first president of the University College at Aberystwyth . . .[6]

Thus, the old glory is still alive, though embodied now in new forms, which are also 'higher' forms. And if there has been a continuation and a development from Owain Glyn Dŵr to the present day, we can go on yet again from here 'to higher things' without a break and without an upheaval. This is the great myth of Progress, and it makes a revolution unnecessary. For Emrys ap Iwan the present is unsatisfactory, and is the result of some betrayal. There has been a break and a loss, and the task is now to go back, to rediscover something which has been neglected and forgotten, to rescue it, as it were, from the dead. With Emrys ap Iwan, Welsh political nationalism becomes divorced from the myth of Progress and becomes a revolutionary movement.

When the idea of evolution or progress is cast aside, the idea of the inevitable is challenged also, and the ideas of will and choice re-assert themselves. To the Anglo-maniacs in Wales who claimed that they were only preparing for the inevitable, Emrys replies that 'the Inevitable is not the high tower of the wise, but merely the sanctuary of the timid.' Whether the Welsh people would continue to exist or not was a question on which they, and they alone, would decide, by their free choice.

---

6. Op. cit., pp. 16–17.

To Emrys, this was the only political question that a Welshman should lose any sleep over, and its outcome hinged on the fate of the Welsh language. He did not give much consideration to the very obvious fact that language is not always an essential constituent in nationhood; enough for him was the equally obvious fact that it had always been so in the case of Wales. 'The Welsh language,' he declares, 'is the only defence between us and annihilation, and he who breaks down this defence by speaking the language of his conqueror without necessity and without cause is guilty of that negligence which shows a total loss of self-respect; and when a man ceases to respect himself, that man has, to all intents, ceased to be.'

Emrys himself was a rare kind of Welshman, a man of undivided loyalties. Face-to-face with the English, it was not in his nature to take up a defensive attitude. In his youth he had travelled on the Continent, living in France, Germany and Switzerland, teaching for his living and spending his free time learning languages. He urges all young Welshmen to do likewise, to acquaint themselves with peoples and literatures 'less insular than those of Britain.' When they have spent a period of time in a European country, he suggests, they will discover that 'the English are not quite as high in other peoples' estimation as they are in their own.' Saunders Lewis, Ambrose Bebb and others followed his example, and it became something of a tradition up to the Second World War that the Welsh nationalist should adopt France as his second country. As well as many valuable new perspectives, this brought with it several small and harmless follies such as a belief in the innate superiority of coffee over tea, and of wine over both; and a tendency to fly into raptures over everything French.[7] It brought also an unwillingness to believe that the imperialism of European powers fighting against England could possibly be as bad as that of England herself.

Through a maternal great-grandmother who had come to Abergele as the companion of a rich lady, Emrys could claim a small drop of French blood in his veins, and it is well known that he was exceedingly proud of it. This has often, and no doubt correctly, been regarded as explaining, in small part, the attraction

---

7. R. T. Jenkins, reviewing one of Bebb's books on France, offers the following bit of dialogue between a member of the Nationalist Party and a learned gentleman from a small European country:

> LEADING MEMBER OF PLAID CYMRU (*hopefully*): What would you say, Doctor, is the national drink of Baconia?
> DOCTOR (*surprised*): Why, tea, of course.
> (*Mute silence.*)

which, from an early age, he felt towards Europe, and also the note of independence which characterizes his manner of addressing his Welsh readers. Like Saunders Lewis (for a different reason) and like so many great national leaders, both good and bad, in history, he had the advantage of being able to look at his people from the outside. Whether the method be direct polemic or irony and satire, his aim is always to disturb. The aim is achieved not by raving and ranting, but by a cool and controlled discourse, spiced with a caustic humour. Emrys never sounds hurt or offended. He never makes pathetic appeals on behalf of Wales or the Welsh language. His attitude is a simple take-it-or-leave-it one: if the Welsh are interested in their own survival, there are steps they can take to ensure it; if they are not, that is that.

By the time that Emrys was writing, Liberalism in Wales had come to identify itself clearly with national sentiment and the struggle for Welsh rights. The *Cymru Fydd* or 'Young Wales movement', which was unofficially linked to the Liberal Party, as well as generating enthusiasm for Welsh cultural and educational advancement, talked hotly but vaguely about home-rule.[8] This was not good enough for Emrys ap Iwan. From the start he saw that *Cymru Fydd* was little more than a shop-window for the up-and-coming, and that Liberalism was by now identified with respectability and success. Once or twice in his articles he called for the creation of a nationalist party which would give absolute priority to working for self-government and to extending the Welsh language. There is no evidence that he took any further steps towards realizing this aim, and a letter from Michael D. Jones, inviting him to co-operate in starting such a movement, does not seem to have drawn any positive response. He bequeathed the task to another generation, to be tackled in 1925. With it, he bequeathed a belief that the rival claims of social classes, and the issue of left and right, as these terms are conventionally understood, are secondary matters which can safely be deferred until the survival of the Welsh nation is assured. Generally accepting this, Saunders Lewis nonetheless applied himself to remedying one of the great defects in Emrys's legacy, by evolving a policy on social justice and the distribution of power and

---

8. In 1895 an official liaison was established between the movement *Cymru Fydd* and the North Wales Liberal Federation, but the South Wales Liberal Federation refused to co-operate.

On this background, the authoritative discussion is Dr. Kenneth O. Morgan's *Wales in British Politics*, 1868–1922 (1963).

responsibility within a country. These are issues which interested Emrys hardly at all, although it is clear that the bent of his mind is against capitalism and against the utilitarian values—he refers with scorn to 'the educational code conceived by a monoglot and uneducated businessman named Forster.'

Notwithstanding the lack of a social policy, Emrys ap Iwan's bequest to Welsh nationalism is a considerable one. It includes a style, an attitude of mind, and a few clearly-defined preoccupations which determined its character in a most unmistakable way: the concern not with the 'success' of the Welsh nation, but with her identity, her life; the belief that the ultimate determining factor will be the fate of the language; the insistence that this question will be decided by the free choice of the Welsh people themselves, and not by any inescapable trends; the abandonment of historicism and the evolutionary view, and their replacement by an appeal to a past greatness; the abandonment also of self-congratulation and flatulent pride in the present, and in particular the belittling of some of the puritan virtues in which Victorian Wales claimed to excel; the total break with the idea of Empire and the advocacy of Europe as the sphere in which Wales should find contacts; the view of the nation as a moral person with a conscience, which is to be roused not by flattery but by plain speaking; the appeal not to self-interest but to honour, and to the heroic and aristocratic, self-assertive values. In all these aspects the nationalism of Emrys ap Iwan, and afterwards that of the early Welsh Nationalist Party, stands in bold contrast to the variety which was cultivated within the Liberal Party just before 1914. Saunders Lewis's blistering attack on Lloyd George in *Canlyn Arthur* underlines all the differences between the old nationalism and the new. And if Mr. Lewis determined from the start, as seems evident, to become a political leader as unlike Lloyd George as possible, Emrys ap Iwan is the man most directly responsible for that choice. It was he who determined that Welsh political nationalism should be, in one sense of the term, a reactionary movement, one setting out to challenge prevailing assumptions and to reverse the trend of affairs; and that it should be an existential commitment, promising little and demanding much, viewing the achievement of freedom not as something which will bring material benefits, but as a duty imposed by our humanity.

*　　*　　*　　*　　*

Was it a wise and proper policy to insist so firmly on starting with a clean slate? Or did modern Welsh nationalism, in the nineteen-twenties, start off on the wrong foot by either rejecting the recent political tradition of Wales or failing to understand it? Would its contribution have been greater—and its success quicker—if it had spoken less of the Middle Ages, aristocracy and Catholic civilization, and regarded itself from the outset, as it tends to do today, as a continuation of the radical protest? Such questions are occasionally raised, and they are deserving of consideration. To answer them is not so easy.

The first hurdle is that of terminology. If to be radical means to challenge old attitudes and to call for far-reaching change, as indeed it does in its original application, then Saunders Lewis's message is nothing if not radical, and the most valid objection to it may be, as W. J. Gruffydd once suggested, not that it fails to be radical, but that it fails to be traditionalist. As Gruffydd put it, of what avail is a tradition that does not tradite? However, when people say that Saunders Lewis's teaching is a departure from the radical tradition (and to say so can imply either censure or approval) what they usually mean is that its socio-economic themes are, in certain important respects, different from those of nineteenth-century radicalism: the earlier meaning of the word 'radical' is not in question. Further, when this remark is made as censure, it usually comes from one of two quarters: either the classical liberal individualist or else the socialist egalitarian.

In considering, however perfunctorily, whether this censure has substance in it, we must face a further complexity. In his early writings, Saunders Lewis often emphasizes the newness of his brand of politics, and evidently regards it as a clean break with the immediate past. At the same time exactly, he speaks of seeking a synthesis. How do we understand this? I believe we may rightly interpret it as meaning that the newness of post-1925 nationalism consists not in the absence of radical protest, or of any fundamental truth brought to light by the radical fathers, but in the fusion of these things with other truths, acquired on the one hand from a study of classical Welsh literature and the character of Welsh society prior to the Union and on the other from contemporary Catholic social criticism. The new formula, we must believe, is genuinely meant to be more inclusive than the old. Just as, according to a commonplace of criticism in the nineteen-twenties, and one which Saunders Lewis echoes, the new classical ideal should be large enough to include romanticism within it, so should the new ideal of social responsibility include, complete and fulfil what is best in the legacy of democratic protest.

The difficulty is that the end product does not, at first sight, look like a synthesis. It requires some scrutiny to see that it is one. The first impression given is that not all elements in the synthesis are regarded as being of equal value. It may be a wrong impression, but we can understand how it occurs: the heritage of the immediate past, democracy, liberalism and the movement towards equality, are taken for granted and not regarded as requiring much comment, favourable or otherwise; whereas the values which have to be sought from the past, and are brought in to correct the balance and complete the programme, are advertised with all the enthusiasm of having made a momentous discovery. The same exactly is true of Maritain. Unlike his mentor Léon Bloy, and unlike most Catholic apologists of Bloy's generation, he does accept the history of the last two centuries as a *fait accompli*, and accepts that the modern world, for all its aberrations, has brought to light certain truths which the ages of faith had managed to overlook. But whenever these facts are mentioned, and whether Maritain has meant it to be so or not, they have about them the sound of a concession; not a grudging concession, a generous enough one; but not something which has behind it the whole weight of the writer's emotional commitment. We are never allowed to forget that the most lasting memorials of Voltaire, Kant and Rousseau are their Great Errors; and while it is not expressly denied that there may have been villains in the world before the sixteenth century, we are not often reminded that there were any. It is for this reason, the uneven distribution of the writer's enthusiasm, that what is supposed to be a marriage—what is, indeed, quite genuinely a marriage—looks at first more like a divorce. A fair examination of the contents of their teaching will show that Maritain, and with him Saunders Lewis, are sincerely concerned with making a synthesis in which old graces would be reconciled with new realities, and old freedoms retained while meeting new economic demands. Politically, the problem which occupies them is that inherited from the great and wise visionary Alexis de Tocqueville. Tocqueville offered neither an answer nor an ideology to go with his far-seeing analysis of modern society, and all worth-while effort in the social criticism of this century has been an attempt to continue from where he left off. Within this movement of thought, Welsh nationalism is not without its contribution.

The political tradition which evolved in nineteenth-century Wales—unlike nineteenth-century France—was that of a moderate radicalism, imbued with a good measure of *pietas*. While it called vigorously for new freedoms, there were old loyalties which it was loth to cast away. It was bound to religion, and it stressed loyalty to hearth, family and neighbourhood: so many of its values, in fact, were those which in France became the property of radical conservatism. As the century wore on, and as the influence of European democratic nationalism came to be felt, these conservative influences grew stronger; radicalism came to be increasingly allied with a cultural aspiration, and came to be accompanied with a sense of history and tradition—something which up to the 1860s had tended to be the monopoly of Tories such as Glasynys and Talhaiarn. By the last quarter of the century, Welsh radicalism had come to include something quite recognizable as nationalism. This is to be seen most clearly of all in the work of Michael D. Jones (1822–98), the last and the greatest in the noble succession of Victorian radical *Annibynwyr*, or Independents. Fully implied in his message and programme for Wales is that wholeness of vision on a nation's life which the two Methodists, O. M. Edwards and Emrys ap Iwan, were, each in his own way, to make more articulate. In his thought, the struggle for the Welshman's confidence and self-respect becomes quite inseparable from the fight for personal freedom and social justice.

During the 1880s and 90s much of the programme of Michael D. Jones came to be adopted by a new generation of professional politicians. In the process it was inevitably watered down. By the mid-1890s we find it incorporated in *Cymru Fydd*, that short-lived movement which was seen by nationalists of a later generation as the test of whether the utilitarian values of bourgeois individualism could work effectively with patriotism and social responsibility. The result was negative. It was a failure which symbolizes, for us today, the floundering of the great Victorian aspiration, and one which thinking Welshmen through the ensuing seven decades have not forgiven. If it had failed completely to get off the ground, posterity might have been kinder to the Liberal radicalism of the last century; because it achieved much, and promised more, its eventual atrophy is all the more noticeable. And for the young generation of nationalists who had come under the influence of Emrys ap Iwan, the failure of *Cymru Fydd* carried more symbolic weight than did all the indisputable achievements of radicalism in the field of personal rights and national self-respect. It had not obtained a parliament, or made any real show of trying to obtain one. It had not stemmed the decline of the Welsh language. The survival of the Welsh as a people was, if anything, more in doubt after the *Cymru Fydd* experiment than it was previously. Some of the young men who founded Plaid Cymru—not all of them—in assessing the worth of the old-style nationalism and the radicalism which contained it, judged them by their fruits and found them lacking.

It is for this reason that the traditional themes of radicalism do not figure prominently in Saunders Lewis's programme, although, as I have tried to suggest, it was a radicalism which gave itself so naturally to the kind of synthesis which he sought. But if not exactly in the foreground, the radical tradition is present, sure as anything. It is not often that Mr. Lewis speaks of it at all—it is remarkable, to say the least, that Ieuan Gwynedd, Gwilym Hiraethog and Michael D. Jones should occupy so small a place in the mythology of a nationalist—but when he does refer to it we see that he is not blind to some of its good fruits. He can admire the spirit which informed the great Patagonian venture of 1865. He has several times spoken appreciatively of the Bethesda quarrymen's stand during the 'Great Strike' of 1900–1903. He calls the establishment and growth of the North Wales Quarrymen's Union 'one of the social achievements which all patriotic Welshmen can be proud of.' He writes of the miners' unions of South Wales as having, in their pioneering days, 'brought conscience and a respect for the working-man's humanity for the first time to stem the viciousness of free competition and the greed of profiteers.' Reviewing a life of Tom Ellis, he shows a greater understanding of Ellis's dilemma than was shown by many of his Liberal colleagues when he accepted the post of Party Whip and, in the view of some people, compromised the cause of Wales. Nowhere, ultimately, is Saunders Lewis's moderation more evident than in his treatment of the radical legacy. He finds it inadequate, yes, and seeks, in continental thought and in the past of Wales, something that will complement it. But he does not dismiss it as being of no value. A comparison of his attitude towards it with that of an Eliot or a Wyndham Lewis—not to say a Barrès or a Maurras or a Bloy—can only show how reasonable he has been. Implicitly he accepted radicalism. It may be the one great unacknowledged debt of his career, but we can be sure that, without it, his political programme would have been quite different from what it is, and that the action at Penyberth in 1936 would not have taken place. The colleagues with whom he freely chose to work, in the establishment of the Nationalist Party, were nearly all the children of radical dissent, and they did not come into the new party without bringing something with them. Saunders Lewis, true enough, started out in the company of Julien Benda's *clercs trahisants*. But, like Maritain, he betrayed them, and compromised dangerously with Freedom and Reason.

* * * * *

A related question is that of élitism. Like Yeats and Eliot, Saunders Lewis has made no secret of his quarrel with the ordinary. He has always accepted as incontrovertible that a society, a country, a nation must have an élite, political, cultural and spiritual, whose rôle is not to enjoy any special privileges but to shoulder tasks with which the ordinary man cannot be expected to cope—to set the tone of a society's culture, and 'to lead a country by suffering for it and thinking for it.' All this has evoked a good deal of virtuous disgust from the left.

Among the Labour politicians of Welsh Wales and among that breed of men known as 'Good Welshmen' (which, for the benefit of the uninitiated means 'non-political Welshmen') there is a long-established habit of using the tradition of O. M. Edwards as a stick to beat Saunders Lewis and the heirs of Emrys ap Iwan. Praising *Urdd Gobaith Cymru* (The Welsh League of Youth) is a standard way of chastising the political nationalists (the fact of a considerable overlap in the active membership of both movements is conveniently overlooked, except when it seems advantageous to accuse Plaid Cymru of 'infiltrating' other organizations). The reprimand has two main themes. First, non-political nationalism is respectable and well-behaved. It does not protest. It does not blow anything up. It does not indulge in negative criticism, which means any criticism, of the Labour Party. It does not challenge Labour's divine right to represent Wales for all eternity. Instead of all this, it does—to quote another of the in-phrases of the Welsh family quarrel—*Gwaith Tawel Diymhongar dros Gymru* (Quiet Unassuming Work for Wales). Secondly, and this is what primarily concerns us here, the tradition of O. M. Edwards is regarded as being in tune with the democratic character of Wales, and the opposite of élitism.

Now there is a sense in which this is true. Owen Edwards did apply himself, and with indisputable success, to the great task of fashioning cultural media which would provide an entertainment and an inspiration, an education and a platform, for the ordinary literate Welshman; and his resolve, resourcefulness and imagination were equalled by his son, Ifan ab Owen Edwards, who created for Wales a democratic youth movement in which class, means or background counted for nothing. But there is one factor about this tradition of cultural inventiveness which is often overlooked—and this is the chief distinguishing factor between it and political nationalism. The essence of the O. M. Edwards tradition, which has its forerunners in the great cultural mandarins of Victorian Wales, Thomas Gee and Lewis Edwards, is that one man with a vision gets on with the job, either on his own or accompanied by others of like mind. His fellows may be few or many—that does not alter the principle. The essence of Welsh political nationalism, on the other hand, is that it asks for the consent of the ordinary Welshman, all the way, and stakes everything on his awakening. It cannot, and will not, go anywhere without him. With its roots in evangelical Christianity, it could not be otherwise. As the hero of the play *Buchedd Garmon* declares:

Upon us, the day of defending,
The day of twofold defending,
The day for keeping the frontier and building the faith.
And how shall we hold the city,
What habitation shall we make,
What building, together, as brothers, what watching together,
Unless we be one in Adam, and one in Christ?
And here the fault of Pelagius,
To break the unity of our nature, and that new-found unity in grace,
So that scholar and pauper may not be of one stock,
But that each gain, of himself, his own heaven,
In self-satisfaction unshaken
On the day that the Goth rides in.

Saint Augustine speaks in these words. Two centuries of evangelical Calvinism speak in them also. Saunders Lewis could never be an out-and-out élitist. He is too much of a Methodist.

We are now in a position to see that the Calvinistic Methodists, in Wales, dominate the main literary tradition of the last two centuries. In their respective ways Saunders Lewis, T. H. Parry-Williams, Kate Roberts, Ambrose Bebb, R. T. Jenkins, John

Gwilym Jones—a clear majority of the important Welsh writers of this century—belong to it and continue it. The relationship of the various religious denominations to the literary tradition of the past hundred years is a fascinating subject, and no less interesting is their relationship with politics.

Up to the Second World War, Plaid Cymru was popularly thought of as being the Pope's party, and the old joke from Northern Ireland, which identifies Home Rule with Rome Rule, was imported to Wales and bandied about with some effect. The president of the Nationalist Party was a Catholic, a small core of Catholics were active within it, and some of its policies showed the clear imprint not only of lay Catholic thought (such as that of Maritain) but also of the Pope's encyclicals, two in particular.[9] But then all those policies had been endorsed, and with but very little argument, so far as we can gather, by those nonconformists who made up the overwhelming majority of the party's members from its earliest date. After all, what can a nonconformist do? If an idea seems to him true, makes sense and meets a need, shall he reject it merely because it comes from the Pope? After the war, the leadership of the party reverted to the nonconformists, and in particular to the old dissenting sects with a long tradition of radical liberal protest, the Baptists and the Independents, this again a natural enough development, taking place peaceably and without wrangling. When we look at the forty-five years of Plaid Cymru's history, a first impression would suggest that the axis is that of Rome–*Llanbryn-mair, and that the intermediaries, such as Anglicans and Methodists, are by-passed. But this is only a first impression. Anglicans such as Arthur Price and A. W. Wade-Evans have made a distinct contribution. And as for Methodism, a closer look will show that exactly as in the radicalism of the last century, so in the nationalism of today, it has worked as an indispensable catalyst. Nothing has been more crucial in determining the character of Welsh nationalism, and nowhere is this more evident than in the case of Saunders Lewis who was himself, let us not forget, a Calvinistic Methodist for many years of his life, and was the son, the grandson and the great-grandson of distinguished Methodist ministers.

Mr. Lewis, and Emrys ap Iwan before him, have spoken dismissively of 'evangelism' in religion. One suspects that what they refer to is a travesty of the real thing. Be that as it may, their

---

9. *Rerum Novarum* (1891) and *Quadragesimo Anno* (1931).
* Here associated with the Congregationalists.

approach to politics is nothing if not evangelical. Their mode of addressing the national 'person' is conditioned through and through by Methodism. William Williams, Pantycelyn, had founded in Welsh literature a new tradition of self-knowledge and self-discovery. And as a first step Welsh nationalism calls upon the nation to know herself, to take stock of her situation and to cast away illusions. Then it calls her to repentance. This is the old religion of personal salvation, to which Methodism had chiefly borne witness, when it was somewhat discounted by the radical Dissenters, and now applied metaphorically to the state of a nation. But as well as the 'national being', conceived metaphorically, it concerns the ordinary individual Welshman too. It involves a hope, we may even say a faith, that he is not doomed to remain ordinary; that there is in him, somewhere, a *bonedd*, a streak of something aristocratic, which may yet be awakened; that the old alchemy may yet work, and that straw may be turned into gold.

* * * * *

To 'save the soul of a nation' more than one method may need to be employed. One method is to talk and reason. No one, except Gwynfor Evans, has talked more with the Welsh people, and at them, than has Saunders Lewis. In books, pamphlets and many hundreds of articles, he has explained and justified his policies to them, addressing them as discerning citizens, appealing to their reason and their critical faculties. But this method has definite limitations, because it can reach only the literate, and because there is more to man's mind than intellect. In some crises a means must be found of appealing to a faculty in man which is deeper than his reason, and includes it. 'Conscience' is perhaps as good a word as any. To reach and awaken this, in a nation as in an individual person, an act may be necessary that will shock her, remove the scales from her eyes, and force her to think in a completely new way about her condition. Such is the justification and the logic— or one might say the strategy—of the Welsh Language Society's campaign today. Such was the meaning of the Burning of the Bombing School.

There were several reasons for opposing the setting up of this 'Weapons and Training' Establishment in the Llŷn Peninsula in 1936. One was concern about the effect it might have on the surrounding area: it was seen as both an anglicising influence and an embodiment of an advanced stage of modern industrial barbarism, threatening 'the harmonious continuity of the rural Welsh tradition of Llŷn, unbroken for fourteen hundred years.' Welsh feeling on the matter was accentuated by the knowledge that several locations in England had been spared from harbouring the bombing-range either because of their historical connections or their special position as nature reserves. Pacifism provided another objection, possibly the most important for a majority of the many thousands of people who supported the protest. Saunders Lewis is not, and never was, a pacifist, and reading what he wrote at the time we see that pacifism was not the starting-point of his objection, although it is clear that he believed the form of warfare practised at Penyberth to be a particularly dastardly one. His condemnation of aerial bombing is that of one who respects the soldier's calling and clings to the idea of a gentleman's war. His crucial contribution in the struggle was to instil the grand concept of honour—or perhaps we should say *honneur*—into the movement of opposition. When, in the company of D. J. Williams and Lewis Valentine on that September night in 1936, he set fire to the buildings of the Bombing School, two hopes prompted the act. One was to impress the government, which hitherto had contemptuously ignored all constitutional protests, with the strength of opposition to the scheme in Wales. A more immediate, and a more practical, motive was to appeal to the Welsh people's sense of honour by placing before them a clear choice. In his address to the jury at Caernarfon, Saunders Lewis made it doubly clear what the nature of the choice was. It was a choice between two philosophies—the dominant philosophy of our time, which denies the existence of anything except matter; and on the other hand the belief that there is such a thing as a universal moral law, natural and real, binding on all men. To act in the name of that law was the only practical way of testifying to its existence.

The same applies to the spiritual reality of Welsh nationhood. In effect, the only proof that Wales exists is that someone is willing to act as though it existed. For that reason, nothing is predetermined or guaranteed. Welsh nationalism regards tradition not as a static, once-and-for-all thing, but as something to be reaffirmed and revivified by personal action. Freedom and tradition co-exist in a dynamic inter-relationship. Time after time someone has to step into the breach, to accept on his own shoulders the weight of tradition and the responsibility for spiritual values, to act for them, sometimes to suffer for them, to interpret them existentially and thereby bring them yet again alive. And what can prompt such a choice except honour, 'that unreasonable virtue,' as Camus said of it, 'that takes the place of justice and reason when they have become powerless'?

The appeal did not go entirely unheard. A Welsh jury at Caernarfon failed to find the three nationalists guilty, and the case had to be taken to the Old Bailey some months later before a conviction was obtained. The action of Saunders Lewis's employers in dismissing him from his post before he was even found guilty, and the failure of one or two of his senior academic colleagues to make any kind of stand on his behalf, have, in the mythology stemming from the affair, tended to dwarf the importance of the true moral victory gained at Caernarfon.

Wales is still trying to assimilate the meaning of the fire at Penyberth, and will continue to do so for many years to come. All the themes and all the complex message of Welsh nationalism converge in this action, and there were both irony and aptness in the fact that it took place exactly four hundred years after the act of Union.

It announced a revolution with world-wide implications, and we do not know yet whether that revolution will be brought to fulfilment. One thing is certain—it is too early to declare that it has failed. The 'failure' of Saunders Lewis is one of the commonest folk-beliefs to be found among thinking Welshmen in the last thirty years and is, incidentally, a belief which Mr. Lewis himself has done much to put about. Seeking reasons to explain this failure, we often overlook what is perhaps the most obvious reason of all, that Saunders Lewis asked the Welsh people to do something rather difficult, something they had forgotten how to do, and something which people generally would rather avoid—namely to accept their selfhood and their freedom, and to accept responsibility for their own fate. It is not in one generation or in two that such a challenge will be met.

*   *   *   *   *

One effect of the fire in Llŷn was to establish Saunders Lewis firmly in the public mind as the prophet of direct action and not-so-civil disobedience. Those who had always regarded him as an extremist had their suspicions confirmed, to their own satisfaction. What of this charge of extremism? It is a safe conjecture that if Saunders Lewis's nationalism had been of a cruder kind, if it had appealed more often to mass prejudices, if it had offered a means of escape from the responsibility of personal choice, and if it had been less discriminate in its use of violence, it would have gained support more rapidly. Looked at from a purely realistic and pragmatic point of view, one of the great deficiencies in Welsh nationalism from the start is that it has not had a leader with a distinct streak of madness in him. It is perfectly true that Saunders Lewis has made a liberal use of the word 'revolution', and true also that his followers today, the young men and women of the Welsh Language Society, refer to themselves with some pride as 'extremists'. But it is an ironic pride, part of the Society's banter and self-critical leg-pulling. It comes from the knowledge that they have not yet earned the label, and provides a good hint that they will never do so. The words 'extreme' and 'extremist', among intelligent Welshmen today, are always used with an ironic twist, reminding one that they mean, in Wales, the opposite of what they mean everywhere else. To use them unironically one must be either brainless or fanatically committed to the cause of respectability. Future generations may see that one of Saunders Lewis's greatest services to Wales has been to teach her the meaning of moderation. Moderation is the most important single factor in the psychology of Welsh Wales today. Usually it is carried to ridiculous extremes, and is used as another name for cowardice, indifference or inertia. Saunders Lewis, following the main tradition of Christian humanistic ethics, has taught us to use moderation moderately. Used in that way it becomes not a negative virtue but a positive one, that which the men of the Middle Ages called *temperantia*, and placed second in the scale of the Cardinal Virtues. The Greeks knew it as σοφρωσυνη (*sophrosyne*), a term which implies ordering or arranging: it consists not in the readiness to sacrifice one ideal but in the ability, the discipline, the inventiveness, to reconcile two or more. Once again the key concept is not compromise but synthesis.

The fault of Saunders Lewis's political philosophy lies not in an over-abrupt rejection of the democratic radical tradition, not in any élitism, and not in any extremism. It lies, if anything, in its neatness. Extreme, it is not. Doctrinaire it is. Both things, though in essence they are different, may look similar and may lead to the same results. In assembling a clearly-defined doctrine and insisting that it should be whole and consistent, Mr. Lewis was obviously correcting one of the deficiencies which had been the undoing of

the old-style *Cymru Fydd* nationalism. The exercise was very necessary. But when divorced, as it unavoidably was, from the real use
of power, the end product has about it an aesthetic perfection which
does not accommodate itself easily to actuality. It excludes too
many possibilities and dismisses plain and obvious facts when they
do not fit in with the theory. Nowhere are the dangers of this
neatly-rounded coherence more evident than in Saunders Lewis's
reading of history and current events.

In 1939, having resigned the presidency of the Welsh Nationalist
Party, Saunders Lewis undertook the writing of a weekly column
of political comment in the Welsh newspaper *Baner ac Amserau
Cymru*. 'Cwrs y Byd' (World Affairs) continued to appear almost
without a break for the duration of the war, and for six years
thereafter. It is a column of enormous interest and much brilliance,
bold, independent and original. Whether one agrees or not with
its conclusions, one can but recognize in it a major landmark of
Welsh journalism, a sustained attempt to foster an attitude on
world affairs which would in no way be derived from England, and
which would be immune from the war propaganda of both sides.
The central message of 'Cwrs y Byd' during the war years was to
argue the standpoint of neutralism. This incurred the sharp scrutiny
of the censorship authorities (though rarely, so far as we know, their
active intervention) and it led also to many wild accusations of
'supporting fascism.' These charges do not stand. Saunders Lewis
had condemned Hitler at a time when Churchill and Lloyd George,
Lord Rothermere and Lady Astor, could still find things to say in
his favour. What is true is that his criticism of the Nazis, while
thorough on its own level, remains, until a very late date, on an
oddly academic plane. Certainly he had not 'fallen for' fascism,
as poor Ezra Pound had, but he gives an impression of not being
sufficiently frightened by it. He held that Hitler would sooner or
later have to be accepted as the inevitable result of Versailles and
of the Depression in Germany, and that some accommodation with
him would have to be found. He argued for a negotiated peace in
1941, and then after Alamein, and showed much sympathy for the
Vichy government. 'Cwrs y Byd', for all its brilliance of argument,
was journalism cut off from real sources of information; for all the
things it dared say there were so many things it did not know.
Its strategy was of the armchair variety, its assessment of events and
personalities was, to say the least, no more correct than those of
newspaper columns generally, and its reading of the issues involved

in the war was, in the main, quite wrong. It was all based on too neat a thesis, which said not only that the war aims of the allies were mercenary and imperialistic (which they may well have been —no doubt were, among other things) but, further, that there was no real choice between the two imperialisms involved in the clash. This was an English war, whose outcome was of no consequence to Wales. Nazi occupation of France or Poland or Czechoslovakia was no different in principle from the occupation which Wales had known for four centuries. One can even agree with the 'in principle' part, and still believe that it required a good measure of either blindness or obstinacy not to admit that here was a case in which the factor of principle was somewhat outweighed by the factor of degree.[10] 'Cwrs y Byd' was not setting out to mislead. Its fault lay in its being hopelessly encumbered by theory. In its favour, it must be said that it was invariably humane; it argued the claims of suffering humanity on both sides in the conflict, and kept vigil against the encroachments of the totalitarian spirit on the Allied side.

'Cwrs y Byd' provides ample proof, if any were required, that a moderate, humane and sensible political philosophy is not in itself a guarantee against serious errors in interpreting the vagaries of history. But the converse is also true, that the mistakes of 'Cwrs y Byd', grave as some of them are, do not invalidate the philosophy of *Canlyn Arthur*. What they do is to confirm a very old suspicion, one voiced by Plato in his old age, that the work of conceiving a political ideal, which will inspire men and hold out to them a hope, differs,

---

10. Over the issue of the war, Saunders Lewis and Ambrose Bebb have switched sides. Bebb, disagreeing with most of his fellow-nationalists, saw reason in the Allies' determination to continue the fight. Saunders Lewis is now found in the same camp as Maurras, and Bebb is found with Maritain, Mauriac and Bernanos. This still does not make Saunders Lewis a Maurrasian, and an attempt by the Rev. Gwilym Davies to prove that he is one deserves to be reprinted today as an example of unprincipled mud-slinging. This article, which appeared in *Y Traethodydd* (*The Essayists*) in 1942, claims that Saunders Lewis is seeking to create in Wales a state which will be 'Independent, Totalitarian, Fascist and Papist.' W. J. Gruffydd, who during the same crisis left the Nationalist Party and became Liberal M.P. for the University of Wales (beating Saunders Lewis in a famous by-election), shows an intuitive grasp of the issue involved in the war, and a healthy fear, to which most Welsh intellectuals at the time were frighteningly immune, when confronted with the menace of fascism. At the same time—Gruffydd would be Gruffydd—in between attacks, passionate and sound, on the Axis powers, he found time, in one of his editorial essays of 1941, to indulge in an anti-Jewish outburst! The learned and plausible Sir Emrys Evans, Principal of the University College of North Wales, was another who strongly criticized the Nationalist attitude towards the war. But for one unfortunate paragraph which prompted Saunders Lewis to write a poem, his article 'Y Rhyfel a'r Dewis' (The War and the Choice), published in *Y Llenor* (1941) carries weight and conviction. Battles long ago!

in a way frequently experienced but never properly defined, from the work of ensuring justice in the here-and-now. The truism of politics being the art of the possible becomes, for established parties in Wales as elsewhere, an excuse for doing nothing, and it is essential that it be challenged repeatedly. Plaid Cymru has been doing this for close on fifty years, and has had some success in making people alter their ideas of what may be possible. Meanwhile, in the same degree as it is rewarded with success, it compromises with the idea which it sets out to challenge. Since 1966 we have seen the incipience of something new in Wales, a breed of Nationalist politicians with a professional, as opposed to a philosophical, attitude towards the search for power and the use of it. Time alone will tell whether the new style and the new formula will obtain quicker or more concrete results than did the old, but it seems natural and necessary that it should emerge.

* * * * *

In 1962, with his radio lecture *Tynged yr Iaith* (*The Fate of the Language*), Saunders Lewis opened a new offensive. It was the BBC Welsh Region's annual 'Radio Lecture' for that year, and illustrates well the comically dual rôle of the Corporation in Wales. No other agency since the Tudor revolution has done more to deepen the Welshman's schizophrenia and to induce in him a militant provincialism. And yet, if and when a history is written of a national awakening in Wales, the BBC will have to feature in that story too, because, if it is to reflect the Welsh scene at all, it is bound, in some degree, to reflect what intelligent Welshmen are thinking.

Tynged yr Iaith represents a major change of strategy on the part of Saunders Lewis. Instead of offering a whole philosophy, he is now offering one aim, to represent it. Instead of appealing indiscriminately to all Welshmen, he is setting a task for a small élite and sending them out to save the others. It is not that he is compromising the ideology or settling for less than he had originally hoped for. As always, he wants purity of doctrine and he wants results. But one item is now selected as the key to the whole. *Tynged yr Iaith* is unmistakably a restatement of Emrys ap Iwan's message, and an attempt at bringing Welsh political nationalism back to where it began, to the language, the *sine qua non* not of Welsh nationality but of Welsh nationhood.

The movement which arose in response to this challenge is now ten years of age, and it has grown into something bigger than the lecture envisaged. In fact, the lecture envisaged no new movement at all: Saunders Lewis was later to explain that he meant it to be understood as a message to the branches of Plaid Cymru in the Welsh-speaking areas. Around the original and central aim, which is to obtain official status for the Welsh language, *Cymdeithas yr Iaith Gymraeg* (The Welsh Language Society) has evolved a body of policy on other relevant matters, in particular the future of broad-casting in Wales, the character of education, and the ownership of Welsh land and property. It is now clearly established as the vanguard of the nationalist movement and the most advanced development of Welsh radicalism. It is often critical of Plaid Cymru, but has not set itself up in rivalry to it; it recognizes Plaid Cymru as the constitutional arm of political nationalism, and as deserving of support within its own area; Plaid Cymru in turn has recognized the Society as an indispensable ally, and while refusing to emulate its methods of action has on the whole withstood temptations to condemn its venturesome spirit. The way that these two movements have found a *modus vivendi* is yet another instance of the moderation of Welsh Wales.

Like Emrys ap Iwan, and for that matter like the greatest of the Old Testament prophets, the Language Society has assumed from the start that you cannot save a people without offending them. It has practised this belief with a vengeance. It is a sign of growing maturity in Wales, and a basis for hope, that a movement has been able to court unpopularity day by day for ten years and emerge at the end of that period with a wider ambition, a greater resolve and a far larger measure of popular support than it had at the beginning. It would be incorrect to call the Language Society a 'popular' movement, but during the last few months there have been small signs that it may become one. The success of its ten years of campaigning is to be measured not only in terms of the actual concessions (in the form of bilingual official signs and documents) it has obtained from government departments and local authorities, but also in terms of the new spirit it has brought into being. Not for five centuries have Welshmen shown such disregard for what Englishmen may think of them. To forecast the outcome would be too risky, but at this stage it can be reported that events are developing in a standard and predictable way. The language campaigners have provoked the system into displaying its inade-quacies in the broad light of day, and so brought home to the ordinary Welshman the four-hundred-year-old fact that the law under which he lives was not made with his dignity in mind (how deeply he is moved it is hard to gauge because, contrary to popular legend, he is an undemonstrative fellow); the provincial or anti-Welsh establishment within Wales, the paramount chiefs and jacks-in-office, are provoked into articulating their stupidity; and the Englishman, poor dab, becomes a pawn in the game, being forced yet again to display that colossal incomprehension, almost endearing in retrospect but effectively exasperating in the present, which has always characterized his dealings with other peoples.

When a revolution comes, compromise will be part of it. The Wales which is rebelled against will continue to be part of whichever Wales takes its place. Just as the myth of Progress and the myth of the Return function side-by-side in the Welsh nationalism of today, so do the idea of continuation and the idea of regeneration coexist, illogically but understandably, in contemporary Welsh literature. The instincts to which modern Welsh nationalism appeals may not be rationally consistent with one another, but they are universal and powerful. One is the instinct to stay alive. Another is the urge to bring something back, as it were from the dead, a profound wish, embodied in the most potent of myths. It is the easiest thing in the world to shoot large holes in one particular portrayal of the Golden Age, as R. T. Jenkins did with such skill and such glee. One can agree also with Alun Llywelyn-Williams, when he says that the particular version of the myth which Saunders Lewis offered was not rooted in the immediate experience of the Welsh people. But the dream is rooted in man, and will not be eradicated. Third is the instinct to complete and to make whole. There is in Wales an identity, going back over many centuries, and it includes several of the constituents which are normally recognized, more by instinct than by categorical definition, as being those of nationhood. But somehow, for various reasons, some of them quite well-known, others more obscure, it has about it a feeling of incompletion. The hope of nationalism is to complete it, to finish it off into a national identity, as that is understood at the present stage of Western man's experience. It is part of the hope also that, in this process, something will have been done to alter nationalism itself, in the direction of greater humanity.

*   *   *   *   *

It often occurs with a literary artist for whom politics matter greatly—with a Yeats or an Eliot, a Sartre or an Auden—that some of his creative literary work may show the true nature of his political hope in a profounder and more balanced way than any political opinions he may directly express. This is true of Saunders Lewis. In conclusion, I shall mention some literary works of his which seem to penetrate to the core of the political problems with which he has been involved.

Looking at the original plays of Saunders Lewis we see that he has strayed afar, over continents and centuries, in search of situations and plots. This is especially true of his work of the forties and fifties. During the sixties he suddenly returned to Wales and wrote several works dealing more or less directly with a contemporary Welsh political problem. The last time he had done this was in 1936. *Buchedd Garmon* was written between the trial at Caernarfon and the trial at the Old Bailey, and together with the stress of the moment it expresses all its hope. It is based on the life of St. Germanus of Auxerre, the soldier-scholar who came over to Britain in the fifth century to support the Christian communities against external and internal threats—barbarian attacks on the one hand and the Pelagian heresy on the other. As in the original *vita*, the saint wins every round. The heretics capitulate before his eloquence, and the barbarians are routed by a brilliant stratagem and a minimum of violence. In *Buchedd Garmon* the whole of the dream is realized. It is total victory.

By the 1960s things have changed. *Cymru Fydd* (*The Wales to Be*) was the commissioned play of the National Eisteddfod at Bala in 1967, and the first performance will be remembered because the hall caught fire half-way through the second act. No one was injured, and D. J. Williams was much amused. Otherwise, metaphorically speaking, the play did not immediately set the house on fire; with *The Playboy of the Western World* and *Waiting for Godot* it shares the distinction of being somewhat disliked by those who first saw it. It came mid-way through the period of hope and success which the Welsh Nationalist Party enjoyed from 1966 to 1968, and shattered many illusions.

The hero of this play, too, has the name of one of Wales's saints, none less than Dewi. Dewi is a young man newly graduated at university. Like Saunders Lewis he is a son of the manse, and a prodigal son who came home in an unexpected manner. Like other plays by Mr. Lewis dealing directly with a contemporary Welsh situation, *Cymru Fydd* includes elements of parody on motifs which were popular in the tradition of Welsh kitchen drama in the early years of this century, a tradition intimately related to liberal progressive thought. Here, it is the return of the wandering boy. Dewi has been sent to jail for petty theft, and the play shows the events following his escape from jail and his return home. He is a young man with a highly logical mind. His tragedy is that of logic without honour, faith or memory. Dewi is a certain kind of nationalist, or, more accurately, he would be a nationalist in certain kinds of situations. Like Kipling (and, I cannot resist the temptation to add, like the Barrès who said '*Je ne peux vivre dans une société sans drapeaux.* . . . *J'aime la république, mais armée, glorieuse, organisée*'), he is prepared to serve his nation if he can be quite sure that it is there, and if it gives him certainty. Dewi's lover is Bet, a vicar's daughter. Her nationalism is that which a Camus or a Simone Weil would understand (though they might not even call it nationalism), that which involves suffering for the nation and with it, accepting that the existence of the nation is not, in practical terms, something that can be taken for granted, but that which must be re-possessed through faith and risk. As her name suggests, she stands for the acceptance of uncertainty. That is possible for her because she remembers.

Cymru Fydd refers openly to some recent events in Wales and particularly to an incident in the town of Dolgellau in the autumn of 1965 when a group of young nationalists, demonstrating for the official use of the Welsh language, were rather viciously set upon by some local thugs (an occurrence since repeated, incidentally, in this dangerous little town). Bet was one of those who took part in the demonstration. Dewi, without sharing her political conviction, had gone with her, just to see what would happen. What he saw put the tragedy in motion. For him, it was conclusive proof that there is no Wales:

> DEWI: I saw the policemen carrying you and the others out of the Post Office and throwing you down on the square. I saw the riff-raff of Dolgellau kicking you and pulling you by the hair. . . . I saw how the policemen let them carry on, and a crowd standing by just as I did myself, without lifting a finger to protect you.
>
> BET: I wasn't badly hurt, Dewi.
>
> DEWI: Perhaps not. But I went there to see whether Wales could give me a thrill in life. I came away cursing all and sundry, cursing Wales. And the Sunday night after that, I broke into a garage and stole twenty pounds.

Dewi is at pains to stress that his action was in no way a political protest, and that it was not meant to avenge any wrong. He did it in order to cut himself off from society and from all responsibility. 'What has a man got left,' he asks, 'when he has no country, nothing to believe in, nothing to be loyal to?' He suggests an answer, not an original one, but a standard one in the thought and literature of our century:

> There's only one thing left, except Communism. One's self. I can't become a Communist. Wales has had more than her bellyful of Puritanism already. Communism is just Puritanism without God. And there is still nuclear war to destroy its foundation. No. I must create my own meaning in life. I must make a choice, and in choosing to stand alone in the face of life and of society, I must turn life into a challenge and a thrill. To challenge society, to challenge law and opinion, to choose the life of a criminal and an outlaw. That is the answer to the Great Absurd. Hitler had a country and a nation to play with and to give him the thrill of living. And then he died of his own choice. But I have nothing. Except my own life. I am Young Wales.

This speech exemplifies the play's two levels of reference. Symbolically Dewi represents all those people, to be found everywhere, but thicker on the ground in Wales than in most places, who do not see that to receive an inspiration from one's country demands a certain effort of understanding and faith on the part of the individual person, and that a nation's heritage and tradition are things to be revitalized by each generation in its turn. On the literal level, the tragedy is that of an intelligent boy who respects logic as though it were the only thing that matters.

Dewi's parents try to convince him that only by going back to prison and completing his sentence will he be able to start a new life—that 'the prison door is also the door of hope' (this again, in another context, is part of Saunders Lewis's political message to Wales). Bet argues likewise, and Dewi gives a promise, which he never intends to keep, that after a night of love he will, on the following morning, give himself up to the police. When the police come for him on the following day, he climbs to a rooftop and throws himself down to his death, having first of all gibed cruelly at Bet for her efforts to 'save' him.

Is this *Cymru Fydd*? Is this the Wales of tomorrow? Many were dismayed at the suggestion. What is certain is that there is a Wales of this kind; that, indeed, this is the Wales of the majority today.

It will not face the challenge to be. It lives in fear of its freedom. Because there is no certainty it sulks, falls in love with death, and turns viciously on those who would offer it life. Nothing will save Dewi. All persuasion and all sacrifice on his behalf will be in vain. Death is his choice. Yet, at the end of the play, there remains the one possibility, that in the union between Dewi and Bet a child may have been conceived. *Cymru Fydd*, this time in a new sense. What the child will be like we can only guess, but it is reasonable to expect that it will be like Bet in some things and like Dewi in others. *Cymru Fydd*, like all the best tragedies, is an unpleasant piece of work, but in the totality of its theme it suggests the possibility that all may not be lost. It shows the making of a compromise, and hints at the partial victory which rewards most attempts to save or transform society.

The making of a deal, a bargain, in the life of Wales is the subject also of the excellent short novel *Merch Gwern Hywel* (*The Daughter of 'Gwern Hywel'*) which appeared in 1964. Sub-titled 'an historical romance,' it is a love story occurring at a crucial point in the history of Welsh Methodism. Sarah Jones, the daughter of Gwern Hywel, a large farm in the county of Denbigh, elopes with a young Methodist preacher, William Roberts of Amlwch, when her mother has forbidden their marriage. Interwoven with the love story there is the story of a crisis in the religious and cultural history of Wales. It is soon after the Calvinistic Methodists, by ordaining their own ministers in 1811, had broken away from the Anglican Church and set themselves up as a nonconformist denomination. The problem is a Tocquevillian one. A new élite is coming into existence in Wales, a new generation of leaders, middle-class and Methodist: will this new élite retain some of the graces of the old, and ensure the continuation without which society collapses? This is the social or cultural crisis, and this is one reason why Sarah Jones must marry William Roberts: into the individualistic and mercantilist world of the Methodists she, a descendant of one of the old landed families of Wales, will carry over a sense of tradition and social responsibility and some of the aristocrat's style and ease. Then, there is the theological crisis. William Roberts is destined to become an influential man in Methodist circles, high up in the counsel of John Elias, the mighty preacher and leading exponent of High Calvinism. Roberts's rôle in Methodism is to be a moderating influence, countering John Elias's heresy and preserving a link between the new movement's theology and that of the Anglican Church. In all this, he is going to need the help of Sarah Jones. By marrying her he will anchor himself to the old Wales, and to the 'tradition' both social and spiritual. Thus, by breaking away, by escaping, from the Wales that she knows, Sarah Jones will be ensuring a fruitful continuation of its values: it sometimes happens that a man's revolt against his tradition may simultaneously mean a re-possession and a renewal of it. It happened in the life of Saunders Lewis when he turned to Rome. His revolt was not without a precedent among his ancestors: for Sarah Jones and William Roberts were his own great-grandparents.

Merch Gwern Hywel is a work of great simplicity and elegance, dealing with the whole man, engaging all the reader's faculties, alive with seriousness and gaiety. The characters are drawn in such a way as to undermine many a stock image of the Methodist fathers; they have humour, panache and daring; to connect them with the idea of romance is strikingly bold and strikingly apt. As in *Cymru Fydd*, the making of a valid compromise is seen not as a cowardly self-effacement but as a positive act involving faith, risk and decisive commitment of oneself. Different as they are in mode, both works are concerned with the same question. They explore the possibilities of a bargain that will ensure continuance. Their conclusion would seem to be that where there is risk there is hope.

The last work I want to mention is a very short poem, unashamedly autobiographical, which says something about the nature of hope and despair. It was published in the Spring of 1970. I have presumed that a rough translation* may give a better idea of the theme than would a prose summary:

> Young, I loved. And love
> Kills a whole world at a move:
> There is none but my love.

> The myriad lights above
> In that moment cannot live:
> No sun, no moon save my love.

> And now, I know despairing.
> Despair, despair, the sound of its knell
> Shatters all being.

At the first reading it may seem to be a simple contrast between erstwhile hope and present despair. The despair, we are safe to

---

* For another translation of this poem, see p. 194.

assume, concerns not the validity of the early vision but the hope of its realizing; the poem, or so it would seem initially, confirms Saunders Lewis's verdict on his own endeavour, found in the interview of 1961 to which I referred at the beginning of this article:

> I had a desire, not a small desire, but a very great one, to change the history of Wales. To change the whole course of Wales, and to make Welsh Wales something living, strong, powerful, belonging to the modern world. And I failed absolutely.

But is it that straightforward? As often occurs with an artist who has also been a man of action, his creative work is not only a kind of compensation for some failure in practical affairs (in the same interview Mr. Lewis readily agrees that he has shared this quite common experience); it is also something which places the failure in a kind of perspective. Art, in transforming the world of actuality, questions all its accepted concepts. What is hope? What is despair? From the poem's two statements arise these questions, leading to a tentative answer, then back to questioning, and so on, open-endedly. If the light of young love could make a man that blind, may it not be that the tolling of today's despair makes him, in the same degree, deaf? The suggestion is not mine. It's in the poem.

DAFYDD GLYN JONES

His Theatre

It.is as the *doyen* of Welsh dramatists that Saunders Lewis is best known to the Welsh public. Since 1921 he has written some twenty plays, for stage, radio and television, and the wide range of subjects in his theatre—often controversial in treatment—bears witness to an intellectual breadth and depth unmatched elsewhere in the Welsh theatre. The theatre has always been his first love. As a student at Liverpool University he reviewed plays for the *Wallasey Chronicle*, and Lascelles Abercrombie the playwright was among his University teachers. His favourite reading included the Anglo-Irish dramatists (especially Yeats and Synge) and other contemporary dramatists such as John Masefield and Gordon Bottomley. During 1919–20 he wrote a series of articles in the *Welsh Outlook* and the *Cambria Daily Leader* on the Welsh theatre, which was then still in its infancy, stressing the need for professional standards of elocution, movement and stagecraft in general. As he has said more recently (in 'Dylanwadau' ('Influences'), a T.V. interview printed in *Taliesin*, Christmas 1961), the fact that there is no professional theatre in Wales still makes him doubt whether it is worthwhile writing plays in Welsh: 'It hurts me to write plays I know no one can act . . . but the only sort of creative writing that appeals strongly to me, is drama.'

Nevertheless, during the inter-war years he sacrificed his interest in writing for the theatre to the demands of political life, and wrote plays only sporadically. In them we see Saunders Lewis experimenting with a variety of topics and modes of expression.

His first play, *The Eve of Saint John* (1921), is a curiosity: his only play in English. It is a whimsical one-act comedy set amongst the peasantry of nineteenth-century Wales. The influence of Synge is plain. The author says: 'I have tried to suggest in English the rhythms and idioms of Welsh, and the play is practically a translation' (Foreword). But in reality, as he admits, 'Anglo-Welsh . . . is something more hideous than parody can suggest' and the type of speech used in the play, with its 'muscled rhythm and vivid imagery' was quite unrealistic. Anglo-Welsh, he came to realize, is a dialect, and tends to limit the dramatist to purely parochial matters. Contrary to the prevalent fashion in Welsh theatre, Saunders Lewis sought to get away from the 'folk' drama in which all Welshmen were peasants and the servile lackeys of an Anglicized squirearchy. In one or two articles written in 1947 on the great French Classical playwright Pierre Corneille, Saunders Lewis wrote: 'From time to time I have lived years with Corneille's plays and more than once tried to transfer a Cornelian dilemma to a Welsh setting or background. A Cornelian dilemma, i.e. a clash between love and family loyalty, is what I tried to depict in my first (*sic*) play, *Gwaed yr Uchelwyr*, and there is a similar situation in *Amlyn ac Amig*.'

Of the two plays mentioned the first, *Noble Blood* (1922), has features common enough in the sentimental popular plays of the day: a tyrannous squire, a malicious steward, a love affair between the farmer's daughter and the squire's son, an oppressed tenantry, attempted arson—all these could be found in any popular melodrama, but Saunders Lewis gives the hackneyed plot an original—and unpopular—twist.

The year is 1827. Rolant Gruffydd is a tenant on an estate of which his ancestors were once the rightful owners before going into exile. In London his daughter Luned, the heroine, has fallen in love with Arthur, the squire's son. On their return, a trivial squabble with the villainous steward, Robert Puw, leads to a threat of eviction. Arthur begs his father to be less harsh, and he relents, but on terms too humiliating for the proud Rolant and Luned to accept. They prepare to emigrate to America. Meantime the farmlads set fire to the steward's hayricks. The magnanimous Rolant persuades them to save Puw's home and put out the fire. The one hope of staying— and ultimately of regaining the estate—is for Luned to accept Arthur's proposal of marriage, and her mother urges her to follow the call of duty to her lineage, to her parents and to her own affections. But after the arson the Squire refuses to let them stay on any terms whatever. Though Arthur offers to marry her and accompany them into exile, she refuses.

Thus there is no happy ending, but a decision as mysterious to the audiences of the day as it is to Arthur. Luned sees that she has been on the point of contracting a marriage which risked *seeming* dishonourable—people might have thought she was marrying merely to save the family home. The Squire's final decision frees her hands and resolves her dilemma: 'Thank God,' she says, 'for freeing me from unbearable temptation. Now I'm free, free to choose my own life. My life shall be an altar for the memories of my race. I shall be a nun for my country. And my family shall die with me, but without betraying their ideals or their traditions.' In retrospect

Luned's words seem to express an unhealthy death-wish; precisely the malaise that Saunders Lewis was later to condemn and reject in his more recent plays (e.g. *The Wales to Be* and *On the Train*) as being defeatist. Luned's heroic self-sacrifice, her preference for eventual death rather than even apparent dishonour, her rejection of happiness at the cost of compromise, all anticipate the values expressed by the heroines of Jean Anouilh (e.g. Antigone), but to Welsh audiences this high idealism was mystifying, and Mr. Lewis's theatre in this critic's opinion shows an evolution away from this uncompromising austerity—it is a luxury that Wales, for instance, can scarcely afford in its parlous condition. Perhaps this is why Mr. Lewis has more or less disavowed his first Welsh play.

Apart from *Doctor er ei waethaf* (1924), a rather stilted translation of Molière's *Le Médecin malgré lui*, Saunders Lewis wrote nothing for the stage for another quarter of a century. However in 1937, while awaiting trial at the Old Bailey for his part in burning the bombing school in Llŷn, he wrote a radio play, *The Life of Saint Germanus*, based on the semi-legendary visit of the saint to Wales in the year 429 to combat the dangerous heresy of Pelagianism— the doctrine that man is perfectible, and can by his own unaided efforts, achieve salvation. The Britons, custodians of the Roman church and civilization in these islands at this time, are threatened by two dangers: disunity within, arising from the heresy; and the attacks by pagan barbarians from without. The Britons guard the very frontiers of civilization itself. Germanus defeats the Pelagians in disputation, rallies the Britons and leads them, ex-general as he is, into victory over the pagans in the 'Hallelujah Victory' of 430. Despite its remote historical setting, it is clearly a fable for the times; the moral for Wales, racked by disunity and threatened by materialism, is plain. Saunders Lewis felt that in 1937 European civilization was facing the same crisis as that depicted in the play. To him the bombing school had been an example of a literally ungodly thing, created by a government which set itself above God's moral law.

The play, in *vers libre*, is spare and powerful: it contains what are generally acknowledged to be some of the author's most stirring and impressive passages. Its many liturgical elements and the use of various types of chorus, inevitably remind one of the success of *Murder in the Cathedral* a few years before, which perhaps provoked Saunders Lewis into experimenting anew with verse as a theatrical medium.

Amlyn and Amig is based on a medieval translation of the French legend of *Amis et Amiles*, and is another example of the Cornelian dilemma.

As boys Amlyn and Amig were as alike as twins and, when baptized by the Pope, were each given identical precious goblets. As youths they swore an oath of loyalty to each other, never to let each other down. Amig risks his life to gain for Amlyn the girl he loved. The play opens on Christmas Eve, many years later. Amlyn, his wife Belisent and two little sons are happily celebrating the feast when a leprous beggar calls. From the goblet he bears, Amlyn recognizes his old friend and welcomes him warmly. That night an angel tells Amig that he may be healed if he tells Amlyn to kill his sons and anoint him with their blood. Amlyn overhears part of this, and forces Amig to tell all. Though horror-struck to the point of blasphemy, he feels bound by his oath to help his friend, and in black despair 'without God, faith, hope or charity' he kills his sons and anoints Amig. By morning, a miracle: Amig is healed. Yet another: the boys are alive and well.

The third and most important miracle is a psychological one: Amlyn's soul is saved. With its happy ending, the play is in a sense a comedy. Amlyn had been smugly content with his wife and children, and his faith had become perfunctory and meaningless. In his family he adored himself rather than God's goodness. Through them God smote Amlyn with Amlyn's own hand. When his faith is tried, it is found wanting. He is saved only by his oath. There is something 'existentialist' about his action: he acts 'as if' there were some supernatural force which made the oath meaningful: it is a 'gamble' that, despite the frightful appearances, God does exist, life is not absurd. This 'existentialist gamble,' this 'leap into the dark' is a theme we shall find recurring frequently in Saunders Lewis's theatre, though seldom with the same optimistic and confident aftermath. The medium of the play is the *vers libre*, and as the author has chosen to link the tale with Christmastide, much use is made of carols and other liturgical elements.

During 1923–25 Saunders Lewis had made an abortive attempt to write a verse play, and in 1947, having retired from active political life, he turned to the stage again and rewrote and finished *Blodeuwedd*, long held by many to be his finest play. It is based on one of the legends known as the *Mabinogi*, and the heroine is so powerfully conceived as to put one in mind at times of Phèdre or even Lady Macbeth.

Llew Llaw Gyffes, lord of Ardudwy, labours under a doom laid upon him at birth by his mother: he shall bear no name or arms, and never find a woman to love him nor have a child. However by sorcery of his uncle Gwydion, this curse has been overcome; Gwydion has conjured up a lovely wife for him, Blodeuwedd, from the flowers of the forest. The play opens with Llew departing, leaving his wife lonely and terrified: not that she loves him—he has never aroused love in her passionate soul—but, after all, she is not human and has no kin apart from her husband: the human world, with its talk of 'family', 'tradition', 'kinship' is alien to her. She is the amoral passionate spirit of Nature incarnate, resentful at being caged in flesh and forced to be a wife before being a maid, looked on as a possible bearer of children rather than loved for herself. Gronw Pebr, lord of Penllyn, calls and in him she sees the lover she craves. He has a choice between the ecstasy and folly of adultery, or the security of an orderly family existence. He succumbs to her, and together they plot Llew's death. This is difficult, for only in certain secret circumstances is Llew vulnerable. On Llew's return Blodeuwedd pretends affection and wheedles the secret from him, in a scene full of dramatic irony arising from the heroine's equivocations. The making of the spear must take a year, and be done only at the hour when Mass is sung: i.e. Gronw must put his soul in jeopardy even to make it. A year elapses. Blodeuwedd lures Llew to the fatal spot where Gronw kills him, takes his mistress and usurps the lordship.

A year later, Llew, resuscitated by Gwydion's sorcery, returns to exact vengeance. Ironically, Gronw is more than ready to take his punishment, for he had had a surfeit of illicit love, and wishes to return to his fellow men: if this entails submitting to their justice and moral code; so be it. Blodeuwedd pleads movingly for her life: she has never been human, she was given human form against her will, and should not have been bound by a human moral code. Llew admits the justice of this, and instead Gwydion banishes her to the forest, transformed into an owl, a bird of ill-omen.

The theme is one adumbrated in *The Eve of Saint John*: the clash between *serch* (*eros*, romantic love, carnal and often illicit, always anti-social) and *cariad* (*agape* love transcending *serch*, spiritual and in harmony with the social order). Blodeuwedd is a tragic figure who inspires pity and revulsion; as she is amoral, and as her passion is intrinsic to her nature, not willed by her, she cannot exactly be adjudged guilty. Though the forces and desires she incarnates are dangerous and anti-social, the heroine herself, as the author has more recently admitted, has all her creator's sympathies. Gronw, on the other hand, does have freedom of choice, and knows he is doing wrong. The raptures of *serch* are intense but fleeting; they cloy and leave a bitter after-taste.

The idea of dramatizing ancient legends probably came to Saunders Lewis from his reading of the Anglo-Irish dramatists, and of plays like *Gruach* and *Britain's Daughter* by Gordon Bottomley; by the late forties, the practice of staging ancient myths, with a novel ethical content or interpretation, had become familiar in the plays of Anouilh and Cocteau among others. Ironically *Blodeuwedd* has today a significance probably undreamt of by its author in 1947— it strikingly depicts the catastrophic results of 'scientific' meddling with the natural order of things! The danger of this revival of old myths is that the dramatist may be unable to get through to an audience unfamiliar with the myth. As Saunders Lewis comments drily: 'It would be a help to understand the play and the characters if the Welsh audience were as familiar with the Mabinogi as the audience of the Greek dramatists were with their myths' (Preface). Alas! Few Welsh spectators are well acquainted with their own literature.

Siwan (translated as *A King's Daughter* in 1954), originally a radio play, is, says the author, 'a creative poem, not the work of an historian,' but is based on the true story of the adulterous liaison between Siwan (Joan), daughter of the English King John and wife of Prince Llywelyn the Great, and her lover Gwilym Brewys (Guillaume de Braos), a powerful Norman Marcher Lord. The lovers are caught *in flagrante delicto* and Gwilym is hanged publicly— a shameful execution for a nobleman. This vengeance puts in jeopardy all the Prince's carefully laid plans for his domain. A year later, husband and wife are reconciled.

Striking resemblances exist between *Siwan* and *Blodeuwedd*. Both heroines are aliens, both passionate women wed against their will to husbands who seem to prize policy above love. Both turn to men who will love them for themselves. In each case the lover is executed, dying bravely to atone for the affront to society. There is the same clash between *serch* and *cariad*, but in *Siwan* the historically true political considerations loom larger. Llywelyn uncharacteristically, so it seems, gambles the fate of his country, his life's work, to show his wife that he does *not* place policy above honour, as she insultingly implies when she begs him to pause and think of the state. *Siwan* is a tragedy of recognition—in the poignant last act, both realize they have tragically misunderstood each other. They are reconciled for the sake of the state—but there will always be a hanged man between them. As in many great tragedies—*Hamlet, Macbeth, Phèdre*—it is a case of the public weal being threatened by a grievous error or crime, often sexual, within the ruling family; as in them, there is a happy ending, in the sense that once the truth is out, and the crime purged, order is restored in the state, though inevitably the tragic heroes must suffer for it. A sense of fatality broods over the majestic and tragic figure of Siwan, reinforced by the frequent ironic allusions to the legend of Tristan and Iseult, to whom Siwan and Gwilym are compared, as lovers doomed against their will to fall in love tragically. The characterization in *Siwan* is a great advance on that in *Blodeuwedd*; the second act is a veritable *tour de force* of the dramatist's craft, and *Siwan* is arguably Saunders Lewis's finest play.

Have a Cigarette? (1955) is a highly controversial play based on the Khoklov affair, a sensational incident in the war of espionage between East and Western Europe, when an agent, sent to assassinate with an explosive cigarette case, defected to the West instead because of his Catholic wife's scruples.

The play is a study of martyrdom and salvation, and in many ways recalls Pierre Corneille's masterpiece, *Polyeucte*, which Mr. Lewis profoundly admires. Marc, the hero, is placed by his wife in a truly Cornelian dilemma. If he fails in his mission he will lose Iris to the secret police; if he carries it out, she has vowed never to see him again, rather than have an assassin as husband, even though this breaking of her marriage is a mortal sin. For him, the whole mission is a journey through Purgatory and Hell (a theme discreetly reinforced by the allusions to Dante's poetry); Marc desperately tries to act on a gamble that Iris's vow is meaningless, i.e. that there is no God. But as Phugas tried to explain later, such a gamble is an absurdity: he uses Pascal's famous argument that by gambling one's life on the existence of God, at least one stands to lose nothing one would not lose anyway. Marc is not convinced, and his reaction on realizing his wife's death, is attempted suicide. His final conversion may seem improbable, but to spectators not endowed with faith it can adequately be rationalized as Marc's attempt to show that his wife's death was *not* meaningless and worthless, but valid self-sacrifice. We have come a long way from the confident faith shown at the end of *Amlyn and Amig*. The plight in which Marc and Iris find themselves is an example of the evil and suffering in the world. How can such suffering be reconciled with faith in a loving God? Even Phugas admits the problem of evil is beyond explanation.

Saunders Lewis is here facing a question posed by other great
writers of our day, notably Albert Camus in *La Peste*; as Mr. Lewis
has stated more recently, the question of whether God exists, whether
life is absurd or not, is not only currently the most important, it is
ultimately the only question of *any* importance. One criticism to
which the play is open is that Communism is depicted almost
uniquely as merely atheism or materialism; the social and economic
aspects are scarcely raised. Marc is not a convinced Communist;
nowhere indeed is it so much as hinted that there *are* Communists
whose beliefs are just as sincerely and fervently held as those of Iris.
Critics have argued justifiably that the play amounts to a biased
debate between religion and Communism, with the author's weight
thrown on one side, a criticism not easily refuted. The fatalism hinted
at in *Siwan* is here more explicit: the dialogue is full of unconscious
irony on the part of the characters who often seem to be forecasting
the dire things in store: future events cast their shadows before.
The very form of the *dénouement* seems to argue that there *is* some
good purpose in the apparently cruel and inscrutable workings of
Fate: Marc, an ex-pilot, is brought to Phugas just when Phugas
needs a new pilot, to carry on the good work of the Church
Militant, the new Underground. As the author says in the foreword: 'Only in a tragedy can Providence be seen achieving
everything this side of the veil.' Iris's martyrdom has been for
Marc's salvation and the greater good of the Church.

The difficulties presented by the source have led to certain
gaucheries in the play, notably the creation of Calista solely to
speak on Iris's behalf, and the need for a 'cameo' scene in the last
act. On the other hand the exposition in the first act is a miracle of
dexterity, and the characters have a life of their own. It is a play
which repays repeated readings.

Saunders Lewis's commitment to the values of tradition and of
European civilization has led him to find them in unexpected places.
His sombre *Treason* (1958), a 'historical tragedy', is set in Nazi-
occupied France at the time of the abortive *putsch* against Hitler
in 1944. All the characters, members of the Officers' Corps, are
involved in the plot, and the play reveals their motives, and their
reactions to their failure. Von Hofacker, a Christian, has come
to believe that 'Hitler is the Devil's instrument to bring Germany
and Europe to ruin' and has an almost Manichean belief that 'Evil
is a person, an Archangel, an immortal spiritual genius, second only
to God Himself . . . sworn to turn the whole cosmos into a shambles

. . . There's the mark of the Archangel of Chaos on the man (Hitler), a supernatural force and destructive will, the Arch-foe of God and Man . . . I have a nightmare that the angels of Evil are watching over Hitler.' To him the old and honourable tradition of the Corps is a part of European civilization; only by killing Hitler can they save Germany.

Like many others of Saunders Lewis's heroes, he has made an apparently hopeless gamble: 'This is the last chance to save Germany from ruin with Hitler. We had to take the risk. It's our *country*. We had to take the risk though it's almost hopeless . . . one must struggle to the last minute as if it were reasonable to hope. It isn't.' Against this moral conscience is set the brutal cynicism of Albrecht, the Gestapo chief, who sneers: 'Don't you know it's the twentieth century and there *are* no rules of war? Nothing but right is might and the weakest goes to the wall. All other morality is a fairy-tale and hypocrisy.'

Kluge is an example of the man who, given the rare opportunity to gamble on becoming a hero for posterity, by defying Hitler, arranging a truce, and thus saving his beleaguered armies, refuses the challenge and so inevitably loses all. Despite the anguished pleas that the fate of Germany and of Europe is in the balance, that he could save Eastern Europe from being over-run by Asiatic hordes, Kluge's oath of loyalty to the Fuehrer, his respect for authority and discipline, seem too strong. He hates having his hands tied by the premature and unauthorised arrest of the Gestapo men. But in fact his hands are already tied—not by tradition but by a personal debt to Hitler.

Albrecht, disillusioned that his idol, Hitler, is crumbling, bargains with Else, Hofacker's mistress—a night of love in exchange for Hofacker's safety: as the Allies close in, he has nothing left but 'revenge on all the aristocrats . . . I must have revenge and pleasure . . . there's nothing left to live for but the brief and eternal pleasure of sex.' This note of black nihilism will be heard again, in the rôle of Dewi in *The Wales to Be*.

Hofacker accepts martyrdom, however, by refusing to flee. 'My duty is to take my part of the revenge and punishment with the rest. I've no right to safety . . . to escape from pain. For Germany's sake, to spare some of the shame. I've no right to life.' But when Else tells him 'You've no right to kill yourself . . . your life has cost too much' and the truth of her bargain comes out, Hofacker too is disillusioned: even the most precious personal relationship has been betrayed. 'I have nothing to believe in now.'

This is undeniably Saunders Lewis's most cynical and pessimistic play, and deliberately so, for the characters of Albrecht and Else, the love affair between Else and Hofacker, are complete inventions of the author. The historical situation has been deliberately darkened, and—as the Foreword points out—these are not the only changes. The play has been widely criticized for the assertion that there may have been something 'honourable' in the tradition of the Corps, but some at least of its officers appear to have thought so, and in any case their concern for their country's future is surely credible enough. Hofacker's gloomy prophecies about the future of Germany and Eastern Europe draw on the author's hindsight and incidentally betray the idea that Russia is not really European. Hindsight has rendered the central premise of the play much less cogent: the assertion that Kluge would have changed the subsequent history of Europe seems far-fetched, and the arguments in the second act sound academic. The love-interest is almost incidental —not to say gratuitous—and, despite the similarities between the two plays, *Treason* is not as poignant as *Have a Cigarette?*

Esther (1958–59), based on the story in the Old Testament and in the Apocrypha, was written when a wave of anti-semitism had swept Europe. As James Bridie pointed out in his adaptation of the story (*What Say They?* 1939) the original story is not religious at all (in the Old Testament story, God is never mentioned). The story only has meaning if a member of a subject race manages to regain his dignity and position in the face of extreme hostility. The theme is thus a political one, bound up with a love-interest.

> Haman, Prime Minister of Persia, detests Mordecai, the Jewish gatekeeper, and persuades the King Ahasferus to proclaim that all Jews be put to death, having told him that they are plotting against his life. Haman little knows that Esther, the king's bride, is a Jewess and cousin of Mordecai. The king too has forgotten that Mordecai once foiled an attempt on his life. Meanwhile, Esther pines; Ahasferus has not summoned her for a month and she fears she may have lost his love. Instant death is the penalty for entering the king's apartment unbidden, unless the king extends his sceptre in token of forgiveness. Mordecai persuades her to run this risk, for only she can save the Jews. She interrupts dramatically when Haman is on the point of denouncing Mordecai. The king is reminded that Mordecai had saved him, and tells Haman to lead him in honour through the city. Esther invites the

king and Haman to a banquet, where she denounces Haman for
plotting against her life, and accuses him of having instigated the
attempt on the king's life. Haman pleads for mercy, but in vain.

This is a powerful and ruthless play, with a strong vein of
cynicism running throughout. Mordecai does not scruple to play
on Esther's feelings to force her to plead with the king, taunting her
with lack of faith in the king's love. Like Phugas, he uses Pascal's
argument—she must gamble her life, for otherwise she will lose it
anyway when the proclamation comes into force. He refuses to
compromise with Haman, though cynically expecting Esther to put
up with the king's other concubines. The *dénouement* is presented
as a meting out of poetic justice. Early on, Esther asks Haman:
'Have you any room for mercy?' to which he replies 'In politics,
only force counts. Mercy is the start of one's downfall.' In the final
scene this boomerangs on him as Esther ironically hurls these very
words in his teeth as he grovels for mercy. Harbona, his confidant
and apprentice, is cynically the first to turn on his mentor, and begs
to be allowed to hang him. No wonder the *dénouement* leaves a
bitter taste in the mouth. Haman is depicted as a villain of demonic,
Hitlerian dimensions, but his hatred of Mordecai is not irrational
anti-semitism. It is revealed in the last act that Mordecai knew
enough to incriminate him and is a danger to be disposed of.
Moreover, the author clearly uses Haman as a mouthpiece for cynical
conclusions of his own, including covert allusions to Wales: 'every
subject race is cowardly to the marrow . . . You can drown their
country, and they'll snivel and accept charity.' Like Esther, he too
risks his life—and loses. But not in a fair fight. Esther flings a charge
against him which is pure bluff—she has not a scrap of evidence to
support it. Evidently any unfair means is justified by the end. We
have travelled far from Luned in *Noble Blood* who shrank from any
action which might even seem dishonourable. Since here both sides
use underhand methods, the distinction between 'good' and 'bad'
seems blurred and arbitrary.

The same conclusion might be drawn from *The Wales to Be* (1967),
an extraordinarily interesting and gripping play.

> Dewi, a minister's son, has escaped home from jail. His girl friend,
> Bet, begs him to surrender to the police; eventually he agrees, but
> only on condition that she sleeps with him that night. She reluct-
> antly consents. But Dewi is a cynical liar and cheat. Bet phones
> for the police in the morning, but Dewi hurls himself to his death
> from the roof rather than submit.

Though the play is not quite an allegory, Bet and Dewi undeniably are more than just individuals—they speak the thoughts of two differing camps of opinion in Wales. Bet is an idealist who believes in the value of our traditional heritage, religious and cultural, and has suffered being kicked by hooligans when she demonstrated with the Welsh Language Society in favour of the Welsh language. This sight has sickened Dewi who has revolted against Welsh bourgeois society by turning to crime—only to find that the criminal society in a prison is even more appalling. He sneers at Bet: 'You devote yourself to dead or dying things—God, religion, church or chapel, Wales, Welsh—that's your world.' Like Jimmy Porter in *Look Back in Anger*, his is the cynicism of a disillusioned idealist. We even hear him envying Hitler his chance to remould a nation. Dewi's father comments: 'It's Dewi who's normal. Eight out of ten Welshmen believe as he does, that there's no such thing as truth,' and the hero himself, while claiming to represent 'Wales tomorrow,' says 'The voice of the majority is the voice of God . . . Everyone in Wales believes that. . . . I can't be a nationalist where the nation is dead, long dead . . . believe me, Capel Celyn drowned is a parable of the fate of Wales and all its chapels.' What alternative is there? Rather like Lafcadio in Gide's *Les Caves du Vatican*, Dewi tries to create a new ethos for himself: 'I must create my own meaning for life. I must choose, and by choosing stand in the face of the world and society, turn life into a challenge and a thrill. Defy society, defy law and judgement, choose the life of a felon and outlaw. That's the answer to the problem of absurdity.' But is it? He seems to incarnate the death-wish that afflicts Welsh life, and his mother shrewdly says that his ideas are 'An escape from living,' and the father adds 'from inability to live. An escape from failure, from the endless daily tedium. He frightens me. For I can't condemn him.' This is the older generation admitting its moral bankruptcy. Logically, there can be only one outcome of Dewi's cynical despair and *jemenfoutisme*—suicide. The idealistic struggle of people like Bet for the survival of Wales may seem hopeless, but the alternative is extinction. To quote Saunders Lewis's foreword: 'Pascal's *pari* is still reasonable. Perhaps that is why the girl in my play took the name Bet . . . But if we do not want Wales' old faith, or Wales herself, nor want to fight for the things that made Wales . . . then will you tell me what is unreasonable in my Dewi's life and choice?' The author's compassion for his creation is clear. The hope presented by the play is that from the illicit mating of the lovers there *may* be born a bastard child—'Cymru Fydd'. As Bet tells

Dewi: 'You see, if there's no Welsh nation to claim your loyalty, I want to create one, and live it too.' But a question mark hangs over the end of the play.

The same thesis is put even more succinctly in the little radio play *On the Train* (1965), in which a seemingly crazy passenger finds himself alone with the ticket-collector on a train hurtling non-stop through the dark, possibly to destruction. He has no ticket, no warrant to be on the train, was put on it against his will and does not know his destination, except that he is going into 'the night of Wales.' It is impossible to turn back, but at least, he says, 'one can choose the terminus' and leaps to his death from the train. As Mr. Lewis admits, this was written shortly after reading Sartre's poignant autobiography *Les Mots*, in which Sartre often talks of his life in terms of being a passenger without ticket, i.e. *raison d'être*—on a train travelling to a destination where he knows 'there is no one waiting for me.'

Despite the great variety of settings and topics in his plays, Saunders Lewis's theatre forms a cohesive whole. His preference has always been for a dramatic situation where a clash between public and private life generates tension; latterly the situation has nearly always been a political one, and as Mr. Lewis has stated, this is partly compensation for his own failure in political life. A constant moral code or set of moral values is implicit in all his theatre. He is committed to values which stabilize society and make life meaningful—tradition, religion, culture, honour, loyalty, the family, the European civilization. For his heroes, loyalty to such values entails a blind act of pure faith, often seemingly hopeless, in the face of opportunism, cynicism, nihilism, atheism and defeatism—all of which are literally dead-ends. Pascal's famous wager lies behind many of his best plays, but of late the note of irony, of disillusionment, of cynicism even, is voiced more keenly, and the author now shows ever more indulgence for his nihilistic characters. Despite the author's faith, there is a sense of the absurdity and futility of life in recent plays—even in the comic libretto *Love's the Doctor* (1958) the leitmotiv is 'Let's pretend there's some point in life'. Indeed, the term 'existentialist' could well be applied to the fundamental issues raised in his work.

It is to the Continent, not to England, that one looks for playwrights comparable to Saunders Lewis, and the influence of France has been especially great on him. He has an obvious affinity with Pierre Corneille; he has translated Molière and written a pastiche of him, *Love's the Doctor*: he has translated Beckett's *En Attendant Godot* and adapted Balzac's *Le Colonel Chabert* as a moving radio play. *Amlyn and Amig* is based on a French legend, and in *Siwan* constant allusions are made to Marie de France's poem about Tristan and Iseult.

A single chapter can be only a superficial introduction to a theatre worthy of a whole book. Space has not permitted discussion of his comedies: *The Bodran Eisteddfod* (1950), a satire of minor poets and Eisteddfodau; *Take It Easy* (1952), an urbanely comic episode taken from the Mabinogi; the libretto *Love's the Doctor*, and *The Problems of a University* (1968), a comedy rather in the manner of Oscar Wilde. *Excelsior*, a satirical study of a young and ambitious politician who sells his nationalist ideals to contract an advantageous marriage and forge a political career, led to a threat of libel proceedings: hence it has not yet been published. St. David's Day, 1st March 1971, saw the televising of his latest play, *Branwen*, the tragic heroine of one of the Four Branches of the Mabinogi. After fifty years, Saunders Lewis appears to be in his prime as a dramatist; the flow of works, and their quality, is unabated.

BRUCE GRIFFITHS

His Criticism

It was as a literary critic that Saunders Lewis first took me captive; and this perhaps has sharpened my impression that it was as a literary critic that he first made a decisive impact on his contemporaries in Welsh literary—and religious—life. But the impression is substantially accurate. It happened with the publication in 1927 of his miraculous study of Pantycelyn, in many ways a more amazing achievement than his clinical novel *Monica* which outraged some of his readers when it appeared in 1930 with a word of tribute to Pantycelyn as the only begetter of that sort of writing. He had, of course, been known to the discerning before this: as one of the new patriots who had launched the frail craft of the Nationalist Party, as the author of two plays, one in Welsh and one in English (or rather in the most Syngean of Anglo-Welsh), as the translator into Welsh of Molière's *Le Médecin malgré lui*, and indeed as a literary critic who had published some notably fresh studies in a new literary magazine which he had helped to found and also a first-rate, though not dazzling, work of scholarship, *A School of Welsh Augustans* (1924). Some were speaking of him as one on whom had fallen the mantle of Emrys ap Iwan, who had with Gallic detachment and incisiveness mocked at the religious and cultural parochialism of an earlier Welsh generation. But no one seemed to be prepared for the magic transformation of Williams Pantycelyn, 'the sweet singer of Wales,' venerated by the pious for his evangelistic activities and evangelical hymns, into a romantic who was to be bracketed with Rousseau into a pioneer of sexual psychology (and, naturally, the clinical novel) and into an ecclesiastical statesman of the subtlest kind who sought through the *seiat brofiad*[1] of Methodism to restore the ancient heritage of confession and ghostly counselling.

More than forty years have gone by since *Williams Pantycelyn* was published: and the new Pantycelyn who was then so complete a stranger has become a familiar and even an accepted figure. He may still seem quaint to someone who approaches him with traditional English literary prejudices. Apart from the normal unwillingness of English literary historians to acknowledge that there can be any literary masterpieces in the Welsh language

---

1. A non-conformist chapel meeting in which public confession plays an important part.

(a prejudice which, in so far as it arose from crass ignorance, is now beginning to retreat) there is the curious reluctance of English critics to consider hymns as literature at all, a disastrous blind spot which has excluded from the anthologies of English verse pieces like Isaac Watts's 'There is a land of pure delight' or Charles Wesley's 'Come, O Thou Traveller' which are superior *as literature* to a considerable proportion of the poems most frequently anthologized. Pantycelyn, of course, offers us more than his hymns: his long poems *Theomemphus* and *Golwg ar Deyrnas Crist*[2] alone would have been sufficient to justify most of Lewis's claims for him. Pantycelyn is certainly one of the key figures of eighteenth-century literature in Europe since his rich and ardent mind combines three trends of the period which are usually kept in separate compartments: the passion of evangelicalism, the self-awareness of the romantics and the enlargement of human horizons by the achievements of contemporary science.

Saunders Lewis was able to look at Pantycelyn anew because he was at the same time moving towards his own aesthetic standpoint —or perhaps I should speak rather of his 'standpoints', for his utterances reveal certain tensions which have possibly not even now been finally resolved. To understand him we have to remember that he was, most emphatically, a conscious and deliberate European, drawn especially to.the literatures of France and Italy and finding in the Catholic heritage of both cultures the matrix of European civilization. He had a strong academic interest in English literature in his early days as a critic and was well read in the English 'Augustan Age' which had gone to school with the classicism of France, and in his *A School of Welsh Augustans* he had been chiefly concerned with English influences on the Welsh eighteenth century. Indeed, in his quest for such influences he tended to ignore what was most distinctive in the Welsh writers; and this is particularly apparent in an early study of the Welsh satirist Ellis Wynne, contributed to *Y Llenor* in 1923, a sufficiently penetrating piece of work but now regarded by its author in a contribution to *Ysgrifau Beirniadol* (*Literary Essays*), 1969, as impercipient. Yet very soon, as he read more and more deeply into the vast (but little understood and only partly published) output of Welsh poets before the Reformation he began to see it as an unique expression of the

---

2. The first is a long poem on the spiritual life of Theomemphus; the second title may be translated as *A Sight of Christ's Kingdom*.

philosophia perennis of Catholic Christendom and to find the English literary tradition less and less relevant to the interpreting of it. I cannot think that he has banished English literature so fanatically from his purview as the writer of an *Observer* 'profile' in 1954 (8th August) indicated, but there is little doubt that he quickly found somewhat distasteful the English combination of bourgeois compromise with the sentimental cult of the genius who rebels against it.

Yet his first theoretical utterances were not entirely 'classical' in purport. It is true that his appreciation of Williams-Parry (in 1922 in *Y Llenor*) reveals interests which became all-important in his mature critical outlook—Christianity with its heritage of devotion and its proclamation of the principle of eternity, Art with its heritage of the classical and the aristocratic. But side by side with this we have a declaration of the 'egoism' of the true poet whose only function is self-portraiture; and in a later study (in the same year of *Y Llenor*, 1922), on 'The Standards of Literary Criticism,' he gives us a seemingly uncompromising description of art as the 'expression of personality,' each work of art being a unique expression of a unique personality. Literary criticism, he says, is a particular form of art and thus is the expression of the critic's personality rather than the application of 'standards' in order to assess the value of the work studied. It is time and time alone that winnows literature, he concludes, having quoted an observation of Emrys ap Iwan to the effect that in our estimates we must pay heed to what is old and universal—a doctrine by which the 'standards' shown out through the front door in the bulk of the essay re-enter through the back. Now the idea of art as expression was dominant in the nineteenth century, springing from the subjectivism of Kant and the Romantic Revival. It influenced the critical method of Sainte-Beuve, who felt it necessary to explore the mind and experiences of the author in order to understand his work. Saunders Lewis remained permanently affected by Sainte-Beuve's example—consciously so, as the title of a collection of critical pieces later on—*Ysgrifau Dydd Mercher* (*Wednesday Articles*), echoing the *Lundis*—makes quite certain. But the method presupposes a 'romantic' rather than a 'classical' approach to literature.

Nevertheless, Lewis's critical stance quickly became on occasion provokingly anti-romantic, so much so that his name has sometimes been coupled with that of T. S. Eliot. He certainly did not altogether escape Eliot's influence but equally certainly he would

have got where he did without it, for he had direct access to the
French sources of modern neo-classicism; while his pilgrimage was
a progress, or regress, in regions very different from those traversed
by Eliot. It is possible to suggest French influences which did not
affect Eliot to anything like the same extent, like the patriotism of
land and language represented by Barrès—Barrès rather than
Maurras whose name was subsequently bandied about in ill-
conditioned attacks on Lewis as a reactionary and near-Fascist.
Lewis himself, roused to self-defence, insisted that the chief contemporary French influences upon him were Claudel and Mauriac with
the literary critic Jacques Rivière and the Thomist philosophical
historian, Étienne Gilson. Rivière must have provided stimulus
rather than a ready-made critical theory, for, beckoned by both
Gide and Claudel, he was still exploring his own path. I think that
there can be no doubt that the profoundest influence on Saunders
Lewis's brand of neo-classicism has been the unique tradition of the
ancient poetic art of Wales and especially those of its practitioners
who belong to what Lewis himself has called 'the Great Century',
the period 1435–1535, ending with the Act of Union which pronounced the sentence of death on the social conditions which made
the fullness of the old tradition possible. And I think it must be said,
with all due respect to his predecessors and contemporaries, that it
was Lewis who first adequately interpreted the tradition and made
it possible for us to begin to appreciate it. Others had endeavoured
to continue the art and after its decay to restore it with patriotic
fervour or antiquarian zeal. John Morris-Jones negatively established its canons and carefully set forth its techniques; W. J. Gruffydd
attempted to distinguish between the poetic personalities of some
of its masters. It was left to Saunders Lewis to expound its ethos
and to initiate us into the secret of its peculiar glory: as of a long
sustained artistic tradition in which a succession of greatly gifted
minds, bound together by cords of influence and discipline, sought
to express the ideal of a Christian society resting upon a sense of
kinship, of mutual obligation, of heritage, of the responsibility
involved in all privilege, all liberty, all ownership, and of the
consecration of the poetic art to the praise of patterns of conduct
that have been sanctified by the Eternal for the social harmony
of mankind.

We find this interpretation of the medieval classicism of Wales
first persuasively set forth in a study of the poet Dafydd Nanmor in
Y Llenor in 1925. Dafydd's half-humorous, half-exultant praise of

his patron's hospitality is shown to be an aspect of the poet's delight
in the Welsh *gwareiddiad*, a word usually rendered 'civilization' but
to be understood in the sense of a disciplined and gracious common
life. The head of the Tywyn family is portrayed as the pattern of
the *perchen tŷ*, the house-owner, the focal point of the social order,
and as the exemplar of *bonedd*, the nobility that grows out of sound
root or stock. Lewis develops the idea further in the first chapter of
his book on Pantycelyn, on Welsh aesthetics. Here he describes the
period 1330–1640 as the Classical Period in Welsh literature, with its
own succession of aesthetic theorists from Einion Offeiriad (Einion
the Priest) to Simwnt Fychan. The classical idea of the poet's function in Wales was the voicing of praise, the delighting of courts, the
entertaining of gentlemen and of maidens—a social art resting upon
a common philosophical acceptance of what is important in human
life and a sacramental principle by which the poem yields its sweet-
ness to the ear and so 'from the ear to the heart.' The theme of true
poetry is perfection—in the heavenly courts and in the courts of
earth—and so satire, which treats of the imperfect, is properly
excluded from it. Lewis's sympathy with this outlook is abundantly
evident, despite his intense admiration for Williams Pantycelyn
whom he sees as the first romantic poet and the first modern poet in
Europe. He tries to save Williams towards the end of his book, main-
taining that he won through to a position not far from the old Welsh
classical principle, to a conception of authority which reconciles
the mystical experience of the individual with the demands of
society and of an objective revelation, a true classicism which
subsumes rather than abolishes romanticism. I suspect that there is
a little more of Saunders Lewis than of Williams Pantycelyn in this
final synthesis.

His exposition of the aesthetics of Welsh classicism is further
extended in his *An Outline of the History of Welsh Literature to* 1535,
published in 1932. The title suggests that it was intended to be a
serviceable and popular textbook, but the work is a rousing sequence
of interpretative essays done with bewildering critical virtuosity.
Sometimes Lewis ventures too far, as in his attempt to explain some
famous ancient Welsh verses as exercises by promising or unpromis-
ing pupils in the bardic schools; sometimes he overstates his case,
as when he compares the typical court poets of the princes in the
twelfth century with Mallarmé and Valèry as exponents of *la poésie
pure*. But his general explication of the nature of the ancient Welsh
poetic art is sound. He shows that it transcends the personality of

the individual poet and in this respect resembles medieval art generally as exemplified in the masterpieces of sculpture at Chartres. The creation of an anonymous, impersonal beauty is the aim of medieval art, he says. 'Whereas an artist today uses art to manifest his personality, the artist of the Middle Ages used his personality to enrich Art.' There may be an inconsistency here, for whether the resultant art could be called 'impersonal' is questionable. In any case, the emphasis contrasts glaringly with that of the 1922 essay which saw art as the expression of personality. The tradition of eulogy Lewis traces back to Taliesin's sixth-century portrait of Urien, Prince of Rheged, as the heroic defender of his homeland and as the wise ruler, the courteous host, the generous patron; though the origins go back far into the pre-history of the Brython.

In the early fourteenth-century bardic grammar associated with the name of Einion Offeiriad we find a religious, philosophical and social analysis of the discipline of poetic praise, and this in its essence is an application of the Platonic realism of the Middle Ages with the help of those two contrasting classifiers, Aristotle and the Pseudo-Dionysius. By this time the art had become patterned in such a way that it was susceptible to this treatment; and although it would be wrong to suppose that the Welsh poets were conscious medieval philosophers there can be no doubt that the upholders of the discipline worked within this scheme of values. Whether or not Einion was educated at a Cistercian school in Wales, as Lewis suggests, I think it entirely probable that the platonizing of Welsh bardism is one of the debts we owe to the Cistercian movement in its Welsh guise. That the poets after Einion's time became conscious of the social content of their word-weaving is abundantly clear in the work of men like Iolo Goch, Dafydd Nanmor, Tudur Aled. Praise is not mere flattery but involves the proclamation of the responsibility carried by heritage and endowment. Against the background of this poetic mission, Saunders Lewis sees fresh significance in the work of those who would not be bound by its aims, especially the incorrigible Dafydd ap Gwilym who brilliantly pursues themes cherished in the lamentably lost underworld of the *clerwyr*, the poets who were deemed inferior and whose work was therefore not preserved, and Siôn Cent, who voices the disillusionment of a later, post-Glyndŵr, generation under the influence, so suggests Lewis, of the European swing from realism to nominalism.

It will be clear that Saunders Lewis was a conscious exponent of classicism before T. S. Eliot in 1928 made his public confession that he was a royalist in politics, an Anglo-Catholic in religion and a classicist in literature. Lewis was evidently moving to his position in the Dafydd Nanmor study of 1925 and had avowedly arrived there in his book on Pantycelyn in 1927. His pilgrimage had been, in this latter phase, profoundly Welsh. It may have owed something initially to his interest in the Neo-Classicism (in some quarters called Pseudo-Classicism) of the English 'Augustans', but I cannot believe that they, or those whom they influenced in Wales, or the Eisteddfodic tradition that took its rise in the work of these, ever truly possessed Lewis's intellect and conscience. A Neo-Neo-Classicism was unquestionably in the air when he began to think artistically. French Symbolism, though historically rooted in romanticism, had developed classical affinities, so that we find Remy de Gourmont, one of the most vocal of its champions, denying that true art is the expression of personality. There was a similar anti-romantic side to the Imagist movement launched by Ezra Pound in 1912, and this was linked, too, with the late-Victorian aestheticism of England. T. E. Hulme, who died in the First World War in 1917, peremptorily spoke out for a revived classicism, complete with a doctrine of Original Sin and asserting that poetry is a craft and not self-expression. His influence did not become significant until after the publication of his *Speculations* in 1924; but in the meantime Pound in 1919 had hailed de Gourmont as one who had restored 'the light of the eighteenth century,' and Eliot in the same year, in his 'Tradition and the Individual Talent,' had gone so far as to say that the poet *qua* poet has no 'personality' to express. It would be idle to pretend that Saunders Lewis, always sensitive to the contemporaneous, remained unaffected by all this. On the other hand, as we have seen, Wales had its own exponent of a classicism of a less raucous kind, John Morris-Jones, who had wielded power on the Eisteddfod platform for a generation before his *Cerdd Dafod (Welsh Poetic Art)* was published in 1925. Morris-Jones —although in his war against vapid platitude and sentimental moralism he had opened the way for narrative themes of which young romantics like W. J. Gruffydd were quick to take advantage —had consistently taught a concrete, undidactic, academically respectable classicism derived from Aristotle; while even before him Emrys ap Iwan had pointed (with classical implications, though his critical method had its romantic affinities), to the tradition of dignified, scholarly and polished Welsh prose-writing (not by any

means always original or ambitious in respect of subject matter)
which some strange providence had bestowed on Wales between the
Renaissance and the eighteenth century, the 'Welsh Classics.'
This, too, meant much to Lewis; but I think that there can be no
manner of doubt that it was the medieval poetic tradition of Wales
that brought him safely to his destination—together with the
stimulus of the French Catholic contemporaries to whom he
acknowledged his indebtedness.

Saunders Lewis's classicism is his own—if I am not guilty of a
contradiction in terms. At least it is not Eliot's. It is not accompanied
by royalism (of the English kind) in politics or by Anglo-Catholicism
in religion. It is not impossible that he sympathized with elements
in the teaching of French writers who had monarchistic leanings,
but there is no evidence that he liked their monarchism. The willing-
ness of the Welsh Party under his leadership to aim at 'Dominion
status' rather than 'independence' for Wales points to his consistent
belief in the interdependence of nations rather than to any sentiment
of loyalty to the English Crown. You may surmise that if there were
a surviving Welsh princely house with unimpeachable credentials
(of which the most important would be an understanding of the
old Welsh virtue of *perchentyaeth*) he might sing its praises as felici-
tously as he has sung to R. O. F. Wynne of Garthewin, but I feel
sure that he would not reward it with royal status in any constitution
for a future Welsh state. Likewise, his religious persuasion is far more
organically related to his critical canons than Eliot's was to his.
Without passing any judgement on Eliot's motives I think it accurate
to state that having well outdistanced Ezra Pound (*il miglior fabbro*)
in the race for fame with the decisive success of *The Waste Land* in
1922 (a success not due entirely to the intrinsic excellence of that
fine and compelling poem) the poet proceeded to add to his prestige
as a brilliant experimentalist the further prestige of holding political,
religious and critical opinions that were more than acceptable to
the 'establishment' in his adopted country; and it proved an
infallible recipe for a Westminster Abbey type immortality. Lewis's
classicism has been far more radical. It drove him to a prison cell,
deprived him of a post which he had filled with unique distinction,
inflicted upon him years of economic insecurity, singled him out for
victimization by political malice and religious prejudice. Eliot's
philosophy of culture sought merely to perpetuate the refined
conservatism of Burke and Coleridge in a very different age from
theirs without truly challenging the might of the Mammon he had

disdained in some of his early verses. Lewis called upon his nation to 'follow Arthur' to join in a great endeavour to realize the good society of mutual obligation and creative faith.

Saunders Lewis's classical view of art is thus closely bound up with his moral involvement in the crisis of Wales and Europe and the world. If Eliot condemned the American 'humanists' Irving Babbitt and Paul Elmer More as 'Imperfect Critics' in that they are moralists not 'primarily interested in art,' what, we wonder, did he think or would have thought of Lewis who is an indissoluble conjunction? I say 'normally' because on rare occasions his regard for the French Symbolists from Mallarmé to Valèry has, as I have indicated once before, betrayed him into that superficial understanding of the doctrine of art for art's sake which rates the arrangement of words higher than the communication of wisdom, thus seeking to divide the indivisible. It was in a review of a book of Welsh poems by the philosopher Hywel D. Lewis, if I remember aright, that Saunders Lewis once quoted the words of Mallarmé to Degas who lamented his lack of success as a sonneteer in spite of an abundance of ideas. 'You don't write poems with ideas, my dear Degas, but with words.' Implied in this is the notion of literature as the craft of word-spinning, the shaping of a kind of beauty divorced from moral or intellectual concerns. The theory is contradicted by everything that Saunders Lewis has written in a creative way—and this covers most of his criticism, too. Of course, his quoting Mallarmé in reviewing verses written to convey ideas is an expression of his distaste for that Victorian moralizing and philosophizing which could be smugly sentimental and conventional. His suspicion of anything that savoured of this in literary criticism may be illustrated by the rebuke he administered to Miall Edwards for venturing to extract from the work of T. Gwynn Jones a philosophy of life.

Lewis's critical dilemma is evident in a remarkable contribution to *Y Llenor* in 1928—in relation to the controversy over the adjudicators' refusal to honour Gwenallt's[3] poem on 'The Saint' in the Treorchy National Eisteddfod that year. This powerfully wrought poem had not then been published and Lewis had not read it, but he shows sympathy with the author's desire to treat the sins of his hero with the utmost frankness. He admits that this kind of psychological realism had no sanction in the Platonic principles of the ancient poetic tradition of Wales: in the Welsh Middle Ages reproof

---

3. D. Gwenallt Jones, one of the most influential of twentieth-century Welsh poets.

and denunciation were for the most part left to the lower grade of bards. With the Renaissance, argues Lewis, there came a new outlook not only in Wales but in Europe generally, a turning away from things eternal to the corrupt and mutable world in which we live. This new interest in humanity and the individual soul manifested itself everywhere, in Shakespeare, in Molière, in Ellis Wynne. The movement did not produce its own metaphysic but instead was deflected into classicism, a process in which Tasso was regarded as more important than Shakespeare. Romanticism, so he develops his argument, was the movement which gave Renaissance humanism its proper metaphysic: a belief in the reality of phenomena rather than the eternal ideas and the need, therefore, for literature to express the experiences of the individual—the heroes of the earliest romantic poetry, Theomemphus, Moïse. The time had come— and let us remember that Lewis wrote this over forty years ago— for this romanticism to ripen into a new classicism. But unlike Paul Claudel who had reverted to the medieval belief that true poetry had nothing to do with the phenomena Lewis declared that he could not repudiate the essential principle of romanticism, that the experience of the individual is the starting-point of all artistic creation—a principle which justified the fullest exploration of the psyche and the frankest expression of human experience even in its most perilous and devious aspects, a principle which justified, indeed, the first canto of *Theomemphus*. And, of course, this was the principle vindicated by Saunders Lewis when about the same time he championed in opposition to the critical 'Tartuffes', Prosser Rhys's courageous treatment of homosexuality in his poem *Atgof* (*Recall*). This is only one of the provocative sallies in a widely read English booklet introducing contemporary Welsh literature and may be contrasted with the gentle chastisement he gave in the same work to Tegla Davies for allowing his studies of human imperfection to become tainted with the mildew of evangelicalism, for wanting to convert his sinners.

All this left Lewis with some unanswered questions. Why is a study of conversion artistically less respectable than a study of wickedness? Is an 'Evangelical' conversion aesthetically inferior to a 'Catholic' one? And, perhaps more fundamentally, is it consistent to retain a 'romantic' preoccupation with individual experience and at the same time to advocate a new classicism? If the new classicism is to embrace what Lewis calls the essential principle of romanticism, is it to have an essential principle of its own? What is the nature of the synthesis which is to harmonize the insights of realists and nominalists, the claims of society and the soul, the attractions of the sacred and the profane? Saunders Lewis has never fully set forth his synthesis. His utterances suggest a veering from one emphasis to another. It may be that if he ventured to finalize his aesthetic he would draw quite as heavily on the pre-Christian 'classics' of Greece and Rome as on medieval scholasticism. If in 1934 (in an article in *Y Traethodydd* (*The Essayist*), reprinted in *In the Steps of Arthur*, 1938) he could with Eric Gill deplore the tendency which had separated the artist from the craftsman so that the artist aspired to be a 'prophet' and the craftsman was reduced to the status of a 'hand' or a 'proletarian', he redresses the balance in 1939 in a review of a handbook on Greek philosophy written in Welsh by D. James Jones, a deeply felt review which provides a startling corrective to any tendency towards an amoral aestheticism. Here he praises what he takes to be the Greek conception of the poet or writer as a teacher and a sage, and holds up for our admiration the poet-lawgiver Solon and the tradition of philosophical didacticism in verse which came to full flower in the Latin poet Lucretius. Lewis himself as an artist is clearly much nearer the puritan epicurean Lucretius than to the *fin de siécle* epicurean of the type of Wilde or even the far subtler Pater.

That literature for Saunders Lewis is not to be separated from the themes of faith, from moral values, from personal experience, from social obligation, shines clear in the critical studies he has written on certain individual Welsh writers after the publication of his *Williams Pantycelyn*. These include important presentations of three writers—Ceiriog, Daniel Owen and Glasynys—as exemplars of the 'Artist in Philistia,' the Philistia of the Welsh nineteenth century, as well as shorter contributions on Tudur Aled, Gruffydd Robert, Morgan Llwyd, Charles Edwards, Ann Griffiths, Ieuan Glan Geirionydd, Eluned Morgan, Emrys ap Iwan and others. The range is catholic, the approach always fresh and sometimes startling, the context consistently European.

From the shorter pieces three major interests emerge. One is his desire to work out in greater detail the course of the Welsh medieval poetic tradition. Thus, in the study of Tudur Aled in *Efrydiau Catholig* (*Catholic Studies*), 1946, he examines the period in which the old social pattern began to be calamitously betrayed and brings into relief the poet's plea for united thought and action among those who had inherited the responsibility for upholding it. A second aim, as is apparent in his treatment of Morgan Llwyd and Ann Griffiths, is to deliver us from any over-emphasis on a romantic individualism in our understanding of figures such as these, who are frequently described as 'mystics'. He bids us consider the *milieu* and intellectual content of their thought. And his third concern is to bring out the significance of some of the manifestations of Renaissance humanism in Welsh literature as in his 'Gruffydd Robert' and in the somewhat overdone thesis of the persistence of Renaissance Stoicism into the early nineteenth century piety of Ieuan Glan Geirionydd.

The three Artists in Philistia between them display profusely and splendidly Saunders Lewis's powers of critical interpretation. The *Ceiriog* is a delicious application of the method of Sainte-Beuve—is it the best critical essay of its kind in Welsh?—to the life and work of the once prodigiously popular poet John Ceiriog Hughes. It reads in part like an historical novel and is not without its psychological and sociological interest. We see the promising young man's susceptibility to feminine influences, his mother's at first and then those of the fashionable young ladies of the middle-class Welsh colony at Manchester; his progress from the cruder form of materialistic self-help to the desire to achieve success as a purveyor of Welsh verse; the impact made upon him by Creuddynfab, that strange lover of literature who detested the arid rules of Caledfryn and the tavern ditties of Talhaiarn and directed him to excel in the drawing-room sentiment of the songs of Thomas Moore and the popular verses of Tennyson; his joy in his craft and his idealization of the old country culture of Wales. In Lewis's introduction to his selection of the stories of the unjustly neglected Glasynys, a writer who had been drawn to the Tractarians before his interests became predominantly literary, we have another discerning study, less belletristic in manner than the *Ceiriog*, of a romantic, of tenuous but indubitable genius, who escaped from Philistia into an Arcadia conjured out of his country's past. If we have to give a label to Lewis's critical approach in these studies of two minor romantics the word must surely be romantic.

Lewis's monograph on the great novelist Daniel Owen (1936) portraying yet another artist in Philistia, acutely traces the growth of his artistic purpose and his struggle for artistic freedom. At that time Lewis was studying the Welsh *cofiant* or biographical memoir, a form of literature which in the nineteenth century enjoyed its golden age; and he shows us how a man of genius with a gift for social comedy broke through the conventions of his society by writing an imaginary autobiography, *Rhys Lewis*, of which the hero becomes little more than a key-hole through which the author eavesdrops on the human scene (except in some passages in which the hero has his living share of the dialogue). After this Owen was free to give us his comic Everyman in the person of the titular hero of *Enoc Huws* together with the gigantic comic villain Captain Trefor, and, when his health was failing, the tamer but sweeter confection named *Gwen Tomos*. Saunders Lewis hesitates to rank Daniel Owen with the supreme novelists of Europe. I disagree, while cordially wishing that Owen could have lived longer to write more and so to place his standing beyond doubt. Apart from the excellence of that superb grotesque Captain Trefor, I am sure that the tension between Bob Lewis and his mother, the conflict between one moral good and another, is one of the triumphs of the nineteenth century novel and one hard to parallel anywhere. But though we may consider Lewis's restraint in his commendation of Daniel Owen excessive there can be no doubt that he provides us with the key to the understanding of his subject.

Saunders Lewis is too complex a critic to be easily classified. He has shown rare skill and discernment in the application of methods that can be designated historical and biographical, psychological and sociological; but he has never lost sight of the principle that the critic is concerned with works of art rather than with their background and he has never thought of the critic's work as anything less than a creative proclamation of values.

PENNAR DAVIES

His Poetry

Saunders Lewis has not written many poems. He has, of course, written poetic drama and has even called one play, *Siwan*, a poem, but I do not propose to deal with these. His poems are found in the pamphlet *Byd a Betws* (*The World and the Church*) and in *Siwan and Other Poems*; a few more are found in various periodicals. The total number is about thirty.

Although the poems display a surprising virtuosity of construction —there are poems in *vers libre*, in the highly formal Welsh strict metre tradition, there are sonnets and other elaborate forms—most of them can be assigned to the two traditional classifications of verse in Welsh, that is, eulogy and satire. In his short Preface to *The World and the Church*, Mr. Lewis specifically states that the poems belong to these two classes. He proceeds:

> I have put them together now because they are an attempt to set forth, in the middle of the war, a conviction about two societies and two traditions—the two things that I consider to be of most importance in the crisis of our times.

The two traditions and societies referred to here are those of the Catholic Church and of Wales. The title of the pamphlet also refers to two societies and two traditions. The 'world' represents what it has always represented in Christian writing—the unspiritual; the 'church' represents the forces of the spirit and of civilization. What man is, and what society is, depends upon the conflict between these diverse forces; man will either live by the values of Christianity or be engulfed by a spiritual barbarism and materialism; society will reflect the course of the conflict.

As in almost all things that Saunders Lewis has written, the present is naturally the point in time in which he is most intensely involved, but he is aware that there have been other times like the present for other people: that is one reason why tradition and history are so important for him. It is one reason, too, why history and tradition have for him a vitality that is beyond that of an academic discipline. He has never sat down to his tea and 'academic toast' (as the poet R. Williams Parry put it in a bitter satirical poem inspired by Lewis's imprisonment) and looked at the spiritual struggles of the past with a cold eye. He has recognized what seemed to him to be this conflict in his own time and become involved in it, he has also identified the cause with that of spiritual struggles in the past. His poems show that Lewis is and has been intensely concerned about the spiritual and political condition of his time and about the national life of his own people.

Some of Mr. Lewis's poems—as, for example, 'Against Purgatory' —are 'personal', but in many of his poems he speaks with a 'public' voice. There is some truth in the popular notion of the Welsh poet as a public figure; certainly the idea of the poet as a public figure has more meaning in Wales than it has in England. The poet as a public figure means that, up to a point, he deals with matters that are of public concern. In *The World and the Church*, Lewis refers to the horrifyingly visible evidence of the crisis of the times, namely the war, and what led up to it. But Lewis manages to present public matters in a personal way, and in a way that is almost always related to the traditional values of the Catholic Church and what can, in short, be called the classical European ideals of civilization. It can be said that Lewis takes upon himself certain responsibilities and is concerned for certain values and principles almost on behalf of his people. In a way it is a kind of *noblesse oblige*; it is certainly poetry in the classical Welsh tradition. The public aspect of the poet's function is the legacy of the medieval classical tradition to modern Welsh poetry. Two other vital factors in the medieval tradition—namely its hierarchical view of life and its Catholicism— were not passed on. As far as one can generalize about a poetry which has a great deal to do with the personalities of the poets, one can say that modern Welsh poetry is democratic in its view of society and Nonconformist in its religion. Saunders Lewis went back to the Catholic classical tradition of the Middle Ages, and this has set him apart from practically all other Welsh poets of his time.

This is especially true of *The World and the Church*. What is probably the most important poem in the pamphlet, 'The Deluge 1939', commences with the ghastly landscape of the depression in Wales and with what that landscape mirrors, the degradation and dehumanization of men. There is a brief interlude in which a classical beauty and the beginnings of Christianity are evoked, but this is soon drowned in the squalor of things. The third section of the poem is an analysis of how the depression came about and refers to public events and figures. Lewis describes the machinations of usurers with a savagery that matches Pound's (one should, perhaps, point out here the elementary but essential difference between the denunciation of the Jewish usurers referred to in the poem and a denunciation of the Jews in general); he refers to the collapse of Wall Street, the rejection of Bruening, the hunger marches of the thirties, the signs of war. He does not think that the real cause of the catastrophe, the deluge of despair, will be found in any economic system, but that it concerns man's evaluation of himself. The responsibility for the situation is shared by all who acquiesced. Although Lewis is primarily interested in the leaders of society, he says that the ordinary people are not without blame because they glutted themselves upon unreality:

> A'r frau weirnos, y demos dimai,
> Epil drel milieist a'r *pool* pêl-droed,
> Llanwodd ei bol â lluniau budrogion
> Ac â phwdr usion y radio a'r wasg.
> (And the frail rabble, the halfpenny *demos*,
> The issue of the dogs and football pools,
> It filled its belly with pictures of sluts
> And with the rotten husks of the radio and newspapers.)

Because of such sections as this, more than one critic has accused Lewis of displaying in this poem a basic lack of sympathy with people. This is justifiable if one is willing to excuse facts in the face of suffering, as most of us would, I suppose—most of us would tend to justify the escape from wretchedness that people found in cinemas, for example. But not Saunders Lewis; he sympathizes with the people's wretchedness:

> Arllwysodd glaw ei nodwyddau dyfal
> Ar gledrau meddal hen ddwylo'r lofa,
> Tasgodd y cenllysg ar ledrau dwyfron
> Mamau hesbion a'u crin fabanod,
> Troid llaeth y fuwch yn ffyn ymbarelau
> Lle camai'r llechau goesau llancesi;
> Rhoed pensiwn yr hen i fechgynnos y dôl.

> (Rain poured its assiduous needles
> On the soft palms of the old hands of the coalface,
> The hail scattered upon the leathern breasts
> Of barren mothers and their withered babies,
> Cows' milk was turned into umbrella sticks
> Where rickets bowed the legs of lasses;
> Young lads on the dole were given the pension of old men.)

and he put his sympathy into action by arranging for those with the means to help those in need. But he refuses to justify the moral helplessness that he saw. This may make him appear to be lacking in human warmth, but it is consistent with a belief in a man's being responsible for his own actions. This is a responsibility which can lead a man to prison, or even to death, but it is a responsibility which must not be shirked. Lewis's standards do not easily accommodate human weaknesses, and this may appear as a kind of arrogance in his work. Most people find such adherence to standards rather embarrassing. But, then, most people are not willing to believe in anything to the extent of being imprisoned for their beliefs.

Intense exasperation can turn into disgust or despair. 'The Deluge 1939' is a poem of tragic satire: in 'A Scene in a Café' there is a black despair and more than a touch of the sardonic. The poem has a nightmare quality, a surrealistic imagery that shows the world as a horrifying shambles, as a place of 'The living dead.' It is the state of things in general and of Wales in particular (it is noticeable that the condition of Wales is the subject of more than one satirical poem) that generates the dark power of this poem and of 'The Carcass'. The satire has a more clearly defined target in the poem to Dr. J. D. Jones and in the two later poems 'A Parliament for Wales' and 'The "Have You Heard?" Stanzas'. The first two engender disgust by the association of reprehensibilities, as one might put it. The persons lampooned are vilified by being associated with unsavoury grease and with defecation so that they appear rather like Gerald Scarfe caricatures. These are succinct, savage and scurrilous poems. Their succinctness adds to their savagery for every syllable is barbed. The third poem depends upon verbal wit, and especially upon rhymes which are so unexpected as to be comic, in order to deflate. The form recalls that of a series of old Welsh stanzas, the 'Have You Heard?' *englynion*, and the satire achieves its end through laughter.

In 'A Scene in a Café' there is a line which parodies the high style of Welsh usually associated with noble subject matter:

> Fuaned oedd gweini'r forwyn
> (How swift was the maid's attendance).

In its context the line is, of course, ironic; it points to a lost world. That lost world is also evoked in the second section of 'Indian Summer 1941'. It is a meditative sadness that pervades this poem and not satire. This is an Indian summer, the break that comes before the winter of catastrophe. In its conclusion the poem becomes a profound prayer, a prayer in time of war, a prayer in despair— although that despair is expressed in a minor key and is certainly

not the fierce despair of the satirical poems. Despair of the same kind
is found in 'June Moon'. It breaks out again, more vehemently, in
the recent poem 'Return'. Love joyfully destroys all things but its
own object: despair, too, in its own way destroys but, unlike love,
it destroys everything—it is a 'return' to an utter nihilism.

One need not, of course, be surprised to find despair in the work
of a writer who is a Catholic. There is nothing odd in the fact that
the same man composed 'Return' and 'Mary Magdalene'. There is
a despair, a profound despair, in 'Mary Magdalene'. She faces the
spiritual death that came out of the cry 'It is finished' on the cross.
But there is a double resurrection in that poem: Christ alive brings
Mary out of her spiritual darkness. The despair is turned into the
strong joy of the conclusion—the strength of the joy is the reason
for the eagle, the image of power, at the end. This is associated with
Dante's vision of the divine love that moves the universe. Despair
is isolated in 'Return', it is part of a spiritual experience and is van-
quished by joy in 'Mary Magdalene'. The poet does not feel any
compulsion to propagate mechanically a Catholic view of life: he
presents to us spiritual experience which includes the seemingly
final despair of 'Return' or the doubt of the *cywydd*, 'Emmäus, as well
as the more orthodox 'Mary Magdalene' or 'To the Good Thief'.

A sensuous joy shines out of some of Lewis's poems where he looks
at flowers or trees, birds or butterflies, as in 'The Dance of the Apple
Tree', 'A Daisy in April', 'August Jottings', 'The Pine', 'Ascension
Thursday'. In 'The Pine' and 'Ascension Thursday' the joy of the
senses takes on another dimension because of the spiritual allusions
in the poems. Even the arrogance of the reference to 'council houses'
in the latter poem does not damage it. The heightening effect of this
two-level reference in these poems recalls, but does not in any way
imitate, Dafydd ap Gwilym's poem 'Mass in a Grove'. Allusions to
classical gods and goddesses make 'The Dance of the Apple Tree'
exquisitely beautiful, they enrich the sensuous response. The
goddesses in this poem and 'the Father kissing the Son in the white
dew' of the other bring us back to the great power that moves in
the work of Saunders Lewis, the Christian and classical tradition of
Western Europe.

Mr. Lewis has always emphasized the involvement of the Welsh
literary tradition in this greater tradition, perhaps at the expense
of minimizing the importance of what is specifically Celtic and
indigenously Welsh in that tradition. His *awdlau* (poems in the
Welsh strict metres with *cynghanedd*) to Robert Wynne of the old

house of Garthewin and to His Grace the Catholic Archbishop of Cardiff assert the value of the old aristocratic and Catholic ideals sung by the poets of the great period of the Welsh bardic tradition. But in his *awdlau* these ideals have fallen upon bad times. It is this realization that keeps them from being exercises in nostalgia.

The elegy to Sir John Edward Lloyd, the eminent Welsh historian, is a vision of Welsh history seen in the context of the sixth book of the *Aeneid*. The pattern is not that of the traditional Welsh elegy where eulogy and lament are combined, nor has it been composed—like his elegy upon the death of the Welsh poet, T. Gwynn Jones—in traditional metre with *cynghanedd*. In his mode Lewis has once again asserted the connection that he sees between the Welsh tradition and the classical past. He has also looked at the lives of men in the great shadows of time and, more specifically, looked at the suffering of his own people, a people condemned, as he says, to perform the task of Sisyphus in the world. And after he (as the first person of the poem) has been led about the past 'Like he who climbed the splinterings of the land of despair,' he asks whether the people of Wales will keep alive their language, the last relic of the past and the last link with the greatness he associates with Cunedda (Cunedda was the founder of a royal dynasty in Wales and may well have had connections with the late Roman Empire in Britain). But his guide cannot help him here. The sadness of things is that after so much suffering there is so little hope. This conclusion takes on an additional intensity for anyone who is familiar with the story of Mr. Lewis's own life.

We are here recalled to what was mentioned at the beginning, in the quotation taken from the preface to *The World and the Church*, that is, 'the crisis of our times'. The crisis did not end with the end of the Second World War. There is now a greater danger that the spiritual and cultural values celebrated in Mr. Lewis's poems will be swamped by a twentieth-century barbarism. In their immediate context the questions that have consistently presented themselves in this poetry are 'Can Wales be saved?' and 'Can Europe be salvaged?', but what Lewis has really done is to indicate that the crisis is not only one of our own time but that it is the old conflict of the spirit and civilization—of the 'church'—against the 'world'. In reading some of these poems we are moved to apprehend the universality of the conflict through the intensity of one man's experience of it in his own time.

GWYN THOMAS

Selections of Saunders Lewis's Works

I. ESSAYS

    The Caernarfon Court Speech
    The Fate of the Language (trans. G. Aled Williams)
    Welsh Literature and Nationalism
    The Tradition of Taliesin
    The Essence of Welsh Literature
    Dafydd ap Gwilym
    Welsh Writers of Today
    The Poet

II. SELECTED POEMS (trans. Gwyn Thomas)

    The Deluge 1939
    A Scene in a Café
    To Dr. J. D. Jones, C.H.
    The Carcass
    Against Purgatory
    The Last Sermon of Saint David
    To the Good Thief
    The Choice
    Indian Summer 1941
    Elegy for Sir John Edward Lloyd
    The Dance of the Apple Tree
    Lavernock
    The Pine
    Ascension Thursday
    Mary Magdalene
    The Milky Way
    June Moon
    Return
    Et Homo Factus Est. Crucifixus . . .

III. THEATRE

    Blodeuwedd (trans. Gwyn Thomas)
    Siwan (trans. Emyr Humphreys)
    Treason (trans. Elwyn Jones)

I. ESSAYS

The Caernarfon Court Speech

13TH OCTOBER 1936

*Inside the courtroom, after making his protest against the way in which the
address of one of the other defendants had been destroyed by its having to
be translated in bits and pieces, Mr. Lewis then started to address the jury
in English.*

The fact that we set fire to the buildings and building materials
at the Penrhos bombing range is not in dispute. We ourselves were
the first to give the authorities warning of the fire, and we proclaimed to them our responsibility. Yet we hold the conviction that
our action was in no wise criminal, and that it was an act forced
upon us, that it was done in obedience to conscience and to the
moral law, and that the responsibility for any loss due to our act
is the responsibility of the English Government.

We are professional men who hold positions of trust, of honour,
and of security. I must speak now with reluctance for myself.
I profess the literature of Wales in the University College of Wales
at Swansea. That is my professional duty. It is also my pride and
delight. Welsh literature is one of the great literatures of Europe.
It is the direct heir in the British Isles of the literary discipline of
classical Greece and Rome. And it is a living, growing literature,
and draws its sustenance from a living language and a traditional
social life. It was my sense of the inestimable value of this tremendous heirloom of the Welsh nation that first led me from purely
literary work to public affairs and to the establishment of the Welsh
Nationalist Party. It was the terrible knowledge that the English
Government's bombing range, once it was established in Lleyn*,
would endanger and in all likelihood destroy an essential focus of
this Welsh culture, the most aristocratic spiritual heritage of Wales,
that made me think my own career, the security even of my family,
things that must be sacrificed in order to prevent so appalling a
calamity. For in the University lecture-rooms I have not professed
a dead literature of antiquarian interest. I have professed the living
literature of this nation. So that this literature has claims on me as
a man as well as a teacher. I hold that my action at Penrhos aerodrome on September the eighth saves the honour of the University
of Wales, for the language and literature of Wales are the very
raison d'être of this University.

---

* An alternative spelling of Llŷn.

And now for my part in Welsh public life. I speak briefly about it. I have been for ten years President of the Welsh Nationalist Party, and editor of its organ *Y Ddraig Goch* (*The Red Dragon*). I have been a member of the Advisory Committee of the University of Wales on Broadcasting, the chairman of which has been the Pro-Chancellor of the University, the Bishop of Monmouth. I have made a special study of the economic problems of Welsh unemployment and reconstruction, and was the originator of the Welsh National Industrial Development Council. In South Wales I have been in constant touch with my unemployed fellow-countrymen, and have successfully founded a club, the membership of which is growing and spreading over Wales, whereby on Thursday of every week a man whose position in life is comfortable gives up his dinner and sends the price of it to provide a three-course dinner for an unemployed fellow-Welshman whose larder on Thursday is empty.

Now, if you examine these activities and if you examine our record, you will find that our works, our programme, our propaganda have been entirely constructive and peaceful. There has never been any appeal to mob instincts. In fact, our leadership has been accused of being too highbrow and academic. I have repeatedly and publicly declared that the Welsh nation must gain its political freedom without resort to violence or to physical force. It is a point I wish to re-affirm today. And I submit to you that our action in burning the Penrhos aerodrome proves the sincerity of this affirmation. Had we wished to follow the methods of violence with which national minority movements are sometimes taunted, and into which they are often driven, nothing could have been easier than for us to ask some of the generous and spirited young men of the Welsh Nationalist Party to set fire to the aerodrome and get away undiscovered. It would be the beginning of methods of sabotage and guerilla turmoil. Mr. Valentine, Mr. D. J. Williams and I determined to prevent any such development. When all democratic and peaceful methods of persuasion had failed to obtain even a hearing for our case against the bombing range, and when we saw clearly the whole future of Welsh tradition threatened as never before in history, we determined that even then we would invoke only the process of law, and that a jury from the Welsh people should pronounce on the right and wrong of our behaviour.

The Judge interrupted: 'You are telling the jury—and I say this in your own interests—the reasons why you took the steps you did and burnt down the aerodrome; and I tell you that that is no excuse in law, and that the more you persist in telling the jury your ideas about Welsh nationalism and Welsh culture, the less excuse there is for having committed this act. So far your argument has been totally irrelevant to the charge.'

Mr. Lewis answered: I thought I was speaking on it the whole time. I am sorry. *And he continued with his address:* We ourselves, public men in Wales and leaders of the Welsh Nationalist Party, fired these buildings and timbers. We ourselves reported the fire to the police. We have given the police all the help we could to prepare the case against us. Is that the conduct of men acting 'feloniously and maliciously'? I submit that we are in this dock of our own will, not only for the sake of Wales, but also for the sake of peace and unviolent, charitable relations now and in the future between Wales and England.

It is charged against us that our action was 'unlawful'. I propose to meet that charge by developing an argument in four stages. First, I shall show with what horror the building of a bombing range was regarded by us and by a great number of Welsh people in every part of Wales. Secondly, how patiently and with what labour and at what sacrifice we tried and exhausted every possible way of legitimate persuasion to prevent the building of the bombing range. Thirdly, how differently the protests and remonstrances of Wales and Welsh public men were treated by the English Government, compared with similar protests, though less seriously grounded protests, made in England in the same period. Fourthly, I shall try to put before you the dilemma and the conflict of obedience in which the Government's cruelty placed the leaders of the crusade against the bombing range, and the limits to the rights of the English State when it transgresses the moral law and acts in violation of the rights of the Welsh nation.

In an English pamphlet stating the case against the bombing school in Lleyn, Professor Daniel has expressed with pregnant brevity the heart-felt fear of all thoughtful Welshmen.

The Judge again interrupted: 'What Professor Daniel said has no bearing on the case. I only say this in your own interest, that if you go on addressing the jury as you have done, you are—so far from putting up any defence—making the case against you worse.'

Mr. Lewis continued: It is the plain historical fact that, from the fifth century on, Lleyn has been Welsh of the Welsh, and that so long as Lleyn remained unanglicized, Welsh life and culture were secure. If once the forces of anglicization are securely established behind as well as in front of the mountains of Snowdonia, the day when Welsh language and culture will be crushed between the iron jaws of these pincers cannot be long delayed. For Wales, the preservation of the Lleyn Peninsula from this anglicization is a matter of life and death.

That, we are convinced, is the simple truth. So that the preservation of the harmonious continuity of the rural Welsh tradition of Lleyn, unbroken for fourteen hundred years, is for us 'a matter of life and death'. I have said that my professional duty is the teaching of Welsh literature. My maternal grandfather was a minister of religion and a Welsh scholar and man of letters. He began his ministerial career in Pwllheli. He wrote the greatest Welsh prose work of the nineteenth century, *Cofiant John Jones Talsarn* (*The Biography of John Jones of Talsarn*). One of the most brilliant chapters in that book is the seventh chapter, which is a description of the religious leaders of Lleyn and Eifionydd in the middle of the nineteenth century. It is impossible for one who had blood in his veins not to care passionately when he sees this terrible vandal bombing range in this very home of Welsh culture. On the desk before me is an anthology of the works of the Welsh poets of Lleyn, *Cynfeirdd Lleyn, 1500–1800* (*Early Poets of Lleyn, 1500–1800*), by Myrddin Fardd. On page 176 of this book there is a poem, a *cywydd*, written in Penyberth farmhouse in the middle of the sixteenth century. That house was one of the most historic in Lleyn. It was a resting-place for the Welsh pilgrims to the Isle of Saints, Ynys Enlli, in the Middle Ages. It had associations with Owen Glyn Dŵr. It belonged to the story of Welsh literature. It was a thing of hallowed and secular majesty. It was taken down and utterly destroyed a week before we burnt on its fields the timbers of the vandals who destroyed. And I claim that, if the moral law counts for anything, the people who ought to be in this dock are the people responsible for the destruction of Penyberth farmhouse.

At this, applause was heard in the court, and the Judge ordered everyone to be quiet, and the officers to take anyone who made such a commotion again outside. Mr. Lewis continued: Moreover that destruction of Penyberth House is, in the view of the most competent of Welsh observers, typical and symbolic. The development of the bombing range in Lleyn into the inevitable arsenal it will become will destroy this essential home of Welsh culture, idiom and literature. It will shatter the spiritual basis of the Welsh nation.

It was the knowledge of the catastrophe that the proposed bombing range would bring to Welsh culture and tradition in this, one of the few unspoilt homes of that culture, which led to thousands of Welshmen not normally interested in political affairs to protest vigorously against such an outrage. I have to show now that these protests were on a national scale, that they were representative of the Welsh nation, that nothing was neglected or left undone to convince the English Government of the seriousness of the occasion, and that efforts of peaceful, legitimate persuasion were exhausted in our endeavour to prevent the catastrophe. I shall summarize the story of the protests as briefly as possible.

It was in June 1935 that the Air Ministry's proposal to establish a bombing range in Lleyn was first announced. Immediately the Caernarfonshire branches of the Welsh Nationalist Party held a delegate committee and sent to the Ministry a statement of their unanimous objection to the plan.

In January 1936 the campaign against the bombing range was renewed with urgency, and from that time on it ceased to be a matter of local interest. It was taken up throughout Wales and became a national concern. Protest meetings were organized generally in Lleyn and Caernarfonshire. Resolutions of protest were passed by Welsh churches and representative meetings of the religious bodies throughout Wales.

Protests were equally general from all the Welsh secular societies and institutions, the University of Wales Guild of Graduates and the Welsh national youth movement (Urdd Gobaith Cymru), as well as Welsh Cymmrodorion societies in Cardiff, Swansea, Llanelli, Aberystwyth, and representative meetings of Welshmen living outside Wales, in London, in Liverpool, Manchester, Birmingham. Before the first day of May more than 600 Welsh societies and religious bodies had passed unanimous resolutions demanding the withdrawal of the bombing range. These resolutions were sent on to the Air Ministry, and the agitation in the Welsh press was a sign of the widespread approval of the protests.

We kept the Prime Minister and the English Air Ministry fully informed of our opposition. On March the thirty-first I wrote to the Prime Minister, begging, in view of the gravity of the affair, for an interview. I said in my letter: 'An important body of Welsh people regard this proposal as one to prevent which even liberty, even life itself, might properly be thrown away.' The Prime

Minister declined to grant an interview, and sent in answer a stereotyped statement exactly similar to that sent to all other protesters.

On May the first I broadcast a talk through the national wavelength of the British Broadcasting Corporation, on Welsh Nationalism. I took the opportunity to make an urgent appeal for the saving of Lleyn from this bombing range. The Government continued to ignore every appeal.

We organized a plebiscite of the people of Lleyn. It was conducted entirely by voluntary workers giving their spare time to tramping the scattered villages and farmhouses of the peninsula and paying their own expenses in food and bus fares. Over five thousand of the electors of Lleyn signed the petition to Parliament and to the Prime Minister asking for the cessation of the bombing range. Our workers were welcomed everywhere. They met with a practically unanimous sympathy, and with time they would have obtained the signatures of almost the entire rural population of Lleyn. Similar plebiscites were conducted in Llanberis and among the Welsh of Liverpool, where five thousand adult Welsh men and women also signed petitions. Before the end of May well over one thousand Welsh churches and lay bodies, representing over a quarter of a million Welsh people, had passed resolutions of protest.

On May the twenty-third we held a final national demonstration at Pwllheli. It was attended by seven or eight thousand people, and they had come in motor buses from all parts of Wales, as well as from centres outside Wales. The meeting received much notice in the English newspapers everywhere because of the attempt of a gang of some fifty drunken roughs in Pwllheli to prevent the speeches from the platform.

The platform represented the whole of Wales, leaders of religion, of scholarship and public life. The chairman was the most eminent literary man in Wales, Professor W. J. Gruffydd. Professor Gruffydd put the resolution calling on the Government to withdraw their plans for Lleyn and inviting the Prime Minister to receive a deputation on the subject. A show of hands revealed an overwhelming majority in favour of the resolution. The negative did not exceed fifty.

On June the fourth the request was sent to the Prime Minister to receive a Welsh national deputation. It was sent on behalf of the five thousand petitioners of Lleyn, the thousands of petitioners outside Lleyn, and the fifteen hundred bodies representing nearly half a million Welshmen who had resolved to protest against the Lleyn bombing range. The letter requesting the Prime Minister to receive a deputation was signed by over twenty eminent Welsh leaders. They included the principals of Aberystwyth and of Bala and of Bala-Bangor theological colleges, the secretary of the Honourable Society of Cymmrodorion, the Bishop of Menevia, moderators of the Presbyterian Church of Wales and the chairman of the Congregational Union of Wales, and the professors of Welsh Language and of Welsh Literature at the University Colleges of Bangor and of Aberystwyth.

A secretary to the Prime Minister replied that 'the Prime Minister does not feel that any useful purpose would be served by his acceding to the request that he should receive a deputation.'

On June the fifteenth the English newspapers circulating in Wales reported thus: 'More than 200 acres at Penyberth Farm have been cleared and levelled for an aerodrome site. The contractors are beginning to erect an aerodrome today.' Thus ended peaceful persuasion along legitimate democratic lines. There only remained now the way of sacrifice.

But the effect of the English Government's contemptuous rejection of this nation-wide protest from Wales, both on Welsh national sentiment in general and on the Reverend Lewis Valentine, Mr. D. J. Williams and myself as the accepted leaders of the crusade, cannot be properly gauged without considering also the contrast between the Government's treatment of Wales and their treatment of England.

Let me recount briefly the story of bombing range sites proposed to be set up in England at the same time as the Lleyn establishment. One was at Abbotsbury in Dorsetshire. It is a well-known breeding place for swans. Because of that, and because English writers and poets were allowed space in *The Times* newspaper and generally in the English press to express their passion for swans and natural beauty of scene, the Dorsetshire site was moved.

Then came Holy Island in English Northumberland. Mr. G. M. Trevelyan wrote a letter to the press to explain that Holy Island was a sacred region: it was a holiday resort for city workers; it had historical associations with Lindisfarne and St. Cuthbert; it was the most important home of wild birds in England. He argued that

Northumberland duck were no less sacred than Dorset swans. He was supported by leaders of English scholarship and letters. The Air Ministry summoned a public conference to consider the matter, and the bombing range was withdrawn.

Will you try to understand our feelings when we saw the foremost scholars and literary men of England talking of the 'sacredness' of duck and swans, and succeeding on that argument in compelling the Air Ministry to withdraw its bombing range, while here in Wales, at the very same time, we were organizing a nationwide protest on behalf of the truly sacred things in Creation—a nation, its language, its literature, its separate traditions and immemorial ways of Christian life—and we could not get the Government even to receive a deputation to discuss the matter with us? The irony of the contrast is the irony of blasphemy.

On June the twenty-second, at the Union of the Congregational Churches of Wales at Bangor, the chairman, the newly appointed Archdruid of Wales, the Reverend J. J. Williams, speaking to a resolution condemning the Lleyn bombing range, said: 'It is our intention to prevent the establishment of this bombing school by every legitimate means possible. But if legitimate means finally fail, I believe there is enough resolution in the Welsh nation to remove the bombing camp by other means.'

He spoke for Wales. But—and I come now to a crucial point in my argument—he spoke also for the universal moral law (what we call in Welsh *y ddeddf foesol*) which is an essential part of Christian tradition and is recognized by moral theologians to be binding on all men. 'Remember that the God who created men ordained nations,' said Emrys ap Iwan, and the moral law recognizes the family and the nation to be moral persons. They have the qualities and the natural rights of persons. And by the law of God the essential rights of the family and the nation, and especially their right to live, are prior to the rights of any state. It is part also of the moral law that no state has the right to use any other national entity merely as a means to its own profit, and no state has a right to seek national advantages which would mean genuine harm to any other nation. All that is universal Christian tradition.

It is also Christian tradition that men should obey the moral law rather than the law of a state whenever the two should clash.

The Judge said: 'I have to administer the law of the land, and you are making statements which are inaccurate.'

Mr. Lewis continued: It is universal Christian tradition that it is the duty of members of a family and of a nation to defend the essential rights of the family and of the nation, and especially it is a duty to preserve the life of a nation, or to defend it from any mortal blow, by all means possible short of taking human life unjustly or breaking the moral law. That is the Christian tradition.

It was in the clear light of this fundamental principle of Christendom that Lewis Valentine, D. J. Williams and I resolved to act at Lleyn. The responsibility of leadership was ours. We could not shirk it. We saw the English state preparing mortal danger to the moral person of the Welsh nation. We had exercised the greatest patience in attempting every possible means of persuasion and appeal to prevent the wrong. We had the unanimous voice of all the religious leaders of Wales with us. The English Government took no heed at all. The bombing range was begun. Building was proceeding.

We resolved to act. We determined on an action that would proclaim our conviction that the building of this bombing range in Lleyn is by all Christian principles wrong and unlawful. We resolved on an act that would compel the English Government to take action at law against us. We went and gave ourselves up to the police authorities and compelled them to take action against us. We made absolutely sure that no human life would be endangered. You have heard the pitiful story of the night-watchman. The only true statement in all his story is that he suffered no harm at all.

We damaged property. It is valued at some two thousand pounds odd. Exactly by that action we have compelled the English state to put us in this dock. Only by appearing in this dock on a charge sufficiently serious to allow a maximum sentence on us of penal servitude for life could we bring the action of the English state to the bar of conscience and of Christian morality. Every other means had failed. But we have put our lives in the balance against this act of Government iniquity. It was in preparation for this day and this hour, when we should appear before you twelve, our fellow-Christians and fellow-countrymen, and should explain all our action to you and the meaning and significance of that action, and should ask your judgement on us—it was for this and in the belief that we could prove the moral justice, the absolute justice, of our act, that we have lived and hoped from the moment that our decision was made.

It is perhaps necessary to say something about the amount of the damage we caused by our fire. It exceeds two thousand pounds, we are told. It is obvious that the damage caused is frivolous compared with the harm that the successful establishment of this bombing range in Lleyn will cause. Actually, if it were practicable to estimate in terms of money the cost to us of the efforts we all expended in our crusade to persuade the Government to withdraw the bombing range, the cost of the time and labour freely given by all our fellow-workers and by Welsh religious leaders who travelled to and fro addressing protest meetings, it could be shown that the bombing range has already cost us very many hundreds of pounds.

But the loss that this bombing range, if it be not withdrawn, will cause to Wales is not a loss that can be estimated in thousands of pounds. You cannot calculate in figures the irreparable loss of a language, of purity of idiom, of a home of literature, of a tradition of rural Welsh civilization stretching back fourteen hundred years. These things have no price. You cannot pay compensation for them. It is only in Eternity that the destruction of these things can be valued. We were compelled, therefore, to do serious damage to the bombing school buildings. Only serious damage could ensure that we should appear before a jury of our fellow-countrymen in a last desperate and vital effort to bring the immorality of the Government's action before the judgement of Christian Wales.

You, gentlemen of the jury, are our judges in this matter, and you have to give a verdict on a case that is not only exceptional but a case that is of momentous importance. I suppose there is no previous example of the leaders of a struggle for the defence of a nation's culture against an alien and heedless state staking their freedom, their livelihood, their reputation and almost their lives, and putting themselves in the dock in order that a jury of their countrymen should judge between them and the brute power of the state. To do this is to show our trust not only in your justice as the jury, but also in your courage. We ask you to have no fear at all. The terminology of the law calls this bombing range 'the property of the King'. That means the English Government. It means these bureaucrats in the Air Ministry to whom Wales is a region on the map, who know nothing at all of the culture and language they are seeking to destroy.[1]

But there is another aspect to this trial that gives it special importance. We have said from the beginning, and it was the point we emphasized in our letter to the Chief Constable of Caernarfonshire, that our action was a protest against the ruthless refusal of the English state even to discuss the rights of the Welsh nation in Lleyn. Now, everywhere in Europe today we see governments asserting that they are above the moral law of God, that they recognize no other law but the will of the government, and that they recognize no other power but the power of the state. These governments claim absolute powers; they deny the rights of persons and of moral persons. They deny that they can be challenged by any code of morals, and they demand the absolute obedience of men. Now that is Atheism. It is the denial of God, of God's law. It is the repudiation of the entire Christian tradition of Europe, and it is the beginning of the reign of chaos.

The English Government's behaviour in the matter of the Lleyn bombing range is exactly the behaviour of this new Anti-Christ throughout Europe. And in this assize-court in Caernarfon today we, the accused in this dock, are challenging Anti-Christ. We deny the absolute power of the State-God. Here in Wales, a land that has no tradition except Christian tradition, a land that has never in all its history been pagan or atheist, we stand for the preservation of that Christian tradition and for the supremacy of the moral law over the power of materialist bureaucracy. So that whether you find us guilty or not guilty is of importance today to the future of Christian civilization and Christian liberty and Christian justice in Europe.

If you find us guilty the world will understand that here also in Wales an English government may destroy the moral person of a nation——

The Judge said: 'That is absolutely untrue'.

---

1. In the copy of the address duplicated before the Trial (and afterwards published) the sentence ended like this: '. . . who know nothing at all of the culture and language of Wales, but will desecrate our sanctuaries like a dog raising its hind leg at an altar'. This copy was in front of Mr. Miles and Mr. Edmund Davies: they saw these words shortly before Mr. Lewis arrived at them, and started to become restless. He didn't see their signs, but he passed the words without reading them.

Mr. Lewis continued: You declare that the Government may shatter the spiritual basis of that nation's life, may refuse to consider or give heed to any appeal even from the united religious leaders of the whole country, and then may use the law to punish with imprisonment the men who put those monstrous claims of Anti-Christ to the test. If you find us guilty——

The Judge said: 'That is untrue. Will you stop? I am not going to allow you to make statements which are not only untrue but almost blasphemous'.

If you find us guilty——

'You are not to say that again!'

I wasn't going to. If you find us guilty, you proclaim that the will of the Government may not be challenged by any person whatsoever, and that there is no appeal possible to morality as Christians have always understood it. If you find us guilty you proclaim the effective end of Christian principles governing the life of Wales.

On the other hand, if you find us not guilty you declare your conviction as judges in this matter that the moral law is supreme; you declare that the moral law is binding on governments just as it is on private citizens. You declare that 'necessity of state' gives no right to set morality aside, and you declare that justice, not material force, must rule in the affairs of nations.

We hold with unshakable conviction that the burning of the monstrous bombing range in Lleyn was an act forced on us for the defence of Welsh civilization, for the defence of Christian principles, for the maintenance of the Law of God in Wales. Nothing else was possible for us. It was the Government itself that created the situation in which we were placed, so that we had to choose either the way of cowards and slink out of the defence of Christian tradition and morality, or we had to act as we have acted, and trust to a jury of our countrymen to declare that the Law of God is superior to every other law, and that by that law our act is just.

We ask you to be fearless. We ask you to bring in a verdict that will restore Christian principles in the realm of law, and open a new period in the history of nations and governments. We ask you to say that we are Not Guilty.

Thank you, my Lord.

[*The Caernarfon jury failed to agree on a verdict.*]

(*Tân yn Llyn*, Dafydd Jenkins, Gwasg Aberystwyth, 1937, pp. 126–141.)

The Fate of the Language
(1962)

I have to start writing this and have to finish it before the returns of last year's census of the Welsh-speaking population of Wales are published. I shall presuppose that the figures which will shortly be published will shock and disappoint those of us who consider that Wales without the Welsh language will not be Wales. I shall also presuppose that Welsh will end as a living language, should the present trend continue, about the beginning of the twenty-first century, assuming that there will be people left in the island of Britain at that time.

Thus the policy laid down as the aim of the English Government in Wales in the measure called the Act of Union of England and Wales in 1536 will at last have succeeded. To give the Government its due, throughout some four centuries of governing Wales, despite every change of circumstance, despite every change in parliamentary method and in the means of government, despite every social revolution, it has never wavered in applying this policy of excluding the Welsh language as a language of administration from office, court and legal writing. A lawyer said in a court of law in 1773:

> It has always been the policy of the legislature to introduce the English language into Wales.

Matthew Arnold, an Inspector of Schools, said in his official report in 1852:

> It must always be the desire of a Government to render its dominions, as far as possible, homogeneous . . . Sooner or later, the difference of language between Wales and England will probably be effaced . . . an event which is socially and politically so desirable.

And even in the second half of the twentieth century, in 1952, in the Charter of the British Broadcasting Corporation, despite all the change there had been in the attitude and thinking of educational and cultural leaders, care was taken not to specify the Welsh language as an essential attribute of the Controller and Chairman for Wales.

I do not forget that there has been an enormous change in the schools. Today the Welsh Department of the Ministry of Education fosters the Welsh language and urges it on the schools more earnestly than the Welsh local authorities. I shall speak later on about the significance of that. But outside the world of the child and the school it is English only which is essential for every post or administrative office in Wales. The principle of the Act of Union has not been relaxed at all, although there has been an important change in the Government's attitude of mind.

Matthew Arnold was writing four years after the publication of the Blue Books of 1847. His purpose was to support the recommendations of the Blue Books, and he laid emphasis on the fact that the extermination of Welsh was a political policy. Let us turn therefore to the Welsh people themselves, lest the mote in the Englishman's eye causes us not to see the beam in the eye of the Welshman. If you read the historical section of the report on *The Welsh Language in Education and Life* (1927) you will see today that the account of the sixteenth century hopelessly misinterprets the meaning of many of the Welsh Humanists' complaints about the condition of the Welsh language. But as to the quotation from the famous preface of Morris Kyffin who complained about the Welsh cleric

> Who said that it were not proper to allow the printing of any Welsh book whatsoever, but he would that all the nation should learn English and lose their Welsh.

—that is' fair evidence of the opinion of the great majority of Welsh clerics and gentry concerning Tudor policy. William Salesbury and Bishop Morgan wrote in a similar vein. Siôn Tudur said as much in a *cywydd*. We know today that what was said in public and in print was not the true opinion of many of the subjects of Elizabeth the First. Her state was that of the sheriff, the spy, and the catchpole, and the wise man did not speak his mind. Besides, we have to interpret the Humanists' vocabulary.

It is proper that we should acknowledge two facts. First, that from the death of Elizabeth until the threshold of the twentieth century there was neither an attempt nor an intention by anyone of importance in Wales to undo in any way the bond that united Wales to England, nor opposition of any account to the principle of a united indivisible kingdom. After 1536 the concept of Wales as a nation, as an historical unit, ceased to be a memory, an ideal, or a fact. Secondly, as a result neither was there any political attempt until the twentieth century to restore the status of the Welsh language or to win for it recognition in any way as an official or an administrative language. All Wales was satisfied with its complete suppression.

These two facts are closely connected. If England and Wales are one totally united kingdom—*homogeneous* is Matthew Arnold's word—then the existence of an historical Welsh language is a political stumbling-block, a reminder of a different state of affairs, a danger to the union. That was precisely what was said in the Act of Union, in the Blue Books, and many other times. But after the age of Elizabeth the First it was not said as often in Welsh. Welsh literature accepted one principle, it accepted the United Kingdom. The first major classic of the United Kingdom in Welsh is the *Bardd Cwsc*[1]. The heroine of that classic is Queen Anne, with the Statute Book of England in one hand and the Bible in the other. Let us turn to a period which is much closer to us, when the Welsh national awakening demanded the Disestablishment of the State Church in the 1880 General Election. This was what a great-uncle of mine, John Thomas of Liverpool, said in an address at Caernarfon:

> We are one great British nation, under one Government, repre-
> sented in one common parliament, and our true strength lies in
> our unity . . . and I must say that I have but little sympathy with
> the cry raised these days for a Welsh parliamentary party.

His standpoint was identical with that of Matthew Arnold, except that Arnold was more logical—it was in English he spoke and he wished that Welsh should die.

By the eighteenth century there is plenty of evidence of the effects of the Act of Union on the language. In a Latin letter written in 1700, Thomas Sebastian Price of Llanfyllin said that Welsh had ceased to be used by that time by anyone except the common folk of low degree. At the time Ellis Wynne was finishing his translation of Jeremy Taylor's *Rule and Exercises of Holy Living*. In the third chapter he comes to a discussion of the duties of 'those who have been given their share of high office,' and he says:

> The duties of kings, judges, and rulers of Church and State, apart
> from their being long and complicated, are also irrelevant, more's
> the pity, where the Welsh language is concerned.

I bless Ellis Wynne for that 'more's the pity', although he is just as inconsistent as John Thomas. You will remember that in the

---

1. Reference to *The Visions of the Sleeping Bard* (1703).

Bardd Cwsc he shows Welsh as the language of ambassadors and of the letters of kings. But, more's the pity however, those kings are the King of Hell and the King of Death: by this time they were the only rulers the Welsh language possessed.

So it was that the Act of Union excluded Welsh from the courts of rulers and the noble houses of the kingdom, and from the world of the leaders of society where every learning, skill, art and science were expounded. Mr. Alwyn Prosser has shown that Williams of Pantycelyn complained in a similar fashion:

> Of all the arts which other countries study, and in which they have achieved great perfection, there is hardly a book in Welsh which shows what one of these arts consists of . . . How long will the Welsh tolerate such ignorance?

The Welsh did tolerate it. *The Constitutions of the Society of Cymmrodorion* (1755) were another attempt to restore breadth of interest and the culture of nobility to the Welsh language. In a letter to William Vaughan, Richard Morris said of them:

> We, the Cymmrodorion, shall reveal to the world the value of this old language in such beautiful colours as it will be reckoned an honour henceforth to speak it amongst the learned and the nobility of the kingdom, aye, in the King's court, as was the custom of yore.

But Richard Morris, too, was disappointed and embittered. The Cymmrodorion failed to nurture a cultured Welsh-speaking middle class. And the next important document concerning the position and influence of Welsh is R. W. Lingen's large section in the Blue Books of 1847. The Betrayal of the Blue Books was the name given in Wales to this report. In his book *Welsh and Scottish Nationalism*, Sir Reginald Coupland maintains that it was the Betrayal of the Blue Books which stung Welsh nationalism awake. Indeed, Coupland is the only historian who has discussed the report in a fair and balanced manner. Hardly a single Welsh writer has yet acknowledged the truth, that these Blue Books are the most important nineteenth-century historical documents we possess, and that they contain a store of information that has not yet been used. All I shall do now is quote a page which is in direct descent from Ellis Wynne, Richard Morris and Williams of Pantycelyn, except that Lingen was writing in the middle of the industrial revolution in South Wales when thousands of the agricultural poor of rural Wales were flocking to the coal-mining and iron-working valleys:

My district exhibits the phenomenon of a peculiar language—here
peculiar means belonging to a place or a group of people as distinct from any other—isolating the mass from the upper portion of
society; and as a further phenomenon, it exhibits this mass engaged
upon the most opposite occupations at points not very distant
from each other; being, on the one side, rude and primitive
agriculturists living poorly and thinly scattered; on the other,
smelters and miners, wantoning in plenty, and congregated in
the densest accumulations. An incessant tide of immigration sets
in from the former extreme to the latter . . . Externally it would be
impossible to exhibit a greater contrast . . . than by comparing
the country between the rivers Towi and Teifi with Merthyr,
Dowlais, Aberdare, Maesteg, Cwm Afon . . . Yet the families
which are daily passing from the one scene to the other do not
thereby change their relative position in society. A new field is
opened to them, but not a wider. They are never masters . . .
It is still the same people. Whether in the country or among the
furnaces, the Welsh element is never found at the top of the
social scale . . . Equally in his new as in his old home, his language
keeps him under the hatches, being one in which he can neither
acquire nor communicate the necessary information. It is a
language of old-fashioned agriculture, of theology, and of simple
rustic life, while all the world about him is English . . . He is left
to live in an under-world of his own, and the march of society
goes . . . completely over his head.

It is Lingen's accuracy and keen perception which strike us
today. A little over half a century later Mr. D. J. Williams went to
the coal mines of the Rhondda valley. There is nothing in his
portrait of Ferndale at the beginning of the twentieth century in
Yn Chwech ar Hugain Oed (*Twenty-six Years of Age*) which conflicts
with the general picture drawn by Lingen in 1847. Neither the
circumstances, nor the quality of life, nor the mode of living have
changed very much. Lingen's description of Saturday and Sunday
nights in Merthyr is astonishingly similar in essence to D. J.
Williams's description of those nights in Ferndale. It is true that
D. J. gives of his abundant sympathy and his love for human nature
whatever its condition, and that Lingen analyses coldly without
mincing his words. Lingen told the harsh truth about what he saw
and heard, and he revealed the inevitable fate of the Welsh
language and of Welsh-speaking society after three centuries of
being kept with

> the devil under the hatches,
> safe, my lad, under lock and key.

Recently Professor Brinley Thomas has been showing that it was the industrial revolution which kept the Welsh language alive in the second half of the last century. Were it not for the coal-mining valleys and the industrial undertakings of the South the drift of people from rural Wales would have been the death of Welsh just as the famine in Ireland was the death of Irish. By 1911 considerably more than half the Welsh-speaking population of Wales was in the coal-mining areas, in Lingen's words 'wantoning in plenty,' and that was why Thomas Gee's *Gwyddoniadur* (*Encyclopaedia*) and the extensive publication of works in Welsh was successful. Already in 1847 Lingen had observed this and foreseen more. The Welsh, he said, had no interest in politics. One witness told him that the Welshmen from the hills who went to join Frost's Chartists believed that their aim was to make for London, to fight one great battle there and win the kingdom. That, I think, is a connecting link with the poems of prognostication and the battle of Bosworth, and with the propaganda of the poets of the Wars of the Roses which carried Henry Tudor to London. Fare you well, Geoffrey of Monmouth, we have heard the final echo of your Brut! In one way this is the strangest and most exciting of the Blue Books' revelations. But as to contemporary politics, Lingen said that all political unrest in the Welsh coalfields was due to incoming Englishmen, thus anticipating the anglicization of the Labour movement which was to bring Keir Hardie from Glasgow to be a leader of the Welsh. The industrial areas did not contribute anything new either to Welsh social life or to the literature of the eisteddfodau. Life in the densely populated valleys was organized on the pattern of that of the rural areas, with the chapel as it focal point. Welsh Nonconformity was the bond which united town and country. And which at the same time kept them standing still.

It was the reaction against the Blue Books which initiated Welsh nationalism in the second half of the century; it must be confessed, too, that it was the Blue Books which triumphed. Despite the anger and wrath they engendered, despite the fervent protest provoked by their dark picture of Welsh Nonconformity, strangely enough the whole of Wales, and Welsh Nonconformity in particular, adopted all the policy and main recommendations of the baleful report. The nation's leaders, both laymen and ministers, devoted their energies to the utmost to the establishment of a thoroughly English educational system in every part of Wales, ranging from primary schools to normal colleges and three university colleges

with a University Charter crowning it all. The money of the Welsh
worker was collected towards the University Colleges. 'He gave his
scanty penny to the college' so that his own son might not know his
father's language or the tales of his forefathers or anything of 'the
echo of the songs of his distant youth.' It has often been said that
the difference between the colleges of the University of Wales and
the universities of the commercial and industrial cities of England
is that the English institutions were created by the captains of
industry and commerce whilst the colleges of Wales were built with
the pennies of the ordinary people. Doubtless, there is truth in that;
it only makes the tragedy more bitter. For the University of Wales,
the principal creation of the national awakening of the ordinary
people of Wales, is an ironic and bitter tragedy. Look at the
University of Jerusalem today where Hebrew, which was a dead
language long before Christ, is the medium of all instruction in the
most subtle and modern sciences. Consider the universities of
Switzerland, and those of Ghent and Louvain in Belgium. Then
look at the University of Wales, now with its six colleges. What
shall we say about the Welsh-speaking Welshman in the four
principal colleges? What shall we say about the departments of
Welsh themselves, despite all the attempt of the Board of Celtic
Studies to create technical vocabularies? In cold blood one can only
say what Lingen said in the Blue Books:

> Equally in his new as in his old home his language keeps him
> under the hatches . . . His superiors are content simply to ignore
> his existence. He is left to live in an under-world of his own, and
> the march of society goes completely over his head.

That is the truth about the Welsh language in the University of
Wales today; and it was Welsh Wales which created it, supported
it, doted upon its honorary degrees, and is satisfied that its diploma
of honour is a token of the degree of the language's degradation.
The University of Wales is more responsible than any other
institution for the fact that it is impossible for Welsh literature today
to portray civilized life in full. The policy of the University of Wales
is the policy of the 1536 Act of Union and the policy of Matthew
Arnold and the Blue Books; and Welsh Wales is satisfied.

If we turn to the political aspects of the Welsh awakening in the
last century we shall see exactly the same disregard for Welsh.
Although the language was subjected to the ridicule and attack of
judges, bishops and civil servants, no one arose to demand its rights
in parliament or on platform. The anti-Welshness of the bishops

and clergy of the State Church and their hostility towards the Welsh Language constituted a large part of the argument in favour of Disestablishment, and it contributed also to the Tithe Dispute. But the subject of Emrys ap Iwan's satire in 1891 was *Cymru Fydd*:

> I ought to tell you that even many a Dic Siôn Dafydd had enrolled in half-Welsh societies of the *Kumree Fidd* type before 1890 . . . In order to gain publicity and in order to ride on the back of Welsh feeling onto committees, councils, and into Parliament, they condescended to end each speech by saying in partly understandable Welsh 'The Welsh language for ever.' But that was all.

It may be that it was because of this that the *Cymru Fydd* societies included 'The appointment of public officials who were proficient in Welsh' in their programme in 1894. Two years later at the *Cymru Fydd* conference there was a statement by the president of the Cardiff Liberal Association, an English businessman named Bird:

> Throughout South Wales there are many thousands of English people . . . a cosmopolitan population who will never submit to the domination of Welsh ideas.

Thereupon *Cymru Fydd* was seized with apoplexy; soon afterwards, without having revived and without fuss, it departed this life.

Is there any tradition of defending the Welsh Language through political means? I am not asking if there is a tradition of praising the language in political speeches or by politicians on eisteddfod platforms. Rather I mean seeing the language as the English Government has always seen it, as a political matter, and from seeing it so raising it as a battle-standard.

The late John Arthur Price maintained that there was something of that spirit in the legal action brought by the churchwardens of Trefdraeth in Anglesey in 1773 against the appointment of a monoglot Englishman as parish priest. But it is in the letters and poems and tracts of Evan Evans (Ieuan Brydydd Hir) that we find explicit propaganda against the policy of turning the parish churches into means for extirpating the Welsh language. His friends feared for him, and he retorted:

> The tract against the *Anglian Bishops* is, doubtless, too harsh; and it would be a little thing in their sight to cut me into two pieces . . . But I certainly wish that something of that kind had been published . . . One Richardson has published a book on behalf of the Irish, who suffer the same wrong as we do . . . I have a small

> paper . . . written in Latin . . . the Letter of the Reverend Father
> Ioan Elphin, Apostolic Nuncio of the Society of Jesus to the
> Papist Welsh . . . in which he pours forth at length concerning the
> State of Religion in that country . . . This is exceedingly sharp.

In the following century there was the leadership of Michael Jones
and the heroic experiment of the Welsh Colony in Patagonia:

> There will be a chapel, a school, and a parliament building there,
> with the old language as the medium of worship and commerce,
> of teaching and government. A strong nation will grow there in
> a Welsh home.

Revolutionary words, a revolutionary programme. To this day our
want of national consciousness and our lack of the pride of nationhood prevent us from understanding the significance and heroism
of the Patagonian venture. Emrys ap Iwan was in the tradition of
Michael Jones. As Evan Evans had attacked the Anglian Bishops
so did Emrys attack the English causes of his denomination and
go on to argue that the Welsh language was Wales's foremost
political issue and the essence of her being, and that every political
problem was secondary compared with that. So it was that he
wrote the famous political pamphlet *Breuddwyd Pabydd wrth ei
Ewyllys* (*A Papist's Dream according to his Wish*), and is it not perhaps
correct to suggest that it was Father Ioan Elphin of the Society of
Jesus in Ieuan Brydydd Hir's satire who gave Emrys ap Iwan the
idea of Father Morgan of the Society of Jesus who tells the story of
the revival of Welsh Wales in *Breuddwyd Pabydd*.

Coupland does not mention Ieuan Brydydd Hir except as one of
the poets of the Morris circle. Michael Jones is to him 'a somewhat
eccentric Independent minister' and he does not have a word about
Emrys ap Iwan. That shows in all fairness how ineffectual, how
powerless, and how unimportant in Welsh political life and in the
development of Welsh thought the tradition of defending the Welsh
language has been. Its advocates have been considered odd, 'somewhat eccentric' people treading a narrow path, the narrowness of
nationalism and the narrowness of language, instead of the broad
highway which leads to Westminster. The tradition of defending
the Welsh language politically is a tradition of suffering, obloquy
and persecution. In Wales everything can be forgiven except being
seriously concerned about the language. That was the experience
of Ieuan Brydydd Hir, Michael Jones and Emrys ap Iwan. Their
only connecting link with the vast majority of their fellow-
countrymen is the most untruthful national anthem in Europe.

Let us therefore turn to the present situation, the crisis of the language in the second half of the twentieth century. It is a weak situation. There was a time, in the period of the awakening of the ordinary people between 1860 and 1890, when it would have been practical to establish Welsh as the language of education and of the university, as the language of the new county councils, and as the language of industry. Such a thing did not enter the minds of the Welsh. Between the two World Wars I believed that the thing was not impossible, given time and a consistent policy followed for a generation or two. Today it is not possible. There have been enormous social changes in Wales in the last quarter of a century. Welsh in Wales is now a language in retreat, the language of a minority, and that a decreasing minority.

Let us consider again the present-day attitude of the Whitehall Government towards Welsh and then the attitude of people in Wales. The change in the Government's attitude has been greater than any change there has been in Wales. To be sure, Government interference with social life in the Welfare State is more far-reaching than was imagined possible in the last century. It is not only education of every kind and at every stage which is under Government care nowadays, but also all kinds of leisure activities, youth clubs and camps, adult education, theatres, art, and radio and television which reach almost every home in the kingdom. The culture of every area and region enjoys a certain amount of patronage. The Arts Council recognizes—although it does not do so generously—the claims of Welsh culture.

The result is that the Government has changed its attitude to a considerable degree. Matthew Arnold's assertion no longer represents the creed of Whitehall. The Welsh language is not considered a political stumbling-block any more. If a letter were written in Welsh and sent to the office of any Welsh local authority it is more than likely that the reply would be in English. If it were sent to any office in Whitehall or in Cathays Park,[2] it is more than possible that the reply would be in Welsh. Welsh can be offered for the Civil Service examination. In the schools it is now the Ministry of Education which urges the Welsh to become a bilingual nation, and so win the best of both worlds, the world of the English upper deck, and the world of the second-class Welsh deck, not quite under the hatches. By far the great majority of Welsh educational leaders,

---

2. The Administrative Centre of Wales in Cardiff.

amongst them Welsh writers, see this as a magnanimous and worthy ideal. I am one of the stupid minority who see in it a respectable and peaceful death and a burial without mourning for the Welsh language.

One important lesson can be drawn from the Government's attitude. If Wales seriously demanded to have Welsh as an official language on a par with English, the opposition would not come from the Government or from the Civil Service. Naturally there would be a few muttered curses from clerks looking for a dictionary and from girl typists who were learning to spell, but the Civil Service has long since learnt to accept revolutionary changes in the British Empire as part of the daily routine. The opposition—harsh, vindictive and violent—would come from Wales.

But lest my flattery of the Government make anyone suspect that I aspire to the House of Lords, may I add another point? There is no hope of the Whitehall Government ever adopting a Welsh standpoint. It is no part of the Ministry of Education's task to force the Welsh language on the schools of Wales, nor even to enforce the effective teaching of Welsh. It will urge, support and encourage, certainly. But offend the Carmarthenshire County Council? I doubt it. *De minimis non curat lex.* The Government will not lift a finger to save a minority which is as politically ineffectual, as wretchedly helpless and as unable to defend itself as is the Welsh-speaking minority in Wales.

Consider the question of the Tryweryn valley and Capel Celyn. What reason was there for the people of Wales to oppose Liverpool Corporation's plan to drown the valley and the village and turn the locality into a reservoir to serve the city's industries? It is true that the economic gain for Liverpool Corporation is enormous. It is true that co-operation between the county councils of North Wales a quarter of a century earlier could have established a better procedure to the advantage of their localities. It is the custom of the Welsh county councils to refuse to co-operate with each other unless they are forced to do so, and to reject as far as they can every attempt to change their constitution and procedure. But that was not the reason for rejecting Liverpool's plan either. The project would destroy a monoglot Welsh-speaking community in one of Merioneth's historical rural areas. To defend it is to defend a language, to defend a society, to defend homes and families. Today Wales cannot afford the destruction of Welsh-speaking homes. They are few and weak. Conferences of all the local authorities of Wales under the presidency of the Lord Mayor of Cardiff, protested against Liverpool's measure. The measure went through Parliament with ease. Liverpool is a great and populous city with immense political influence. What Government could weigh a small and poor Welsh rural community in the balance against the economic interests of Liverpool Corporation? It was not childish but dishonest to blame the Minister for Welsh Affairs because he did not block the measure. Tryweryn was our concern, our responsibility, and ours alone. But 'We are not Irishmen,' said the journal of the people who were defending. Do you suppose that that was not observed in Government offices and noted there together with the other classical Welsh slogan 'Bread before beauty'? What has been the result? Wales is today rent in twain on Sundays, Welsh-speaking Wales and English-speaking Wales. That is but proof that the Government has taken the measure of the feebleness of Welsh Wales and knows that it need not concern itself about it any more. And Gwylfa, the Menai and Snowdonia are now to be desecrated to feed Lancashire with electricity.

There is another reason why the Government need not concern itself about Welsh-speaking Wales. It can leave that to the Welsh local authorities and to the political parties in Wales. It was some of the Welsh members of Parliament who pressed upon the Government that Welsh was not essential even in posts in Wales connected with Welsh culture. The attacks made on the National Eisteddfod by several Welsh local authorities in South Wales are extremely significant. They refuse to contribute towards it or to give a grant towards it because it is a Welsh language institution. They demand that one out of its five days should be turned into an English day before they will contribute towards its maintenance in an honourable fashion. This is the type of spiritual and mental perversity which is the psychiatrist's bliss, but this spirit is on the increase in South Wales and can hasten the end of the Eisteddfod. It is not an official, legal or administrative institution. It is the creation of Welsh-speaking Wales, the only remaining symbol of the historical unity of the Welsh nation, the only Welsh mythos. But several of the leaders of the political parties and local authorities in Wales are full of poison towards the Welsh language. And many thousands of steel, coal and nylon workers and workers in the various new industries do not even know of the language's existence any more.

The attitude of mind of the county councils and local authorities of the Welsh-speaking parts is just as threatening. They have but one answer to the problem of the decline of the rural areas, that is to press on the Government to bring them factories and industries from England, and to invite the corporations of cities like Birmingham to establish satellite towns in Anglesey, Merioneth or Montgomeryshire. The Minister for Welsh Affairs does what he can with the aid of civil service departments to promote this policy; and not in vain either. But Lord Brecon himself has said that it is a pity that the Welsh-speaking districts do not do more to set up industries themselves instead of calling continually for aid from outside. I shall only say this about the present policy: it is another nail in the coffin of the Welsh language. There is no need to add that the whole economic tendency in Great Britain, with the ever-increasing centralization of industry, is to drive the Welsh language into a corner, ready to be thrown, like a worthless rag, on the dung-heap.

Is the position hopeless? It is, of course, if we are content to give up hope. There is nothing in the world more comfortable than to give up hope. For then one can go on to enjoy life.

The political tradition of the centuries and all present-day economic tendencies militate against the continued existence of Welsh. Nothing can change that except determination, will power, struggle, sacrifice and endeavour. May I call your attention to the story of Mr. and Mrs. Trefor Beasley? Mr. Beasley is a coal-miner. In April 1952 he and his wife bought a cottage in Llangennech near Llanelli, a district where nine out of every ten of the population are Welsh-speaking. All the councillors on the rural council which controls Llangennech are Welsh-speaking: so too are the council officials. Therefore when a note demanding the local rates arrived from 'The Rural District Council of Llanelly' Mrs. Beasley wrote to ask for it in Welsh. It was refused. She refused to pay the rates until she got it. She and Mr. Beasley were summoned more than a dozen times to appear before the magistrates' court. Mr. and Mrs. Beasley insisted that the court proceedings should be in Welsh. Three times did the bailiffs carry off furniture from their home, the furniture being worth much more than the rates which were demanded. This went on for eight years. In 1960 Mr. and Mrs. Beasley received a bilingual note demanding the local rates from *Cyngor Dosbarth Gwledig Llanelli*, the Welsh on the bill being just as good as its English. It is not my right to say what was the financial cost of all this to Mr. and Mrs. Beasley. Friends, including solicitors and barristers, were very loyal. Their trouble became the subject of the country's attention, and the newspapers and radio and television plagued them continually. The court cases were interesting and important. For example, the rating officer's reply to Mr. Wynne Samuel: 'The Council is not under any obligation to print rate demand notes in any language except English.'

In the middle of the last war, in October 1941—as a result of *Undeb Cymru Fydd*'s (*Union of the Wales to Be*) most important campaign—a petition was presented to Parliament, a petition signed by approximately four hundred thousand Welshmen, appealing for a law

> placing the Welsh language on a footing of equality with the English language in all proceedings connected with the Administration of Justice and of Public Services in Wales.

But after the great labour, the collection of signatures, and the conferences, the Welsh members of Parliament went into conclave with Mr. Herbert Morrison, the Home Secretary at the time. The result was the Welsh Courts Act of 1942, a parliamentary Act which disregarded the whole purpose of the petition and which still left English as the only official language of the courts and all the public services. That was what the Llanelli rating officer was referring to.

The Welsh language can be saved. Welsh-speaking Wales is still quite an extensive part of Wales territorially, and the minority is not yet wholly unimportant. The example of Mr. and Mrs. Beasley shows how we should set about it. During Mrs. Beasley's eight years of endeavour only one other Welshman in the rural district asked for a rate demand in Welsh. This cannot be done reasonably except in those districts where Welsh-speakers are a substantial proportion of the population. Let us set about it in seriousness and without hesitation to make it impossible for the business of local and central government to continue without using Welsh. Let it be insisted upon that the rate demand should be in Welsh or in Welsh and English. Let the Postmaster-General be warned that annual licences will not be paid unless they are obtainable in Welsh. Let it be insisted upon that every summons to a court should be in Welsh. This is not a chance policy for individuals here and there. It would demand organizing and moving step by step, giving due warning and allowing time for changes. It is a policy for a movement, and that a movement in the areas where Welsh is the spoken language in daily use. Let it be demanded that every election communication and every official form relating to local or parliamentary elections should be in Welsh. Let Welsh be raised as the chief administrative issue in district and county.

Perhaps you will say that this could never be done, that not enough Welshmen could be found to agree and to organize it as a campaign of importance and strength. Perhaps you are right. All I maintain is that this is the only political matter which it is worth a Welshman's while to trouble himself about today. I know the difficulties. There would be storms from every direction. It would be argued that such a campaign was killing our chances of attracting English factories to the Welsh-speaking rural areas, and that would doubtless be the case. It is easy to predict that the scorn and sneers of the English gutter journalist would be a daily burden. The anger of local authority officials and those of many county councils would be like the blustering of those in the Llanelli Rural District. Fines in courts would be heavy, and a refusal to pay them would bring expensive consequences, though no more expensive than fighting purposeless parliamentary elections. I do not deny that there would be a period of hatred, persecution and controversy in place of the brotherly love which is so manifest in Welsh political life today. It will be nothing less than a revolution to restore the Welsh language in Wales. Success is only possible through revolutionary methods. Perhaps the language would bring self-government in its wake—I don't know. In my opinion, if any kind of self-government for Wales were obtained before the Welsh language was acknowledged and used as an official language in local authority and state administration in the Welsh-speaking parts of our country, then the language would never achieve official status at all, and its demise would be quicker than it will be under English rule.

Translated by G. ALED WILLIAMS.

(BBC Publications, February 1962.)

Welsh Literature and Nationalism

Welsh literary critics are shy of emphasizing what distinguishes Welsh literature from other literatures in Europe and especially separates it from its neighbouring English. This is perhaps because the discordant elements are not in the modern world fashionable. I take two modern examples in this essay.

The religious revival of the eighteenth century made Wales, for a century and a half, a Nonconformist and Calvinist community. There are historians and critics who are rather sorry about this. Today, Nonconformity is in sad and sullen retreat and Calvinism is almost a dirty word.

For English people of the upper-middle class—that is, the literary English—both Nonconformist and Calvinist have been rather smelly lower class attributes since the eighteenth century. That is the gulf that divides nineteenth-century Welsh literature from English.

The Methodist revival gave Welsh prose and verse a separate character, a new idiom. One may complain that the nineteenth-century Welsh literature lacks the broad secular liberal interests of French or German or English. True enough. True also of the nineteenth-century Spanish literature; even of modern Italian letters. Welsh literature since the sixteenth century has been a minor literature. Nevertheless, it is unique. It tells of an experience no other nation knows in the same fashion; and no other literature relates.

For Methodism was the form that the Romantic revolution took in Wales. Williams Pantycelyn and Ann Griffiths are for us what Blake and Wordsworth are for the English, what Manzoni is for the Italians. There are no religious hymns of the eighteenth century in the *Oxford Book of English Verse*. That may be a correct judgement.

On the other hand, the greatest Welsh lyrics of the eighteenth and nineteenth centuries are certainly hymns. Their grandeur and intellectual power make them major poetry. These are national characteristics that a literary historian, be he Christian or unbeliever, must in loyalty to objective truth maintain.

I take my second example from a more recent past. It is now forty years since the Welsh Nationalist Party began its career at Pwllheli. By the 1930's it had become an established phenomenon in Welsh life. How much it has influenced Welsh political development and Welsh political thinking is a matter of petty dispute. Historians who rely on statistics are not impressed. Welsh socialist members of Parliament deny it an atom of importance. Welsh nationalists of an ardent optimism claim that only they have put the Right Honourable James Griffiths[1] where he now is.

I make what I believe to be a statement of fact: the majority of Welsh poets and writers, novelists, dramatists, critics, have since 1930 onwards been avowed members of the Welsh Nationalist Party.

This is not a political argument. This is not a political article. I don't proclaim this as a challenge or in the least as a proof of the rightness of the nationalist cause. I am ready to grant that these men and women may be as daft as Sligo crofters thought W. B. Yeats. What interests me here and now is that this political allegiance has been a gulf between Welsh writers and their English and other contemporaries.

In the 'thirties, English poets and writers, from the public schools and from Oxford and Cambridge, were frenziedly trying to proletarianize themselves, engage themselves, joining the Communist party and the Left Book Club, enlisting for war against Franco in Spain. The influence of that period in English drama and poetry remains today, even if today it is an influence of disillusion.

In the same period, Welsh creative writing was profoundly moved by the development of the nationalist party. It was the period of Williams Parry's great sonnets. Then came the poetry of Gwenallt and Waldo Williams and of Euros Bowen and the generation of Bobi Jones. It is the crisis of Wales that has given this period of poetry its *angst*.

It shows equally in the prose of D. J. Williams, the plays of John Gwilym Jones, stories and novels from Kate Roberts to Islwyn Ffowc Elis.

---

1. At this time he was Labour M.P. for Llanelli, the first Secretary of State for Wales.

Propaganda is not what groups these writers together. Only one or two write at all on politics. Dr. Kate Roberts, whose unfailing activity is a joy, does much political journalism, but she rigidly shuts the door on the least breath of propaganda in her stories and novels.

What these writers and poets have in common is an awareness that the Welsh nation may be dying of indifference and sloth and that a literature of a thousand years may end with a whimper.

In that they have, as it were, an epitome of what now overhangs all Europe, of what threatens humanity, a destruction of civilization through apathy.

There is no longer any faith that makes the deferment of the nuclear war very urgent. So that a particular Welsh experience of this century, the crisis that the Welsh Nationalist Party evokes and was organized to avert, takes on universal reference and significance. Civilization must be more than an abstraction. It must have a local habitation and a name. Here, its name is Wales.

Alas, there is one sad difference between the Welsh Nationalist Party of the 1960s and the Welsh Methodists of the 1760s. The Methodists in their day roused hate, violence, persecution, prison. That is why they triumphed.

(*Western Mail*, 13 March 1965.)

The Tradition of Taliesin

A young poet, Mr. Anthony Conran, has translated into English a selection of Welsh poetry from the sixth century to today, and his translations are to be published this year in a popular series.[1] It seems a moment to discuss a main tradition of Welsh medieval verse-making, the panegyric tradition that has its source in the sixth-century poetry of Taliesin.

Taliesin is the first known poet of the Welsh language. Tradition associates him with the court of Maglocunus or Maelgwn Gwynedd, king of North Wales. But the poems safely attributed to him belong specially to a more northern kingdom, the kingdom of Rheged which is the modern north-west of England from the Solway Firth southwards and perhaps across the Pennines to the Swale river.

The first certain reference to Welsh poets is in the well-known work of Gildas, a Latin treatise on the Ruin of Britain, *De Excidio Britanniae*. It is a moral tract, containing some history and much severe condemnation of five local Welsh kings, and most especially of Maglocunus, the king of North Wales. Until recently it was thought that this mightiest and most interesting of Gildas's tyrants had died in the year 547. But Count Nicolai Tolstoi, in a newly published study has given valid reason for putting his death at 575. This allows us to place Gildas's *De Excidio Britanniae* in the third quarter of the sixth century, and not a few previous difficulties are removed.

There is one recognized anomaly in Gildas. After describing the Ruin of Britain he turns to attack the morals of his contemporary Welsh regional kings. There are five of them, from the king of Devon in the South to the great ruler of North Wales. But the Welsh lands of Britannia in the second half of the sixth century extended much further north than North Wales. Our earliest poetry is associated with the North-West of England and the Scottish lowlands. On the kings of these regions, on the king of Rheged in particular, which perhaps bordered on North Wales, Gildas is utterly silent. While he was writing his indictment of the other rulers, his contemporary, Taliesin, who could have been among the

---

1. *The Penguin Book of Welsh Verse*, 1967. *Quotations used are early versions of the translations.*

poets he lashes for their false flattery in the North Wales court, was actually singing, in the very manner he condemns, the praises of Urien, king of Rheged. It is unlikely that Gildas penned his fierce attack on the Welsh rulers in any territory where they had jurisdiction. Welsh sixth-century kings were not as liberal as all that. 'Many have they bound in prison and ill-used with heavy chains,' says Gildas, thanking his lucky stars. He needed security and protection, *dinas pellennig* (*sanctuary for the traveller*), to write his accusations. His silence about Rheged becomes understandable. It suggests that he wrote his arraignment of the other kings in the safe refuge of Urien's kingdom—he may indeed have been a native of it—and that while he penned his scorn of the poets of North Wales, Taliesin himself was teaching just that sort of panegyric to the courtiers of Rheged, and that their coincidence was not fortuitous.

Panegyric, poetic praise of the ruler in his court, be he emperor or king, was an ancient Latin tradition. It survived in such Latin poets as Sidonius in the fifth century and Fortunatus in the sixth. Frankish kings in Gaul took over this court custom from their defeated predecessors. In the Welsh language, as one would expect, it is our earliest, our sixth-century poetry. I have translated from Welsh to English a poem in praise of Urien by Taliesin as an example of this court panegyric:

Urien of Yrechwydd,   most generous of Christian men,
much do you give   to the people of your land;
as you gather   so also you scatter,
the poets of Christendom   rejoice while you stand.
More is the gaiety   and more is the glory
that Urien and his heirs   are for riches renowned,
and he is the chieftain,   the paramount ruler,
the far-flung refuge,   first of fighters found.
The Lloegrians know it   when they count their numbers,
death have they suffered   and many a shame,
Their homesteads a-burning,   stripped their bedding,
and many a loss   and many a blame,
and never a respite   from Urien of Rheged.
Rheged's defender,   famed lord, your land's anchor,
all that is told of you   has my acclaim.
Intense is your spear-play   when you hear ploy of battle,
when to battle you come   'tis a killing you can,
fire in their houses ere day   in the Lord of Yrechwydd's way.
Yrechwydd the beautiful   and its generous people,
The Angles are succourless.   Around the fierce king
are his fierce offspring.   Of those dead, of those living,

```
of those yet to come,      you head the column.
To gaze upon him        is a widespread fear,
gaiety clothes him        the ribald ruler,
gaiety clothes him        and riches abounding,
gold king of the Northland    and of kings king.
```

Now, direct from that paean I want to move to the quite elaborate character study of Maglocunus, king of North Wales, that we find in Gildas. It is unlike his attacks on the other four kings. Those are brief and black. Of Maglocunus he reports exceptional qualities, royal virtues, but yet, and constantly, worse faults and infamies. Listen to Hugh Williams's translation of the opening paragraph:

> And thou, the island dragon, who has driven many of the tyrants previously mentioned, as well from life as from kingdom, thou last in my writing, first in wickedness, exceeding many in power, and at the same time in malice, more liberal in giving, more excessive in sin, strong in arms, but stronger in what destroys thy soul, thou Maglocunus . . .

You notice, of course, the antitheses, 'exceeding many in power, at the same time in malice, more liberal in giving, more excessive in sin.' I want to drop these rhetorical antitheses, though they have a touch of Tacitus about them, and examine only the theses. I make a list of them:

> Island dragon (*insularis draco*)
> overthrower of rulers (*tyrannorum depulsor*)
> exceeding many in power (*major multis potentia*)
> more liberal in giving (*largior in dando*)
> strong in arms (*robuste armis*)
> superior to almost all the kings of Britain, both in dominion and in physical stature (*tam regno quam status liniamento editiorem*)
> accompanied by soldiers of the bravest whose countenance in battle appeared not unlike that of young lions . . .

I don't think that anyone acquainted with the poems of Taliesin can doubt, after this catalogue, that here in Gildas's Latin we have all the themes and imagery of the poet's panegyric taken up, put into Latin, and made the basis of Gildas's character study of the king of North Wales. In the poem that was quoted above you will find phrase after phrase corresponding with the Latin phrases of eulogy in Gildas. It was, I conclude, the Taliesinic poems of panegyric that Gildas took as the basis of his moral condemnation of Maglocunus; he would be hearing them in the very court of Rheged; and it is to Taliesin and his school that he points when he speaks of 'False tongues of flatterers singing at the top of their voice.' I would even submit that these coincidences cannot be utterly ignored when the period of the Taliesin poetry is in question.

Gildas writes of Maglocunus with an intimate knowledge both of his court and his career. It is accepted as probable that they had been pupils together in the monastic school of Saint Illtud in South Wales. That will explain a personal note in which he reproaches the king for not listening to him in spite of the difference of status between them. The king, Gildas tells us, had once abdicated and returned to become a monk. His vows, however, had failed to hold him; he had abandoned the monastic choir and the praise of the liturgy, and had resumed his throne. But he had had a Latin education under the most distinguished teacher of his age. Scholars have always looked askance at Gildas's prolix and unclassical Latin prose. Yet Gildas knew large parts of his Vergil by heart and if the Ruin of Britain is also somewhat a ruin of Latin, there are very frequent phrases and echoes from the *Aeneid* throughout the first thirty-six chapters of the book. The king of North Wales had had a training that allowed him to appreciate the Vergilian echoes. He had shared in the same teaching. And it is impossible not to ask, what of Taliesin?

We know nothing of Taliesin except through such poems as are with confidence attributed to him. But when one reads the poems and Gildas's Ruin of Britain together, one notices more than one simile and many a phrase where the Latin and the Welsh are strikingly akin, and where the Latin is certainly a reminiscence of Vergil or of later Latin historians borrowing from classical Latin. A simile in Taliesin is apt to fill a line, as when he sings of invaders coming—

Like waves with mighty roar over the grounds.

It is a Vergilian simile, and Gildas has this description of Roman soldiery in attack: 'Just like a mountain torrent, swollen by numerous streams after storms, sweeps over its bed in its noisy course.' This is a direct borrowing from lines 496–99 of the second book of the *Aeneid*. This book, with its tale of the fall of Troy, is constantly in Gildas's mind throughout his account of the Ruin of Britain, as, for instance, when he speaks of 'swords gleaming on every side and flames crackling.' And has not something of it rubbed off on to many phrases of Taliesin, who tells of 'fire in their houses ere day in the Lord of Yrechwydd's way'. Gildas tells of the

Saxons admitted to Britain 'like wolves into the fold,' while after the Roman withdrawal the Irish had leapt 'like rapacious wolves into the fold' and had cut down their victims, 'reaping them like ripe corn.' These figures all have their models in the *Aeneid*, and we find them again in Taliesin, for whom Owain ap Urien is 'reaper of his foes' and punishes them 'like wolves ravening sheep.' The Romans are said by Gildas to have exhorted the Britons 'to fight bravely so as to save their land, property, wives, children, liberty and life.' Taliesin describes Urien addressing his troops in Roman general style before battle—'If there is to be a fight for our kinsfolk.' But let us quote the entire poem in Anthony Conran's English version; it is both scholarly and poetry, and the poem has a Roman ring.

THE BATTLE OF ARGOED LLWYFAIN[2]

There was a great battle Saturday morning
From when the sun rose until it grew dark
The fourfold hosts of Fflamddwyn invaded.
Goddau and Rheged gathered in arms,
Summoned from Argoed as far as Arfynydd—
They might not delay by so much as a day.

With a great blustering din, Fflamddwyn shouted,
'Have those hostages come? Are they ready?'
To him then Owain, scourge of the eastlands,
'They've not come, no! They're not, nor shall they be ready!
And a whelp of Coel would indeed be afflicted
Did he have to give any men as a hostage!'

And Urien, lord of Erechwydd,[3] shouted,
'If they would meet us now for our kinsfolk,
High on the hilltop let's raise our ramparts,
Carry our faces over the shield rims,
Raise up our spears, men, over our heads,
And set upon Fflamddwyn in the midst of his hosts
And slaughter him, ay, and all that go with him!'

There was many a corpse beside Argoed Llwyfain;
   From warriors ravens grew red
And with their leader a host attacked.
For a whole year I shall sing to their triumph.

---

2. For the author's version, see p. 152.
3. The forms Yrechwydd and Erechwydd are both possible.

I would not be thought to claim that Taliesin borrows his Vergilian lines from Gildas nor at all directly from the *Aeneid*. But the evidence is there that Gildas and Taliesin were in touch. Hitherto Gildas has been left entirely to the historians. Welsh literary criticism has taken scant notice of him. I submit that Taliesin cannot be read apart from Gildas; the *De Excidio Britanniae* provides not only a key to the understanding of the Taliesinic panegyric, but reveals the mental climate, the cultural background and body of traditional imagery, in which the earliest Welsh poetry that we know had its formation. It belongs to the main stream of European literature rather more than we appreciate.

Finally I turn to Taliesin's picture of this Northern Welsh king, Urien of Rheged. Panegyric, in spite of Gildas, is not merely or mainly fulsome flattery. It is also idealization; it establishes an ideal, a standard of behaviour. So it is essentially creative. Taliesin's picture of Urien is the poet's greatest achievement, his major creation. Urien became, through Taliesin's portrayal, the accepted model of the Welsh Christian king, of the Welsh leader of his people. He is no adventurer. He does not win a kingdom. He is the acknowledged heir, the inevitable defender of his inheritance, his country's anchor, its shelter. He has the example and the qualities of his father and grandfather, and around his throne and his table are his sons, especially Owain, who learn from him, go to battle with him, take over from him, continuing the line and the tradition. He is renowned for riches, for his exuberant generosity, for his physical strength, for his immensity in battle, for his victories, for his delight in poetry and song, for his rewards to warrior and bard. His nobles are like young lions around him.

This picture of the ideal Welsh king became the foundation of the entire Welsh poetic tradition for a thousand years, right up to the sixteenth century. It was the basis of the poetic schools. But I do not believe that we can study this portrait of Urien, considering its background, considering the impressive evidence of Gildas, without remembering another idealization, another heir and re-founder and father of kings, great in war as in generosity, the hero of Vergil's *Aeneid*. Taliesin's picture of Urien is far, far slighter, far less subtle, but it is in that mould, in that tradition; it has that inheritance. Let me end, then, with Mr. Conran's translation of the most classical of Taliesin's poems, his short elegy on the prince or king, Owain ap Urien. It is one of the big things of Welsh poetry, and it has a Horatian quality:

DEATH SONG FOR OWAIN AB URIEN[4]

God, consider the soul's need
　Of Owain son of Urien!
Rheged's prince, secret in loam:
　To honour him was honour!

A strait grave, a man much praised,
　His whetted spear the wings of dawn:
That lord of bright Llwyfenydd,
　Where is his peer?

Reaper of enemies; strong of grip;
　One kind with his fathers;
Owain, to slay Fflamddwyn,
　Thought it no more than sleep.

Sleepeth the wide host of England
　With light in their eyes,
And those that had not fled
　Were braver than were wise.

Owain dealt them doom
　As the wolves break sheep;
That warrior, bright of harness,
　Gave stallions for the bard.

Treasure as from miser's greed
　For his soul's sake he gave.
God, consider the soul's need
　Of Owain son of Urien!

---

4. For the author's version, see p. 153.

Possible Variations to Anthony Conran's Translations

THE BATTLE OF ARGOED LLWYFAIN

There was a great battle Saturday morning
From when the sun rose until it grew dark.
The fourfold hosts of Fflamddwyn invaded,
Goddau and Rheged gathered in arms,
Summoned from Argoed as far as Arfynydd—
They might not delay by so much as a day.

With a great blustering din, Fflamddwyn shouted,
'Have these the hostages come? Are they ready?'
To him then Owain, scourge of the eastlands,
'They've not come, no! They're not, nor shall they be ready!
And a whelp of Coel would indeed be afflicted
Did he have to give any man as a hostage!'

And Urien, lord of Erechwydd, shouted,
'If they would meet us now for a treaty,
High on the hilltop let's raise our ramparts,
Carry our faces over the shield rims,
Raise up our spears, men over our heads
And set upon Fflamddwyn in the midst of his hosts
And slaughter him, ay, and all that go with him!'

There was many a corpse beside Argoed Llwyfain;
   From warriors ravens grew red
And with their leader a host attacked.
For a whole year I shall sing to their triumph.

DEATH SONG FOR OWAIN AB URIEN

God, consider the soul's need
  Of Owain son of Urien!
Rheged's prince, secret in loam:
  No shallow work to praise him.

A strait grave, a man much praised,
  His whetted spear the wings of dawn:
That lord of bright Llwyfenydd,
  Where is his peer?

Reaper of enemies; strong of grip;
  One kind with his fathers;
Owain, to slay Fflamddwyn,
  Thought it no more than sleep.

Sleepeth the wide host of England
  With light in their eyes,
And those that had not fled
  Were braver than were wise.

Owain dealt them doom
  As the wolves devour sheep;
That warrior, bright of harness,
  Gave stallions for the bard.

Though he hoarded wealth like a miser
  For his soul's sake he gave it.
God, consider the soul's need
  Of Owain son of Urien!

(Originally intended as a BBC Third Programme Talk.)

The Essence of Welsh Literature

During the wars of Napoleon there was a country squire of the name of Lloyd living in the old house of Cwmgloyn, inland a little from Trefdraeth (or Newport on the English maps) on the north coast of Pembrokeshire. He was a justice of the peace. His father had been high sheriff of the county in 1771. The family had been much concerned with the sea, and squire Lloyd had ships built for him at Trefdraeth and at Aberystwyth. One of these, the *Hawk*, was a fifty-ton schooner made from his own woods at Trefdraeth, partly for trade, partly for his pleasure voyages. It was later sunk by the French. At its launching a local poet, one Ioan Siencyn, wrote a poem to greet it and its captain, and its squire-owner. After a finely imaged description of the *Hawk* breasting the sea, the poet visualises squire Lloyd on board, travelling to England and Ireland, but especially visiting his friends in North and South Wales. There the gentry and local poets come to meet him, and one verse describes their welcome to him:

> Around their tables laden with steaming dishes,
> He shall hear histories of those good men, our ancestors,
> And *cywydd* and *englyn* and odes of Taliesin,
> And he shall drink his fill of golden barley beer.

That poem was written close to the beginning of the nineteenth century. It speaks simply and naturally of odes of Taliesin and *cywydd* and *englyn* as part of the pertinent welcome to squire Lloyd of Cwmgloyn. Taliesin was a poet of the sixth century. *Cywydd* and *englyn* were metrical forms of the Welsh Middle Ages. But for Ioan Siencyn at the very end of the eighteenth century they were all necessary for the proper entertainment of the Welsh squire in any Welsh country house. Poetry was part of the tradition of hospitality.

Now will you imagine with me that a poet of the fifteenth century, some great figure such as Tudur Aled, had been released to revisit Pembrokeshire at the launching of the *Hawk*, and had listened to the reading of Ioan Siencyn's verses to squire Lloyd. What would our fifteenth-century master have thought or said? He would note with warm approval the occasion of the poem. Just such an event, the completion of a new house or a new ship had in his time also been the appropriate moment for a complimentary poem to the

154

head of a family. And Tudur Aled would have relished Ioan
Siencyn's development of the image of the *Hawk* as it was launched
on the water:

> Spread now your wings, forget the green woodlands,
> Learn to live mid the mouthing of seas.

When Siencyn calls on Neptune and Triton to protect the schooner,
Tudur Aled would remember that he, in the early sixteenth century,
was beginning to learn the use of those Greek gods from his friends
in the circle of Cardinal Wolsey; and then when the poet returns
to his bird-schooner and describes the *Hawk*:

> Your wings playing high as the clouds,
> Your breasts cleaving the salt billows,
> Let your beak pierce the waves, your belly furrow them,
> Your rudder scatter them in spray-suds.

the fifteenth-century poet would have recognized it as just that
serious playing with image that was part of the technique of poems
inspired by manual craft in his own day. And as the poem grew to
the final eulogy of squire Lloyd and his society, to the reference to
Taliesin and talk of the deeds of his forefathers storied over the
yellow beer on the laden dining table, Tudur Aled might well
exclaim: 'My art still survives in this last decade of the eighteenth
century and the great technique and the old mastery are not all
forgotten. This country poet, this Ioan Siencyn, is truly an heir of
our ancient discipline; he also sings the immemorial ideals and the
pattern of behaviour of the leaders of the Welsh people, and
I recognize him as a poet of the long line that began with Taliesin
in the North.'

There, I think, we capture something essential in the progress of
Welsh poesy. We call it the literary tradition of Wales. It means
you cannot pluck a flower of song off a headland of Dyfed (South-
West Wales) in the late eighteenth century without stirring a great
northern star of the sixth century. And all the intermediaries are
involved. The fourteenth century gave the technique of *dyfalu* or
image-making, the sixteenth century brought in the Vergilian echoes,
the seventeenth gave the measure. The whole body of Welsh poetry
from the sixth century onward has contributed directly to Ioan
Siencyn's verses. And, mark you, the poem I am discussing is an
obscure piece of work by a little known poet whose name is in no
history of Welsh literature nor in any anthology. It was last published in a forgotten volume at Aberystwyth in 1842. Why do I use

it as a peg for this talk? Because it reveals the nature and continuity of the Welsh poetic tradition and because it reveals its quality and creative virtue: for the virtue of that tradition is that it may enable a quite minor poet to write a major poem.

Sir Idris Bell has written recently that 'the unique contribution of Wales to the world's literature, the poetry which, because it *is* unique, most obviously deserves and requires interpretation, is the classical great tradition of the Mediaeval bards.' I accept that, save that I hold that the tradition remained the main Welsh literary tradition down to the nineteenth century. But the Middle Ages are the ages of its energy and splendour. Up to the death of Llywelyn, Prince of Wales, in 1282, that tradition was Taliesinic. It was heroic verse, and its matter was praise of God and the saints and the king or prince. Poetic praise, as with the Greeks, is the portrayal of an ideal which is the bond of unity of tribe or society or nation. That is the function of eulogy in heroic poetry and in primitive society. It is in that sense that heroic poetry is the main educational factor in primitive, aristocratic communities. It was so in Wales. But with the death of the last Llywelyn, the Welsh poetic tradition faced a crisis in its development. What now, without the Prince, was to be the theme of heroic verse? Had the tradition of Taliesin to be abandoned?

The crisis was resolved by two clerics. For simplicity's sake let me talk only of Einion the Priest as the teacher and saviour of the tradition and author of the first text-book of the master-poets that has been preserved for us. Today it is easier for us to understand Einion's contribution to Welsh poetic thought than it was fifteen years ago when I first dealt with this matter. The close connection of medieval philosophy with poetry is now widely recognized. In 1936 Arthur Lovejoy published an important book in America on the Great Chain of Being.[1] Then, inspired by Lovejoy, Dr. Tillyard of Cambridge published in 1943 *The Elizabethan World Picture*. I think that the chapters on the Chain of Being in Tillyard's book are the best available English introduction to the matter of the great classical poetry of medieval Wales from the time of Einion Offeiriad. Tillyard shows that the idea of order in the Creation was basic to all medieval thought, and it was considered under the image of a great chain or ladder of degrees of being, starting from the very throne of God. 'The idea,' says Tillyard, 'began with

1. *The Great Chain of Being*, Cam., Mass., 1936.

Plato's Timaeus, was developed by Aristotle, adopted by the Alexandrian Jews, spread by the Neo-Platonists, and from the Middle Ages till the eighteenth century was one of those accepted commonplaces more often hinted at or taken for granted than set forth.' Then Tillyard quotes from some of the medieval exponents of this conception, and finally shows how profoundly the doctrine affected the poetry of Spenser and Shakespeare and Milton.

Now it is this Great Chain of Being that is the main content of Welsh poetry from the fourteenth century to the sixteenth. It is a logical enlargement of the Taliesin tradition. It is set forth in those chapters of the grammar-book of the poets which discuss *How all Reality is to be praised in poetry*. And there is a sixteenth-century treatise called the *Graduelys* which is the fullest Welsh discussion we possess of the Chain of Being. The Chain starts with the Trinity and descends through Our Lady and the Saints and down all the celestial hierarchies. Then we find described the corresponding orders of the Church Militant on earth, from Pope and Cardinal down to parish priest and beggar friar. There follow the hierarchies of the laity, the emperor, the kings, the Princes of Wales, dukes, lords, knights, esquires, freemen. The grammar books tell what are the appropriate excellencies of each grade and how they are to be praised. It is this universal order, this graded plurality of God's creation, that is the theme of the classic poets of Welsh *cywydd* and *awdl*. It accounts for the confidence and grandeur of their song. It is the explanation of almost all their imagery. For their comparisons and metaphors come also from the philosophy of the Chain of Being. Medieval natural philosophers held that as each grade of men had its peculiar excellence, so also in the natural world. The lion is king of beasts for his might, the stag has primacy of speed and pride, the eagle is king of birds as the oak tree is of the forest and salmon of fish; air is higher than water which in its turn is above the land. All nature is linked thus in the Great Chain and there are correspondences in all the orders.

In the fifteenth century at Tywyn, near the mouth of the river Teifi in the extreme south of Cardiganshire, a young heir of the great house, Rhys ap Rhydderch, had fallen into mischance. An old poet who had lived with the family, one of the learned among Welsh poets, Dafydd Nanmor, wrote a *cywydd* to cheer and encourage the young man to raise his head, make good, and emulate his father and forefathers. He addresses him as the Rose of Tywyn (the rose was primate of flowers in the books), he bids him consider how the stag leads the race uphill, how the young salmon leaps the fall, the eagle's flight to the topmost branch of the oak tree, the urge of the lion for the hills, the inevitable soaring of the hawk and the flowering of the highest branch of the tree. Do not fear, says Dafydd Nanmor to the lad, but become what you must be and what you are; gain your own place and rank in the chain of being; you are founded in a noble stock, you are the offering and sacrifice of all South Wales. Every line of the poem, every comparison is drawn from the doctrine of the Chain. That is what makes it one of the supreme educational poems. Dafydd Nanmor summons the entire world-view of the Ages of Faith to sustain his young pupil. The examples he offers are not lucky or pretty similes. They are not fortuitous. They are the detailed and pertinent elaboration of a doctrine of correspondences that run through all creation. The salmon must leap the fall because his sire leapt; so Rhys with such a sire and such a grandsire and such ancestors, must attain his allotted station in life. That is not modern exhortation. It is deeper. It is an appeal to the implicit faith in God and God's purpose in creation. The effect is to give the young heir confidence and assurance of his part in the vast ladder of universal order, and hence courage to fulfil his rôle.

Poetry is great and classical when a high seriousness of function in society and profound philosophic content meet with a form that is unique and subtle and richly expressive. That is true of the great centuries of the *awdl* and *cywydd*. If this classical poetry of the Welsh bards is, as has been claimed, unique, the explanation is that their matter, their explicit and implicit theme, is the philosophic conception of an integrated Christendom taking its place in the great realm of divine order, and that the *cywydd* and *awdl* were shaped by fearless artificers into bright mirrors of that order. There is in European poetry only one thing that can compare with it, and that is *The Divine Comedy* of Dante.

(First published in *Wales*, VII, 27th December 1947, pp. 337–341.)

Dafydd ap Gwilym

Until recent years Dafydd ap Gwilym was the only Welsh poet with a high reputation outside Wales. This was not so strange. He fitted into the conventional picture of medieval poetry. He shared themes and modes with Guido Cavalcanti and with Thibaut de Champagne. He stretched a hand to Rutebeuf and another to the early Chaucer. Sir Idris Bell tackled English translations; Stern treated him as a Welsh *Minnesänger*; a Dutch scholar, Theodor Chotzen, killed later in a Nazi prison, had in 1927 published his *Recherches sur la poésie de Dafydd ap Gwilym*, a large volume which remains still a most valuable survey of much of the poetry of Northern Europe in the fourteenth century. Now Professor Parry, of the University College of North Wales, Bangor, gives us the long-awaited edition[1] which is based on a study of all the manuscript sources. One must not speak of a final edition, for the simple reason that oral tradition admits of very little finality; but here are the text and critical apparatus that will be the starting point of study for the rest of this century. What I propose to attempt now is to give English readers a glimpse of Dafydd ap Gwilym from the point of view of the Welsh literary tradition.

This is no longer too difficult. The first volume of *The Growth of Literature* by H. M. and N. K. Chadwick—a great and noble work despite necessary lacunae and some errors—has revealed to English students the tradition of heroic panegyric that is the main stream of Welsh poetry from the sixth century onwards. The Welsh poets themselves used to call it the tradition of Taliesin, from the sixth-century poet of that name. The Norman conquest of England and the consequent threat to the Welsh that began in the closing years of the eleventh century gave fresh impetus to the heroic praise of the defending princes in the three princedoms of Wales. The struggle and its verse lasted till 1282 and later; but with the extinction of the principality and of the North Wales dynasty, the poetic activity that had made panegyric of the princes its main theme and heroic lyric its mode came to a difficult period.

---

1. *Gwaith Dafydd ap Gwilym*, ed. Thomas Parry, University of Wales Press, Cardiff, 1952. Thomas Parry was then Professor of Welsh at Bangor.

For some two generations, say 1290 to 1330, there was multifarious and robust confusion. It is a still uncharted patch of Welsh literary history. The poets were professionals, organized in a *confrérie* that had points of likeness to the French corporations, or *puys*, and the Chief of Song exercised offices not dissimilar from those of the *Roi des ministraux* of the French and Anglo-French thirteenth century. But the high rank and the panegyric function of the *prydydd* or court poet seemed (or seems) at this period to be merging with those of the bohemian *ioculatorum turba*. Then out of the confusion came, before the middle years of the fourteenth century, two strong movements of renaissance.

The first was a reorganization of the poets' corporation and a re-statement and enlargement of the tradition of panegyric. I must deal with it summarily, since it is a big matter. It is represented by a new chapter in the official grammar books of the poets, a chapter that describes the function of each class of poet and the appropriate modes of high panegyric. This reorganization with its emphatic separation of the noble panegyrist from the miming and railing clown, is akin to the only little earlier movement of poetic reform in France, that is specially reflected in the work of Watriquet de Couvin and Jean de Condé. There are moral exhortations in Watriquet:

> *Menestrieus qui veut son droit faire*
> *Ne doit le jongleur contrefaire,*
> *Mais en sa bouche avoir tous diz*
> *Douces paroles et biaus diz*

and again in Jean de Condé:

> *Sois de cuer et nés et jolis*
> *Courtois, envoisiés et polis*
> *Pour les boines gens solacier*

which have their exact equivalent in the sentences in the Welsh grammar books that describe the moral qualities required of the poet of panegyric. Moreover, panegyric itself, the tradition of heroic praise as the highest poetic function, was now attached both to the *Laudes* of the daily Office and to the dialectic taught in the Cistercian schools, and so given new significance and *raison d'être*. Thus reorientated it became the basis of the great *cywydd* and *awdl* poetry of the next two centuries. That corpus of poetry is the major glory of Welsh literature.

The second movement, contemporary with this, is the work specially linked with the name of Dafydd ap Gwilym. Baldly, this response to the predicament was a turning aside from the tradition of heroic panegyric in order to embrace what Dafydd himself called the 'art of Ovid.' This meant all the varieties of invented love lyric and 'feigning' that stemmed from the *Roman de la Rose* or found in it (particularly lines 2265–2580 in Langlois' edition) their widest-known exemplars. It was a turning from what the Chadwicks have called the tradition of the Northern Islands to the continental and classical modes of *jongleur* and *trouvère*. Dafydd ap Gwilym himself, very aware of the challenge he was involved in, proudly maintained the equal dignity and honour of the Ovidian tradition he had elected for his own:

> The dignity of feigned love-song, however resisted,
> Is no less than that of panegyric.
>
> (Nid llai urddas, heb ras rydd,
> Na gwawd geuwawd o gywydd[2])

How came he to make his choice? Let us say that it was all around him. We shall not get a proper idea of the cultural climate of the late Middle Ages in Britain unless we recognize that Anglo-French and Middle English and Welsh were all cheek by jowl in the Welsh Marches and Crown Lordships. In the thirteenth century Brother Simon of Carmarthen writes French didactic verse that seems to betray the influence of the monorhyme of the Welsh *awdl*. Dr. Carleton Brown has shown that the most remarkable English lyric poet of the late thirteenth century was a Welsh-speaking Welshman 'between Wye and Wirral' who makes the North Wind his love-messenger:

> Blow, Northern wind,
> Sent thou me my suetyng,

and whose curiously contrived *Annot and Johon* is notably influenced both in imagery and technique by the Welsh love *awdl*.[3] Dafydd ap Gwilym was nurtured in a household that belonged to the king's service, did the king's business, and met with political trouble. Pembroke and Carmarthen and Cardigan were within easy reach,

---

2. I have to disagree with Professor Parry's reading and interpretation of this most important poem (p. 392).

3. No. 76 in Brown's *Lyrics of the Thirteenth Century*. See the notes, but Dr. Brown fails to observe the *concatenatio* between the last half-line of the monorhyme and the first half-line of the final couplet throughout the poem.

a busy, turbulent, polyglot region. One might hazard the suggestion that it is in the verse of Dafydd ap Gwilym that French-Flemish-English-South Pembrokeshire makes its most signal contribution to Welsh literature. Certainly he was early acquainted with castle and abbey, town and tavern. He learned the cosmopolitan fashion of minstrel and *jongleur* and wandering poor clerk. He sings the courtly high-born love-song, esoteric and learned with literary allusion. He sings as often the broad song of tavern druery and all the irreverent parody and farce and adventure of the goliard tradition. There is nothing that can precisely be called *fabliau* in his work, but his spirit is frequently that of the *fabliaux* writers. He is the gay, insouciant hero of his own misadventures, and so brilliantly master of the mood and manner that he turns *l'esprit gaulois* into *esprit gallois* and gives it for two centuries the freedom of Welsh verse.

Yet the tale of misadventure is rarely the purpose of a poem by Dafydd ap Gwilym. Unlike the *fabliaux* writers he is a true poet, and what is most typical of him, what imposes itself as the chief device of all his verse, is as ancient as the Heroic Age. The Chadwicks have a chapter on the riddle poetry of Old Norse and English and Welsh. It was a species of descriptive poetry, and they give this riddle of a fog as a Norse example:

> What is that huge one that passes over the earth, swallowing lakes and pools? He fears the wind, but he fears not man, and carries on hostilities against the sun.

There is a kindred but longer and more elaborate riddling of the wind in old Welsh, the only early Welsh example surviving. The Welsh poets of the fourteenth century, and Dafydd ap Gwilym especially, developed this riddling description into clusters of metaphor and fantastic simile bound together metrically by strong *concatenatio*, a poetic junction of intense rhetoric and contemplation. He walks over the moor to meet his mistress and a bramble catches his foot; the bramble becomes the theme of his riddle. He rides at night in a strange country, perhaps Cheshire, and he and his horse stumble in a peat-pit, and the bog is wondrously riddled. Mist blocks his love journey or the stars light it, thunder frightens his lady; or an echo, icicles and a gander disturb his serenade; a ruined house on his road where once he made love, his own heart and his deep sigh, they all—and a score more—become themes of his riddling. And, of course, his love-messengers, stag or wind or wave or bird:

Flashing gull on the full tide,
Hue of snow or white moon,
Speckless in loveliness,
Ball like a sun, fist of foam,
Gaily-winged fish-swallower,
There at anchor I'd have you float
Linked hand with mine, sea lily,
Like a paper glistening,
A nun cresting the flowing tide.

It is as compulsive as Dylan Thomas for the English. All Dafydd's themes seem to rise like Goethe's songs out of moments of experience, realized with swift intensity, accidents, and occasions for incandescence. At the very same time Petrarch was teaching all Europe a slow and measured pace for poetry, but Dafydd ap Gwilym's verse is as nimble as his imagery; his mind is all turned out to see, to hear, to be with the fox and hare and blackbird, to climb the sky with the skylark, in a rapture of entranced living. They tell us his life was short. It could not but be so.

(First published in *Blackfriars*, March 1963.)

Welsh Writers of Today

I shall presume in this article on Welsh writers of today that the reader cannot read Welsh. If I were writing in Welsh I could presume a background of knowledge in the reader. Writing in English to non-Welsh readers I shall not discuss particular writers in detail; I'll try instead to give some sort of general picture.

If I were writing a history of Welsh literature in the twentieth century I should divide the sixty years into two periods. The first period would be from 1901 to 1940, and I'd call that the reign of Sir John Morris-Jones. John Morris-Jones was Professor of Welsh Language and Literature in the University College of North Wales, Bangor, from 1895 till his death in 1929. It is quite fantastic and incredible that there is no published biography of him.[1] It is one of the ominous signs that the Welsh nation doesn't take its own history seriously and doesn't believe in its future. John Morris-Jones was much more than a great scholar. He took hold of the platform of the National Eisteddfod and he turned it into a lecture-room for all the literate population of Wales. He gave them a standard spelling for the language. He went back to the seventeenth and eighteenth century classics and gave Welsh prose a standard of correct idiom, so that Welsh prose of say 1920 to 1940 is more uniformly clean and classical and civilized than it had been for a hundred years, and more than it has been since. He imposed a standard of correctness and a standard of classic elegance on Welsh poetry and established the fifteenth century as the norm for Welsh metrics in the old bardic verse-forms. He was aided, of course, by a generation of extraordinary genius—I beg you to believe that I am not romancing but talking bald truth—but the man who achieved all this was John Morris-Jones; the others, greater poets than he, were proud and glad to acknowledge his primacy. The standards he set were established and gained their general acceptance chiefly through the medium of two quarterly magazines; the first was *Y Beirniad* (*The Critic*) which he himself edited from 1910 to 1919, and the second, *Y Llenor*, was edited by his friend and disciple W. J. Gruffydd up to 1940: actually it lasted a little longer, but

---

1. A short biography by Dr. Thomas Parry was published by the University of Wales Press in 1958.

1940 was its effective end. To be a contributor to these journals during their great period was to have made the grade as a Welsh writer. Their reviewing had much authority and a poet accepted in their pages had no need of chair or crown. There were times when there'd be a thrill of excitement throughout Welsh-speaking Wales because a new lyric by Robert Williams Parry had appeared in *Y Llenor*.

Then came the war, to which the First World War was only a prologue. In all Europe it is the Second World War that has made the abyss of difference, and just so in Wales. 'Welsh writers of today' means Welsh writers after the war, writers of 1945 to 1960.

They fall into two groups, the old and the young. The old are still a respectable remnant. They are not as productive as they were in the thirties, yet many of their major works have appeared in the last ten years. That is especially true of the prose writers. Prose is a *métier* in which experience tells. Mr. Griffith John Williams, most widely learned of all Welsh scholars, has given us a biography of Iolo Morganwg that is a work of art. Dr. D. J. Williams of Fishguard has published an autobiography in two volumes that is probably the greatest prose work of this century in Welsh. One is tempted to say that works such as these can never appear in Welsh again. That mastery of idiom and vocabulary, that rootedness in both literary tradition and in a monoglot Welsh community with its richness and rightness of dialect and phrase, have they not passed or are they not in the moment of passing away for good? I was inclined to think so in the last weeks of 1960, and then a new book was published, an account of the Llŷn Peninsula in Caernarfonshire, by Mr. Gruffydd Parry, a man still in the prime of life, I think. When you suddenly come across something new that you know at once to be a masterpiece, doesn't it make you want to shout, to get hold of the telephone and sing to the operator about it? This is how I felt when I'd finished Gruffydd Parry's book. The old brigade of John Morris-Jones's formation is by no means dead yet. Even sureness of dialect is not yet utterly lost. Mr. John Gwilym Jones's dialogue in story and in play unites the most vivid modern speech with a profound culture.

Yet there's no denying that a vast impoverishment has happened. So let us look at the younger generation of Welsh writers, those who started writing after the war or thereabouts. I think it would be fair to say that only a minority among them comes from a predominantly monoglot community. For a writer that is unmitigated loss, disability, even calamity. I know all the Welsh education authorities are kidding themselves that a bilingual Wales is an excellent ideal and a possibility. I think it is just not true. It is only the Welsh-speaking people of Wales that you can make bilingual, and they will only be bilingual for a transition period. Once all the monoglot Welsh are gone the bilingual Welsh will quickly turn monoglot English. We are now in the transition period. For a young writer it is an unhappy predicament. Dr. Kate Roberts has recently deplored the degenerate idiom of our younger writers and of their society. It hasn't got the raciness of phrase, the instinctive sureness of syntax, the creative gift of noun-making to welcome new inventions, that come naturally to a living monoglot community. English idiom enters unconsciously into Welsh speech today. It is all about us, even in the remotest countryside, in radio set and television screen and daily newspaper. Inevitably there's a landslide of deterioration. Even literary standards seem lost. You see it at once if you compare the quarterly of the young writers, *Yr Arloeswr* (*The Pioneer*), with the quarterlies of the John Morris-Jones epoch.

It is a dark picture; this is no time for facile and dishonest optimism. Yet I don't think the rot has yet gone too far to be checked. The surprising thing is that there's undoubted vigour and there's a kicking life in the young Welsh writers of today. Stranger still, some of the most fertile and prominent among them have learnt Welsh at school or college or later, and have set themselves to write in Welsh like professionals. I think of a German lady, an Egyptologist and classical scholar, possessing also the German literary tradition from the eighteenth century to Thomas Mann, who has written novels and short stories and essays in Welsh and has in journalism published her own first-hand impressions of post-war conditions in Eastern Germany and in Russia. Others of these are poets, novelists, dramatists, in Llangefni, in Aberystwyth, in Llandeilo, in Swansea, some of them with a quite turbulent abundance of output—and abundance, of course, is one of the surest marks of creative genius. Why did they choose Welsh and just at this time of day? Did they fall in love with it? Perhaps it was love, but I think they would also, if pressed, say to the Welsh language:

> I could not love thee, dear, so much,
> Loved I not honour more.

There's a cavalier gaiety about the kissing of these new Welsh writers. You say we're for the dark, that our language is doomed? Alright my bonny, be it so—and how long is your own expectation of life? At any rate we, here in Wales, will make it the end of a lovely party:

Leaving great verse unto a little clan

to quote your own poet who also thought his name was writ in water. So let's look at their achievements. First, poetry. The John Morris-Jones period saw the establishment of a Welsh poetic vocabulary, of a poetic idiom and style, of a formalized lyric and of regular, standardized rhythm and metrical structure together with a noble and firmly correct revival of the great medieval bardic verse-forms. It was a splendid period, romantic in spirit, classical in exactness of form, and it gave us the poetry of Thomas Gwynn Jones and Robert Williams Parry, which is some of the greatest verse of all the centuries.

But it was Parnassian. As I've just said, Morris-Jones believed that some words were poetic, some not. His disciples and colleagues believed with him in the importance of formal precision and regularity of verse structure and in metrical smoothness. Syncopation was something they simply couldn't understand. W. J. Gruffydd printed some free verse in *Y Llenor*, but he only tolerated it. The story of Welsh poetry from 1930 to 1960 is of the breaking down of these prejudices. The poetic vocabulary was swept away. Perhaps the early English work of Ezra Pound and Eliot helped here. But T. H. Parry-Williams had started his pioneering before Eliot's early work was known. Even more important was the metrical development. That *vers libre* should establish itself in Welsh as in other European languages was not remarkable. But Parry-Williams began using intimate conversational phrases, dialect expressions that suddenly were not dialect, a short unparagraphic, staccato verse. This was carried further by Gwenallt Jones and Waldo Williams. Gwenallt Jones was the major influence on poetry in the period 1940–1950. Waldo Williams's importance in the technical development of verse is not yet properly appreciated. It is a nuisance that he is perhaps the most beloved figure in Wales today. It makes critical assessment very difficult. He is an uneven poet, spoils a lot of his work by preaching and emotional rhetoric. But many of his lyrics have extraordinary density and power, an abrupt syncopated rhythm and subtle variations of tempo and line. He has been followed by Bobi Jones, another uneven poet who throws off impossible stuff and marvellous stuff with speed and fertility. He is the most exciting poet of the last five years. Flauntingly Christian, outrageously romantic and realist, tingling with the thrill of being alive and in Wales and actually thinking in Welsh, he is the antidote to depression, the poet of generosity and joy and occasional howlers, but especially the poet of the alarming adventure of married love. I think his poem in Dantean *terza rima* on Isaac and Rebecca, *Isaac's Dream*, one of the big things of Welsh literature today. And with it the revolution in style and rhythm is complete. The romantic Parnassian ideal that was enshrined in W. J. Gruffydd's anthology *Y Flodeugerdd Gymraeg (The Welsh Anthology of Verse)*, published in 1931, is today as dead as the dodo.

What of the novel? For the novel tells more about the present moment than poetry. Certainly there's a striking difference between the pre-war novel or the novel of the older school of writers and the new school. The pre-war novel had three marks: first, it was regional; secondly, it described a social group in a fixed environment, a community; third, it had a normal background of traditional poverty. That would be true of Mrs. Puw Morgan, of Rowland Hughes and of Dr. Kate Roberts, three important novelists. Let me suggest a comparison between Kate Roberts's *Traed Mewn Cyffion (Feet in Fetters)* and the Prince of Lampedusa's novel *Il Gattopardo*. Both are concerned with a family in a fixed region in the nineteenth century, one in Sicily, one in Caernarfonshire. In both there is a study of family tradition and of change: one is aristocratic, the other is quarryman-peasant inured to poverty. But the sense of family and relations, of soil and rock and the impact of weather and patient animals, of established convention of family meals and of regulated order and mode of life and daily ritual, all this is common to both novels; and one suddenly discovers that, haunted by the tang and damp of poverty as Kate Roberts is, she is nevertheless, perhaps unconsciously or semi-consciously, no less than Lampedusa describing a remnant of an aristocracy.

Turn to the post-war novel and the young novelists. The change is startling, and if you are sensitive to the atmosphere of novels you find it frightening. The fixed environment, the traditional and ancient poverty have all but vanished. It is quite a different scene, a different Wales, a peninsula of the Welfare State, this Wales of the new novel, full of university colleges more appallingly staffed than the real ones. If you come to it abruptly from the Wales of Mrs. Puw Morgan or Dr. Kate Roberts or D. J. Williams you find yourself shocked and lost; you have stepped from yesterday into today. It is always more difficult to do it in art than in life.

You can make the passage more gently by following the work of Mr. Islwyn Ffowc Elis who knows both the old Wales and the new. He is the most professional of the young writers and his Welsh is admirable. Miss Eigra Lewis is the youngest, but she also knows a traditional society. A masterly intruder is Mr. Emyr Humphreys who two years ago published his first Welsh novel, then turned it over into English and took the Hawthornden Prize with it. If you read his *A Toy Epic*, in Welsh *Y Tri Llais* (*The Three Voices*), you'll get a picture of the Welsh predicament and the Welsh novelist's predicament. For the new Welsh novel is intensely political. I use the word 'political' in its primitive sense. These novelists seem to feel that merely to write in Welsh now is a political act. It throws Wales at you as an inescapable personal problem. For the language is the only Welsh thing left in Wales. It alone compels you to consider the history that gives your life a meaning. That seems close to the theme of novels by Islwyn Ffowc Elis and Gerallt Jones and Bobi Jones. The community's gone, the religious traditions and the life centred on the chapel have gone, the bond of place and family has been snapped. Only the language remains, and human nature. Enough for the novel. It mirrors the Welsh predicament.

The strangest, perhaps the most phoney, of the new novels is Dr. Pennar Davies's *Anadl o'r Uchelder* (lit. *A Breath from on High*). The period is about 1970. Great Britain has been incorporated into the United States, and this new empire is governed by a neo-Nazi hierarchy of Party Gauleiters; there are regional fuehrers for North and South Wales. Nazi tyranny, framing of political victims, secret trials, assassination, death by poison and by medical experiment, control of the press and of religious meetings are the normal thing. Sexual perversion with licensed pervert-brothels is a prominent feature of the ruling class of life. Those who know too much are proved to be agents of an Eastern power beyond the Strontium Curtain and they disappear.

Against this background we are given a picture of a Welsh religious revival in the nineteenth-century style. But the methods used by the revivalist have all the features of an Elmer Gantry–Aimee MacPherson American stunt evangelist. However, the revivalist himself is converted to a passionate arraignment of the government, and his preaching campaign and revival becomes the centre of an anti-government Welsh passive Resistance. He, as the Resistance leader, is arrested and killed. The novel seems to discover a function for Welsh Nonconformity in today's world drift towards totalitarianism. I ought to say that the novel is as learned as Joyce's *Ulysses*: it is comic and fantastic and melodramatic and brilliant. The Welsh novel started less than a hundred years ago as a picture of nineteenth-century Welsh Nonconformity. Dr. Pennar Davies finds a function for Welsh Nonconformity in the darkening years of possibly the last of the centuries.

(BBC Welsh Home Service, April 1961)

The Poet

Inviting me to take part in this symposium, Mr. Todd wrote: 'I am inviting you to contribute as a poet. Your contribution could include some indication of how in your view art mediates truth, both to the artist himself and to those who listen to his work. How would you describe the experience of artistic creation?'

May I take that as my agenda? The fact that none of you knows anything at all of my work is an obvious advantage; it gives me a sort of anonymity. I can say 'he' as though it were 'me'.

I suppose it is normal to begin writing verses in adolescence, perhaps in the last two years of school life. It is a consequence of being taught poetry. A poet is a schoolboy who likes poetry even after being taught it. Lines and verses stick in his mind, are exciting, and he tries to do something similar. Then he discovers that the most absorbing of all verse is that of his slightly elder contemporaries. Poets are largely formed by their seniors, whether in their image or in revolt against it.

May I pass-by the question, how does a poem start? There are so many answers by so many poets in as many languages. I venture a generalization: however the poem starts, what sets the poet working at it is the realization that what is vaguely in his mind has the promise, the shapeability, of a poem. A poet is a man who has formed the habit of making poems. By practice he acquires proficiency in recognizing and collecting the sort of material that is capable of being shaped into a poem. He lives on the watch for it. In medieval Wales and Ireland the material of poetry was part of the curriculum of the poets' schools. Today it depends on the caprice of fashion and the caprice of the individual.

But whatever it be, the matter of poetry is not an unwritten poem in the poet's mind. It is not a completed experience for which the poet has to find adequate symbol. A poem is not the expression of anything already existing, nor of anything that has already occurred unexpressed.

When you are making a poem you are aware of two activities, both essential and continuous. The first is complex. Your poem has started, perhaps a line, perhaps more, perhaps—in spite of

Mallarmé—an embryo idea. So you begin churning up, inventing, discovering, phrases, half-lines, lines, sentences that grope into the right rhythmic shape, or else that won't, and your poem builds up. You depend, of course, on what the doctors call your foreconscious for memories and associations of all kinds and periods of your life, and you find you are fed with images and suggestions of matter appropriate for that or this particular point of your poem. You don't know what may not turn up. It is not that you've got an idea but cannot find the right word for it. It simply is that you haven't yet the idea, you are suspended, waiting, willing, experimenting, evoking, perhaps by chanting a phrase repeatedly to yourself, fishing for the thing, despairing; and then when your headache is so bad that you give up and think to go to bed, suddenly it comes—or no, it doesn't come, but there it is, proton-like and Proteus-like, having crossed no intermediate space, impossibly virginal, nothing like anything you expected, but so absurdly inevitable that with glaring untruthfulness you dub it *le mot juste*.

So the poem is not the completion of anything foreseen or preconceived. It is not the carrying out of a previous intention. Certainly it is necessary to have some initial intention, but you launch your intention, you entrust it to the co-operation of all that seems chance or at least is unknown and incalculable in the foreconscious and the unconscious. So that the poem does not recollect or recreate an experience. The poem is the experience: it creates the experience for the poet just as much as for his first audience. The Dante of the *Inferno* was not a man who *had been* through Hell, but a man who went into Hell a-making.

Yet I must not suggest that it is all a game of tennis between the conscious mind and the foreconscious. There is a third player; let us call him *technique*. Poetry is normally made in verse, all kinds of verse, from such strict forms as sonnet or *englyn* to *vers libre*. Verse, all and every verse, implies rules, relations, semantic and phonetic relations, formal constructions, both rhythmic and metric. These are never ornaments of verse, in the sense of being superfluities, but essential and major concerns. No craftsman of verse can give his constant attention to these factors without observing that they profoundly and incalculably contribute to the texture, to the themes, to the development, to the ultimate shape of the product which is the poem. Paul Valèry once wrote that Racine would change the character of one of his *dramatis personae* if a rhyme demanded it. That is not a *boutade*: it holds truth, though it might

be more carefully said. It is not that a rhyme for Racine modifies
a character already decided, already entire, but rather that the
rhyme discovers the character, contributes to the character, adds
its own unforeseen quality to the character. When Monime tells
Mithridate:

> . . . *cet aveu honteux, ou vous m'avez forcée,*
> *Demeurera toujours présent à ma pensée.*
> *Toujours je vous croirais incertain de ma foi;*
> *Et le tombeau, Seigneur, est moins triste pour moi*
> *Que le lit d'un époux qui m'a fait cet outrage.*

both Racine and Monime are surprisedly discovering that she has
become this kind of person, that there are in her these unplumbed
depths, and hence to the end of the play he has to treat her
accordingly.

Characters don't have the same sort of life in the dramatist's
mind before he starts writing and after starting. Characters take
flesh from the words fastened to them, from the rhymes they find,
out of the unfolding situation. They grow into and through the
technique.

Some modern critics have written blame of Aristotle because in
his discussion of tragedy he said that the thing of first importance
was the plot. They are shocked that he did not give priority to
characterization. That is a sadly academic criticism. Aristotle was
examining how plays were made. He was analyzing tragedy from
the point of view of the practical maker, and I think he was right
and most percipient to put plot first. Plot also is technique, and for
the working playwriter it is the exploration of the plot that contributes most to the shaping of the tragic hero. I remember reading
the advice of an English literary critic to young aspiring play-
writers. Put half a dozen living characters together on the stage, he
advised, get them talking, and then see what happens to them. For
my part I cannot imagine even a Pirandello play being written that
way. You don't put living characters into a play. You start your
plot with mere ciphers or ghosts. You fasten words to them while
you fasten them into a plot. Then, if your words have life, they may
emerge from the plot living characters. I think that is as true of
Uncle Vanya as of *Oedipus Rex.*

Technique, in this view, is the poet's major ally; the technical
controls of verse, far from being restrictions or impediments, are
an ever-present fount of happiness. Rhymes create character and

alliteration may tangle a hawk in a sprung rhythm. The poet is a craftsman who has learnt to trust technique. This, I suspect, is a point at which I ought to bow to the ballet dancer.

The second constant activity in the making of a poem is that of critic. 'Would he had blotted a thousand,' said Ben Jonson rightly of his better. You cannot control what the foreconscious offers. Half-lines leap up, phrases, new combinations of words; images and memories take word-shapes, sometimes nimbly, sometimes sluggishly. But there you are, the appraising critical you, alert, watching, rejecting, selecting, moving the pieces about, building the chosen into a satisfactory unit, testing them on your ear, speaking them in different tones, scrutinizing them on the paper. Have you got the necessary patience? Can you reject steadfastly enough or do you surrender to what you know is second-rate? Can you lie in wait long enough, like a fisherman over a dark pool? Is the critic in you—the essential poet in you—resolute enough, inflexible, fine and subtle enough? Everything depends on that. Making poems, like making a picture, is applied criticism. A single line may destroy a lyric or a painting. Even to recognize when your poem is finished is a vital critical decision. For I have said that I do not understand a poem as the reproduction of anything previously complete in the mind. Therefore to find the poem finished is to be critically satisfied with the whole shape of it, since there is no criterion outside the poem itself. That is why fixed forms such as sonnet or *ballade* are so tempting, and why success in them is now all but impossible. Technique can also betray. One needs immense critical sureness to succeed with the fixed forms.

Mr. Todd's second question was: how does art mediate truth? I am no philosopher and I must try to avoid the snares of the metaphysicians and the analysts. The account I have offered of poetic composition posits that the poet does not 'tell the truth.' He is not a witness in any legal sense. He is not relating or recollecting or symbolizing a previous experience. The fact that memory provides very much of the unshaped material of a poem does not, I trust, invalidate this account. One may remember the Abbé Brémond's theory of the relation of poetry to prayer. It seemed to me a most depressing theory in its implication for poets. I am anxious to avoid giving my two nouns, poetry and truth, capital letters, and I am more interested in poems and in plays than in poetry. And yet, truth in poetry—the phrase has its honest meaning, just as it is sound sense to talk of sincerity in a poem. Any poem, even the slightest lyric, is a complex thing. Let me go· to neutral territory and consider for a moment 'The Banks o' Doon' by Robert Burns:

> Ye flowery banks o' bonnie Doon
> How can ye blume sae fair!

It is a hackneyed theme. In six simple verses the poet uses images that had been used a thousand times before him. Nothing is new; the rhymes are most obvious, the rhythms those of commonplace song. Yet it is one of the lovely and immaculate things. Truth and sincerity are words you need to describe its quality. An adjective too literary, a smear of sentimentality, might have toppled the thing into a falsehood. Burns goes serenely by his dangers and achieves a song that is as pure as a crocus.

So I would offer for your consideration that the truth of a poem is the recognition of the poet's critical control. It is the criterion of the poem's spiritual unity. The truth, the integrity—and I thank goodness for this—are not all in the poet or in his mode of life or even in his immediate mood, but they are in the poem, in the thing made, which, once completed, stands independent of the poet. Integrity is not a virtue of the poet transferred to the poem as though the style were indeed the man, but is a quality achieved objectively in the poem through the poet's craftsmanship and critical control. Even so, I do not offer that as a dogmatic statement about all poetry. I offer it as a means of protecting my own integrity. Poets are not as good as their poetry and are not served by being identified with their poems. There is a wisdom in *Hamlet* that there never was in William Shakespeare. The truth of the poem depends on no reference outside itself. Its validity is its one-ness, and its truth is its being. It has the truth of a thing, a *res*.

I do not deny, of course, that there is a large body of poetic work in many languages that is autobiographical, that poets have had experiences which they have recorded in poems. What I am trying to maintain is that the making of the poem changes, transforms the experience, frames it in a new context so that its truth now is the truth of the poem. It cannot be veracious, it cannot be witness, just because art demands an absolute unity, and every poet knows that in composing he surrenders his experience to the poem. I venture to maintain that this is true even of the Song of the Ascent of Mount Carmel.

A good poem is an impersonal thing; whereas bad verse is personal. I wonder will the dancer tell us that at the supreme moment of a well-achieved dance she is like Wordsworth's Lucy:

> She neither hears nor sees;
> Roll'd round in earth's diurnal course,
> With rocks, and stones, and trees.

I believe it must be a common experience for a poet, having some time written something good, to read it again after an interval and to say to himself 'How did I ever happen to write that? I cannot imagine myself today thinking or saying anything at all like that.' When you come out of the dance you are just ordinary and normal. It is when you surrender your being to the technique that you achieve things beyond your knowledge of yourself.

I stop here. I know that there are implications unexplored in more than one of my paragraphs, but I have tried not to trespass on the philosopher's ground. Nor have I discussed 'poetic vision' as a means of approaching Truth. Frankly, I do not know what poetic vision means. It is the adjective that I don't understand.

(*The Arts, Artists and Thinkers:* An Inquiry into the Place of the Arts in Human Life. A Symposium edited by John M. Todd. Longmans, Green and Co., London. 1958. II. The Witness of the Artists.)

II SELECTED POEMS

(*Translated by* GWYN THOMAS)

THE DELUGE 1939

The tramway climbs from Merthyr to Dowlais,[1]
Slime of a snail on a heap of slag;
Here once was Wales, and now
Derelict cinemas and rain on the barren tips;
The pawnbrokers have closed their doors, the pegging clerks
Are the gentry of this waste;
All flesh had corrupted his way upon the earth.

My life likewise, the seconder of resolutions
Who moves from committee to committee to get the old country
    back on its feet;
Would it not be better to stand on the corner in Tonypandy
And look up the valley and down the valley
On the flotsam of the wreckage of men in the slough of despair,
Men and tips standing, a dump of one purpose with man.

Where there have been eyes there is ash and we don't know that
    we're dead,
Our mothers thoughtlessly buried us by giving us milk of Lethe,
We cannot bleed like the men that have been,
And our hands, they would be like hands if they had thumbs;
Let our feet be shattered by a fall, and all we'll do is grovel to
    a clinic,
And raise our caps to a wooden leg and insurance and a Mond
    pension;
We have neither language nor dialect, we feel no insult,
And the masterpiece that we gave to history is our country's
    M.P.s.

II

The dregs rose out from the empty docks
Over the dry ropes and the rust of cranes,
Their proletarian flood crept
Greasily civil to the chip shops,
It crawled as blood about the feet of policemen
And spread into a pool of silicon spittle
Through the faceless valleys of the industry of the dole.

---

1. The places named in the first section are in South Wales.

Rain poured its assiduous needles
On the soft palms of the old hands of the coalface,
The hail scattered upon the leathern breasts
Of barren mothers and their withered babies,
Cows' milk was turned into umbrella sticks
Where rickets bowed the legs of lasses;
Young lads on the dole were given the pension of old men.

And yet the moon kept her ways
And Apollo washed his hair in the dew
As when the wise men had their respite
Between the hills of the Sabines centuries before;
But Saturn, Jove, and the golden age of the Babe,
In their turn came to an end; the clumsy destruction
Of the ashes of chimneys and the vain birth
Have drowned the stars under the slime of the dole.

III

In the beginning, it wasn't like this we saw things:
We thought that it was only the redeeming ebb and flow, the
    thrifty dislocation
That our masters blessed as part of economic law,
The new scientific order that had cast out natural law
Like Jove usurping Saturn, the summitless progress of being.
And we believed our masters: we put the vestments of priests
    upon them,
Tortoise-shell spectacles and plus-fours to preach,
To preach the sanctity of the surplus of the unemployed and the
    flexible providence of prices;
And one day in seven, not to break a courteous ritual,
We offered an hour to the sweet magic of the old world
And in the Pantheons of the fathers we sang psalms.

Then, on Olympus, in Wall Street, nineteen-twenty-nine,
At their infinitely scientific task of guiding the profits of fate,
The gods decreed, with their feet in the Aubusson carpets,
And their Hebrew snouts in the quarter's statistics,
That the day had come to restrict credit in the universe of gold.

Earth's latest gods did not know
That they had breached the last floodgates of the world;
They did not see the men marching,
The clenched fists and angry arms,
Rank upon rank through the anguish of Vienna,
The deaf fury of the wrangling in Munich,
Nor the dragging feet or the weak twittering of the march
Of the somnambulent unemployed and their stunned agony.

But it had been; the woe of mothers wailing,
The noise of men like the noise of dogs moaning,
And multitudes casting themselves without hope
To the starless ditch and the mute sleep.
The mind of leaders, it lapsed,
There was a sowing of dragons' teeth in Europe,
Bruening went out from their seething passions
From the sniggering of Basle and its foul usurers,
The husks and shells of that rout of Geneva,
To his long silent fast and exile.
And the frail rabble, the halfpenny demos,
The issue of the dogs and football pools,
It filled its belly with pictures of sluts
And with the rotten husks of radio and newspapers.

But in the region of Ebro the sky grew dark,
Blood turned to wine for our hungry passions,
And paralysis of will froze over the defect
Of the powerless wretches of Basle and Geneva.
We saw we'd been betrayed. The power of our gods
Was the vile illusion of fiends festering our end;
Felling and raping the excellence of reason
And our peerless idol, man without fetters;
The splendid religion of the masters of the planet,
Man's faith in man—that was extinguished:
We the hard-faced great ones—computers
    Of stars and suns above,
     The journey was without gain,
     All ecstasy vain,
Our black refuge is the deluge of despair.

And from over the sea comes the noise of tanks gathering.

A SCENE IN A CAFÉ

From the rush of the uniformed garrison
And their noise in Great Darkgate Street,[1]
In the midst of the crowd that was poured out of the market and
  the college
And from the vestries of the chapels and the taverns,
In the midst of the mottled throng,
The sad throng that had lost the goodness of understanding,
The living dead,
In the midst of unhappy guffaws and the red clutches of females
And their chops like a wanton nightmare tearing
The sleep of their gorilla faces,
In the midst of the throng fleeing,
Fleeing the death from the sky and the life from the bomb,
In the midst of the articulate skeletons, the walking ash,
We pushed through the café doors
Hiding our empty skulls behind our fig leaves,
And snatched the corner of a table against the host of Babel,
And shouted above the bones and the tea dishes
To a waitress nearby.

How swift was the maid's attendance—
She brought us oysters and Kosher vinegar and the burial service
  on toast.
The rain fell like a parachute on the street,
But the urban guard of dustbins stood
Like policemen in a row by their houses.
And an old hag went, with a rope around her neck,
From bin to bin in the rain, lifting every lid,
And found them, every coffin, empty.
And at the bottom of the road,
Before that gluttonous ash in the café,
The ash that had escaped from the bins,
The lard-bellied women of Whitechapel, the Ethiopians of
  Golder's Green,
On a convenient lamp-post, and with her cord, the hag croaked
  herself.
We saw her pins turning in the rain,
And we knew from her white gloves with their smell of camphor

---

1. In Aberystwyth, Cardiganshire.

That she came from the old country.
She was buried undenominationally by the BBC
On the waveband of the empire.

TO Dr. J. D. JONES, C.H.

(Late of Bournemouth)

From your feathered pulpit your tallow sermon
Dropped upon the gluttons,
The lard-droppings of your greasy English
Was a service for the guzzlers.

Now you return to the land of the poor
That's sore under the thumb of the blusterer,
With your harsh ranting to a fragile nation
To bend to the yoke and the cord.

THE CARCASS

('Many, and among them Welshmen, ask why it should be allowed to
live.' From *Y Llenor*, Summer 1941.)

The carcass of Wales lies in outrage
    With few to weep her shame,
The sorry slave of her conqueror, served yesterday
    His taste, and is dirt today.

To lick her disgrace and to foul her underfoot
    A barren swine-herd of justices
Gathers, grunting over her blood,
    And the wrathful, parliamentary bitches.

What stench moves beneath her flesh?
    Tape-worms, a host of public servants
Battening on the death of a poor motherland;

And on her forehead behold a black toad
    Croaking before judgment day
The trembling call to the brazen putrefaction.

AGAINST PURGATORY

Death, when you come, don't strike me like a dog
With gunshot or bomb suddenly,
Nor in my sleep, that I may not slip into your claws
Without shiver or summons or cry or any fear;
Don't wait either until the winter of weariness comes
When all zest that may rise is unruffled
And the sap of old passions sleeps under my withering
Until I stir in the new spring of a new world;
But like a canny woodsman choosing a tree,
Come to me; with your axe sing an earnest warning,
And strike once, twice, until the scales
Start, and the branches shake, and bend their weight;
Uproot me from the earth, before the furnace
Firework of those cremators there.

THE LAST SERMON OF SAINT DAVID

It was a strange sermon that David[1] preached
After the Sunday mass before the first of March
To the crowd that had come to him to mourn his dying:
'Brothers and sisters, be joyful,
Keep the faith, and do the little things
That you saw and heard from me.
And I shall walk the way our fathers went,
Fare thee well,' said..David,
'And never more shall we meet again.'
That is how the anchorite of Llan Ddewi Brefi records the
    sermon,
A fuller version than the Latin of Rhygyfarch,[2]
And it may be that it was from the recollections in the memories
    of rustic believers
Who had wandered the banks of the Teifi like prayers
Slipping one by one through the fingers of the centuries,
That the version the anchorite put in his parchment was found.

---

1. The patron saint of Wales. The saint's day is the 1st of March.
2. Was twice bishop of Tyddewi (St. David's) in the eleventh century. He wrote a 'Life of St. David.'

No sunset was ever more imperial
Than the journeying of David from the senate of Brefi
To his death in the dawn and the vale of roses.
A week before this day, in the morning service,
The proclamations of his release were announced to him
By a choir of angels; and by an angel
Was the news spread through the churches of Wales and the
     churches
Of gentle Ireland. There was an assembly at Saint David's,
The saints of two isles came to bury their saint;
The city was filled with tears and weeping
And wailing, woe that the earth does not swallow us,
Woe that the sea does not cover the land, woe that the mighty
     mountains
Do not fall upon us.
And the first of March
To the weeping church came the victorious church,
And the sun, and the nine orders of heaven, and songs and
     perfumes:
David went from wonder to wonder to his God.

That is how Rhygyfarch records the story
In the hour of his heaviness in Llanbadarn Fawr,
In the hour of the anxiety of canons and the anguish of a
     country,
With the old writings of David in his chest
And the old chronicle and the relics of the clerks,
The remnant of the greatness that had been and been dear,
In the sorrowful cloister, in the reminiscent cell.
And likewise, two centuries later, is the story
According to the anchorite who copied it by the hill
Where Brefi's senate was and the feet of the saint and the
     miracle.
But neither miracle nor angel was found in David's sermon
After the Sunday mass before the first of March
To the crowd that had come there to mourn his dying,
Nor the summoning of the cloister as witness to the glories;
But an exhortation to the humble ways, be joyful
And keep the faith and do the little things
That you saw and heard from me.

To historians the rule of David has been awesome
And the Egyptian whip of his abstinence and the heavy yoke,
The lord of saints, great-grandson of Cunedda and the purple.
But his last words, the sermon that nestled in the memories
Of those who prayed on the banks of the Teifi through centuries
Of terror, through war, under the scowl of the vulture castles,
Through the ages when the grasshopper was a burden,
They are the words of a maid, the gentleness of a nun,
The 'little way' of Teresa towards the purification and the union,
And the way of the poor maid who saw Mary at Lourdes.

TO THE GOOD THIEF

You did not see Him on the mountain of Transfiguration
 Nor walking the sea at night;
You never saw corpses blushing when a bier or sepulchre
 Was struck by his cry.

It was in the rawness of his flesh and his dirt that you saw Him,
 Whipped and under thorns,
And in his nailing like a sack of bones outside the town
 On a pole, like a scarecrow.

You never heard the making of the parables like a Parthenon
 of words,
 Nor his tone when He talked of his Father,
Neither did you hear the secrets of the room above,
 Nor the prayer before Cedron and the treachery.

It was in the racket of a crowd of sadists revelling in pain
 And their screeches, howls, curses and shouts
That you heard the profound cry of the breaking heart of their
 prey:
 'Why hast thou forsaken me?'

You, hanging on his right; on his left, your brother;
 Writhing like skinned frogs
Flea-bitten petty thieves thrown in as a retinue to his shame,
 Courtiers to a mock king in his pain.

O master of courtesy and manners, who enlightened you
 About your part in this harsh parody?
'Lord, when you come into your kingdom, remember me,'—
 The kingdom that was conquered through death.

Rex Judaeorum; it was you who saw first the vain
  Blasphemy as a living oracle,
You who first believed in the Latin, Hebrew and Greek,
  That the gallows was the throne of God.

O thief who took Paradise from the nails of a gibbet,
  Foremost of the nobilitas of heaven,
Before the hour of death pray that it may be given to us
  To perceive Him and to taste Him.

THE CHOICE

The last holocaust is ended. The world's united.
No more riots, no rebellion,
But order like a railway where before there was blood,
Every knee bending tamely and every face subdued.
Out of his proud belligerence the Dictator arose;
With five continents under his feet in obedience
He could exult in the feat that was done
And among his mute subjects walk at ease.

And to a forlorn hill he came, where there was a cross
And on it someone dying. The tyrant laughed,
'If you're the Son of God, descend out of your agony,
Let the world choose between us; save yourself.'
And the Sacrifice under the iron nails replied,
'Here shall I be whilst there is either man or world.'

INDIAN SUMMER 1941
(Lit. *The Little Summer of St. Michael*)

Spring there was none, and the glint of the sun was scanty
On the blue brightflash of the swallow under the bridge;
The grain sprouted in August in the heads of corn
With the wet, sultry summer:
Women with their ears fixed to a voice in a box,
And the post so slow from Egypt, from Singapore,
'Killing's heavy in Russia, I should think,'
And the rain like anxiety falling day after day
On backs that sooner showed their grief than words;

That's how the war was in our village,
The blackness of thunder turning and turning
About us and above us, a wall approaching,
Roaring and gathering and holding its bolts;
And, on the mantelpiece, a voice in a box bragging,
And the postman delaying his story from door to door
And the familiar names, Cardiff . . . Swansea . . . The South,
A meaningless fear lingering; strange faces, strange tongues;
No one says his mind, no one
Thinks; the voice in the box brags about
Our navy, *our* air force,
And we suspectingly believe that our is ours,
And go like people bewitched to the close and the field
Where our hands feel the comfort of old certain things
In the rain in August.

But the wind changed. A mist came in the early morning
And was broken by a royal and unhurried sun,
An expansive afternoon and a sunset under banners,
And the Great Bear like a girdle on the waist of the night;
The drays were loaded in the cornfields,
And in the orchard, between green apples,
Dewdrops sparkled on the still gossamer;
Michael raised for us a hill of restoration,
A glade of warmth and balm in late September,
Before winter, before the trial, before the whirling of the night,
Before raising anchor and sailing like Ulysses
Beyond the last promontory in the land of the living:
'Friends, do not deny either this experience
To the time, O how brief, that is yet to be
For us to see and feel of the world's splendour and its squalor . . .'
And he turned his ship to the unknown stars . . .
And Dante saw him with Diomede.

Michael, who loves the hills, pray for Wales,
Michael, the friend of the sick, remember us.

ELEGY FOR SIR JOHN EDWARD LLOYD[1]

I read how Aeneas long ago went
Through the cave with the Sibyl, to the land

---

1. J. E. Lloyd was Professor of History at the University College of North Wales, Bangor.
He wrote *A History of Wales*, 1911.

Of Dis and the shadows, like a man journeying
At night in a forest under the unsteady moon,
And there in the mild dark
Beyond the river and in the Field of Lamentation
He saw the old heroes of Troy, the ancestors of Rome,
The wounded Deiphobus, the brave men of the earth,

The sons of Antenor and grey Adrastus;
And they would lead him, and stay close
Until they came upon a cross-road, where there was a gate,
And where his face was washed, the golden bough endowed,
And a field opened and fair
Groves under the stars and a clear purple sky,
Where Dardanus, Ilus and the undejected dead
Were at their ease in green meadows.

And I, one evening, guided by the old magician of Bangor
Went down to the river, ventured the boat,
Left the shallow wave of the present where there is no anchor
And crossed the water which is in the depth of night like ash,
To the darkness of the caves
Where between the trees harsh ghosts peered
Whispering the dead feeble cry of dead huntsmen
That we hear not; for they are only images on the walls of a cave.

Then came a light and shape like a dawn smiling,
A helmet and cuirass sparkling and an eagle of brass
And the felling of wood, ponies under the flood in the Menai,
Hills paved and forts roped in a row:
Tu . . . regere populos,
I saw the form of Agricola standing
On the shore in Môn,[2] murmuring the prophecies of Vergil,
And the brine at night on the edge of the toga like a drift of snow.

And behind him I could see a man turning
From the road into the forest, to clear a patch
And sow his corn and set a table and cover it;
And in his posture was a secret. He slowly
Made the sign of the cross,
And uttered words of remembrance over the bread,
And lifted up a cup slowly towards the dawn,
Knelt and beat his breast, communed with pain.

---

2. Anglesey.

I hesitated: 'I know, while Europe lasts
The memory of these will last; they will not die,
The carpenters of the empires of the Cross and the Eagle;'
Their dream it was that tied under one toll,
One people to one rock,
Môn and Cyrenaica, that was the foundation of the hoping
Of Dante and Grotius, it was a shadow over the ravaging
Of Frederick the Second and sad Philip of Spain.

But here in the land of shadows is a race
Condemned to the pain of Sisyphus in the world,
To push from age to age through a thousand years
A nation of stone to the top of the hill of Freedom, and when—
O bitter progeny of Cunedda,—
The crest of that same hill is seen, through treachery or by
    oppression
The rock into the valley's thrown and the attempt lost,
And the Birds of the Abyss laugh at their latest pain;

Where are these?' And behold a baneful hall,
A bed in the middle, an archbishop, archdeacon,
Tonsured monks, the priors of Chester, Shrewsbury,
Anointing the dark eyes of an awesome leader-dragon,[3]
And he looking out of his antiquity
Upon a Scandinavian fjord, the ships of Gothri at large,
The Cave of Ardudwy, the gaol of Hugh the Fat, Bron yr Erw,[4]
The troubles of the saga of an age and its pain anointed.

And on a green I saw a gallows[5] and proud hands
Reaching towards it between iron bars,[6]
Until there came a ship from Aber and mute oarsmen,
Torches on the water and ash on a king's head
And a cross between hands on a shrine . . .[7]
And behold a head on a lance,[8] the hair of horses
Dragging in the dust of Shrewsbury behind their harness
The wounded body of the last, the weakest of his line.[9]

---

3. A play on the name Uthr Pendragon.
4. There are several references to places and events of historical importance in this section.
5. The gallows of William de Braose (see Lloyd, *A History of Wales*, II, p. 670.)
6. The hands of the imprisoned Siwan, or Joan, the wife of Llywelyn the Great.
7. Refers to the burial of Siwan (Lloyd, p. 686).
8. The head of Llywelyn the Last on the Tower of London. He was killed in 1282.
9. The cruel treatment of David, the brother of Llywelyn the Last. He was killed in 1283.

And for a moment, like the shaft of a lighthouse beam
Over the flood of night, the clefts of the fort that stands
On a rock in Harlech flashed, the heir of the two houses
Of Wales leading a crown, a dance for the heir;
Then by Glyn y Groes
A second Tiresias in the dawn of Berwyn
Gave the sentence of fate's oracle, and there was an end:
His shadow dissolved in the mist that covered him.[10]

Like he who climbed the splinterings of the land of despair,[11]
I too turned to my guide, 'Can your mind
Ascend the precipice of time and discover hope?
Their language they will keep,[12] can this prophecy be trusted?
Will the last relic
Of Cunedda be kept from the journey of pain of all his sons?'
But the lamplighter of all the centuries
Was there no more, nor his lamp nor his word.

THE DANCE OF THE APPLE TREE

The apple tree dances under its flowers,
The bride of the perfumes of May;
A lamp singing an enamelled carol
And pink-coloured in a flame of crystal
Like snow; sweet conjurer
That draws the swarms of bees and their golden agitation
To crown her hair with their music
Gushing between the emerald and the cambric white.

The September apple tree's enticing;
I see under it the daughters of Atlas
Raising their hands, Erytheis,
Hespera, Aegle, Arethusa,
Towards the green round lanterns
Like moons or the hidden breasts of the shining maids
That shepherd the winterless gardens;
It is the dance of goddesses under apples that I see.

---

10. Refers to Owain Glyndŵr (*c.* 1315–1416).
11. Refers to Dante, whose guide disappears when he meets Beatrice.
12. Refers to a prophecy about the Welsh made by the Old Man of Pencader, as he is called.

LAVERNOCK[1]

Moorland and sea, the song of a lark
ascending through the freedom of air,
and we standing, listening
as we listened before.

What remains, what riches
after our journey's dismays?
Moorland and sea, the song of a lark
descending through the freedom of air.

THE PINE

The lake of night is still in the valley,
In its windless trough;
Orion and the Dragon[2] sleep on its leaden face,
The moon rises slowly and swims drowsily on her way.

Behold now the hour of her ascension.
Immediately you shine before her with the lance of your leap
From root to tip under her journey
Shooting to the heart of darkness like the Easter Candle
     under its flame:
Hush, the night stands about you in the cool chancel
And the bread of heaven crosses the earth with its blessing.

ASCENSION THURSDAY

What's on this May morning in the hills?
Look at them, at the gold of the broom and laburnum
And the bright surplice on the shoulders of the thorn
And the intent emerald of the grass and the still calves;

See the candlestick of the chestnut tree alight,
The groves kneeling and the mute birch a nun,
The cuckoo's two-notes over the shining hush of the brook
And the form of the mist bending from the censer of the meadows:

---

1. In Glamorgan.
2. Constellation Draco. Part of the moon's path which lies south of the ecliptic.

Come out, you men, from the council houses before
The rabbits scamper, come with the weasel to see
The elevation of the unblemished host
And the Father kissing the Son in the white dew.

MARY MAGDALENE

'Touch me not'

About women no one can know. There are some,
Like this one, whose pain is a locked sepulchre;
Their pain is buried in them, there is no fleeing
From it and no casting it off. No ebb
Nor tide of their pain, a dead sea without
Movement upon its depth. Who—is there anyone—
Who will take away the stone from this sepulchre?

See the dust on the path lamely dragging:
No, let her be, Mary moves towards her peace,
Deep calls unto deep, a grave for a grave,
A carcass drawing towards a carcass in that unhappy morning;
Three days was this one in a grave, in a world that died
In the cry in the afternoon. It is finished,
The cry that drew blood from her like the barb of a sword.

It is finished. Finished. Mary fell from the hill
To the emptiness of the last Easter, to the pit of the world
That was no other than a sepulchre, with its breath in a mute
     grave,
Mary fell into the startling death of perdition,
A world without a living Christ, the horrifying Sabbath of
     creation,
The abyss of the hundred thousand centuries and their end,
Mary lay down in the grave of the trembling universe.

In the hollow of the night of the senses, in the cauldron of smoke;
The great hair that had wiped his feet turned white,
All the flowers of memory withered except the rain of blood;
Cloud upon cloud upon her, and their foul odour
A cinder in her throat, wasting her sight
Until with their sharp horror God was extinguished,
In the dying together, in the burying together, frowned upon.

See her, Christ's Niobe, drawing with her towards the hill
The rock of her pain from the leaden Easter
Through the dark dawn, through the cold dew, through the heavy
    dust,
To the place where there is a stone that is heavier than her torn
    heart;
Uneasily the awkward feet find their way over thorns
With the annoyance of tears doubling the mist before her,
And her hands reaching out to him in barren grief.

One luxury only under the heavens remains,
One farewell caress, the gentleness of memory, one
Last carnality, sad-consoling, dear,
To weep again over His flesh,
Anoint the feet and wash the harsh wounds,
To kiss the ankles and wipe them once more with her hair,
To touch Thee, Rabboni, O Son of Man.

Let us have pity upon her. He did not pity her.
Beyond pity is that burning, pure love,
That steels the saint through pain on pain,
That pursues the flesh to its stronghold in the soul, and its home
In the heavenly spirit, and its lair in the most holy,
That burns and kills and tears unto the last scrimmage,
Until it bares and embraces its prey with its steel claws.

Little did she know, six days before Easter,
Whilst pouring the wet, precious nard upon him,
That truly 'it was against the day of my burying she kept this;'
She did not think, so dear was his praise of her task,
That he would never ever again touch her with feet or hands;
Thomas could put hand to his thigh; but she, despite her weeping,
Henceforth under the woe of the Bread would come to her the
    broken body.

Behold her in the garden at the first colour of dawn;
She turns her eyes to the cave; runs,
Runs to the remains of her joy. Ah, does she believe,
Does she believe her eyes? That the stone is down,
And the sepulchre empty, the grave bare and silent;
The first lark rising over the bald hill
And the nest of her heart empty, and escheat.

Her moan is as monotonous as a dove's,
Like Orpheus mourning Eurydice
She stands amongst the roses and cries without mourning
'They have taken away my Lord, taken Him away,'
To disciple and angel the same cry
'And I know not where they have laid Him,'
And to the gardener the same frenzy.

Made wild. Broken. She sank within herself in her grief.
The understanding reels and reason's out of joint, until
He comes and snatches her out of the body to crown her—
Quickly like an Alpine eagle falling on its prey—
With the love that moves the stars, the power that is a Word
To raise up and make alive: 'and He said unto her, Mary,
She turned herself and said unto Him, Rabboni.'

THE MILKY WAY[1]

(Owain's soliloquy before meeting the Abbot[2])

I saw the night closing its wing over the moor,
Over a few frail homesteads, fallow land, infrequent furrows,
And the stars came and the Milky Way, a dense miracle,
To spatter the feathers of the firmament with their myriad peacock
    eyes.

I spread the wing of my dream over you, my country,
I would have raised for you—O, had you willed it—a joyful
    stronghold;
But my lot is like a shooting star that's cast out from among the
    stars
To stain the darkness with its hue and to burn out.

(From *Y Ddraig Goch*, March 1947)

---

1. Lit. The Fort of Arianrhod.
2. Refers to the story where the Abbot of Valle Crucis meets Owain Glyndŵr early
   one morning on the mountain, Berwyn. 'You're up early,' Owain said. He answered,
   'No, it's you who's risen early—a hundred years before your time.' With these words
   Owain disappeared.

JUNE MOON

Last night at mid-night
The moon was full in a firmament,
In the void with no stars, no nebula,
In the abyss of no night.

No shadow stirred, no owl hooted
In the lunatic desolation.
The world was dead.

Longing in the nightmare of sunlight
For the meaningless grave of a moon.

(From *Y Ddraig Goch*, August 1950)

RETURN

I loved young. Love in an instant
Kills a world of people.
No one lives but my love.

Creation's myriad lights
Extinguished in that moment:
There's no sun or moon but my love.

Now I know despair.
Despair, despair, all life to ashes
It tears down with its knell.

(From *Y Traethodydd*, April 1970)

ET HOMO FACTUS EST. CRUCIFIXUS . . .

And was made man. Was crucified.
What other way, what other fate
Was there for the son of heaven?
Man's first instinct is to kill,
It is the amoeba's urge;
Lays of pain and peril have been
The most intense songs of the myriad preys
Since stone axes were first hewn
In the openings of caves,
The millions of generations of woe
Of an insignificant planet
Lost in the endless emptiness of being.

And here in the pit of darkness
In the earth's winter,
In the ultimate hell of the history of our broken line,
We light a candle for the birth to us of a son
And raise him from his cradle—
How heavy the weak babe,
He bears the weight of all the aeons of sin,—
But we raise him and kill him,
I Caiaphas,
You Tiresias,
And set him above
As an altar hewn
Out of the world's agony
To one who is, without him, an unknown God.

(From *Y Traethodydd*, April 1972)

III THEATRE

Blodeuwedd

translated by GWYN THOMAS

PRONUNCIATION OF WELSH NAMES

Blodeuwedd	Blod-I-weath (as in *weath*er). The name means 'flower features'.
Llew Llaw Gyffes	'Llew' is also the Welsh for *lion*. This ambiguity is fairly extensively used in the play: all this has been lost in translation. Lèoo (*e* as in *spend*). Lau (rhyme with *Mau-mau*) Gúff-ess.
Gwydion	Gooéed-yon.
Gronw Bebr	Grów-noo Bébb-er.
Rhagnell	Rág-necl (*cl* as in *cl*ue).
Penllyn	Pénn-clin (*cl* as in *cl*ue).
Ardudwy	Are-díd-we.
Gwynedd	Gwín (as in *win*) - eth (*th* as in *the*).
Gilfaethwy	Geel (*g* as in *gull*) - vaieéth - we.
Math	Math (as in *Math*ematics).
Caer Dathal	Cauyer (rhyme with *buyer*) Dath (to rhyme with *hath*) - al (as in *Al*).
Caer Siddi	Cauyer (rhyme with *buyer*) See-thee.
Pryderi	Prood (to rhyme with *flood*)-air-ee.
Dyfed	Dóve-edd.
Bryn Cyfergyr	Brin (to rhyme with *in*) Cuv-érr-geer
Cynfael	Cun-va-ell.
Caer Arianrhod	Cauyer (rhyme with *buyer*) Are-ián-rode.
Nantlle	Nán-clay (*cl* as in *cl*ue).
Arfon	Are-von.
Meloch	Méll-och (*ch* as in *Bach*).
Tryweryn	Tru (*u* as in *unto*)-wére-inn.

FOREWORD

The first two acts of this play appeared in *Y Llenor* in 1923 and 1925. Then, for several reasons, I put it aside. In 1947 the Garthewin Players asked me for a play to perform. I went back to *Blodeuwedd* and revised the style of the first two acts somewhat and completed the work. I was glad of the opportunity.

It would be a help to understand it and to understand the characters if the Welsh audience were as familiar with the *Mabinogi* as a Greek audience was with their old tales. In spite of this I hope that the play tells its story plainly enough for everyone. I changed as little of the original story as would satisfy the requirements of a theatre. As for the language and the versification I shall only say this: I attempted to make the literary language and the unrhymed metre suggest the modes and rhythms of the speech of people who think and feel deeply when they talk. The poetry of drama is the poetry of conversation.

I have kept the forms of the proper names Llew Llaw Gyffes and Gronw Pebr, although Lleu is the correct form of the first and Gronw Pybyr or Pefr of the second. But for a modern play, Llew is a familiar name and Gronw Pebr is striking. It was a temptation to spell *Nantlleu* (in that way) to call the association to mind, but it would be an obstruction on the stage. *Earl* and *Lady* are used, although the terms belong to a much later period in our history.

DRAMATIS PERSONAE

BLODEUWEDD
LLEW LLAW GYFFES
GWYDION
GRONW PEBR
RHAGNELL
THE STEWARD OF THE HOUSE OF PENLLYN
SOLDIERS AND SERVANTS

Three days elapse between the first and the second act, and a year between the second and the third, and another year between the third and the fourth.

BLODEUWEDD

Act I

(A fort in Ardudwy. Gwydion and Llew Llaw Gyffes.)

LLEW *(clapping his hands)*:

Here, someone come here . . .   *(a servant approaches)*
Are the horses ready?

SERVANT: The horses and the host, my lord, are ready,
And the golden arms and the silk, your gifts.

LLEW: Where's my lady?

SERVANT: In her chamber, my lord,
Embroidering, with her maids, and listening to the
     harp.

LLEW: Go to her, tell her,
We'll travel three hours today while there's light,
Gwydion and I and the soldiers with us;
Bid her come quickly to say good-bye.

SERVANT: I will, my lord.   *(Goes.)*

LLEW: Ah, my uncle and foster-father,
You'll not find in Gwynedd a more wretched man
     than I.

GWYDION: Tut, tut. Don't talk nonsense. Be quiet.

LLEW: There's no one on this earth more wretched than I,
With my mother's hate and the fate she ordained for
     me
From the womb to this day, hate and wrath and
     malediction.

GWYDION: I'm surprised to hear you of all people speaking like
that after enjoying such great friendship. You, a
bastard thrown over the theshold before you scarcely
breathed, and more frail than a chick newly-hatched?
You who had upon you the three most awesome
destinies in the world, and I breaking them all,
giving you a name, and arms, and the most wonderful wife that was ever created, and the fairest
lordship in Math's kingdom? Shame on you.

LLEW: No one ever had a better friend than you, Gwydion.

GWYDION: No, and no one had the trouble I've had with friends. There's my brother, Gilfaethwy, because of whom I lived for years with wild beasts, without knowing my part in the world, being masculine and feminine in turn, with a scarcely mentionable family. And look at you, who knows what evil will come to me because of you, with your own mother eager to kill you if I did not prevent her.

LLEW: A mother's vengeance is stronger than your love.

GWYDION: How so? All her plans were frustrated, weren't they? When she refused to give you a name, I caused you to be named. She ordained a fate for you that you'd not have arms, and I caused you to be armed by her own hands. She ordained that you would never take to wife any daughter of man: I created for you out of flowers the most beautiful girl that eyes ever saw.

LLEW: But still, I did not escape my mother's wrath— Blodeuwedd is not like other girls.

GYWDION: Of course not. I am old and highly experienced, and in my time I've loved many women and wild beasts, but I've yet to see a girl that's like other girls.

LLEW: Gwydion, listen, she has no children.

GWYDION: You're lucky. The last child I had—he was a wolf.

LLEW: Never, I never will forget the morning
When I first saw Blodeuwedd;
You and Math walking across the lawn,
And between you, naked like the flowers of the dawn,
With the dew still wet upon her cold breasts,
Breasts as chaste as a lily's heart
When the night turns to her bosom, she walked
The spirit of the virgin spring in a body of flesh.
I looked upon her, and she upon me,
And I dressed her nakedness with hot kisses;
And these arms, the lustful arms of the young—
My arms that had been so empty—held her steel waist.

GWYDION: The old story. I've loved all the girls.
And believe you me, on a spring morning there's not much difference between the skin of the softest maid and a boar's bristle.

LLEW: But, my Lord Gwydion, she was cold, cold.
My heart that beat upon her breast broke
Like the breaking of glass on crystal. In her face
I never saw a blush, nothing but a moon's beauty
Rising without caring over the world.
Her blood is strange and foreign. One night
Of awesome wind and rain, she fled
From my bed into the fury of the storm;
I followed her, angry and suspicious,
With a sword beneath my cloak. But no one came
 to her,
No wolf ventured from his lair that night,
But she danced in the wild tempest.

GWYDION: It's difficult to pull a man from his own.

LLEW: Frightened, I shouted to her, but she did not hear,
With the wind howling destruction through the
 trees.
I was lost in a world beyond the mind
Where rock and rain and storm and night—
And she, Blodeuwedd, flourished. I ran after her,
And shouted louder, and held her arm:
'You've caught me,' she said sadly, like one
 wakening
From a deep dream, 'You've caught me, let's go
 home.'
And I saw in that tempest
That I had no part in her life.

GWYDION: Here's Blodeuwedd.
(*She approaches slowly.*)

LLEW: Oh, that there's a heart of ice
Beneath breasts that breed love like the first sun
Of June.

BLODEUWEDD: Lord, your message came.

LLEW: My lady, we have to go.

BLODEUWEDD: And Gwydion, too?

GWYDION: I, too my lady.

BLODEUWEDD: The day is short, and it will soon be night.
My lord, stay on; I do not want to be without you
This night.

LLEW: You'll not be lonely,
You have many maids and servants.

BLODEUWEDD: I've never been without you until now.
I'm afraid of being left.

LLEW: Since when?

BLODEUWEDD: I am uneasy. No good will come
If you go today. Wait for the young dawn;
You'll have sunshine on your way to Caer Dathal.

LLEW: No, no. Everybody's ready; we have to go
With Math, the King, expecting us.

BLODEUWEDD (*turning to Gwydion*):
My warlock lord, am I beautiful?

GWYDION: What magic tricks are these?

BLODEUWEDD: No magic and no tricks.
You who caught my spirit in the leaves,
Tell me, did you fashion well?

GWYDION (*looking at her*):
By my sword,
No eye ever saw a fairer thing than you, girl,
You're the crown of all my magic.

BLODEUWEDD: Why then, when I ask my husband
For the only favour I ever sought,
Does he not grant it to me?

GWYDION: The only favour, niece?

BLODEUWEDD: The only favour.

GWYDION: You've been a fool, Blodeuwedd,
You ought to have taxed him with requests
And tired his spirit with a thousand whims;
With men that's the way to find favour.

BLODEUWEDD: Yes,
Serf women know more about men than I.
My lord Gwydion, you did me wrong
When you put chains of flesh and bone upon me;
I do not thank you and I ought to hate you.
But in me there's some instinct to like you;
You also spent summers under the leaves
And you know the scent of wild, wily creatures.

GWYDION: Sh. Don't tell, that's my shame.

BLODEUWEDD: My friend, tell me what is shame? I don't know
How to be ashamed . . . Stay here
Until my lord comes back to me again.
You'll be my protection in the meantime.
(*Servant by the door.*)

SERVANT: My lord, the retinue is waiting,
Everyone is mounted and ready.

LLEW: Yes, let's go.
Come, my friend, it's time we went.

GWYDION: Farewell, my lady. I am old,
And you would tire of my grey company.
The perfumes of May are still about you,
The flowers that came together in your face have
not withered.
Be ever young; farewell.

BLODEUWEDD: My gentle lord,
Will we three ever be seen together again?
My heart is heavy. Farewell . . .
(*Gwydion goes.*)
My Llew,
If you believed me, you would not go today;
I know it in my bones—no good will come of this.

LLEW: I can't live by a girl's whim.

BLODEUWEDD: I know the seasons better than you,
And when the wind and rain and sun will change—
How then should I not know man's seasons?

LLEW: Don't be afraid. It's part of my fate
That no hurt or evil can easily befall me.
Be sensible. Don't wander far from home,
Don't go at night into the lonely woodland,
But stay in the habitable places
With your maids. I wish you joy, Blodeuwedd,
I'll only be three days. Farewell, farewell.
(*Exit. Blodeuwedd throws herself on to a couch and weeps.
Her maid, Rhagnell, comes in and finds her so.*)

RHAGNELL: Blodeuwedd, my lady, what's this crying?
Blodeuwedd, tell me.

BLODEUWEDD: My lord has gone away.

RHAGNELL: What of it?
He'll only be three days. He'll come back again,
And soon.

BLODEUWEDD: Rhagnell, you don't know
The fear I have in my heart.

RHAGNELL: Hush, my lady.
What is there to fear? This is your castle,
And the country's yours, and your word its law,
And there's no one here that doesn't love you.
And if it were necessary
I would give my life for you.

BLODEUWEDD: No, no. It isn't men
I fear, but emptiness and loneliness.
My lord has gone away.

RHAGNELL: What's this?
I've often heard you wishing to escape,
Cursing the man that made you a wife:
Why the change?

BLODEUWEDD: Oh, you will never,
Never, never understand my grief.
You don't know what it is to be alone.
For you the world is full, you have a home,
Friends, a family, mother and father and brother,
So that you're not a stranger in the world.
For you the place where men have trodden is
    homely,
And all Gwynedd, where your forefathers have been,
Is a hearth to you, a roof that was built
By generations of your ancestors;
You're at home in your own land
As in a bed that was spread out for you
By loving hands that had long awaited you;
But I, I have no home
In all the ways of men; search through Gwynedd
And all Britain and you'll never find one grave
That belongs to me, and the world is cold,
Is foreign to me, without any tie of family
Or nation to bind me. That's how I'm afraid—
I'm afraid of my freedom, like a ship astray
On the oceans of humanity.
Listen, what's that?
(*The sound of a hunting horn is heard from afar.*)

RHAGNELL: Some hunters in the woodland there.

BLODEUWEDD: My lord has gone away. No, there never was
Any warmth between us. He knows nothing
Of the tangled passions in my nature,
And I don't know how to live like him, tamely,
Without daring, depending on friends
For every good thing he ever had.
But among men he's the only one
Related to me. There's no one but him
To bind me to the family-men
Who only respect pedigrees. Without him
My life has no pedigree, has no anchor
With the defiance and the danger of nature in my
    blood.
God on my side that I shall not be punished
When this evil comes upon us.

RHAGNELL: What evil, my lady?
Your words frighten me. Tell me
What wild storm drives through your flesh?
(*The sound of the horn nearer.*)

BLODEUWEDD: Hush, listen.

RHAGNELL: The hunt is coming this way.

BLODEUWEDD (*drawing the maid to her and putting her hand on her heart*):
Rhagnell, where's your heart? Oh, as quiet
As the oak's heart in a wet winter.
(*The sound of the horn, very near.*)
Listen, girl. A hunting horn. Hunting in the woods
And the deer thrashing the earth fiercely behind it
Like oars striking a wave. The hounds sniffing,
Leaping to the trail, and the horses' hooves
Like the wind along the miles. Oh, nature's
There, a prodigious joy in the feast of life,
And the hunter himself is made one with the vigour
    of the mountain—
I could love a hunter—
(*The sound of the horn, passing.*)
Go, girl, go,
And ask who is that knight hunting.

RHAGNELL (*after going out and returning to the door*):
My lady, the hunting's over and there's the
    nobleman
Coming this way over the moor.

Isn't it right to offer him lodging tonight,
With the dark pressing upon him?

BLODEUWEDD: What's he like?

RHAGNELL: Young, and supple on his horse
Like a hawk in the wind.

BLODEUWEDD: Give me
Gold cups, and the wine I tasted
The morning of my creation, and give me fruit,
Cherries and sweet, red apples,
And you receive the knight;
And bid that they unrobe him. Give him
Water to wash, and lead him to the hall;
And let there be a feast tonight for this stranger,
So that my lord shall not chastise me
For letting him go, at the day's end, to his country.

RHAGNELL: Here you are, my lady, as you ought to be,
Happy and kind. And I'll go
To invite him and to order fully-laden tables
To welcome him. Be joyful,
Forget your worries. Feasting and dancing
And gentle words are your sisters,
And your friends—anyone who sees you.
(Goes.)

BLODEUWEDD: Be still, uneasy heart, your time has come . . .
Though I have bent a full year under the customs
    of the court
And the rites of men, they will no longer hold me.
My portion is excitement and freedom,
And my law desire, desire that drives the seed
To break the earth that keeps it from the sun.
In me there is a shoot that must also have its day
To grow branches and become great above the
    grove
Without anyone's knife to cut it. And for me
I know this knight is passion's herald.
I know the music of a horn: it is not my husband's
Thin lips that made such vigorous noise,
But full, red lips, lustful, drunken lips,
To match my own.

RHAGNELL (by the door):
My lady, the feast is laid, and Gronw Pebr,
Lord of Penllyn, greets you.

BLODEUWEDD: How bare your words! A horn of brass,
Not a girl's tongue, should announce his name.
Give me your arm and we'll go to receive him.
(*The two go. The lights are dimmed to indicate the passing of the feasting time. Then full lights again, with the scene as before, except that there are wine cups and flowers on a table. Blodeuwedd and Gronw Pebr enter.*)

BLODEUWEDD: Did you have enough?

GRONW: Of food and wine, yes.

BLODEUWEDD: Is there anything else?

GRONW: Don't ask, my lady.

BLODEUWEDD: You're afraid to say.

GRONW: I know no fear
Except the fear of losing dignity and honour.

BLODEUWEDD: Neither stag nor girl was ever caught through fear.

GRONW: My lady, is there a way from here tonight?

BLODEUWEDD: Yes, over the hills where the swift wolves
Howl their famine to the moon.

GRONW: Is there one of your servants who'll show me the way?

BLODEUWEDD: There's no one who would dare, except me.

GRONW: You?

BLODEUWEDD: The night and I are close,
And wolves can't chase the scent of flowers.

GRONW: Is it true that you were made of flowers?

BLODEUWEDD (*taking the flowers from the table*):
You see these? How quiet they are,
You'd say their beauty was forever;
And yet they'll die. They were plucked
And put for a brief hour to adorn a feast,
And arranged and held up like that, but with no root;
Already there is pain in their bitten hearts,
And languor in their stems. In a while they'll bend,
And let to the floor their heap of colour
And dry and wither and die before their time . . .
My lord, would you say I too was fair?

GRONW: The world's rose.

BLODEUWEDD: And yet, I languish,
                      I have no root or earth among men.
                      There's water to kill these flowers' pain
                      And postpone their end; but I was taken
                      By an arrogant hand and put here to die
                      Without one kind element to keep me young.

GRONW: What's your will?

BLODEUWEDD: You tell me your thoughts,
                      And then I'll tell you my will.

GRONW: Since I saw you, I've loved you.

BLODEUWEDD: Because of that you would have left me?

GRONW: You're married, and I've sat and eaten
                      At your husband's table. Had I
                      No obligation then to him?

BLODEUWEDD: And now?

GRONW: I am lost in desire for you
                      So that I no longer know of dignity and honour.
                      Your face, my love, is the fort of wonders
                      That lured me to forget all laws
                      And all the loyalty of nobility. For me
                      You are the end of hope, a haven of my dreams
                      Where I will cast the anchor of my fierce youth.

BLODEUWEDD: Without wanting any more to leave?

GRONW: Never, never more.

BLODEUWEDD: And your nobility and your tradition, the good
                      Ways of your family, and the loyalty of noble
                         blood?

GRONW: I'll forget them.

BLODEUWEDD: No, forget nothing,
                      So that they'll not come to mind again
                      And cool the blood and put out desire's flames.
                      But choose between us, friend, between them,
                      The safe, tame ways of man's civility
                      And all the torrent of my kisses.
                      And think before you choose. With them,
                      The security of family and friend and wife
                      And a placid life on your estate,
                      And a burial in the sepulchre of your righteous
                         ancestors

GRONW:
BLODEUWEDD:

With your children to carry your bier. With me
No security except this point of time.
Whoever loves me must love danger
And all the loneliness of freedom. In his time
He'll have no friends, children will not escort
Him to his secluded grave. But the heavy flood of
   my hair
Will fill his senses for a while, and my breasts
Hide him for a moment from the murmurs of the
   world,
And the instant shall be his heaven . . . Choose.

GRONW: Who knows what will befall him? What does it
   serve a man
To lose his joy tonight for a tomorrow
That only hope can see. Tonight exists, it is a gift;
We have been thrown together; shall I go
And leave all this to be like a dream in my life
And refuse the hour of the gods? I've made my
   choice:
Your beauty to rule in my mind,
Your will from now enthroned in my life.

BLODEUWEDD: All my will is for the passion of desire . . .
(*She pours wine into a cup.*)
Listen, my love: The day that I was caught
And bound tight in my husband's court and bed,
Gwydion gave me to drink a strange-tasting wine
That Pryderi brought from the Other World. This
I tasted and kept, and swore
I would not drink it again until the time
I'd drink with a man freely chosen
At my will. The bowl's been locked away a long
   time;
And I've often thirsted for its taste.
But today, this evening, I heard a horn
Away in the woods, that sounded like a king's
   challenge
That the captive months were over, and I knew
That it was that mouth that called through the
   thicket
That would drink with me from the cup of love . . .
(*Drinking and giving her cup to him.*)
Drink, Gronw, my seal is on the rim.

GRONW: I will, and I swear to you a love that'll last—
BLODEUWEDD: No, my darling, don't swear to me.
                Leave the oaths to them,
                Who guard feeble passions with rituals
                And the timid bonds of their barren religion.
                What would promises be but admission
                That the bliss of this hour's not sufficient?
                Be quiet in our night of joy
                Without suspecting what may be. All the power
                Of nature gathers in me to satisfy you,
                And if I do not tire, neither will you.
GRONW (*drinking*):
                Let this cup where your lips have been
                Be a foretaste of your kisses. This night
                I'd like to die in your arms, my love,
                That I'd never wake in a tomorrow without you.
BLODEUWEDD: Rhagnell, Rhagnell . . .   (*Rhagnell comes.*)
                        Prepare my bed tonight
                In the glazed room, and put upon it
                The whitest, finest linen, as before
                When I slept for the very first time.
                                        (*Rhagnell goes.*)
                My love, what did you see to like in me?
GRONW: Who can ever say? Your face, your form, the way
                    you walk,
                And your body burning like a flame through your
                    dress.
BLODEUWEDD: And nothing else? Didn't you see
                The wonder of my birth? Before you came to me
                This body was a prison about me,
                Like a dead web about a living chrysalis;
                You came like spring where I lay
                And gave wings to my flesh, put dancing in my
                    blood.
                Among families I'll not again be lonely;
                To me your smiles are my lineage and my claim
                Upon humanity. There is one will
                In leaves and men; no feeble ceremony
                Nor custom nor judgement can imprison the heart
                That feels the rays of desire beating. Come, my
                    love,
                Life is ours, and to love is to be free.

CURTAIN

ACT II

(A fort in Ardudwy. Rhagnell, the maid, there, and the Steward of Gronw's house in Penllyn.)

STEWARD: Rhagnell, where's my lord?

RHAGNELL: I don't know.

STEWARD *(with scorn)*:
And it's likely too that you don't know what's on between him and your lady?

RHAGNELL: Is there anything?

STEWARD: How is it, then, that no one except you attends to them? Why does he stay three days from his country? Is there anything on, indeed!

RHAGNELL: He'll return this morning.

STEWARD: Yes, and there are the horses waiting for him. Go and tell him to quit this half-breed witch who's charmed him and come home.

RHAGNELL: I pity him if he hasn't men more loyal than you.

STEWARD: What's he got to do with loyalty? He'll sell his father's home for his lust, and his only virtue is that he's too reckless to know fear . . . Hush, here they are . . . Can you tell me now that there's nothing between them . . . ?

RHAGNELL: Quiet, you churl.
(Gronw Pebr and Blodeuwedd approach.)

STEWARD: My lord, by your leave, the horses are ready.

GRONW: Go to them. I'll come before long.
(Exeunt Rhagnell and Steward.)

BLODEUWEDD: You have to go?

GRONW: Or stay here to be killed.

BLODEUWEDD: No, my love. If there's to be killing,
You'll not be killed.

GRONW: His men are here,
And he returns today with his host.

BLODEUWEDD: Yes, go. Don't delay. His name
Is like a death-knell in my broken heart.
You know, in the thickets in June,
With the warbling on the blackbirds' beaks like
    golden grains,
And the noise of the leaves louder than the brook,
Slap, unexpectedly, there's stillness,
The whistling stops on every branch and grove
And the wood sap in the stems is paralyzed,
And from that moment the leaves grow old,
The weight of summer and its sloth comes to the
    grove;
And that's the death of spring. So, too for me
In the middle of the first measure of desire's dance
His name and the memory of his existence
Trip my step.

GRONW: Blodeuwedd, was it for this
That three days ago I was charmed to seek you,
To see in you my joy and satisfaction,
And then, without hope, to part?

BLODEUWEDD: I've tasted joy like a bite
Hurting my breasts, the pain of desire's birth,
And this, my body, that was to me before
A heap of death, this now is
A garden of all the perfumes of my life's spring,
A new world which you have struck with your
    sorcery
And planted with graces. You, my love—
Not Math, not Gwydion—are my creator.

GRONW: Do you know all things in your world?

BLODEUWEDD: Inexhaustible our bodies. Oh, my Gronw,
The wonder would be to exhaust all their riches,
The mystery of the five awakened senses,
The seasons of our quietness, the peace of sleep
Upon a lover's arm, breathing together.
Desire has a gift of joining flesh together
And between two creates a new, higher life,
Fuller than the two apart, where both
Lose the narrowness of being, and play freely
In the delight of love. And for me
You're the door to this delight. For without you

I can only cry throughout the night
And watch him sleeping by my side,
A cold and strange oppressor.

GRONW: You don't want our love to end today?

BLODEUWEDD: I want to live. Love and life are one;
I've seen the dawn of love with you.
I want to see its noon.

GRONW: And Llew Llaw Gyffes?

BLODEUWEDD: Why name him? Isn't it enough
To know he's like a pillager between us
And love's way?

GRONW: We must look upon our fear
And name it, so that we'll not be afraid.

BLODEUWEDD: Is there any trick or skill
To deceive Llew?

GRONW: Yes. Escape with me
This morning.

BLODEUWEDD: Where to?

GRONW: To my castle,
Here are the horses waiting by the gate
And freedom in the stirrup. Let Llew come
Into his lair and find it empty. From the walls of
    my fort
I'd challenge him safely, let him roar
Threats how he will.

BLODEUWEDD: You don't know
The strength that's in him. With him will come
    Math
And all the force of Gwynedd behind him,
And the warlock Gwydion. There's no fort in the
    world
Can stand against them. And I don't want
To be caught like a deer in the paws of Llew
To have my flesh torn.

GRONW: Blodeuwedd, what's a court,
What's a kingdom to us? Let's flee to Dyfed,
We'll be welcomed there by the enemies of Math,
And find protection and safety.

BLODEUWEDD: No, never.

I can't go begging to strange men.
It's easy for you to trust foreigners
For you're a man like them. I have no claim
On anyone nor trust to anyone's word.
I'm afraid of all strange things.

GRONW: Man's not so unkind
As you believe.

BLODEUWEDD: Not to other men. But to me who am not
One of them, who'll give his trust?
Neither shall I trust them.
If he's not enjoined with me in love's ties
Every man is an enemy to me . . . My only
brother,
Don't take me away.

GRONW: What can we do?

BLODEUWEDD: Kiss and forget and part.

GRONW: Is that your counsel?

BLODEUWEDD: I know none better.

GRONW: Will it be easy for you to forget?

BLODEUWEDD: An apprenticeship in forgetting doesn't take long.
Skill in it
Becomes easier every day.

GRONW: I can't ever forget.

BLODEUWEDD: Everyone's awkward when he begins his work,
Like a student with a task.

GRONW: Do you want to
Forget?

BLODEUWEDD: Do you?

GRONW: When I want to die.

BLODEUWEDD: Kiss me, my love . . . Before long
He'll claim the tribute of my lips,
His unfeeling hand upon my white shoulder
Will rule all my body.
Ah! that I had poison in my teeth,
Then like a serpent I would coil about his neck
And embracing him more ardently than ever
before . . .
Like this . . . like this . . . I'd bite him to death.

GRONW: That's the only way—we'll have to kill him.

BLODEUWEDD: How long you've been in seeing my intent.

GRONW: I wouldn't wish to kill him without need.

BLODEUWEDD: We must, we must. What place is there for him
In a world that knows the tempest of our passions?
Dead wood in a whirlwind's path.

GRONW: Is there a way
To kill him?

BLODEUWEDD: It'll not be easy. His fate is
That no one knows how to kill him;
He himself knows how.

GRONW: Fate too is an enemy
Of love?

BLODEUWEDD: Love's a rare flower
That grows on the precipice of death. Some snatch
it,
Whilst others are like an ox chewing its cud in a
meadow.

GRONW: How fair scorn is upon your lips.
But in the world there is a rose more rare than
love,
Were it not so, I wouldn't venture my life,
I wouldn't plan a betrayal of the innocent . . .
Tell me now,
How can we learn the way to kill him?

BLODEUWEDD: Leave that to me. These fingers can
Play upon his hungry body so cannily
That his suspicions will be charmed into pity
And his secret drawn from his breast.
His anger's a child's sulking,
He'll come back today alone and ill at ease,
And I, I'll kiss him—

GRONW: And win as a prize
His life's great secret?

BLODEUWEDD: A life for a kiss
Is the price too much?

GRONW: This instant,
Had I to choose between the two,
Like a moth to the flame I'd fly to you.

BLODEUWEDD: Yes, my spirit is a burning flame,
And he, who first kindled the fire,
Will be devoured by it . . . How shall we arrange
things after this?

GRONW: The arrangement's my business. If by human
hands
He can be killed, send to me,
And when the day for the plot comes
I'll count each hour of your loving lost,
And in the blow that will destroy him
I'll gather my longing morning and noon and
night
And avenge them on his body.

(*Rhagnell approaches.*)

RHAGNELL: My Lord,
Your men are waiting, and the sun above the hill
Shows the passing of the hours of safety.

GRONW: We must say farewell.

BLODEUWEDD: Will you keep your word?

GRONW: Do you doubt my loyalty?

BLODEUWEDD: Oh, Gronw, what's loyalty to me?
Will you keep your desire? Desire's strong
To keep the will like an arrow to its target
When the bow of loyalty's rusty. Look at me.
Fill your mouth with the taste of this kiss,
And your head with the scent of my breast . . .
Go now.

GRONW: I'll hear from you this evening?

BLODEUWEDD: Before nightfall.

GRONW: It's night now for me with the setting of my sun.
Farewell, my love . . .
(*Exit. Quiet. The sound of horses moving away is heard.
Blodeuwedd sits on a couch.*)

RHAGNELL: I saw dust moving in the distance.
He'll be here soon.

BLODEUWEDD: What did you say?

RHAGNELL: Where do you want me to prepare dinner?

BLODEUWEDD: Who for?

RHAGNELL: For you and the earl your husband.

BLODEUWEDD: In a grave.

RHAGNELL: Is that the strength you talked about
With Gronw before he left? Come, my lady,
Make yourself ready to welcome him. I'll go
To greet him for you at the gate—

BLODEUWEDD: Yes, go.
And tell him all my secrets.

RHAGNELL: You think I'll betray you?

BLODEUWEDD: You're human, born of woman as he is.

RHAGNELL (*kneeling by her side*):
My whole life through I'll be your maid.

BLODEUWEDD: No, I'll not let you mock me. I know
My face can bewilder a young man
And tie him to my will. You're a girl—
And I can't ever chain you.

RHAGNELL: But there's another chain on me.

BLODEUWEDD (*looking at Rhagnell and taking the plait of her hair and
beginning to tie it about her neck*):
Yes, you've got a chain too, girl,
You too are fair, my lass. Your hair
Is like a golden rope falling on your back,
It's soft like silk. But why
Don't you wear it as a torque about your neck
A golden torque, as a gift from your mistress
To you for your loyalty. With this tight,
Tight about you, dear Rhagnell,
You can lie forever wise and mute
And keep my secrets unrevealed.

RHAGNELL (*without moving and quietly*):
You're hurting me. Are you going to kill me?

BLODEUWEDD (*gazing into her face*):
I would like to tie your slender little neck
With this silk, so that not one word of treachery
Shall ever pass your modest lips
That have kissed your lady's hand many a night.
You've served me many times, fair Rhagnell,
And tended to me before sleep. And now I
Can tend to you, and give you to a quieter sleep
Than I have ever had.

RHAGNELL (*again without moving*):
    Alive or dead, I'll never betray you.

BLODEUWEDD: You'll never have the chance, my gentle maid,
    I'll tie your tongue and your pretty lips
    Beyond temptation.

RHAGNELL: Here's the earl.
    (*Llew Llaw Gyffres approaches. The two rise to receive him.*)

LLEW: I came unexpectedly?

RHAGNELL: No, my lord,
    I saw the dust from your host on the hill,
    And I ran with the news to my lady.

LLEW: I hurried on before my men
    To be the first to see Blodeuwedd.

BLODEUWEDD (*going to him*):
          Here I am.

LLEW: My unblemished wife.

BLODEUWEDD: You came safely?

LLEW: The wonder of your beauty is today the same
    As on that morning when between dawn and dew
    You first walked towards me. My handsome girl
    Till I went from you I never knew the greatness of
        your magic.

BLODEUWEDD: You've never been away from me before.

LLEW: And until I die I will not go again.

BLODEUWEDD: True enough.

LLEW: What did you do while I was away?

BLODEUWEDD: Ask Rhagnell . . . Tell him, girl,
    Here's your chance.

RHAGNELL: My lord, ever since the time
    Blodeuwedd first came to Ardudwy
    I've attended to her night and day.
    I never saw a tear on her face
    Nor saw her eyes wet; she was a quiet one
    And long-suffering in sadness. But the hour
    You went away, I found her
    Sobbing on that couch
    And her body weak from pain and fear,
    And to every comfort I whispered to her
    She replied, 'My lord has gone away.'

LLEW:
My wife,
Why have I never known you before this.
(*Exit Rhagnell.*)

BLODEUWEDD: Forget the former pain. This new union is
A new marriage bond between us.

LLEW: I thought you were cold, without desire;
I didn't know that tears of longing
Could cloud the brightness of your fair eyes.
Why did you hide your tenderness from me?

BLODEUWEDD: My lord, I was given to you like booty
Or like a slave, without choice and mute.
You never learnt to love me before having me,
Never had to devise how to win me. In your fort
You have arms and coats of mail
You had to pay for by battle, sweat and blood:
You gaze upon them and remember each one's
day,
And look to see the signs of your valour and the
mark of your arm
In the many dents made in them. And I,
I never cost you an hour's weariness to catch,
And that is why you never took the pain to look
Upon any sore or dent or emptiness in my breast,
Nor the signs of your earnestness in my heart.

LLEW: You are my wife. By you
I hoped to establish my line in Ardudwy,
And to honour you with a father's love to the
mother of his sons.
What greater love could anyone have?

BLODEUWEDD: I was your wife before I'd been a girl,
You'd have the fruit before the flowers bloomed,
But I'm the woman made of flowers, Blodeuwedd.

LLEW: Oh, woman made of flowers, teach me the way
To go past all the petals
To be buried like the bee in your bosom.
Like you I am a stranger to a mother's arms,
My mother cast me from her body before my time
And has pursued me all my life. In all my time
I'd never kissed before I kissed you,
And never had a girl's arms about my neck,
I never felt a brother or a sister's tenderness.

I long for your love, girl;
Teach me how to win you as you'd have me do,
For doesn't love draw to it love,
And one heart another? O my wife, my world,
Why do you keep apart from me?

BLODEUWEDD: My love,
I never kept myself from you.

LLEW: You gave your body, but kept your will.

BLODEUWEDD: I gave you my trust. You're the only one
I have upon this earth. What would I do
If you were killed, and I without a husband or
    anyone?

LLEW: Is it true, what Rhagnell said, that you wept?
                                    (*She is silent.*)
Blodeuwedd, look at me . . . Answer me . . .
Why don't you answer . . . Tell me, are you well?

BLODEUWEDD: The day you went away
Despair nearly broke my heart:
I was afraid I'd never see you alive again.

LLEW: Did you love me that much?

BLODEUWEDD: I have no family except you.

LLEW: My second soul, I now know your love,
And from this time to me my life will be a balm
And your fellowship, tranquillity. We two,
We'll raise a family in Ardudwy
That'll be a grove about us. There
The young shoots will grow together with the
    strong old trees,
And we'll be like a snug and sheltered orchard,
With love as walls between us
And the cold wind of loneliness. And you, my love,
No more will be an exile; I am your patrimony
Your family, and unless I'm killed—

BLODEUWEDD: What if you're killed?

LLEW: My fairest, don't be sad
And do not fret. To kill me isn't easy,
For there is a fate that rules the way I'm killed
And that won't happen easily by any man's hand.

BLODEUWEDD: You're careless and unmindful,
And you'll soon forget. But I,

My care will never let me forget;
Tell me your fate, so that my breast
Will not again be weak with worrying.

LLEW: I'll tell you gladly. A full year must be spent
On fashioning the spear to strike me,
And no work can be done on it except
During the Sacrifice on the Mass on Sundays.

BLODEUWEDD: That's certain?

LLEW: Quite certain.
I cannot be killed, either within a house,
Or on my horse, or with my foot upon the ground,
But must stand on a water trough
Beside a river. If I were there,
And were I stricken in my back with poisoned
spear,
He who'd strike me in that way could kill me.

BLODEUWEDD: Thank God, it will be easy
To avoid that.

LLEW: Many times, Blodeuwedd,
I've longed for my death. But now
Life has a relish like the taste of an apple on the
teeth,
And your love is the throne in Caer Siddi
Whose people cannot be touched by old age or
disease,
And I'm a king there
Without anyone or anything to dispossess me any
more,
Neither fear nor longing nor even death itself,
For love's monarchy's unchanging.

BLODEUWEDD: Among men is there anything that doesn't change?

LLEW: Desire does, because it's frail
And swift like youth. But love
Will grow like the oak throughout life's tempests,
And under it a home, a family,
A country's nobility and government will thrive.
Our love, my lady, it will provide
Security and a roof for Ardudwy,
Provide instruction for the people and nurture for
a tribe,

And we'll be blessed by princes
Because of this hour's firm atonement.
(*Rhagnell comes to him.*)

RHAGNELL: My lord, the water and the towels are ready,
If you want to change and wash off the dust,
For it's very nearly time for food.

LLEW: I'll come, girl. And today we'll have a feast
Like a marriage-feast in my house. Three days ago
I went from here with a heavy heart;
I came back today to a greater joy
Than I have ever known. This day
Is like a standard of protection on my fort,
For I have known what a woman's loyalty is like.

(*Exit Llew Llaw Gyffes.*)

BLODEUWEDD: Rhagnell, I tried to kill you.

RHAGNELL: Yes, my lady.

BLODEUWEDD: Why then did you not betray me?

RHAGNELL: My lady, you're a woman; I'm a woman too,
And I won't betray another woman's secrets.

BLODEUWEDD: I can't understand people. Wherever they are
I hear nothing but talk of traditions,
Loyalty and integrity, family, kind,
Tribe, country, or religion . . . Do you love me?

RHAGNELL: You're innocent, my lady, like a child,
And like a child, destructive. Having known you,
Who wouldn't have pity on you?
I've been given to you as a maid,
And all my life I'll be loyal to you.

BLODEUWEDD: Forgive me. I know you're wise,
And that you know all the lore of women.
And I, I only know how to yearn
And seek what I want with all my might.
Will you take my message to the Earl of Penllyn?

RHAGNELL: I'll go, my lady.

BLODEUWEDD: Tell him
To make a spear of steel and poison,
Without making any of it except
During the Sacrifice at Mass on Sundays;
He must take a year to make it,

And then in a year's time tell him to come
To meet me near Bryn Cyfergyr.
Go, hurry, so that no one will see you,
And give him this ring as a token.

RHAGNELL (*taking the ring*):
    Is that all?

BLODEUWEDD: That's all.

RHAGNELL: And if he asks about you?

BLODEUWEDD: Tell him
How happy my lord is, and that today
There's feasting and dancing and singing in the
    court
As on a holiday. Go and don't delay.

CURTAIN

ACT III

(*A hill in the background. A long water trough in the middle on a river bank.
Gronw and his Steward come in to Blodeuwedd and Rhagnell.*)

GRONW: I've come, Blodeuwedd.

BLODEUWEDD: On time, brave warrior,
Before the sun's risen above Bryn Cyfergyr.
Don't hold me, Gronw.

GRONW: Fair flower,
I've thirsted for a year for your lips
And have long been absent from your arms. And
    you say,
Don't hold me.

BLODEUWEDD: I'm wearing Llew's collar;
I've left his arms to come here now.

GRONW: Into my arms.

BLODEUWEDD: Across his carcass.
While he's alive don't put your hand on me
In case you miss when you strike. Is that the
    spear?

GRONW: I've laboured on it from Sunday to Sunday for a
    year

During the hour of the Sacrifice. This is a costly
  spear,
There's a soul's perdition in its bite.

BLODEUWEDD: Are you afraid of that? There's a road back to
  Penllyn;
A man's fate is not like a river's flow
Or a woman made of flowers. You can choose.

GRONW: Don't trifle with me, woman. Your perilous beauty
Is the fate I've chosen Sunday after Sunday
To this time. It's been a long year
Since I saw you; the rose has withered, the hips
Of the dog-rose have fallen with the leaves; sun and
  moon
Have moved through the cycles of the months: my
  days
Have stood apart from the turning of the seasons
And been nailed to your lips. The passion of your
  kiss
Is the death I sharpened on my spear.

BLODEUWEDD: My Gronw, the year for you was easier than for
  me;
You could mind your passion, count your memories
In the fold of your loneliness; and yield to longing
Without guarding your sighs, without stifling your
  tears.
Neither night nor day was safe to me,
I had the burden of his body and the weight of my
  hate
Crushing my breasts and obliterating your image.
I won't say more; I can tell tonight,
Tonight and tomorrow and after tomorrow, and
  Oh, I'll be free.
But this is the hour to strike.

GRONW: What's your plan?

BLODEUWEDD: Is this your captain?

GRONW: The Steward of the house of Penllyn;
The men are there in the wood, a hundred knights,
With this noble to lead them.

BLODEUWEDD: Brave Steward,
Llew Llaw Gyffes will be killed on this trough.

Go to your horses. Be ready. The instant
He is killed your lord's hunting-horn will sound;
Rush to the fort; Rhagnell will open the gate for
    you;
There will only be a soldier or two to overcome;
Take it and hold it till we arrive.
Tomorrow we'll unite Penllyn and Ardudwy.
Rhagnell, go, tell my lord I'm here
On the bank of the river Cynfael
In the shadow of Bryn Cyfergyr, by the goat-
    trough;
And in accordance with what we said last night
I want to meet him here, now, to talk.

                            (*Exeunt Rhagnell and the Steward.*)

GRONW: Will he come?

BLODEUWEDD: Why won't my loving husband come
To his dear wife?

GRONW: What did you talk about last night?

BLODEUWEDD: A topic that will bring him to me here in haste.

GRONW: How will I kill him?

BLODEUWEDD: It won't be hard:
I'll hide you here under this bank;
He can't be killed with his foot on the ground,
But he must stand upon a water-trough
Upon a river bank. When you see him here
Standing full of pride upon the trough
Rise up and thrust him in the back with the
    poisoned spear,
Sound your hunting-horn, and accept your
    reward.

GRONW: I wonder whether you'll get him to climb upon the
    trough?

BLODEUWEDD: Don't you miss, and I won't fail
To get him to stand on the trough.

GRONW: My cast has been aimed for a year
And it can't miss. The target's not
His death. Beyond his carcass is your kiss,
That's my warrant that my spear won't miss.
I need a long life, Blodeuwedd, to slake
The thirst that grew in me beneath twelve moons.

How long this year is; how short I see
All the years of life I have before me.

BLODEUWEDD: In a year's time how pleasant it will be
To remember this morning.

GRONW: Will it be easy to tame Ardudwy and hold it
quiet?

BLODEUWEDD: Why not? Was there ever any country
That didn't count successful oppression deserving
of success?

GRONW: I've heard that everyone's content with him.

BLODEUWEDD: You kill him, and your welcome won't be any less.

GRONW: Isn't there one among them who'll try to avenge
his wrong?

BLODEUWEDD: Tomorrow be harsh and cruel; and for the rest of
your days
They'll run like little dogs to lick your hand.

GRONW: You've learnt the skill of government, my lady.

BLODEUWEDD: The instinct to govern's in the flea; neither she
Nor I need do any more than follow nature.
Hush, hide, my hunter, Llew is on his way.
Fasten your will to mine
To get him onto the trough. The last encounter
will come;
And then we can laugh and live as we please.
(*Blodeuwedd sits on the edge of the trough after Gronw has
hidden himself. Llew Llaw Gyffes comes to her.*)

LLEW: You've risen early, my lady.

BLODEUWEDD: The shimmering of daybreak
Enticed me like a rabbit to wash in the grass.

LLEW: And you came barefoot like a rabbit too?

BLODEUWEDD: It takes a married man to notice something like
that;
Will you make me a shoe as you did for your
mother?

LLEW: My mother didn't walk in the dew, she was
careful;
She sent servants with the measurements.

BLODEUWEDD: Is that the time you killed the wren with a spear?

LLEW: Not a spear, but a needle; no one could thrust a
                    wren with a spear,
                 It was a shoemaker's needle that I was using to
                    stitch a shoe.

BLODEUWEDD: A needle, of course. How stupid of me.
                 Tell me how you killed the wren.

LLEW: Gladly. But first you tell me
                 Why you called me from bed so early.

BLODEUWEDD: The wren's story first.

LLEW: No, your tale first,
                 Why did you call me here from the fort?

BLODEUWEDD: Can I then have the story of the killing of the
                    wren?

LLEW: Yes, upon my word, but what's the great secret?

BLODEUWEDD: How insistent you are. Didn't I say last night?

LLEW: You said that you'd keep till today some happy
                    news
                 To celebrate the year since my return from Caer
                    Dathal.

BLODEUWEDD: How slow your fancy is in the morning . . .
                 Are you content with your year, my lord?

LLEW: How could I not be content? I've found a nest
                 In your trust; you've been kind and gentle,
                 Not like a wild bird shut in a cage.

BLODEUWEDD: You're still afraid of all wild things, my Llew?

LLEW: My mother was wild. I learnt what hate was from
                    my mother;
                 She pursued me as a child and as a man,
                 And I don't know who my father was. All wild
                    things are cruel,
                 Cowardly and servile, killing a man in the back.
                 You've been like a garden to me; I never spent a
                    year before this one
                 Without fearing the knife of betrayal.

BLODEUWEDD: And now you've defeated all your mother's
                    ordinations?

LLEW: All that she mentioned. There's one she didn't
                    mention.

BLODEUWEDD: What's that, my friend? You've had a name;
You've had arms in spite of her; you've had a wife.

LLEW: When my mother swore that I
Would never have a wife from among the
daughters of men,
Though her contrivance failed and a girl was made
of flowers
And given to me as the fairest maid in the world,
Though where you stand is the daylight sun
And in the night it's my joy to hold you in my
arms,
Though I give thanks for you, my fair Blodeuwedd,
I know I haven't yet escaped my mother's wrath.

BLODEUWEDD: Yes, I understand. But tell me now,
When will you be free of her malice?

LLEW: When you'll tell me the best news I could hear.

BLODEUWEDD: And the news, my love?

LLEW: The news
That I've a son from you to be my heir.

BLODEUWEDD: And that will loosen your mother's bonds upon
you?

LLEW: My mother tried to kill me. She failed.
My birth was her shame, and through me
She spat her vengeance and gall on the world.
She cut me off from men, from the body's delight
And from the joy of any youth,
By forbidding me arms and forbidding me a wife.
I fought against her for life,
For a taste of the sweet things of men's communion.
Gwydion was a father to me, you a wife;
King Math gave me a lordship;
I know the ordinary worries, and through you
This year, I know gentleness. The nightmare that
was there
Is dying from my mind. But, Blodeuwedd,
If once I saw between your arm and breast
A son, my heir, then the last chain
Would fall, I would be safe, the father of a
family,
A giver of life to generations.

BLODEUWEDD: Without that, you can't be content with me?

LLEW: Without that I'll be content; with that
My love and gratitude will turn into a song around
    you.

BLODEUWEDD: That wouldn't be a song for me,
But the poem of your triumph over your mother.
Oh, Llew, how I wish you'd look upon me once
And say, 'You, you are my all.'
If you said that—

LLEW: I'll say it when your son's on your arm.

BLODEUWEDD: A fateful word! Listen to my secret:
I now have here an heir for you.

LLEW: You know for certain?

BLODEUWEDD: As every woman knows.

LLEW: Ah, my queen! Let fate decree that he will be a boy.

BLODEUWEDD: He's a boy, I'll swear it.

LLEW: I didn't dare
Believe that was the meaning of your words last
    night.
My cup's so full; let death now come
When it will, my welcome won't be bitter.

BLODEUWEDD: Death won't come to you easily, the last fate
Is a strong fort to keep you from your mother's
    spear.

LLEW: My mother's wrath won't count when the son
    comes.
My lady, guess what this heir will be like.

BLODEUWEDD: With hot kisses; I can imagine him now
Putting his lips to mine,
And he'll be a hunter frightening the deer with
    his horn,
And dancing on the floor of Ardudwy in his
    gaiety.

LLEW: I'll teach him his father's games.

BLODEUWEDD: Will you teach him to cast a spear and needle?

LLEW: And to row a boat and make shoes for his mother
So she won't go barefoot in the dew.

BLODEUWEDD: Will you tell him the story of the striking of the
    wren?

LLEW: I can imagine him now a child of three
             Listening on his mother's knee to Gwydion's
                 stories;
             And it'll please that sorcerer to astonish
             The lad with the tale of the boat by Caer
                 Arianrhod.

BLODEUWEDD: Tell the story as if to your heir,
             Imagine for a time that this trough's the boat;
             Where was Gwydion standing?

LLEW: Here, in the middle,
             Bending down to my mother's foot.

BLODEUWEDD: And the youth without a name
             Who was sewing the leather, where were you
                 sitting?

LLEW: There, in the stern.

BLODEUWEDD: Did your mother look at you?

LLEW: Yes, closely for a long time, wry-mouthed.

BLODEUWEDD: But without
             Recognizing you?

LLEW: Gwydion had cast a spell upon us;
             She was fair and had her foot on the side of the
                 boat,
             And she stood proudly, without bending, like a
                 princess.

BLODEUWEDD: Like this, with her face to the sea?
             And then?

LLEW: It was spring, and ten feet from the shore
             There was a stone wall; through a low crevice there
             I saw the wren darting in and out
             In his quick way, and then tiring
             And wanting to rest, alighting on the prow of the
                 boat.

BLODEUWEDD: Here? Oh, show me how he stood.

LLEW (*jumping on to the front of the trough and standing, looking out*):
             Now look . . .
             (*Blodeuwedd goes to the middle of the floor to the left and
             faces him. Gronw Pebr gets up on his right, and aims the
             spear.*)
                 My mother and Gwydion were here,

And I was in the stern. It was a tense moment,
With a kind of shimmer of stillness on the water,
And there was the wren. He stood and raised his
    wing
Like this . . . with his head down . . . At that
    moment,
With the needle between my fingers—

BLODEUWEDD: A needle, not a spear—

LLEW: I aimed at him—

GRONW: Like this.
(*Casts the spear into the back of Llew Llaw Gyffes. He
falls with a cry on his face on to the ground. They look at
him.*)
Is he dead?

BLODEUWEDD: He twitched and struck his head
Twice on the grass and became still. He's still now.

GRONW: The poison cannot fail. Gwydion and all his sorcery
Couldn't fend off this fate.
(*He sounds his hunting-horn. The sound of horses is heard.*)

BLODEUWEDD: Come, my heir . . .
(*They embrace. Blodeuwedd laughs wildly.*)
He's a boy, I'll swear it.

GRONW: I never saw a better ending to a tale . . . Yes, he's
    dead.

BLODEUWEDD: How easily a man dies.

GRONW: There's the sun casting light on the hill.

BLODEUWEDD: Let's stay awhile;
I'd never have believed he could die so easily.

GRONW: Let's go to the fort to take possession of it.

BLODEUWEDD: He screamed and went;
Will it be like that for me when my turn comes?

GRONW: Come, Blodeuwedd. This isn't the time to linger.

BLODEUWEDD: I never saw a death before. What'll we do with
    this?

GRONW: I'll send soldiers to bury him this afternoon.

BLODEUWEDD: Hush! I heard a noise in the woods like the
    tinkling of a shield.

GRONW: They're my soldiers.

BLODEUWEDD: They've gone to the fort.

GRONW: It's likely they've left one on guard.

BLODEUWEDD: Has his ghost fled in anger to the woods?

GRONW: His ghost cannot tinkle like a shield.

BLODEUWEDD: He fell like a flower. Will you die
              Like that?

GRONW: Come, girl,
              You're like an owl, and not your sprightly self.
              We must hold the fort and hastily put the country
                  in order
              And then we'll be safe. Let's go quickly.
              (*Exeunt. A moment's respite. Then two soldiers, with
              Gwydion behind them, slip in stealthily. They find
              Llew Llaw Gyffes.*)

SOLDIER: It's worse here than you feared, my Lord Gwydion,
              Here's your nephew dead by the trough . . .

GWYDION: And you fell here, my child,
              Like a great wounded eagle. Come into my lap . . .
              His heart has stopped beating. Oh evil woman . . .
              We'll lift him, men; we'll carry him to the woods,
              And hide him under the oaks. And there my
                  magic
              Can contend for him with warlock death.
              Carefully, now . . . gently . . . quietly . . .

                            CURTAIN

                            ACT IV

        (*A year later, in the hall of the fort, the Steward and Rhagnell.*)

STEWARD: Are you still here by yourself, Rhagnell?

RHAGNELL: By myself. My lady's still in bed.

STEWARD: In Llew's time she'd be the first to rise.
              Hasn't Gronw come back from hunting?

RHAGNELL: No.

STEWARD: Some of the men have come. I've seen them in the
              courtyard.

RHAGNELL: There wasn't a great deal of go in their hunting,
                 I'd say.

STEWARD: There's plenty of go in the whispering among them
                 now.

RHAGNELL: If they have tales, let them keep them for the feast.

STEWARD: What feast?

RHAGNELL: What feast? Where have you come from?

STEWARD: From roaming in Arfon and reconnoitring in the
                 Vale of Nantlle;
                 I didn't hear there as much as a mention of a
                 feast.

RHAGNELL: A year to this day Gronw came to Ardudwy.
                 And I opened the gate of the fort to you.

STEWARD: Will you be the porter today?

RHAGNELL: Stop your foolish chatter.

STEWARD: You'll be surprised at the guests that'll come to
                 your feast.

RHAGNELL: Why annoy me? I haven't done you wrong.

STEWARD: You've opened too many doors in your time.

RHAGNELL: You and your lord came through them all.

STEWARD: I won't come this afternoon.

RHAGNELL: The omen's bad:
                 The men of Penllyn would sooner quit a battle
                 than a feast.

STEWARD: Who will be welcomed here from Caer Dathal?
                 Has Gwydion been invited?

RHAGNELL: Hardly.

STEWARD: I heard in Nantlle that he was on his way.

RHAGNELL: And maybe you heard that Llew Llaw Gyffes was
                 on his way?

STEWARD: Yes, I heard that.

RHAGNELL: You stupid liar.

STEWARD: Liar, perhaps. But why do you call me stupid?

RHAGNELL: You buried Llew Llaw Gyffes yourself.

STEWARD: I, too, have heard that said many times.

RHAGNELL: You said it, not anyone else.

STEWARD: Did you hear me?

RHAGNELL: When the earl and lady came from the slaughter
He ordered you and two of your men
To go to bury the body near the goat-trough.
We'd been in the marriage-feast an hour or more
Before you came and said that your task was done.

STEWARD: Did Gronw or anyone else ask what task was done?

RHAGNELL: The burying of Llew Llaw Gyffes wasn't it?

STEWARD: Have you seen the grave?

RHAGNELL: No.

STEWARD: Has your lady?

RHAGNELL: I don't know.

STEWARD: It's strange that no one asked about the grave.

RHAGNELL: Taming Ardudwy and making it obedient
Was more necessary than raising a stone on a
grave.

STEWARD: There's comfort in a grave, a suggestion of a death
there.
Stones on an enemy's grave let the living sleep.

RHAGNELL: You don't have to worry, Gronw's a pretty sleeper.

STEWARD: Does he sleep as well as Llew by the goat-trough?

RHAGNELL: What do you mean?

STEWARD: Didn't you say
That Llew Llaw Gyffes died there?

RHAGNELL: It was ordained that he would die like that.

STEWARD: No, it was ordained as part of his fate
That he could only in that way be killed.

RHAGNELL: Two and two make four. He was killed, he died.

STEWARD: Since you know that, you're happy.

RHAGNELL: I know it? You buried him.

STEWARD: You've already said that, I don't know why.

RHAGNELL: You don't know? Didn't you bury him?

STEWARD: It's a year since Llew Llaw Gyffes was lost
And no one's asked about that before now.

RHAGNELL: Why enquire, when everybody knows it?

STEWARD: I didn't know it.

RHAGNELL: What? Didn't know it?

STEWARD: If he was buried, I didn't do it.

RHAGNELL: Your men, then, under your command.

STEWARD: Go, ask them. They're there in the courtyard.

RHAGNELL: Llew Llaw Gyffes was killed by the goat-trough.

STEWARD: That's how I understood it, too; I went there;
There was neither carcass nor goat near the place;
I searched the woods and the river, and searched
in vain.

RHAGNELL: Why didn't you tell this to Gronw Pebr?

STEWARD: He's a man who never gave anyone the truth;
It doesn't pay to give him the truth either before
there's need.

RHAGNELL: Perhaps one of his retinue took the body?

STEWARD: It's strange that Gwydion from Caer Dathal
Or that poet from Ardudwy didn't come to sing
above his grave.
I didn't hear an elegy in Nantlle, nor his mother
crowing.

RHAGNELL: You mean that Llew Llaw Gyffes is alive?

STEWARD: That's what I thought. I went to Arfon:
For a full year Gwydion and Math's physicians
Fought against the poison for Llew's life.
Now he's recovered and alive. He'll be here today:
He has a word or two to say to Gronw.

RHAGNELL: I wouldn't be surprised. Is there someone with
him?

STEWARD: His uncle, Gwydion, and three hundred armed
men.
(*Blodeuwedd comes to them.*)

RHAGNELL: Here's news, my lady.

BLODEUWEDD: Happy or foolish?

RHAGNELL: Is it happy or foolish that Llew Llaw Gyffes is
alive?

BLODEUWEDD: Alive? Who said so?

STEWARD: I saw him yesterday.

BLODEUWEDD: Ah, the time has come . . . I've been expecting
this.

STEWARD: You expecting it, my lady? For how long?

BLODEUWEDD: From that moment, a year to this day,
              When I saw your face when you were hesitating by
                the gate
              The day that Penllyn and Ardudwy were united;
              There was scorn in your eyes and on your lips.

STEWARD: I've never done you wrong, my lady.

BLODEUWEDD: You kept silent because you hated me, and that
                silence was a lie,
              To devise the fall and ruin of my frail joy.
              You didn't bury Llew.

STEWARD: I did not.

BLODEUWEDD: Gwydion took him.

STEWARD: How do you know that?

BLODEUWEDD: I know the hand of my sorcerer. It is only he
              Who could call pigs or a man's soul from the
                Other World
              And bewitch death. He'll be here today?

RHAGNELL: Gwydion and Llew and three hundred men.

BLODEUWEDD: Come what may, I too have had my day.

STEWARD: My lady, what's your counsel. Time's short.

BLODEUWEDD: Shall I give counsel to someone's who's planning to
                betray?

STEWARD: I swear—

BLODEUWEDD: That you've already arranged to escape.

STEWARD: Barely forty men can't hold the fort.

BLODEUWEDD: Saddles on the horses, the rattle of shields,
              The noise and bustle of departure, and the earl in
                the woods
              Unaware, with the avenger in his land.

STEWARD: I've sent men to fetch him, I've posted guards—

BLODEUWEDD: You've arranged everything in order to escape
                before he comes.

STEWARD: He must escape, and so must you. The soldiers
              Won't wait for the enemy here in Ardudwy;
              Over in Penllyn we'll have right on our side and
                be strong.

BLODEUWEDD: Do the soldiers have the right to decide for their
lord?

STEWARD: Is that worse than being a woman's slave?

BLODEUWEDD: How easy it was to whip your treason to your
mouth
And hook it to your tongue, false Steward.

STEWARD: Remonstrating won't do with the enemy at hand—

RHAGNELL: Gronw's here now, my lady.
(*Gronw enters.*)

BLODEUWEDD: Have you heard, Gronw?

GRONW: Yes, I've heard everything.

BLODEUWEDD: Your captain's arranged that we flee to Penllyn.

GRONW: How many are there of the enemy?

STEWARD: Three hundred armed men.

GRONW: And our men?

STEWARD: There aren't forty here,
And some of those are subjects of Ardudwy
That can't be trusted to stand firm.

GRONW: You've done well to gather the men and horses,
The fort cannot be held.

STEWARD: The words of a soldier,
Not women's jabber with the battle near.

GRONW: Are the men ready?

STEWARD: Men and horses,
And a fresh horse for you and your lady.

GRONW: When will the enemy arrive?

STEWARD: I've posted guards,
We'll know when the army's at the opening of the
valley.

GRONW: You've always been wise and tenacious.
I give you possession of Penllyn
And the heritage to you and your children,
And I hand to your charge this lady
And Rhagnell her maid; give them shelter
From the terror of Gwydion, from Llew's claw;
And send messengers to Caer Dathal
To King Math, and offer him recompense
Lest he savage your land;

Rule your country wiser than I did.
I'll stay here to satisfy Llew Llaw Gyffes
For his disgrace and shame;
So you can escape in safety.

STEWARD: My lord, there's no need for this. In Penllyn
You have men and a fort and a right to your
    lordship.

GRONW: Do as I say. I'll stand here
To welcome Llew to his lair.

BLODEUWEDD: Gronw, what's this?

GRONW: Go, Rhagnell, hurry
And gather the lady's things for her journey.

(Exit Rhagnell.)

BLODEUWEDD: But you'll come too, Gronw?

GRONW: No I won't,
I've been mad a long time; but I'm not any more;
I won't bring vengeance on my innocent people
Or spoil my father's home.

BLODEUWEDD: Let's flee to Dyfed then,
There we'll be welcomed by Math's enemies
And given refuge and protection.

GRONW: If I did that
Math would let loose his wrath on Penllyn's
    beauty,
And I'd be in a woman's arms escaping in fear.

STEWARD: It's high time, my lord, for you to remember
    Penllyn,
But come now and you'll find your country behind
    you.

GRONW: Your admonition's fair, your offer's fair
And it's fair that I refuse. I have a debt
To Llew of Ardudwy, and I'll pay it today
Here, myself, without asking anyone for surety.

STEWARD: I ask as a soldier now, my lord:
Time's short to save the men's lives,
We must choose to fight here or escape through the
    woods
Before the enemy close up the valley; they're
    coming on their horses.

GRONW: You musn't delay—

BLODEUWEDD: Gronw, my Gronw—

GRONW: Don't touch me, woman, the time has come
               For you to go; you've got a journey to make.

BLODEUWEDD: I won't move from here without you
               Or leave you alone in Gwydion's hands.

GRONW: Your husband's alive. He'll be here. You can't
               stay.

BLODEUWEDD: I can't go by myself to strange men.
               They'll kill me without you.

GRONW: Brave Steward,
               I've given you my lordship. Give me
               Your word on oath that this lady will have
               Her part in Penllyn without shame, under your
                    protection.
               (*The sound of another horn. A soldier rushes in.*)

SOLDIER: My lords, the enemy's front line is in the valley's
                    opening.

STEWARD: Mount up! Come now, my lord.

GRONW: Hurry, Blodeuwedd. Where's the maid, Rhagnell?

SOLDIER: Rhagnell went out of the fort a short while ago.

GRONW: Out? Where to?

SOLDIER: I don't know; towards the river.

STEWARD: This isn't the time for anyone to look for a grave.

GRONW: You can't wait for her.

BLODEUWEDD: I must wait,
               Don't ask me to leave you;
               We're joined by blood, we cannot separate;
               I stood with you by the goat-trough,
               I saw your spear aimed, I saw the killing;
               I'll stand to see it again.

GRONW: And why not?
               You came to me across his carcass,
               He'll take you back like Helen of old
               Across my carcass. Steward, go,
               Take your men and flee. Tonight you'll see
               The little waves of Meloch and Tryweryn
               And the smoke rising from Llanfor, when I was
                    a boy . . .
               Farewell, don't delay.

STEWARD: I'll leave two horses for you in the courtyard.
                (*The Steward and the Soldier go out. The noise of horses
                leaving the courtyard. Then stillness.*)

BLODEUWEDD: They've gone, Gronw.

GRONW: Your fort's become a prison.

BLODEUWEDD: There's no one here except the two of us.

GRONW: It won't last long. We'll soon have company.

BLODEUWEDD: I wish Rhagnell would come back!

GRONW: I wouldn't be surprised
                If she came with Gwydion.

BLODEUWEDD: I'm afraid;
                There was never any guile in her,
                She was our love messenger, remember?

GRONW: Remember? I remember too much. There's no
                    pain
                Like the pain of failing to forget in the nightmare
                    of being.

BLODEUWEDD: Why must we stay here? Why must we, Gronw?

GRONW: There's no 'must' for you. 'Must' is part of my fate.

BLODEUWEDD: You haven't got your arms either. Shall I fetch
                A sword and shield for you? Don't you want to
                    fight?

GRONW: It's not my turn to strike now.

BLODEUWEDD: Then will you go down on your knees before him?
                He can't forgive. I know my Llew.

GRONW: I can do without his forgiveness
                If I feel the taste of his spear.

BLODEUWEDD: You want to be killed?

GRONW: How long you've been in seeing my intent.

BLODEUWEDD: What are you looking for by seeking death?

GRONW: Another hour of freedom.

BLODEUWEDD: I can't understand you;
                There are horses still standing by the gate
                And there's freedom in the stirrup. Why don't
                    we go?

GRONW: Freedom's here, here with you.

BLODEUWEDD: Your 'with you' is like wine to my heart;
I was afraid before, Gronw; I see it now—
Your freedom's that we die in each other's arms
And end a marriage-feast of living with defiance to
all order.

GRONW: My freedom's not in your arms,
But in looking at you with my fall at hand
And preferring your sister death to you.

BLODEUWEDD: Casting me aside? Blaming me
For enticing you to murder? Pleading with Llew
That it was a woman's trick that made you do
what you did?
Is that how you'll win freedom, my handsome
Gronw?

GRONW: You needn't be frightened. It's not your death
That would give me life. There is now,
Woman, only a little time left for me, and your
husband will come
And my death will come. I choose that,
And that choice is my full freedom.

BLODEUWEDD: Your freedom now is to escape from me?

GRONW: I can't escape you without dying,
With the poison of your kisses in my blood.
Why should I live? To taste forever
What I've already tasted, the surfeit of the flesh
And the pain and shame in this repeated futile
surfeiting?
Your love's a grave with no tomorrow; no baby
will laugh
On your bosom; there's no cradle in your fort;
But in the night the noise of a mad wretch has been
heard
Howling on firm breasts in the dark,
The biting of filth and the simpering of the owl.
I lost the paths of men to chase a flame
And the magic pipes of the fen, and I sank in it,
Embraced a star, had a bat hang on my lips;
Today a bolt struck me and I woke;
I see Penllyn, I see my boyhood there,
And I see myself now, oh loathsome, and I see
you—

Better your husband's sword than your kiss.
(*Two soldiers rush in and hold Gronw: with them are Llew Llaw Gyffes and Gwydion; then two other soldiers come carrying a bier with a drape upon it.*)

SOLDIERS: Here are the two . . .
To him . . . he's caught . . .
(*They tie Gronw's hands behind his back.*)

GWYDION: We walk through an open gate as to a feast
And the young couple are waiting to welcome us.

LLEW: Where are your men, you traitor?

GRONW: Scattered.
I alone struck you. There's no need
To look for others nor to take your revenge on
anyone but me.

LLEW: Is this a plot . . . Search the fort thoroughly.
(*Two soldiers go.*)

GWYDION: And here's the handsome heir, the son of Gronw
Hir,
Now without a family, tied, and without a spear
in his hand.

GRONW: My lord, there's no need for your men to tie me;
I stayed so you'd have your way; I'll stand in the
face of your vengeance
As freely as you stood on the goat-trough.

GWYDION: That's true, my nephew. I knew his father
And the fort at the lake's side. Untie him,
We must respect a nobleman who is to be punished
by death.
(*The soldiers untie him.*)

LLEW: He has a rope of flax upon his arms;
He tied me with a rope of woman's lies.

GRONW: What do you want, my lord?

LLEW: Your life.

GRONW: You have a right to that. You'll have it gladly.

LLEW: You spent a full year preparing my death,
For a full year you took possession of my bed,
My fort, my lordship, and that half demon
Who was called my wife. It's not because of this
That I want your blood, but because you listened

To the deepest secret in my soul and laughed,
Mocked a young man's pain, and turned to jest
A man's confession as he worshipped the fruit of
    his love.
Your betrayal in that act cut you off from
The family of men, you gave your youth to the
    swine;
The mark of the forest's upon you; you cannot live.

GRONW: My brother, how do you want to kill me?

LLEW: My uncle Gwydion, how shall I deal with him?

GWYDION: This afternoon we'll go together, the three of us,
To the river Cynfael and to the goat-trough;
And he shall stand where you stood
On the front of the trough, and you where he was,
And you'll strike him in his back as he struck you.
And there won't be any laughter there or physician
    either.

GRONW: Or tears, but a welcoming of punishment. I'll
    come back
To the family of men through that common
    gateway
That gathers us all to its shade. I thank you, earl.

LLEW: Take him and keep him till this afternoon.
               (*Exeunt Gronw and the soldiers. Silence.*)

BLODEUWEDD: My uncle, you've travelled far today,
Can I prepare dinner for the two of you?

GWYDION: Your husband's already tasted your poison.

BLODEUWEDD: You need not fear. Rhagnell will soon return,
She can prepare the food and I'll serve it.

GWYDION: Rhagnell has already returned. She's there.
    (*Blodeuwedd raises the drape from the bier.*)

BLODEUWEDD: This is your work? You drowned her?

GWYDION: We found her body by the goat-trough.

BLODEUWEDD: She was a sister to me, the only one
That did not seek to profit by me; she reached out
    her hand,
Forgave, and went to her grave without
    reproaching faults;
Do you wish to drown me too?

GWYDION: I've told you we didn't drown her.

BLODEUWEDD: She was always quiet, and she died without a
             sound.

GWYDION: Like a wise maid, she too anticipated her
             punishment.

BLODEUWEDD: What have I done to deserve punishment?

GWYDION: Poison, betrayal, slaughter, seducing a man to his
             death.
             Trifles of that kind that aren't to everyone's liking.

BLODEUWEDD: Am I the first unfaithful wife?

GWYDION: I wouldn't say that. There are many of your sort.

BLODEUWEDD: You, Gwydion, are a sorcerer, deeply learned,
             Powerful and bold enough to bind nature
             And to play with the powers in the rocks.
             What for? to satisfy an urge. You had a nephew;
             You loved him more than your own children—
             That's easily understood—you made him your heir
             And considered how to raise him to the throne of
             Math
             To be in time a king of Gwynedd and the father of
             kings.
             But his life was subject to conditions,
             He was chained by fate to be set apart;
             There are such men, men separated
             And cut off from all generations. But for you,
             Sorcerer and master of the secrets of creation,
             For you it wasn't easy that your heir had a burden
             of shame;
             You bent the elements to please your pride,
             Defied fate, put spells on the sea's waves,
             Bewitched the spirit of the forest into a woman of
             flesh.
             And so I was tied to serve like a slave
             To give children to your nephew, to establish his
             line,
             And to lull him at night to forget the misfortune of
             his pedigree.
             Answer me, Gwydion, wasn't this the plan?

GWYDION: Is it any violence to expect a woman to give her
             husband a son?

BLODEUWEDD: Thank you, warlock. It was ordained that
                    Arianrhod's son
                    Should be forever without a wife from among the
                        daughters of men
                    And without a son. He would not yield to his fate,
                    Neither he nor you; I was caught to be an
                        instrument,
                    A thing in your hands to outwit fate.
                    Have I been unnatural? Was it wrong for me
                    To act according to my nature? I implored him,
                    The youth not made for love, to look upon me
                    And to love me once for my own sake;
                    But he persisted with a song to his heir
                    And told his last tale to the son of his hope;
                    He would not leave the tomorrow of his dreams
                    To come into the empty present of my heart.

LLEW: Gwydion, this is true. She has suffered wrong.
                    She doesn't deserve to die like the other one.

GWYDION: You say that? You astonish me!

BLODEUWEDD: Gronw chose to die. Rhagnell has died.
                    What good is it to me to stretch out my life now?

LLEW: I came here bitter, to be avenged;
                    I see now that you were always pitiful.

BLODEUWEDD: You defied your fate, and so did I;
                    The two of us have been struggling against
                        necessity.

LLEW: There is necessity in all marriages among men.

BLODEUWEDD: Necessity and grasping is in the nature of my love.

LLEW: Because of that I forgive you,
                    No reasonable being can love like you.

BLODEUWEDD: One could. I gave him to you as an heir.

LLEW: And he chose death to escape from you.

BLODEUWEDD: And out of jealousy you want to kill him
                    Because he could love and kindle love.
                    What will you do without me, poor man,
                    That will never find a wife among the daughters
                        of men?

LLEW: Accept my fate, make a nest of my frustration.

BLODEUWEDD: I can hear the laughter of your mother and her
                    jubilation.

LLEW: You do not hear her sobbing in the night.

BLODEUWEDD: A cold hearth and a cold bed.

LLEW: All of us are exiles; the world a cold hearth;
I'll be a part of human kind in my bitterness.

BLODEUWEDD: Your fate is to be without knowledge of love.

LLEW: The love I had, I gave it to you.

BLODEUWEDD: A sorry remnant of your own generous self-pity.

LLEW: I put my life in your hands. You betrayed it.

BLODEUWEDD: So that I'd have life. Take your revenge.

LLEW: I cannot take revenge. I'll let you go.

BLODEUWEDD: How gracious my lord is. I can go
To my family, my friends, to my love.
And where will you go now? To your mother?

LLEW: I'll go to the goat-trough this afternoon,
I and Gwydion and Gronw Pebr of Penllyn;
Will you come there to laugh as before?

BLODEUWEDD: Gladly, my love. I didn't know you were so merry;
I'll go to the woods until then. Farewell.
And good day to you, uncle.

GWYDION: Yes, my niece,
But listen before you go. In the woods
There is a bird that is fearsome like you
And like you loves the night, and its hooting
Is, like your laughter, an omen of death,
And between it and the other birds there is hostility;
Your sojourn with men has been unhappy;
Go to the woods to the owls,
To the rituals of the moon and the hollow tree. Now,
As you cross the threshold and shelter from the sun
Your laughter shall be turned into an owl's
screeching,
And you will never dare to show your face by
daylight.

BLODEUWEDD: I'll fly to Caer Arianrhod. I'll receive from your
sister
An unusual welcome for a daughter-in-law.
(*She goes out still laughing. Then the laughter stops and
the screech of an owl is heard.*)

CURTAIN

Siwan

translated by EMYR HUMPHREYS

PRONUNCIATION OF WELSH NAMES

Alis	(Alice).
Siwan	(Shée-one).
Gwilym	(Gwéel-im) (Bré-os) Bray-oss (Norm. Fr.).
Llywelyn	(Lle-wéll-in).
Gwladus	(Gladys).
Prydydd y Moch	Pré (*e* as in early) - dith (*th* as in *th*e) y (*e* as in *early*) - Mōch (*ch* as in Ba*ch*, lo*ch*).
Caerleon	(Car-láy-on).
Menai	(Mén-I).
Ednyfed Fychan	Edd-név (*e* as in early) - edd Véch (*e* as in *early*), *ch* as in Ba*ch*) - an.
Gruffydd	(Griffith).
Gwynedd	Gwínn-eth (*th* as in *th*e).
Gwladus Ddu	Gladys *th*ee. Black (haired) Gladys.
Gelert	Géll-ert (*e* as in *e*nd).
Erging	Erg (*e* as in *e*nd) - eeng.
Dolwyddelen	Dole-with-éllen.
Cadwgan	Cad-óog-an.
Bangor	Bán-gore.
Tywi	Té (*e* as in *e*arly) + wee.
Teifi	Tíe-vee.
Rhys	Rees.
Dinefwr	Din-é-voor.
Ystrad	Es (*e* as in *e*arly) - trad.
Cunedda	Keen-éth (*e* as in *e*arly, *th* as in *th*e) - a (as in b*a*d).
Aberffraw	Ab-er (to rhyme with *pear*) + frown (without *n*).
Arfon	Are-von.
Hafan	Há-van.
Dindaethwy	Deen-dái-thw-ee (*th* as in *th*anks).
Llanfaes	Clan-vice.
Aberconwy	Ab-er (to rhyme with *pear*)-con-wee.

DRAMATIS PERSONAE

LLYWELYN THE GREAT, 57 years of age.

SIWAN, wife of Llywelyn, daughter of the King of England, 35 years of age.

GWILYM DE BREOS, 25 years of age.

ALIS, Siwan's maid, 20 years of age.

ACT I

The bedchamber of Llywelyn and his wife, 1 a.m., 1st May 1230

ACT II

A room in the Tower, 6 a.m., 3rd May 1230

ACT III

The bedchamber of Llywelyn and his wife, 1st May 1231

NOTE.—Princess Joan (Siwan in Welsh), daughter of King John, grand-daughter of Eleanor of Aquitaine, was married in 1205 to Llywelyn the Great, ruler of North Wales —'Prince of Aberffraw and Lord of Gwynedd'. In 1216 King John died and Henry III came to the Throne. Princess Siwan died at Aberconwy in 1237. The events in the play are based on historical fact.

Siwan

Act I

Time: 1 a.m., 1st May 1230
*Place: The Court of the Prince of Wales—the Prince's bedchamber in the
Castle*

ALIS: That's the silver dress off at last, madame;
I'll lay it in the chest immediately.

SIWAN: And this crown, Alis . . .
How late is it?

ALIS: I heard the watch cry midnight on the wall
Some time ago.

SIWAN: Have you waited long?

ALIS: Not long. When I came in from the lawn
I turned the hour-glass, and look, the sand
Has only half run out; just half an hour.
Wasn't the dancing on the lawn delightful?
The French knights were in their element.
More than one expressed surprise to find
On a Welsh field the measures of Aquitaine.
They can't be familiar with your court, madame.

SIWAN: The music is dying out. The last lamps are leaving.

ALIS (*at the window*):
The big lantern still hangs there.

SIWAN: The moon? Yes.
It shines in here so well we hardly need these candles.

ALIS: The French carol by moonlight, and with lanterns,
Had all the charm and magic of a fairy dance.
I never saw anything more charming
Than what seemed spirits and the shadows of spirits
Moving in stately rhythm to an unseen harp!
Why didn't you dance, my lady?

SIWAN: And the crown heavy on my head?
And the stiff silver dress around me like a tent?
Even for French dances, Alis, one needs to be more
mobile.

Tonight presiding from my chair and taking the
  Prince's place
In his absence was my duty.

ALIS: I never saw anything more charming.
          If only his Highness had been there.

SIWAN: This was a formal dance
          To celebrate our pact with the French of Hereford
            and Brecon.

ALIS: There's no one can dance the French carol, madame,
            like you.
          When the marriage dancing starts you must take the
            lead,
          As you did at all the other children's weddings.

SIWAN: Gwladus, Margaret, Helen, and now David,
          David, for the gilding of whose kingdom I have given
            my life;
          I shall dance at David's wedding. Indeed I shall.

ALIS: May I let down your hair now and comb it
          Ready for your sleeping?

SIWAN: Do that Alis. The crown has been a burden on my
            head;
          In any case, I like you to comb my hair.
          I'll sit on the smaller stool . . . there we are.

ALIS (*sings quietly as she combs*):
          Le roi Marc etait corrocié
          Vers Tristram, son neveu, irié;
          De sa terre le congedia
          Pour la reine qu'il aima . . .

SIWAN: I do not like your song tonight.

ALIS: Marie de France, madame,
          I learnt it from you.

SIWAN: And I from my mother.
          My grandmother was with my grandfather in
            Gloucester.
          She sang the songs from Aesop and taught them to
            my mother.

ALIS: And your mother heard her singing Tristram's story?

SIWAN: Yes. And she taught me the song. Tonight it's too sad
            a story.

ALIS:　Marie makes the song a country girl's,
Our feelings are in it, our longing and our fears:
Different from the scholarly poets who are clever and
　　cold.

SIWAN:　But she learnt from the scholarly poets . . .

ALIS:　She was as good a poet as Prydydd y Moch
And her French easier for a simple girl than Prydydd's
　　Welsh!
(*Singing again*)
En sa contrée en est allé
En Sud-Galles où il fut né.

SIWAN:　Leave Tristram and Iseult alone
And hurry to finish my hair.

ALIS:　Was Tristram a Frenchman, madame?
He was born in South Wales.
En Sud-Galles ou il fut né.

SIWAN:　Is Caerleon Welsh or French?

ALIS:　When I look at Gwilym de Breos
So young, so gay, so joyful,
I see in him a second Tristram, a . . .
(*Siwan slaps her*)
Madame! What have I said to upset you?

SIWAN:　Will you finish dressing my hair?

ALIS:　Look in this brass mirror, madame.
Two plaits, as fair as Iseult's own.
Your ring cut my lip, madame. My lip is bleeding.

SIWAN:　The taste will trim your tongue.
Did you give my personal guard the wine I left?

ALIS:　Did you not see them, then, as you came in?

SIWAN:　The two were sound asleep.
One each side of the door.

ALIS:　The guard asleep?
Must I wake them?

SIWAN:　Why bother? Let them sleep.
Tomorrow's the first of May.

ALIS:　It is the first of May already.
The young men and the maidens will dance on the
　　hillside

> Hand in hand around the maypole and then
> disappear
> Two by two, before carrying it to the homestead at
> daybreak.
> Country boys and wenches have their sport, madame.

SIWAN: Did you ever go with them, Alis?

ALIS (*a low reminiscent laugh*):
> Of course—when I was fifteen . . .
> Did you never dance around the maypole, my lady?

SIWAN (*suddenly bitter: to herself*):
> I was a king's daughter. At fifteen
> Mother of a prince and ambassador of Snowdon.
> I gave my womb to kingcraft, like every king's
> daughter.

ALIS: How still the trees are: not a sound of the sea.
> The tide is out, the Menai ebbing.
> I'd cast off my cowl of statecraft
> On such a night, such a festival,
> The first of May.

SIWAN: You speak of things you do not understand.
> Take your taper and take yourself off to bed.
> I am not ready for sleeping yet.
> If I need you I shall knock the floor. Go to your
> room.

ALIS: Good-night my lady, and God be with you.

SIWAN: God and Our Lady keep you girl: good-night.
> (*Door closed. Siwan sings softly to herself 'Pour la reine
> qu'il aima'. Knock on door: door opens.*)

GWILYM: Your Grace?

SIWAN: Gwilym? Come inside.

GWILYM: You and your lady-in-waiting kept me waiting.

SIWAN: This day, at daybreak, my brother sails for France.

GWILYM: Henry? The King of England?
> Well, what is that to me?

SIWAN: You are still a small boy.

GWILYM: I'm twenty-five years old and the father of four girls.

SIWAN: To me you will always be a venturesome boy,
> Wounded and captured and brought here for
> attention.
> My eternal youth.

GWILYM: What about your brother the king?
　　　　What if he does sail for France?

SIWAN: Only because that's why I kept my maid here rather
　　　　late.

GWILYM: To delay my coming or to keep me out?

SIWAN: This is Llywelyn's bed. There's danger here.
　　　　If Ednyfed Fychan or one of the Council observed
　　　　You coming this way from the dance, and told the
　　　　　　Prince,
　　　　Who knows, now the king's in France, what
　　　　　　Llywelyn would do?

GWILYM: Don't be afraid, no one saw me come,
　　　　The guards outside your door were fast asleep.
　　　　Was it you who prepared their wine?

SIWAN: Just in case. And you are so bold.

GWILYM: Have no fear at all: I'm one of the family you know:
　　　　The Prince's daughter, and yours, is my widowed
　　　　　　step-mother.
　　　　You married another daughter to my cousin,
　　　　And now I give my daughter to your son David,
　　　　We must be related somehow!

SIWAN: A pity she's so young.

GWILYM: Isabella? But she's eight years old.
　　　　Gwladus was three when my father took her for wife.

SIWAN: But she was his second wife. Your father already had
　　　　　an heir.
　　　　If Isabella is married this year, there will be still six
　　　　　years
　　　　Before she comes here to David:
　　　　And after that a year before there can be an heir.
　　　　That is too long: it threatens the state. Llywelyn is
　　　　　fifty-seven;
　　　　I want to hold my son's son, Llywelyn's heir,
　　　　Above the font, as crown of my endeavour,
　　　　Our policy fulfilled.

GWILYM: David has his many loves.

SIWAN: Consider before you speak.
　　　　The age of haphazard loving and natural sons
　　　　Is over for this royal house. Why did I work

To win the Pope's consent to my own legitimacy
Except to found the house of Snowdon from father
    to son,
A royal line as long and immaculate as Caesar's.

GWILYM: Gruffydd ap Llywelyn has sons.

SIWAN: Gruffydd? A concubine's son.

GWILYM: A Welshwoman's son.

SIWAN: I know.
Twenty years ago I sent him as a hostage to my
    father,
Trusting in my father's way of treating a hostage.
I was disappointed. Yes, Gruffydd has sons:
That is why David must hasten to have a son.

GWILYM: Don't you want this wedding?

SIWAN: This is for the Prince to decide. Of the two purposes
    of marriage
Which is the more important, guaranteeing the
    kingdom's frontiers,
Or the royal succession? It's a long-living breed;
If David lives to his father's age he should achieve
    both.
One political lesson Llywelyn has at least taught me,
That patience is the prelude to success—but patience
    comes hard to me.

GWILYM: And what lessons have you taught him?

SIWAN: You are married, and, as you say, the father of four
    daughters,
You know a wife has nothing to teach her husband.

GWILYM: False modesty! To walk through the courts of
Kings like Helen of Troy, to be first minister and
    plenipotentiary at large, to be the . . .

SIWAN: That is my escape,
My father's passionate energy burns in my blood,
And I have spent it as a man would spend it in my
    husband's cause,
To keep my life intact and keep my sanity.

GWILYM: Do you know what they say about you in the courts
    of Glamorgan and the Marches?
That you've transformed Gwynedd into a French
    kingdom,

Llywelyn has married his sons and daughters
To the sons and daughters of the Lords of France.
You've moulded him to our pattern, Siwan,
And turned Welshmen into knights.

SIWAN: This is hardly the time to say it,
You may as well say Llywelyn loves me your way,
Gwilym,
For it is love that changes men.

GWILYM: You are the first successful politician I have ever
Found intelligent, Siwan.

SIWAN: Government takes no account of the vagaries of
loving.
Only once have I allowed my heart to interfere.

GWILYM: And when was that, my cautious lady?

SIWAN: When I arranged the marriage
Between the heir of Snowdon and wild Gwilym de
Breos's daughter.

GWILYM: The best arrangement you ever made, the most
diplomatic!

SIWAN: The worst, indeed, unless David gets a son.

GWILYM: You astonish me, Siwan.

SIWAN: How do I astonish you? You must tell me.

GWILYM: You know why I came here?

SIWAN: To arrange a marriage between your daughter and my
son David.

GWILYM: Do you know why I want that marriage?

SIWAN: Is it necessary to explain? Your father and your
cousin did the same.
An alliance with Gwynedd is the policy of your house.

GWILYM: Policy, alliance, Siwan, that's council talk,
Not mine.

SIWAN: Be sensible. You still have no heir, no son.
Four daughters cannot keep your Brecon lordship
intact . . .

GWILYM: It wasn't statecraft brought me here tonight.

SIWAN: With you, talking affairs of state is my only
protection.

GWILYM: What protection do you need?

SIWAN: Believing that my life is worth its living.

GWILYM: Are you afraid of the truth?

SIWAN: Not afraid of truth, but afraid perhaps to hear it:
A thing can be couched in the mind that storms in
     the ear.

GWILYM: I'm not frightening you, Siwan? I wouldn't want to.

SIWAN: No, you are not: but there are things in me
That you awaken; they frighten me.

GWILYM: The things that make life sweet.

SIWAN: No, make life bitter.
Things that have been dumb and hidden from my
     own sight.
Because I had no part in them, because I am in
     exile here,
My only worth, my worth to the welfare of the
     realm.

GWILYM: You know then why I came to arrange this marriage?

SIWAN: Do I? No, I do not . . .that can never be.
Business and pleasure are two things apart.

GWILYM: Pleasure. That's not the name for the love I have for
     you.

SIWAN: Your flattery falls rather short tonight!
Is it because I am too old that your love gives you
     pain?

GWILYM: I didn't come here to be teased or to fence with
     words.

SIWAN: You know I am ten years older than you
And the mother of four grown children. That's not
     teasing . . .
My son David isn't far from your own age.

GWILYM: Princess, I was ten years old when I first saw you,
Leading the girl-bride Gwladus Ddu to my father
Waiting at the altar, and the great congregation
In Hereford Cathedral throwing roses in your path.
I never spoke to you, how could I?
My heart stopped and my lips moved, but did not
     speak,

But I stole a rose that had been beneath your foot
And I laughed my kisses on it in the night.
I never saw you again until the day I came here
Prisoner, wounded, held to ransom.
It was a light wound but I had a fever,
I was sleepless, tossing, hot at night:
Then you came among your maidens, walking slowly
As I had seen you walk at the Hereford wedding,
To the head of my bed, you bent so graciously
And kissed my lips. When I fainted . . .

SIWAN: Yes. I remember. You gave us all a fright . . .

GWILYM: It was not because of my wound.

SIWAN: How could I have known then?

GWILYM: Because, that kiss was Fate, like Iseult's kiss.

SIWAN: No, Gwilym. Don't speak of unhappy things.
That story recurs tonight like an evil dream.

GWILYM: There was nothing evil about the dream of my
    recovery
Riding at your side, Siwan, and drinking wine
    among the rocks of Snowdon
And the songs in the afternoon. The halls of
    Snowdonia
Seemed as bright as the hall of Toulouse in those
    happy days:
And in the night, dances and carousal;
And your kiss growing from the kiss of courtesy
Into prologue and promise of this night.

SIWAN: Do you remember,
    'I love her marshlands and her mountains
    Her forts near her woods, her comely domains,
    Her valleys, her meadowlands, and her fountains
    Her white seagulls, and gracious women.'

GWILYM: I remember. That was the night you first put the
    flame in your kiss.
    (*They sing it together.*)

SIWAN: Llywelyn came back next day, bringing your ransom.

GWILYM: The man has a positive gift for coming back.

SIWAN: And after that, only one careful week.

GWILYM: And that is why I came back. I have arranged
This marriage and alliance with the Prince

	Only to return and possess you, Siwan, tonight. You knew that.
SIWAN:	No. I did not know. I didn't dare to know. I could not believe you could give up your castle in Builth, And your daughter—such hostages—
GWILYM:	I would give all that I have for this night with you.
SIWAN:	Everything you have? Like Francis of Assisi? Love and sanctity are as wild and prodigal as each other And both despise this world.
GWILYM:	You follow the fashion of this new saint?
SIWAN:	He preached to wolves. That's a saint for you.
GWILYM:	I heard that Francis was a wild one when he was young, Gambling and taking chances: I like men Who put their lives to the throw and lose with a light heart. If Francis was like that, well, he's the saint for me.
SIWAN:	I shall pray to him for you, to keep you From mischance.
GWILYM:	But not from tonight. Luck is my guardian angel tonight; I'll turn to Francis when I lose my luck, when I lose you.
SIWAN:	You indulge in danger too much! I am a hard woman But your thoughtless daring makes even me afraid for you.
GWILYM:	I am to be taken, Siwan, as I am: my element Is the gamble of war and hunting. I'm a child of chance. That's the way to squeeze the grapes of life And feel the sweet taste in my mouth against the eager palate.

SIWAN (*teasing*):
    Am I one of those—those grapes?

GWILYM (*serious*):
    The taste of things is important to me.

My taste for you is a hot desire, an unslaked thirst
That sweetens as it burns.

SIWAN: Have you breathed a word of this at my brother's
court?

GWILYM: To whom should I speak?

SIWAN: Not to anyone that I
Suggested Easter for negotiating the marriage?

GWILYM (*slowly*):
Perhaps I did: I mentioned it to Hubert de Burgh,
the Chancellor,
When he inquired about the conditions.
Why should that matter?

SIWAN: Matter?
Only that Hubert de Burgh is loaded with more
poison than a snake,
And that my husband Llywelyn was in his company
The day before yesterday.
He will return with Hubert's poison between his ears.

GWILYM: Suppose Llywelyn suspects the worst, he's a politician.
He'd damp his anger until he recovered from me the
castle in Builth—
I know Llywelyn.

SIWAN: That is more than I would claim
And I've been married to him for twenty-five years.
A king can feel like any other man.

GWILYM: Well, leave him be. You give me this one night.
(*They move to the bed.*)

SIWAN: I give you this one night. I give you myself
Tonight in my husband's bed.

GWILYM: You know that I worship you.

SIWAN: A middle-aged matron?

GWILYM: A ruler and a princess from a royal line,
Age has not marked your forehead or your body.
Counting years can't affect my worshipping you.

SIWAN: No, not tonight, if only tonight were all time.
I give you myself for one night—Gwilym de Breos.

GWILYM: Tonight is enough tonight, and tonight for me is all
time.

(*They kiss.*)
Can you not love me, Siwan?

SIWAN: I cannot say, not yet. Tonight to yield is enough.
Tomorrow—who knows. Perhaps I shall love you
tomorrow
When this tonight has become memory and longing.

GWILYM: Tonight you yourself called me to you,
You put the sleeping draught in the watchmen's
wine.

SIWAN: I did it myself. Tonight is my gift to you.

GWILYM: And why, my benefactress, tell me why?

SIWAN: Because you remember the flavour of things,
Because the flavour fades so soon:
Because you laugh at danger
And dangerous living dies:
Because your joy is in my giving
And to give you your joy is sweet,
Because tonight is the first of May.
(*Voice of a Watchman on the walls in the distance.*)

WATCHMAN (*off*):
Two o'clock.
Two o'clock
And all's well.

GWILYM: Listen to the watchman, Siwan,
It is the first of May and all is well.

SIWAN: The first of May and all is well.

GWILYM: The bed waits for us.

SIWAN: Come to the window first,
And breathe in the tender air.
I give my five senses their freedom tonight to do as
they will.
Do you see the old moon waning
Over the woods of Anglesey
And Menai hidden and still;
I can't hear waves on the beach, it's a silent tide.
(*Far-off sound of horses' hooves.*)

GWILYM: Did you hear that in the distance—horses at the
gallop?

SIWAN: Wild ponies perhaps. They graze the lower hill.

GWILYM: Those horses are shod.

SIWAN: I don't hear them.

GWILYM: Nor do I now. Nothing. Strange, too,
           My ear is sensitive to the sound of hooves.

SIWAN: A cloud has crossed the moon. Look far to the right,
           There's the Plough and the North Star,
           And great Arcturus on the other side.
           I wish I could hear their music
           As they turn in their glass spheres.
           They say little children hear them as they sleep
           And the song makes them smile.

GWILYM: Isn't that Mars up there?
           I was born under Mars.

SIWAN: 'The star of blood makes war increase
           Mars' children know no peace.'

GWILYM: 'Nature's strength, the fright of folk,
           His enemies must know the yoke . . .'
           (*They laugh. Dog heard barking in distance.*)

SIWAN: What was that?

GWILYM: Hound baying at the gate. One of the watchdogs.

SIWAN: Gelert!

GWILYM: Which Gelert?

SIWAN: Llywelyn's hound. I know his cry.

GWILYM: But it can't be. He took the dog with him
           To hunt in the Royal Forest on his way home.
           There's a dog for you! I saw him jump in pursuit of
              a deer
           From crag to crag with more mettle than a stallion.

SIWAN: It is strange. I know Gelert's bark.

GWILYM: At night one is easily mistaken,
           Staring into the darkness conjures up ghosts!
           In remote France on a May night
           Witches fly through the air and their dogs bark!
           Why are there no witches in Wales? I never heard
           Here of a Welshwoman before the Bishops' court
           For making love with the devil.

SIWAN: In Wales men are more attractive—especially the
              sons of Mars.

GWILYM: Siwan, my Giver of Great Gifts, these candles are
                burning out
           And the royal bed is waiting:
           May I have my joy before the darkness falls?
           (*She moves towards him and stops.*)

SIWAN: Gwilym! Listen.

GWILYM: I hear nothing.

SIWAN: At the great gate. People are moving.
           The sound of an arrival.

GWILYM: Merely your fancy. There are sounds in every royal
                castle,
           Any hour of the night. Your ears are too acute
                tonight.

SIWAN: I wonder. I hope so. (*They embrace.*) Listen!
           There! Again!
           (*Sound of a heavy door opening and closing.*)

GWILYM: That was the castle gate opening and closing.
           The guard changing. Don't be disturbed.

SIWAN: Soldiers changing guard do not open the door.
           Something's afoot. I hear men running.
           Look there! Torches moving. The courtyard alive
                with shadows.

GWILYM: I wonder?
           (*Noise of brass weapons clashing and soldiers—with a few
           orders.*)

SIWAN: What's happening? Gwilym, what is it?

GWILYM (*concerned at last*):
           Armed men have surrounded our tower.
           You are right, Siwan, something is afoot.
           I'll take a candle and see if the doormen have moved.

SIWAN: Gwilym, have you a sword?

GWILYM: No, not even a knife. I'll not be a second
           Descending the steps to the tower door.
           (*Trumpet announces the Prince's approach.*)

SIWAN: He's here . . . Gwilym . . . Llywelyn is here.

GWILYM: And twenty men armed about the tower door—
           We are betrayed, Siwan. The trap has closed
           While we were studying the stars,
           And it was laid by a master hand.

SIWAN: Could you escape through the window between the
                  bars?

GWILYM: Too narrow! Where is the women's room?

SIWAN: Beneath, on the right side of the long gate.

GWILYM: And what's above?

SIWAN: The Tower platform. That door is locked.

GWILYM (*laughing softly*):
                  There's nothing to be done.
                  We must welcome
                  The Prince to his room
                  And judging by the noise he won't be long.
                  We must make our welcome simple, without fuss.

SIWAN: Come to my arms on the bed. I give you myself, my
                  beloved.
                  (*He joins her and closes the bed curtains. Door bursts open
                  and Llywelyn rushes in with armed escort.*)

LLYWELYN: Tear down that bed curtain. Here he is.
                  Hold him. Tie up his arms.

GWILYM: You need not, I am unarmed.

LLYWELYN: Tie him . . . put him on his feet . . .
                  Gwilym de Breos, I captured you once in battle.
                  As prisoner of war you got from me a courteous
                  welcome,
                  The freedom of my court, an alliance, and the
                  treatment of your wounds.
                  This is your repayment, turning the Princess of
                  Snowdon into a whore
                  And me a cuckold to be laughed at in the courts of
                  France.

GWILYM: The rhetoric of wounded pride, shouting whore and
                  cuckold.
                  I love a married lady, as hundreds of the lords of
                  Christendom do,
                  It's like a tournament, part of a knight's behaviour.
                  You caught me in your bed. Very well. I shall redeem
                  your insulted feelings
                  I'll pay for your wife's violation
                  And give my castle of Builth, and my daughter to
                  your son.

LLYWELYN *(laughing bitterly)*:
You'll pay for a mortal insult. You French lords are
a light-hearted pack!
Your freedom after honourable battle cost you
A third of your wealth, Gwilym de Breos.
But all your wealth could not atone for tonight;
I'll take your castle of Builth. I'll take your life.

GWILYM *(quietly)*:
That, my lord, is more than you dare. I think your
anger
Runs away with your reason. Every baron in
England
And France and the Marches would avenge me,
And ravage your land.

LLYWELYN: If the Pope himself
And all Christendom rise against me, I'll have your
life.

GWILYM: So that's how it is? Oh ho! Oh ho!
So it's not injured vanity or princely dignity.
Only jealous fury! My lady Siwan,
What other princess is there in all Europe
Whose husband . . .

LLYWELYN: Shut his mouth,men!
Gag him! Gag him!
(Smothered laughter from Gwilym.)

SIWAN: My lord, may I ask you a question?

LLYWELYN: You!

SIWAN: Yesterday you saw the king my brother before he
left for France.

LLYWELYN: Your brother the king? What about him?

SIWAN: Then you saw Hubert de Burgh? Was it from him
you heard of this?

LLYWELYN: What if it was? Does that make you less of a whore?

SIWAN: He holds Montgomery and Erging,
He holds the castles of Cardigan and Carmarthen.

LLYWELYN: This is no time to talk of Hubert de Burgh.

SIWAN: You know how sickly the Earl of Gloucester is.
If he dies, Glamorgan too falls into Hubert's hands.

LLYWELYN: And so, what? What are you trying to say?

SIWAN: Gwilym de Breos has no son. He alone stands between
Hubert de Burgh and Snowdonia, only he stands between
Hubert and David your son.

LLYWELYN: See how he stands? Look at your paramour!
He shan't stand long.

SIWAN: If you kill Gwilym his estates will crumble
And the way will be open for Hubert to attack North Wales,
Did you rush home to accommodate Hubert de Burgh?

LLYWELYN: Madame, you make your concern for my welfare
Very clear tonight.

SIWAN: One does not easily shed the discipline of twenty years.

LLYWELYN: You shed your virtue as you shed your clothes.
In a moment you'll be saying it was for my sake
You took this scoundrel to you in my bed.

SIWAN: I have done you wrong. I don't deny it. But I do not see
Giving you a pair of horns sufficient reason for drawing
all your teeth.

LLYWELYN: Adultery isn't enough for you. You've also lost all shame.

SIWAN: I am a Frenchwoman and the daughter of a king,
I find your intense Welsh morality distasteful.
Go and preach to your concubine in Dolwyddelen.

LLYWELYN: You are both French? Is that the implication?

SIWAN: I am defending your life's work against a moment's madness.
Gwilym's life is necessary for your kingdom.

LLYWELYN: You cherish the life of Gwilym de Breos?

SIWAN: Well? If I do?

LLYWELYN: If you do, he dies.

SIWAN: And your kingdom, and the inheritance of David
your son?

LLYWELYN: To the devil with you and the kingdom.
I have lost my wife,
You shall lose your lover . . .
(*To the soldiers.*)
Away with him! Keep him close.

SIWAN: You dare not kill him. The king my brother will
come
Back from France.

LLYWELYN: He shall hang like a common thief.

SIWAN: Gwilym!

LLYWELYN: He shall hang.
(*She runs to Gwilym, but Llywelyn strikes her down.*)
I never thought that I should live to strike you.
Take him away.
Take her and lock her in the tower.

CURTAIN

ACT II

Time: 6 a.m., 3rd May 1230

*A bare room in the castle tower. Sound of scaffold being erected—hammering,
sawing of wood, etc. Noise kept in background for first half of act. Door
opened and closed.*

ALIS (*approaching*):
Madame, are you awake?

SIWAN: I have not slept.

ALIS: Not at all? Not for two nights, madame?

SIWAN: I am not used to being shackled to my bed.
The irons are heavy Alis, Welsh style in bracelets.
Feel the weight, feel the weight of a prince's anger.
(*She drags the chain along the floor.*)

ALIS: Of his disappointment, madame;
His disappointment much more than his displeasure.
Does it hurt very much?

SIWAN: It hurts my pride so much, I don't feel
The pain in my leg.
I have sent men to prison:
I never imagined the shame of feet in chains.

ALIS: The prince has said the chain shall be kept on only
                for today.

SIWAN: Why today and not after today?
                Can today change my condition?

ALIS (*to avoid giving a direct answer*):
                Let me ease your condition madame.
                I have some wine here.

SIWAN: Did he send you here?

ALIS: To serve you and do your bidding.
                I can come and go: bring you things; the porter
                    knows.

SIWAN: The porter is a mute. All day yesterday I saw no one
                But that dumb man at the door.

ALIS: A dumb porter can't spread gossip.

SIWAN: Or carry messages from the prison.
                That's why he was chosen.
                Well, why should I have a maid-in-waiting now to
                    carry messages?
                My condition must change?

ALIS: Will you take some wine?
                (*Wine being poured.*)

SIWAN: This wine is sour: it suits my thirst . . .
                The third of May, is it?

ALIS: Yes, the third, my lady.

SIWAN: Two days and two nights in the cell's silence;
                So long ago it was the first of May.
                Alis, did you ever sleep alone in a chamber?

ALIS: Oh no, madame. I'm not a princess.
                I have slept in my place among the other women, on
                    the floor.

SIWAN: The solitude of a prison is different, and somehow
                    amazing,
                A hermit's world, where the tongue has no function.

ALIS: You were never very talkative, madame.

SIWAN: I know. Having nothing to say
                In the midst of revelling has often been a burden to
                    me.
                But here it is not my own silence I have to bear—

Here it is the dumb walls, the dumb man at the
　　door, the uncertainty
That build the silence.
In daylight, yesterday, I heard nothing here
But my own heart beating hour by hour.
What hour of the morning is it now, Alis?

ALIS:　　The sixth hour, madame.

SIWAN:　　Add those twenty-four, and another twenty-four,
I have been here almost sixty hours.
Once I heard a learned teacher, an Augustinian, say
That in eternity time does not exist. I hope he's
　　right;
Staring out the glare in the eye of time is the start
　　of madness.
In time there is time for everything—so there is no
　　security,
Time is always a threat, like that hammering that
　　began before dawn.

ALIS:　　You have not slept, madame, not for three days.
Or touched the food sent to you.
No wonder you are nervous and distraught.

SIWAN:　　Why were you sent to me?

ALIS:　　To serve you and be at your command.

SIWAN:　　The Prince himself sent you?

ALIS:　　Yes, my lady, the Prince himself.
Otherwise the guard would not have let me pass.

SIWAN:　　I suspect it. He said you could come and go for me
And do my bidding. Can you carry messages
from one prison to another?

ALIS:　　I couldn't say, my lady. He didn't mention that.

SIWAN:　　I have no other message. (*Pause.*)
What is that endless hammering on the lawn?

ALIS:　　Something the soldiers are doing. Some exercise
　　I expect.

SIWAN:　　Didn't you see what it was on your way here?

ALIS:　　I didn't notice. I was told to hurry;
Is the wine warming, madame?

SIWAN:　　Go to the window and look: this chain ties me to the
　　wall

Like a bear to a post. You are not a bitch to bait me,
    girl.
What are they putting up? Stand by the window
    and tell me.

ALIS: They are soldiers, madame.

SIWAN: Soldiers—I know they are soldiers. You've said so
    already.
I never saw soldiers before doing carpentry on the
    castle lawn.
Snowdonia can't go to war because of this: it's no
Preparation for war. Tell me,
What are they building?

ALIS: It's not possible to see between these narrow bars.

SIWAN: Don't lie, girl. I know how much you can see.
I've stared through that window myself before today.
What are they doing? Answer me, girl.

ALIS: O please, my lady, don't ask me that again.
On my knees I beg you, allow me to go from here.

SIWAN: My poor child, what is it? Don't tremble and cry;
Tell me quietly what are they making on the lawn?

ALIS: A gibbet, madame, a gallows.

SIWAN: A gallows?
(*She laughs incredulously.*)
Good for you, Llywelyn. So that's my punishment?
My little Alis, don't cry about that.

ALIS: Not for you, madame, not for you.

SIWAN: What?

ALIS: A gallows for Gwilym de Breos.
(*Siwan falls to the ground in a faint. Chains dragged as she
falls.*)
Gaoler! Gaoler!
(*Alis runs to door and bangs it wildly.*)
Hurry! Open the door! Hurry! Hurry!
(*Door opens and the mute gaoler comes.*)
The Princess has fainted. Help me to lift her.
You take her feet . . . Now . . .
(*They place her on the bed.*)
Some water now. Please hurry . . .
A cup of water, water, do you understand?

(*Exit gaoler.*)
The sweat on her brow! I must use this sheet . . .
(*Gaoler returns.*)
Here's the water . . .
Soak this rag, put it on her brow . . .
That's it. She's recovering . . . madame, madame . . .
Open your lips and try some of this wine . . .
There, now, there. She is coming to herself.
Her eyeballs are still now . . .
You frightened us, my lady.
Leave us, gaoler,
Leave us. She wants you to leave.
(*Gaoler leaves, door closed and locked.*)
He has gone now, my lady. There's no one now
but me.

SIWAN: I'm all right . . . did I faint here on the bed.

ALIS: No. On the floor.
The gaoler and I lifted you on to the bed.

SIWAN: I am ashamed.

ALIS: You have not slept or eaten for three days and the
shock—

SIWAN: How long was I senseless?

ALIS: A few seconds, my lady. Why?

SIWAN: The hammering has stopped.
Nothing has happened yet?

ALIS: No—nothing at all, madame.
This moment, while you were recovering,
The hammering stopped.

SIWAN: That is as well. I would not wish to escape it
Quite so easily. Have the workmen finished?
Go and look.
(*Alis goes to the window.*)

ALIS: They are collecting their tools and sitting on the
lawn.

SIWAN: After the job is done, they say, there's always the
waiting.
How was he condemned? By the judge's court?
Or by
The Prince himself?

ALIS: By mid-day yesterday it was all over.
All morning the court hummed like the mouth of a
   hive
With rumours, stories, whispers; nothing was certain;
And the court servants pale and trembling at every
   summons,
You could see only the whites of their eyes.
Bishop Cadwgan had been with his Highness early,
And we heard that he said he suspected
That the young Earl had been spirited into your
   room
By witchcraft.

SIWAN: The good old Bishop.
Soothing the Prince's anger somewhat
Was his intention.

ALIS: And to comfort him perhaps.

SIWAN: And might it not have been witchcraft?
There is a supernatural impact in such upheavals:
It is well for men that love is rare in this world.

ALIS: Your head is bleeding where you struck the wall.

SIWAN: The bleeding will calm my fever. What happened
   next?

ALIS: Then the Council was called.

SIWAN: Was my son there?

ALIS: No, he was sent to Cardigan the day before.

SIWAN: That was well done. And what did they say?

ALIS: Well, some report
That Ednyfed Fychan pleaded for his life
For fear of the insult it would mean to the King of
   England
And all the Marcher Lords.
When that failed, he argued for a beheading,
The execution due to a man of his birth. The Prince
   wouldn't listen.
He wanted the death of a thief, a daylight public
   hanging:
To argue with him was reasoning with thunder.
When he left the Council, Ednyfed Fychan himself
Was as white as one who had just escaped being
   struck by lightning.

SIWAN: When was the verdict announced?

ALIS: Yesterday in the afternoon, madame. And the
           hanging
           Takes place this morning before the hour of Mass.
           It was announced from Bangor church door yesterday
           Before the market in the churchyard closed.
           The crowd has been waiting two hours at the castle
           gate.

SIWAN: And he knows?

ALIS: Yes.

SIWAN: When was he told?

ALIS: Bishop Cadwgan was with him last night for an hour
           And he's with him now.

SIWAN: Have you heard how he is? Is there some news?

ALIS: No one is allowed near his prison or the men who
           serve him.
           The knights who accompanied him here are under
           lock and key
           Till today. But last night, madame, when the bishop
           had left him,
           I walked secretly beside the tower. I heard him sing.

SIWAN: What did he sing, Alis?

ALIS: Marie de France:
           Le roi Marc etait corrocié
           Vers Tristram, son neveu . . .

SIWAN: Have you ever seen a hanging?

ALIS: Why yes, my lady, several.
           Outlaws and thieves. Haven't you?

SIWAN: No, never. Strange as it may seem.

ALIS: A thief's hanging draws a bigger crowd
           Than a clown at a fair, and if the man's afraid
           There's fine fun pushing him up the ladder
           And putting the rope on his neck,
           And tying the hood on his face. Then there's quiet
           And a few 'Hail Marys' if it happens the priest
           Hears his confession and signs him with a blessing;
           Then the shouting breaks out again, a celebration.
           I saw a pirate once joking on the ladder

And drinking the health of the crowd, and when
    hanged
Still dancing with his feet.

SIWAN: Do they take long to die?

ALIS: They vary, my lady. It depends how the ladder is
    thrown
And how the knot is tied.

SIWAN: Who throws the ladder?

ALIS: The soldiers or the executioners below,
I heard it said once that if the knot was well tied
A man could leap off and kill himself in a second.
I never saw that myself. But a girl I knew told me
She saw it, and that the jump thrusts the tongue out
    past the nose,
And before the leap is finished and the feet still
The backbone breaks in two. But the thieves prefer
The knot to tighten slowly, so that they gain a little
    time
Before the face is squeezed black.

SIWAN: Holy Mary, let him leap like Gelert,
Let him leap!
(*Trumpets and drums.*)
Go to the window Alis. Tell me what happens.

ALIS: O madame. He is your lover.
I never dreamt to see the hanging of a great lord
Come to give his daughter in marriage to Prince
    David.
And he's so young, splashing laughter about him;
He used to tickle my chin sometimes and steal a kiss.
The court of Snowdonia after today will never be the
    same.
(*Wild crowd shouting away. Drums.*)

SIWAN: Get to the window, girl, or I'll break these chains!

ALIS: You'll never bear it, madame.

SIWAN: I won't repeat my weakness,
I shan't faint again, or scream, or even weep,
The whole thing will be over in a matter of minutes.
I'll go through it second by second, with him.
I'll kneel on the bed here by the crucifix.
You stand where you see best.

ALIS: The soldiers are in the square now around the
          gallows
       And the crowd swarms about them.
       (*Crowd shouting*: '*To the gallows! De Breos to the gallows!*')
       They look like the damned, the devils in the picture
       In Bangor church, on the Day of Judgement. More
          loathsome.
       Isn't the human face a filthy thing?
       Looking like that how can we be bound for anywhere
          but Hell?
       The canons of Bangor and the choir are leaving the
          Hall
       Chanting their litanies as they march.
       (*Choir chanting in distance. 'Sancte Francisce ora pro eo.'*)

SIWAN: Saint Francis, pray for his hands to be free
       So that he may leap.
       Saint Francis, brother to the wolf, pray for my wolf.
       (*Crowd and choir alternatively*: '*Omnes sancti, orate pro eo;*'
       '*The gallows! The gallows!*')

ALIS: The crowd sways forward.
       And the soldiers can barely hold them.
       They are beating them back with staves.
       (*Choir and crowd*: '*Devil take him!*'; '*Parce ei, domine!*')
       The court officials. Ednyfed Fychan leads them.

SIWAN: And is *he* there?

ALIS: The Prince? There is no throne prepared so he
          cannot be coming.
       No, he's not with them. He can see all that goes on
          from his room.
       Ednyfed organizes the ranks, yes, Ednyfed Fychan
          presides.
       The mob is quieter under his stern eye . . .
       (*Drums and trumpets again.*)
       Here are the Prince's bodyguard. The prisoner must
          appear now.
       They are making a path from the court to the
          gallows
       For the condemned, each man with his shield and
          lance
       A yard apart, and the path two yards wide . . .

SIWAN: Mary, Mother of sinners, I don't dare to pray.
Make this bargain
For a sinner: I'll spend my life in prison
If you let him leap.

ALIS: Here come the six French knights that came with
Gwilym de Breos.
They walk two by two in black without arms or
armour.
They will bear his body back to Brecon for burial.
(*Crowd shouting. Drums and trumpets flourish.*)
Now. Now here is the Bishop of Bangor with his open
prayer book,
And just after him, here he is, Gwilym de Breos,
Bare foot, and the rope about his neck.
The Steward carries the rope's end in his hand.
His arms are free and his hands!

SIWAN: His arms and hands free! He can jump!
He can make his leap!

ALIS: They are passing beneath us now.

SIWAN: How does he look?

ALIS: To see him you'd think the Steward was going to be
hanged
And proud Gwilym leading him by the rope
to the gallows.
(*Crowd shouting louder: 'The gallows! De Breos to the
gallows!'*)
Now they are on the lawn. The last minutes are at
hand.
(*Drums muffled.*)

SIWAN: Saints of God who dare to pray, pray for him now.

ALIS: He's shaking hands with Ednyfed Fychan and the
Council
One by one like a great lord bidding them welcome
to his table,
A word for each, and each one laughs . . .
Now he's on his knees before the Bishop who makes
The Sign of the Cross over his head.
The mob are dumb with astonishment, and the
Council
Stand like images in stone. Only Gwilym moves.

He tests the ladder, now he feels the rope,
Adjusts it about his own neck, he bows,
He bids farewell, he climbs like a ship's captain
To the top of the ladder, he straightens . . .

SIWAN (*rapidly*):
Pray for him now and in the hour of his death,
Mother of God, pray for him now in the hour of his
death.

ALIS: The executioners don't move to knock away his
ladder.

GWILYM (*his cry is heard distant and clear*):
Siwan!
(*A second's silence then Alis screams.*)

SIWAN (*quietly*):
Is that the end?

ALIS: But the leap he made, the leap!
The rope stretched out like a fishing rod
And the ladder fell among the officials of the court.
Now the body hangs like a log wound up on a crane.
(*The crowd groan. Then bugles.*)
The crowd moves out. For them
The show is over, a shock of disappointment. What
do they know or care
About a widow in Brecon, or of a woman here
Imprisoned in agony. Pain is a leprosy,
A disease apart, a dark lair in the heart of daylight:
No one ever felt sympathy with pain.
Go, all of you, go dance to the fiddle and harp. The
musicians
Are already waiting on the green, their songs wait
On their lips . . .
Madame, is someone coming? I hear soldiers coming.
(*Door opens. Soldiers enter and Llywelyn.*)

LLYWELYN: Strike off those fetters,
The danger is over now.
(*The soldiers remove the chains.*)
Leave us!
(*Soldiers leave. Door closes.*)
It's all over now . . .
So! I wouldn't dare, wasn't it that you said?
I wouldn't dare!

SIWAN: From the pit of hell in my heart, Llywelyn, my curse on you.

CURTAIN

ACT III

(*1st May*, 1231. *Llywelyn's chamber.*)
(*Knock on door.*)

LLYWELYN: Come in.
(*Enter Alis.*)

ALIS: Your Highness. My mistress is almost ready.

LLYWELYN: I sent my son to escort her. Is he with her?

ALIS: He is with her now. She will be here presently.
She sent me to tell you so.
She has not seen him since his wedding-day.

LLYWELYN: She has not seen him for a year—I know that, girl.
Is your mistress well?

ALIS: As well as she can be, my lord, after a year in prison.

LLYWELYN: Seclusion, not imprisonment. She had everything
except her freedom.
Two ladies-in-waiting and a garden in which to walk.

ALIS: Oh yes, sir, she had everything except her freedom.

LLYWELYN: What do you mean, girl? Speak your mind.

ALIS: Your command, sire?

LLYWELYN: My command.

ALIS: Prince David was married. His mother was not at the
wedding,
And she did not lead the dance at the wedding feast.
She was "secluded" among her "memories".

LLYWELYN: My son was married to Gwilym de Breos' daughter
according to plan;
It would have been hard for his mother to dance in
the widow's house.

ALIS: A marriage dance is a ceremonial.

LLYWELYN: For a royal house, life is a ceremony.

ALIS: She has changed, my lord.

LLYWELYN: Everyone changes. Even memories change.
Anger and vengeance change.
How has your mistress changed? What changes have
you noticed?

ALIS: She hasn't beaten me for one whole year!

LLYWELYN: Have you deserved a beating?

ALIS (*laughing*):
I wouldn't know, my lord.
Beating maids is a matter of custom, a ritual rather
than a punishment!

LLYWELYN: And she has given the custom up?

ALIS: My lord, she was so young in spirit before her
imprisonment,
Always so lively.

LLYWELYN: That's not what you mean. Speak your mind, girl.

ALIS: My lord, I have said as much as I dare say.

LLYWELYN: She withered with Gwilym's hanging.
Her liveliness was choked with Gwilym in the noose.
That's what you are thinking.

ALIS: That's my sorrow, sir. You asked me to speak.

LLYWELYN: I must ask someone,
A year without a beating makes you bolder.

ALIS: I'm not a serf's daughter, my lord. My father was a
gentle, a free man.

LLYWELYN: You are married, are you not?

ALIS: I have been a widow, my lord, these three years past.

LLYWELYN: Forgive me. He was one of my troop.
He was killed near Castle Baldwyn: a brave boy.

ALIS: I saw him once before I was given to him for wife:
Then, after a fortnight together, the war came.
He left me, and I never saw him again.
Today it all seems like a young girl's dream.

LLYWELYN: A dream—not a nightmare.
He was killed in an attack on the castle walls.
How did you part?

ALIS: In the early morning.
I gave him a cup of warm milk straight from the
goat's udder,

And he gave me a wet kiss, and the soldiers laughed.
A fortnight. That's all it lasted. Just getting to know
    each other.

LLYWELYN: Every husband and wife are just getting to know each
    other,
Be it two weeks or twenty years.
You are not without courage.

ALIS: Me, my lord?

LLYWELYN: You did not give up living.

ALIS: Had I any choice?

LLYWELYN: Giving up living at one time or another
Is a temptation that assails everyone intelligent and
    brave.
Life is a frightening gift.

ALIS: Even for a Prince?

LLYWELYN: A prince is a man, like any other.

ALIS: Would you say that, sire, to my lady?

LLYWELYN: Does she doubt it?

ALIS: It would help her to hear it.
To govern and make war, affairs of state,
Lap a great Prince in lonely majesty.
But to us women, royal or of low estate,
The urge to mother is the root of love, and a
    woman's first child
Is the husband given her when still a girl;
When she loses the child in him, sir, she herself is
    lost.

LLYWELYN: To be weak is to be human; is that what you mean?

ALIS: Gwilym de Breos was a child, my lord, a little child.

LLYWELYN: And little children inherit the kingdom of love:
You make your point, Alis: I'll try to digest it.

ALIS: Your Highness, I'm only my lady's maid: you made
    me speak,
I was trained in these royal chambers.
I respect and cherish my master and mistress.
This widowed year had left us all bereaved, the
    household and the house.
Excommunication was child's play compared with
    this distress.

LLYWELYN: The Pope's Interdict will soon fall upon us all again—
If that should matter.

ALIS: So the rumour is true?

LLYWELYN: Are there whisperings? What rumours?

ALIS: That once again you are going to war against the
King of England.

LLYWELYN: That shall be settled today, and by your mistress;
She shall decide, war or the end of Snowdonia.
To that end I have called her now from her year of
prison,
The fate of Wales is in her hands.

ALIS: Here comes the Princess, sir.
(*Siwan stands at the door.*)

LLYWELYN: Be at hand in the ante-room.
I shall need you again, I hope, before long.

SIWAN: You sent for me, my lord. Here I am.

LLYWELYN: Siwan!

SIWAN: My lord!

LLYWELYN: Siwan! (*Pause.*)
Siwan . . . I . . . Llywelyn . . . am here . . . Siwan?

SIWAN: Llywelyn?

LLYWELYN: I need you, Siwan . . . I, Llywelyn (*pause*)
I need you, Siwan.

SIWAN: *You* need *me*?
How can that be?

LLYWELYN: Why should it not be?

SIWAN: I have been a prisoner, my lord, for months.

LLYWELYN: A year to this morning. I, too, have counted the
days.

SIWAN: It is May day today? I had lost count.

LLYWELYN: It is the first of May.

SIWAN: Is it necessary to be so indelicate, even to a prisoner?

LLYWELYN: What indelicacy? Explain yourself.

SIWAN: Today of all days, here, to bring me to this room,
Straight from my prison? Why? Why?

LLYWELYN: To continue our conversation of a year ago.

SIWAN (*quietly, self-possessed, with iron control over herself*):

No. No. No. Never again. I can't talk of Gwilym.
Out of your mercy, Prince, order me back to my
  prison.

LLYWELYN: I need you, Siwan. This is an appeal, not an order.
And it is not to torture you I chose this morning to
  make it.
Last night a messenger arrived from the South,
And that is why I called you. Peace to Gwilym's
  soul . . .
Hubert de Burgh is the burden of my unease.
Here, that night, like Cassandra, you prophesied
  about him.
All your words have come true.
I must go to war again, against your brother.

SIWAN: Go to war again? Is that the Council's decision?

LLYWELYN: The Council has not yet met. I ask your counsel
  first. Then I'll call the rest.

SIWAN: And why my help?

LLYWELYN: I have a right to your help.
Neither adultery nor imprisonment can stop that
  right.

SIWAN: Yes. You have a right. I gave you that right.
I gave it, so I cannot refuse it.
But why do you insist upon it today?

LLYWELYN: For my Country's sake, for Snowdonia's crown.
I demand your help and advice in accordance with
  your oath.

SIWAN: So. Not an appeal, but an order, a demand?

LLYWELYN: Very well, if you say so. Let the appeal come next.

SIWAN: Why should you go to war at your age?
In two years you'll be sixty.

LLYWELYN: The messenger last night brought news of the death of
  William Marshall.

SIWAN: God rest his soul. I have been a year without news,
  my lord.
You must forgive my sluggish apprehension. Why,
  may I ask,
Is William Marshall's death a cause for war!

LLYWELYN: Last year Gwilym de Breos's lands were put in his care.

SIWAN: He was Gwilym's brother-in-law . . .
And now?

LLYWELYN: Now those lands have been given to Hubert de Burgh.

SIWAN: Nothing succeeds like success. One of your friends, my lord,
This time last year you did your best for him.

LLYWELYN: Have you heard of the Earl of Gloucester's death?

SIWAN: Gilbert? God speed his soul to heaven. No, I had not heard.

LLYWELYN: He died in Brittany.

SIWAN: The heir is a small child.

LLYWELYN: Yes, the heir is a child,
And he has been put in the charge of Hubert de Burgh.

SIWAN (*laughing*):
Of course, of course. And what of the child's lands?
What of Glamorgan?

LLYWELYN: Hubert de Burgh will hold Glamorgan.

SIWAN: Your old friend waxes uncommonly fat.

LLYWELYN: It has all happened, Siwan, as you said.

SIWAN: That won't undo the knot or bring the dead back.
That night saving a life was my motive,
And your temper was not quite statesmanlike—
Peace to Gwilym's soul. Hubert de Burgh is a fox.

LLYWELYN: His possessions stretch now from Hereford to Cardigan
Uniting Pembroke and Gower, Brecon and Glamorgan.
De Breos and Marshall and Gilbert of Gloucester have become one
In Hubert de Burgh.

SIWAN: Chief Minister of the Crown in England too,
And all the king's might there and in France
Under his thumb.
Would it be wise for you to venture to war?

LLYWELYN (*gives a short laugh*):
Madness, I know. But how can I avoid it?
Consider the lands between the Tywi and Teifi,
I cannot keep the allegiance of the Lords of the
South,
The great Rhys's grandsons,
Without proving my strength to protect or punish
them.

SIWAN: Is Rhys of Dinefwr still alive?

LLYWELYN: Alive and as wild as ever, but faithful up to now.
And only war can keep him so—
Hubert is along his either flank now
Like a wolf stretching his jaws to swallow
Ystrad Tywi.

SIWAN: If Ystrad Tywi is surrounded, Cardigan all goes too.
Hubert's South would be a bigger kingdom than
North Wales;
Two Principalities in Wales are impossible.

LLYWELYN: That hits the nail on the head.

SIWAN: Where is my brother now?

LLYWELYN: The King is in England.
I must attack, even though I know
The strength of the Crown of England and the
Marches
And the power of Hubert de Burgh are all with one
accord against me.

SIWAN: In one accord?
In that case we do not go to war.
Since the day David our son was born, it has been
laid down like a law,
We don't make war or risk making war
When there's peace between the English Crown and
the Marches.

LLYWELYN: True. But never before have Glamorgan and the
Welsh South been one kingdom.
War is inevitable.

SIWAN: So it is,
War *is* inevitable. But we must go to war
In such a way that to win is also inevitable.
David's inheritance is in the balance.

LLYWELYN: Your work and mine are in the balance.
           The burden we have shouldered from the beginning,
           The line of Cunedda, the crown of Snowdonia,
               Wales.

SIWAN: You should have considered that a year ago.

LLYWELYN: A year ago I *did* consider it.

SIWAN: What do you mean?

LLYWELYN: Here, in this room, you foretold the consequence
           Of killing Gwilym de Breos. In the Council afterwards
           I repeated your words. I kept nothing back.
           They were considered and weighed. Ednyfed Fychan
               believed them;
           So did the Bishop; and so did I.
           Knowing the terrible risk to my crown and kingdom,
           The crown of Aberffraw and Gwynedd,
           I sent Gwilym de Breos to his death.

SIWAN: May I ask why?

LLYWELYN: It is well you should know. And it's time that I should
               speak.
           But policy, first, my lady: the old exercise.

SIWAN: Very well . . . What is afoot in England and in the
               Marches,
           Some hope of division? The trace of a crack?

LLYWELYN: There's our best hope. The earls and bishops
           Who went on the crusade are on their way back.

SIWAN: Peter, Bishop of Winchester, is he coming back?

LLYWELYN: He has reached France. He will be in England before
               the summer ends.

SIWAN: Hubert de Burgh's bitterest foe. The Court and the
               Marches
           Will be at odds, at each other's throats.
           Can you put off the war until Peter comes?

LLYWELYN: More's the pity, no. Not that and keep Rhys's
               allegiance.
           If he and his nephews in the South see me hesitate,
           They'll scuttle to Hubert like so many rats.
           I must start to attack before this month ends.

SIWAN: Can you wait until June, the beginning of June?

LLYWELYN: That would do in Powys. What about the South . . . ?

SIWAN (*carefully*):

> Give Rhys licence now to ravage the Breos lands
> And promise him that you'll be with him soon.
> At the same time send envoys to the King
> To put your case before him,
> Affecting peaceful complaints to delay his moving
>   for a month.
> Then the Crusaders will come and they'll see fat
>   Hubert in Hereford:
> You will strike suddenly against Montgomery and
>   burn your way to Monmouth;
> The Marcher Lords will be baying for Hubert's
>   blood;
> With luck you should finish the summer in Cardigan
>   Castle,
> And Hubert's kingdom smashed, a thing of the past.
> (*Pause.*)

LLYWELYN: Your counsel is shrewd and grave,

> It is the tradition; it's the right strategy, the well
>   tried way.
> To win back Cardigan Castle would round off my
>   work like a rich amen.
> I shall take your advice, good lady—on one
>   condition.

SIWAN: Does the condition concern me?

LLYWELYN: I shall take it if you return, today, to my table and
> bed . . .

SIWAN (*brief silence*):

> Does this mean—forgiveness?

LLYWELYN: Will you take forgiveness from me?

SIWAN: To forgive is to overcome. I have not forgiven you.

LLYWELYN: For killing Gwilym de Breos?

SIWAN: I knew that Gwilym de Breos's life would be short,

> And to kill him was perhaps human; I could forgive
>   that.
> But because he loved me
> And because I yielded to his love,
> You doled him the death of a scoundrel and a thief,
> And let loose the rabble of Arfon over these lawns to
>   jeer at him.

You hanged him to show your contempt
And to spit on our love before the whole world.

LLYWELYN: He died well. (*Pause.*) His death was worthy of your
love.

SIWAN: He put your Council to shame,
And shut the mouths of your serfs:
He did it. No thanks to you for that.

LLYWELYN: Has it ever crossed your mind, Siwan,
That I too could be in love with you, like Gwilym
de Breos
In the same way?

SIWAN: You love me? What do you mean?

LLYWELYN: Is the abyss between us so wide?

SIWAN: My lord, I was given to you in marriage
When I was ten years old, and you a prince
And already over thirty.
Four years later I came like a frightened rabbit into
your bed,
And I've been your wife and bedfellow for twenty
years;
I gave you an heir, I gave you daughters,
I presided at your table, I was your ambassador
To plead on your behalf and protect you before my
father
And reconcile my brother to you;
I wore myself out, engaged in the pursuit of bishops
And cares of men of state, travelling in your service;
I built with you this kingdom.
Once, before I grew too old, a youth came,
And the music of his harp revived my tired heart.
You hanged him like a herring on a string.

LLYWELYN: That is true. Today I am sorry for it.
He had to die. He should not have been hanged.

SIWAN: Why then? Why? I could never live with you
And lie in the same bed without knowing why?

LLYWELYN: You cannot understand why, because I don't exist
for you.

SIWAN: You exist as a nightmare exists ever since that
morning.

LLYWELYN: I know that. Your Gwilym was nearer to me,
He saw me as a person,
I had to gag him before he revealed me and my
   secret to your face.

SIWAN: Will you tell me what Gwilym saw?
In the name of twenty years' cohabitation I believe
   I have a right to know.

LLYWELYN: Expose myself to your laughter?

SIWAN: The solitude of one year in prison impairs the power
   to laugh—

LLYWELYN: Our marriage was statecraft,
Between us lay a gap of twenty years.
Well, that is the custom; it founds alliances
And makes possible true concord between nations.
But four years later when you came to me
A virgin, as slim and graceful as a young silver birch,
My heart bounded as if I had suddenly seen the Grail,
And where you walked there was brightness.
But I was afraid of hurting you with my unbounded
   delight,
And when I held you, here, shaking in my arms,
I never bruised you with clumsy kisses,
Nor stained you with the sweat of barbarous
   embraces.
I restrained myself with all my will so as not to be
   loathsome to you:
I was patient, courteous and formal.
And your trembling ceased: this hall became your
   home,
And I a not altogether distasteful part of the
   furniture.
So I worshipped you, mutely, and from a distance,
Unwilling to intrude upon a remote image
That burned beyond my reach.
But I brought you into my public life.
I ordered my house, my family, my kingdom after
   your fashion,
Giving your intellect the freedom of high office.
I remember the afternoon you returned from your
   father:
Your first embassy; my life had been at stake.

You were a girl and yet already a mother.
You brought home my life and my son
And his inheritance. That night
It was you embraced me. I had no words
That could express my delight. I was unmanned
By a joy I had to master, and I mastered it.
But after that night I scattered my enemies.
I gathered Cardigan and Powys and the South
And plaited them about your David's crown,
All for him, primogeniture,
In the face of Welsh custom and the opposition
Of my own house. I fought for his recognition
By the Pope; by the English king.
And the Pope proclaimed the immaculate royalty of
  his descent.
All this, I, the architect of it all,
Planned as your temple and you in the centre
The very shrine . . .

SIWAN: Llywelyn, I didn't know. I never knew.

LLYWELYN: What good would your knowing do? The years
                were mountains between us,
                I understood that, too.
                I am a statesman, I deal in the possible,
                Your integrity was enough for me.

SIWAN: In twenty years of living together you never told me
                this before.

LLYWELYN: In twenty years of living together you never saw it
                before.

SIWAN: Was it jealousy, then, that made you hang him?

LLYWELYN: There may have been jealousy in his killing:
                The hanging was because of you.

SIWAN: Me? Me?

LLYWELYN: During that nightmare journey
                Galloping night and day through Powys
                And the land beyond Conwy, I knew in all the
                  bitterness of disillusion,
                That Hubert spoke the truth, and that I should
                  catch
                The fellow here,
                In your arms, unarmed.

> The journey was long enough to smother the desire
> To plant my dagger in his heart; he should die as a baron
> And under proper sentence.
> So he would have died, but for you.

SIWAN: In God's name, why?

LLYWELYN: You judged in your contempt of me,
That policy alone possessed my soul,
That I would sell my bed for another castle,
And defile my wife to seal a new alliance.
I answered contempt with contempt,
I hanged him to make your warnings come true,
And to show a wife who ignored me
There was one thing for which I would throw away
Even the crown of Snowdonia and imperial Roman Wales.

SIWAN: Out of reckless contempt you brought this war on yourself,
An ageing man. Government is not a gamble.

LLYWELYN: Your contempt for me that night
Tumbled a structure that had taken fifty years
To build.

SIWAN: By the Holy Cross, Llywelyn,
Contempt was no part of my intention.

LLYWELYN: The unintended word unlocks the heart.

SIWAN: There is no key to the human heart,
On this earth there are none who understand each other
Or see each other as they really are;
The man who embraces his wife and the wife
Who returns his kiss are two planets fixed in their separate courses;
Near or far they never even hear each other.

LLYWELYN: And that is marriage—
An unconditional surrender
To an unknown power,
An alliance that takes from both
Without giving to either.
The child and the adult are in the same trap:
Living is always a gamble.

SIWAN: This war, this is your choice, not a gamble.

LLYWELYN: It depends on you—not me.
                Will you return to my bed and table?

SIWAN: What has that to do with your war?

LLYWELYN: War can't be avoided. One could choose to return.

SIWAN: I am a prisoner. Your verdict set me apart.
                Why don't you order me to return?

LLYWELYN: You must come back to me of your own free will.

SIWAN: And if I refuse?

LLEWELYN: Well enough. I go to war.

SIWAN: Without returning? (*Pause.*) The threat is unfair.

LLYWELYN: A queen and a king's daughter?
                Decisions, judgements of life and death,
                Have always been part of daily life to you—
                A sentence to death . . .

SIWAN: I can't come to your bed without having your
                    forgiveness.

LLYWELYN: You know that is to be had.

SIWAN: No, it's not to be had. I won't ask or endure
                Forgiveness from a self-righteous hypocrite . . .
                You see yourself in some inflating mirror,
                Llywelyn the Great, greater than ever, forgiving that
                    weaker vessel,
                His wife, before going out to meet the danger
                That her rash sin aroused.
                I have listened to you and learned that *I* defiled
                    your bed,
                That *I* also hanged my lover, and gave Hubert de
                    Burgh the South.
                I endangered David's inheritance with this war,
                I smashed the image before which the lamp of your
                    life burned,
                You, most hallowed martyr of married love!
                And now before going forth to battle, you receive me
                    back to your bed,
                And with your gracious pardon reduce me to weeping
                    in sack-cloth and ashes,
                While you, your armour flashing in the sunlight,
                Ride off in glory to your beautiful death.

Having borne your body home, Llywelyn, I'll hire
  a painter from France,
To fresco the chapel wall above your shrine
With the Parable of the Prodigal wife and the
  husband as good as God.
(*A moment's silence, then they both burst out laughing.*)

LLYWELYN: I'm not worthy of you, Siwan.

SIWAN: Every wife hears that at one time or another.
That's the moment at which the man's most
  dangerous.

LLYWELYN: Can you forgive me, Siwan?

SIWAN: Llywelyn the Great asking forgiveness from a whore?

LLYWELYN: Spoken in madness, spat out in jealous anger,
My love turned into hate and malice
That terrible night . . .

SIWAN: Hush, don't speak the truth.
This is not a confessional, and I am not a priest in
  a box,
But only a wicked wife itching for the last word.
(*They both laugh again.*)

LLYWELYN: Will you forgive me, Siwan?

SIWAN: For calling me harlot and whore?
Llywelyn, my dear, the name suited me well.

LLYWELYN: But the malice of hanging? The savage joy in your
  pain?

SIWAN: Your misery remains. Gwilym was hanged,
He leaped to his death crying out my name
And our love achieved a bright climax of pain.
So I remember him; we were saved
The hour of disillusion, the bored kisses, the getting
  on one another's nerves.
But you, if you forgive, you must live with the
  wreckage of your idol,
And remember the sleepless nightmare when love
  became hate.
To lie with me in your bed will be
Like sleeping alive in your grave.
Can you endure me, Llywelyn, can you stop hating
  me?

LLYWELYN: Come back to me, Siwan.

SIWAN: If I do, between us in the bed will always be the stench of your love defiled.

LLYWELYN: If you come, between us in the bed will be another body, a corpse hanged by the neck.

SIWAN: What shall we do with them, Llywelyn?

LLYWELYN: Stretch out our arms across them towards each other,
And accept them as souls accept Purgatory!
The best of marriage is the purifying fire.
I am the fire that shrivels up and kills you,
Fire on your skin, an old man, more of an institution
Than a human being, the politician in bed.
You, with your memory of a lad who leaped to your kiss and his death;
Will you come back?

SIWAN: The habit of twenty years draws me back.

LLYWELYN: Your son's inheritance draws you back.

SIWAN: An old man's folly, rushing off to war.
That draws me back.

LLYWELYN: With a bit of luck, in spite of my age
I'll win this war if you come back.

SIWAN: Llywelyn, I wish, I will your well-being and success.

LLYWELYN: That is enough: already you've come back.

SIWAN: Will you have me like that, with nothing except goodwill?

LLYWELYN: To wish well is to love. Siwan, my wife,
I shall go out to war rejoicing, as a giant to win a contest,
The contest of your war.

SIWAN: One word Llywelyn—
I shall see your victory if God wills it.
I shall see the fall of our old friend Hubert de Burgh,
I shall see your kingdom and David's inheritance secure,
After that, my time will not be long.

LLYWELYN: You'll be living long after me . . .

SIWAN: No I shall not. Life is still strong in you,
There is still power in your appetite to create.
That power has left me.
Can I exact one promise from you now?

LLYWELYN: Speak your will.

SIWAN: My last testament. From the window of my prison
Beyond the gallows' lawn and Lafan sands,
Across the Menai, I could see Dindaethwy and
Llanfaes, and the rooks rising and falling above the
trees that hide St. Catherine's church:
To watch their blameless freedom was balm to a
prisoner's heart.
When I am dead,
Will you take my body across the water
And bury it there, in the new graveyard, and give
the land
To the Franciscans to raise a house and a chapel?

LLYWELYN: The Grey Friars? Why to Francis?

SIWAN: I have a debt to pay to the patron saint of cord.
He liked a gamble and was fond of rope.

LLYWELYN: A bitter taste in your testament. It was my hope
To have you lie with me at Aberconwy.

SIWAN: You appealed to the marriage oath;
That ties me to you up to the edge of the grave.
I accept that, and I welcome it.
But the grave cuts every knot, frees everyone.
I want my bones to rot out there alone.

LLYWELYN: It shall be as you wish.
All shall be done according to your wish.
Alis, are you there!
(*Alis enters quickly.*)

ALIS: My lord?

LLYWELYN: Where is the crown of the Princess of Snowdonia?

ALIS: In my lady's coffer.

LLYWELYN: Bring it here to me.
(*Alis brings the crown.*)
This maid complains about you, Siwan.

ALIS: My lady, no! I never complained.

LLYWELYN: She says you haven't hit her for one whole year.
She misses the flavour of your clouting sorely!

ALIS: My lord, for shame on you!

LLYWELYN: Therefore, I take the burden of punishing her upon
myself.
If I return victorious from this war
I'll give you to wife to the bravest youth of my
troop
If you should want him . . . Here's the crown.
Siwan, my princess, I crown you title-holder
To my domain. I give you my right hand.
And I kiss you . . . and we shall go in to dine in the
hall together.
Tonight I shall summon my council
And put before them our country's plans for war.

(*Trumpet flourish.*)

CURTAIN

Treason

Translated and adapted for television by
ELWYN JONES

AUTHOR'S INTRODUCTION

This play is an historical tragedy. It has been based on events which took place in Paris and Normandy on 20th July 1944, and after. Two of the characters, General Stuelpnagel and Colonel Linstow, were hanged in Berlin on 30th August 1944. Colonel Hofacker was hanged on 20th December. Field-Marshal Kluge poisoned himself and died immediately; this was while returning to Germany following his dismissal at the end of August. General Blumentritt is alive today in Frankfurt. I sincerely hope that the portraits given of these characters in this play do not do any injustice to them in any way nor cause grief to their families. I had recently an opportunity to talk (in English) with a relation of Colonel Hofacker about his political ideas. I have also tried not to say anything that was not completely true about Field-Marshal Gunther von Kluge. For example, many historians mention his financial debt to Hitler.

There are two imaginary characters in the play. One is Else von Dietlof, the private secretary to the Military Governor of France. The Military Governor's private secretary at the time was indeed a woman, a married woman, Countess Podewils. She came from a good family. I do not know whether she is still alive. Although there is no law on the matter, I believe it would be odious to create an imaginary love story about a foreign noble woman who is most likely to be alive. The story in this play about the love affair between Colonel von Hofacker and Else von Dietlof is completely imaginary and has absolutely no historical basis. Perhaps I will be told that I had no right to confuse history with an imaginary story. I have been uneasy about this and decided eventually in favour of the confusing for three reasons: (1) that a play without a woman in it is a burden for the audience and less interesting to many actors; (2) that an historical play is not history but creative work—ultimately all the characters are imaginary; (3) because it was only by confusing fact and imagination in this way that it was possible to suggest or symbolize the influence of political events and political activity on personal and private life, and the tremendous tension set up between these two levels of living.

When I say that, I would like it to be clear that the late Colonel von Hofacker in 1944 was married, father of a family, and that he had no love affair in Paris. I have been careful to avoid including anything in this play that would dishonour him. In the play he brings about his own arrest during an air-raid because he delays and refuses the opportunity to escape. That is what happened.

Another imaginary character in the play is General Karl Albrecht, head of the S.S. in France. The real head of the S.S. in France in 1944 was Karl Albrecht Oberg. He is alive, imprisoned for life in France, and the Karl Albrecht in my play is not a portrayal of him. German and English historians show that General Oberg was a more humane, more moral and more philanthropic man than the normal S.S. *Gauleiter*. I had to have a character that would represent the normal type and the views of the Gestapo. It would be unfair to put that burden on a living person who is in prison and unable to defend himself. Sauckel was the *Gauleiter* in 1944 who advocated that the young men of Paris should work in German arms factories. Obviously the Albrecht of my play is a composite character, but I have tried to give him the personal life and pathos appropriate to him. What he says about Hitler and Socialism in the last act is an important part of the play. Our part in Hitler's creation has been forgotten so completely and so easily.

The history of the plot against Hitler, on 20th July 1944, and the *putsch* in Paris is to be found in several books. I have depended heavily on two English historians, Chester Wilmot, *The Struggle for Europe* (1952), and J. W. Wheeler-Bennett, *The Nemesis of Power* (1953), and the English translation of Wilhelm von Schramm's book, *The Conspiracy of the Generals* (1956). It is surprising how these historians and many others, like Gisevius in his famous Memoirs, contradict one another even on important historical topics. I am beginning to understand how the late Sir Reginald Coupland could write so many complete untruths about myself in his book on *Welsh and Scottish Nationalism*. To discover the true facts even about living people and about very famous events is extremely difficult in our own age. I hope no one expects factual accuracy in this play. It contains many deliberate fictions. I will quote examples. The official investigation by the Gestapo into the Parish *putsch* was started on 23rd July, but Hofacker was not arrested until two days later. Colonel Linstow was already under house arrest. And I compressed all this into one half-hour act. Another more important example: Linstow did not accompany Stuelpnagel and Hofacker to the Roche-Guyon on the Thursday evening of 20th July. Stauffenberg's last telephone message did not come to the Roche-Guyon either, but to Paris. Stauffenberg's close friend and relative was Hofacker, not Linstow as in the play. I attributed this to Linstow for the simple reason that I knew little about Linstow and I knew a great deal about Hofacker. So, in order to build up Linstow's character for the play, I transferred to him many of the real Hofacker's characteristics. Schramm and others record his illness, and a photograph of him is included in Schramm's book which shows him to be an extremely fine and handsome young man.

I hope one is free to do this in a play. To take the same liberty with the characters and principles of many who had a dominant part to play in the history of Europe is a different thing. I have attempted to give a fair portrait of Field-Marshal Kluge in the great crisis of his life and a great crisis in the history of the Second World War and the history of

Europe. Historians still disagree to this day about Rommel's character; and I have given the opinion and attitude of the officers of his staff in the play. I also hope that the portrait of General Blumentritt is fair and that I have not wronged Stuelpnagel or Hofacker.

Is the play's interpretation of the spirit and tradition of the German Army Officers' Corps fair? It is not my place to argue about that. The standard English interpretation is Mr. Wheeler-Bennett's book—my debt to his conclusions can be judged from page 689 of *The Nemesis of Power*; it is also evident that Blumentritt and Hofacker say something different in my play's second act. I maintain that their interpretation of the *Corps'* spirit and tradition is one which was held by at least a number of the best officers of staff. But, of course, my task is not to convince historians, but for a short time to convince a theatre audience. Europe's future in the second half of the twentieth century and the battle for Germany's soul—the Germany that is still poised between Europe and Asia—that's the theme of this play. West Germany's future is far from secure today, and for that reason the whole of Europe's future is completely uncertain. I think that this is an appropriate subject for Glyn Ebwy's National Eisteddfod in 1958.

['*Author's Introduction*' *translated by*

Marian Elias.]

DRAMATIS PERSONAE

COUNTESS ELSE VON DIETLOF, personal secretary to the Military Governor of France.

GENERAL HEINRICH VON STUELPNAGEL, Military Governor of France.

COLONEL CAISAR VON HOFACKER, member of Governor's staff.

GENERAL KARL ALBRECHT, Head of the S.S. and Gestapo in France.

COLONEL HANS OTFRIED LINSTOW, Head of Staff in Paris.

GENERAL BLUMENTRITT, Head of Staff of the West and Stuelpnagel's successor as Military Governor of France.

FIELD-MARSHAL GUNTHER HANS VON KLUGE, General in Chief of the Western Armed Forces.

SOLDIERS.

The first two acts take place in the afternoon and evening of Thursday, July 20, 1944, and the last act in the morning three days later.

Treason

ACT I

Scene 1—The Staircase

2.30 p.m., Thursday, 20th July 1944. A pair of boots (jackboots) climbing slowly upstairs to the Military Governor of France's office at the Hotel Majestic, Avenue Kleber, in Paris. The gait must be slow, not uncertain, but deliberate and thoughtful. It must contrast with the heavy, rushing clatter of feet we shall see later.

As the boots reach the top of the stairs we see another pair (the sentry's) come sharply to attention. We see Stuelpnagel acknowledge the salute, and enter his secretary's office.

Scene 2—The Countess' Office

Bare. Table with telephone. Steel cupboard with a catch at the back. Chairs. Portrait of Hitler on wall. Countess Else von Dietlof sits at the table— covered with maps and papers—reading a paper into the telephone. She is about to replace the telephone receiver, after saying:

ELSE: I'll give the message to Military Governor Stuelpnagel immediately.
(*Stuelpnagel walks in.*)
General Albrecht is on his way back to Paris to see the Military Governor and to deliver an important message from Reichsfuehrer Himmler.
(*She hands him the message.*)

STUELPNAGEL: Did you get something to eat?

ELSE: A quick snack. Did you?

STUELPNAGEL: I tried to each lunch. Are all the papers in order?

ELSE: Those I typed yesterday?

STUELPNAGEL: Yes.

ELSE: I worked on them until late last night. I learned the orders for today and tomorrow. Then I didn't put the papers back; I burnt them.

STUELPNAGEL: You burnt them?

ELSE: Yes, you see I am attached to the General and anxious to stay in his service. Look. How many keys are there to the cupboard?

307

STUELPNAGEL: I have one. I gave one to you. There are no others.

ELSE: Are you sure?

STUELPNAGEL: Perfectly sure. I had the lock made in Paris.

ELSE: But there are other keys. I've had my suspicions for some time. They were confirmed this week—beyond doubt.

STUELPNAGEL: I see. Once again I have to thank you Countess. Who is it, one of Albrecht's men?

ELSE: The only things he could lay his hands on now apart from the normal files are the Gestapo records and the letter to Boineberg.

STUELPNAGEL: The letter is to go today, the records are for tomorrow. Then they can be burnt . . . I can trust your memory?

ELSE: Only I have that key.

STUELPNAGEL: Good. Where was Albrecht speaking from?

ELSE: Somewhere near Versailles, I think. He'd been to see Marshal Rommel.
(*Door knock.*)

STUELPNAGEL: Poor Rommel. That won't make him feel any better.
(*Door opens. Hofacker enters and salutes.*)

STUELPNAGEL: Ah. Come in von Hofacker. Countess, Colonel von Hofacker will be with me for the next half-hour. Please see that we're not disturbed. If there's a call from Berlin put that through immediately.

ELSE: Yes.

Scene 3—Military Governor's Office.

HOFACKER: It's nearly a quarter to three and still no word from Berlin. What can be happening there, for God's sake?

STUELPNAGEL: We shall hear before three. Beck is there, isn't he? He's ready?

HOFACKER: Since this morning. He has Goerdeler with him, waiting for the word to take over the Government of the Reich.

STUELPNAGEL: We are ready in Paris. I can set the wheels in motion in half an hour.

HOFACKER: If only the telephone would ring.

STUELPNAGEL: Don't worry. It will come, it will come.

HOFACKER: Noon in Hitler's headquarters. That was the plan. The bomb should have exploded before twelve-thirty. It's more than two hours since then.

STUELPNAGEL: Why are you so nervous suddenly? You've kept us all going, all these long weeks—even Rommel. Without you we should have lost heart long ago. Now the weeks of watching and waiting are over; it can only be a matter of minutes.

HOFACKER: Unless what he claims is true, that Providence protects him.

STUELPNAGEL: Caisar. You don't believe such superstitious rubbish? The Devil's own nonsense.

HOFACKER: I'm some sort of a Christian, but I'm with you there.

STUELPNAGEL: What do you mean?

HOFACKER: I believe that the Fuehrer is the Devil's own, his chosen instrument to bring catastrophe to Germany and Europe. It's Faust's bargain all over again; the Devil owns him, and the Devil keeps him.

STUELPNAGEL: The melodrama of creation? No wonder he gets drunk on Wagner. Give me Mozart every time, a music that's all human.

HOFACKER: Can't you even believe that what I've said may be true?

STUELPNAGEL: Of course there is war between good and evil, an unending war. But it is a human war, man's effort to defeat the beast within himself.

HOFACKER: To me evil is a being—a person, an archangel of infinite spiritual genius, second only to God himself. This genius is bent on turning human history into the Devil's own nonsense as if he had challenged himself to reduce the entire cosmos to confusion.

STUELPNAGEL: You believe that's Hitler's function? The reason for his existence?

HOFACKER: He bears the mark of the Archangel of Chaos, the arch enemy of God and man.

STUELPNAGEL: So that's why you agreed to take part in his murder.

HOFACKER: No Heinrich. Never, never . . . I believe that the German General Staff is responsible for Germany, and to the German people. Today we must choose the lesser of two evils. Therefore, Hitler must be killed. That is the only way to save Germany.

STUELPNAGEL: It is the only way, that is as certain as anything is. To me, you know, there is nothing certain about man's life except that the stars above and the earth beneath are totally indifferent to what we do. (*Looking at his watch.*) Twenty minutes to three.

HOFACKER: I wish I could believe as you do.

STUELPNAGEL: Why?

HOFACKER: Then, if we fail, I could put a bullet through my head.

STUELPNAGEL: Of course, there is no other way.

HOFACKER: There is for me.

STUELPNAGEL: You're odd, Caisar, very odd. There'd be no sense in falling into the hands of the Gestapo.

HOFACKER: I believe in Providence. I believe that life has a meaning. I believe in the Providence of the Devil, too. How else can you explain that every effort to kill Hitler so far has failed?

STUELPNAGEL: *Absit omen.* Don't tempt your Providence with prophecy.

HOFACKER: Think of Rommel.

STUELPNAGEL: Yes, Rommel. With him at the head of the Army it would have been easy. And now he's in hospital, in a bad way too.

HOFACKER: And Kluge in his place.

STUELPNAGEL: Today of all days. All part of Providence looking after Hitler, eh?

HOFACKER: The Devil's Providence. It does exist, Heinrich.

STUELPNAGEL: How much does Kluge know?

HOFACKER: He knows everything except the date.

STUELPNAGEL: We can't turn back, anyway. Can we rely on him?

HOFACKER: If the bomb kills Hitler, yes. He promised to accept the authority of Beck and Goerderer on condition that Hitler was dead.

STUELPNAGEL: The Marshal's a difficult man. He's as brave as Rommel in battle. There's no general more anxious to rush to the front where the fighting's hottest. A brave soldier . . . and yet . . .
(Telephone rings.)

HOFACKER: Berlin at last?

STUELPNAGEL: No. No, it's Normandy Headquarters.
(Telephone picked up.)
Governor of France here. Normandy Headquarters. Yes . . . Von Blumentritt . . . What? . . . Yes. I'll see Fink at once of course . . . You realise I have no authority to move a regiment without the Fuehrer's authority . . . I shall go to Fink myself now and I'll see that you get every tank we have in Paris . . . I'll call you within half an hour.
(Puts down receiver.)
(Stuelpnagel moves R. to mirror.)
The Americans have thrown us out of St. Lo and made a substantial dent in the line.

HOFACKER: They haven't broken through, though?

STUELPNAGEL: Not yet.

HOFACKER: The front must hold. They must hold, if only for a day or two. If Hitler dies and Beck takes command we can ask for an armistice in France tonight. But we cannot ask for terms unless the front holds . . . and is seen to be holding.
(Stuelpnagel moves L. downstage to map table. Hofacker joins him.)

STUELPNAGEL: With Hitler out of the way we could call on the Army in the South of France. There'd be some slight chance then.

HOFACKER: Everything must be done to make the front hold.
(Else opens the door.)

ELSE: General Albrecht is here and wishes to see you immediately.

STUELPNAGEL: I said we were not to be disturbed for half an hour.

ELSE: I know sir. But Albrecht? It's the privilege of the Gestapo.

STUELPNAGEL: To hell with the Gestapo.

ELSE: Amen. He says he has an urgent message from Himmler.

STUELPNAGEL: Very well, Countess, show him in.

ELSE (*calls, but without raising her voice*):
               General Albrecht. Will you go in, please.
               (*Albrecht enters, comes to attention and gives the Nazi salute. Hofacker stands to attention and gives the Army salute. Else exits.*)

ALBRECHT: Heil Hitler.

STUELPNAGEL (*politely shakes hands with him*):
               Well, Albrecht. I can give you ten minutes. Please sit down.

ALBRECHT: Heard about Rommel?

STUELPNAGEL: Of course. He's in hospital at Bernay.

ALBRECHT: He's not. He's been moved to Le Vesinet near Versailles.

STUELPNAGEL: When?

ALBRECHT: This morning. He recovered consciousness and realised he was in a Luftwaffe hospital. He insisted on being moved at once—that's how much he hates Goering.

STUELPNAGEL: It was the R.A.F. that got him into hospital.

ALBRECHT: Is that what makes him angry?

STUELPNAGEL: He is not the only one. Goering's air force has ceased to exist.

ALBRECHT: Goering is not the only one he hates. Marshal Rommel is a strange creature. He has, shall we say, some friends who are unreliable? People like Beck and Witzleben and Goerdeler. Isn't that so, von Hofacker?

HOFACKER: The Gestapo is infallible, sir. Yes, I had the privilege of being one of Field Marshal Rommel's friends.

ALBRECHT (*laughing*):
               O come, Colonel, don't be so touchy.

STUELPNAGEL: You came here on business. I haven't much time, Albrecht. Please take a chair. You too, Hofacker.

ALBRECHT (*hardening*):
               Yes. I have an urgent command from Reichsfuehrer Himmler in person.

STUELPNAGEL (*agitated, and with a quick glance at his watch*):
Is that possible? Himmler's in the Wolf's Lair in North Prussia attending the Reichsfuehrer's weekly conference.

ALBRECHT: Probably. He telephoned me from Berlin this morning before he left.

STUELPNAGEL: So. It can hardly be an urgent message.

ALBRECHT: I came at the first free moment.

STUELPNAGEL: What is the message?

ALBRECHT: You've heard the latest news from the front?

STUELPNAGEL: The enemy is in St. Lô and the front is about to break.

ALBRECHT: It's always darkest before the dawn.

STUELPNAGEL: We can agree that it's pretty dark.

ALBRECHT: I hope you don't question the dawn? Do you dare doubt the Fuehrer?

HOFACKER: Have you no doubts, General?

ALBRECHT: No doubts. When things looked blackest for Frederick the Great, with all Europe closing on him, that was the moment that the Great Alliance broke and he threw them out of Prussia and created the eternal and united Germany. Hitler is greater than Frederick. These Allies will break, too.

STUELPNAGEL: Heil Hitler.

ALBRECHT: You always were a sceptic, General. Let me tell you that this is no time for doubt. It is the hour for fanatical faith.

HOFACKER: Faith is the only thing that will throw the Americans back into the sea.

ALBRECHT: Don't tell me you are a sceptic too, von Hofacker.

HOFACKER: What does my *dossier* say?

ALBRECHT: Time will tell. And perhaps that time is not far off.

STUELPNAGEL: Has this anything to do with Himmler's message?

ALBRECHT: It has, sir. This is a moment of crisis. The Eastern front is weakening with the Russians closing in on us. The British and the Americans are attacking in Normandy. To avoid catastrophe we must form regiments of soldiers from the factories in Germany at once. And we cannot do that without replacing them by other workers. Do you follow me?

STUELPNAGEL: What then?

ALBRECHT: With the specific approval of the Fuehrer, Reichs-fuehrer Himmler has decreed that every Frenchman under twenty-four be conscripted to work in the German factories. A beginning must be made in Paris this week.

STUELPNAGEL: It's Thursday today.

ALBRECHT: This week. That is an order.

STUELPNAGEL: We must have time to consider this, Albrecht. It's fortunate that von Hofacker is here. He is our staff specialist on French matters. Colonel, what do you think of this proposal?

HOFACKER: I shall have to speak plainly, sir.

STUELPNAGEL: That is no more than your duty.

HOFACKER: There are two obstacles. First the scheme is directly contrary to the Geneva Convention and the rules of war . . .

ALBRECHT: Are you mad? The Reich is in peril. In your simplicity do you believe that both sides have not already broken the Geneva Convention?

STUELPNAGEL (*authoritatively*):
General Albrecht. I asked for von Hofacker's opinion. Now I wish to hear it.

HOFACKER: I agree that the Reich is in danger, in even more danger than General Albrecht thinks. We could lose the war.

ALBRECHT: Only through treachery.

HOFACKER: Our function is to face the facts and give the best advice we can. This is not the time to trample the Geneva Convention under foot. We have no desire to give our enemies an excuse, if they win the war, to put German Army officers on trial and hang them. We must keep the Army's hands clean in France.

ALBRECHT: The Reich is in danger. The Reich of the Fuehrer, the greatest political creation in the history of

Europe, is in peril. Even the Fuehrer's own life is in danger—and this fastidious minx, Miss von Hofacker, wants to keep her hands clean.

HOFACKER: Ever since the time of Frederick the Great the military tradition of the Army and its officers has provided the heart and the conscience of Germany. It is a part of European civilisation. It has survived every war and every revolution. Without it there is no chance of re-creating the historic tradition of the Reich. That is why Herr Himmler's order is impossible. Respect for the rules of war even in extreme peril, even in the crisis that exists today, is essential to the survival of the Corps, essential to the reconstruction of Germany and Europe.

ALBRECHT: Are you suggesting that the Fuehrer's days are over? Let me tell you this: the fate of Germany and the fate of Europe are tied hard to the fate of Hitler. If Hitler falls, all Germany and all Europe will fall with him, fall without hope of any reconstruction.

HOFACKER: There you have it. The gangster's threat. That may do for the Gestapo. But the officers' corps is not a gangsters' club.

ALBRECHT: The day you come into the Gestapo's hands you will have cause to remember those words.

STUELPNAGEL: Albrecht, are you threatening my staff?

ALBRECHT: Yes I am, and what's more, General, I am reminding you both that every German Army officer—each one individually—took an oath of loyalty to the Fuehrer, and I am suggesting that you keep that oath and carry out this order. You know the trouble with you lot? Every single member of the grand officers' corps? 'You are all romantics. You talk about honour and the rules of war as though war today was a tournament for the Knights of the Round Table. Can't you get it into your bullet heads that this is the twentieth century and that there are no rules of war? There is nothing but the domination of the strong and the wails of the weak. Blood and iron—iron and blood, that is politics.

STUELPNAGEL: Your second reason for ignoring this proposal, von Hofacker?

HOFACKER: A practical one, sir. Already the French Resistance forces are a problem behind our lines. Only French loyalty to Pétain prevents the Resistance from becoming a major danger. If it is announced tomorrow that Frenchmen are to be conscripted for factory work in Germany, then forty thousand men will disappear to join the Resistance. We shall have a war on two fronts in France.

STUELPNAGEL: Is that a fairy story, Albrecht?

ALBRECHT: It's rubbish. We can throw cordons around every district of Paris and catch the lot.

STUELPNAGEL: The front in Normandy is on the point of collapse . . . I have to see Colonel Fink this afternoon to organise all available tanks and guns. To have to fight on the boulevards at the same time would be disastrous.

ALBRECHT: And that is your answer to Herr Himmler? A refusal?

STUELPNAGEL: Himmler's order entails a new policy . . . You know, and so does Himmler, that I have no authority to change policy, except on the instructions of my superior, Field Marshal Kluge.

ALBRECHT: I shall report to Herr Himmler as soon as he returns to Berlin from the Fuehrer's conference.

STUELPNAGEL: In that case, there isn't so much of a hurry. You have, I hope, plenty of time.

ALBRECHT: Reichsfuehrer Himmler is not a man who expects to be kept waiting.

STUELPNAGEL: I'm not under his authority. I am responsible only to Field Marshal Kluge. I hope to be talking to him within fifteen minutes.

ALBRECHT: Stuelpnagel. The day is not far distant when all the Army—including the officer corps—will come under the control of Himmler.

STUELPNAGEL: You're quite a prophet, General.

ALBRECHT: I shall be back here within half an hour to hear Field Marshal Kluge's reply.

STUELPNAGEL: I shall prepare your welcome carefully.

ALBRECHT (*at attention*):
> Heil Hitler.
> (*Salutes and exits.*)

HOFACKER: He's out for your blood, Heinrich.

STUELPNAGEL: Tomorrow morning, Karl Albrecht will be facing a court martial. Or I will.

Scene 4. The Countess's Office. Int. Studio. Day.

STUELPNAGEL (*coming through door*):
> Nothing yet from Berlin?

ELSE: Not yet, sir.

STUELPNAGEL: If a message should come from Berlin, call Colonel Linstow or Colonel von Hofacker. No one else.

ELSE: What if there's a call from the Fuehrer's headquarters in Prussia?

STUELPNAGEL (*smiling*):
> If there is, take the poison. But don't worry. There'll be no message.
> (*Exit Stuelpnagel.*)

ELSE: What does he mean?

HOFACKER: He was joking.

ELSE: Have you got poison?

HOFACKER: You know that that is no way for me—or for you.

ELSE: I see. If a message does come from Hitler's head-quarters it means . . . we're finished . . .

HOFACKER: Sh. (*They move into Military Governor's office.*)

Scene 5—Military Governor's office. Int. Studio. Day.

HOFACKER: The staff conference was arranged for noon. Goering and Himmler were to be there with Hitler. If Hitler dies every telephone line from East Prussia to the rest of Germany will be cut. Beck will take over in Berlin. Then we shall hear from him . . . At least, that is the plan.

ELSE: And then?

HOFACKER: It depends on Beck. There are two groups in the plot. You know that we believe that an immediate request should be made to the Americans for an armistice, but the others hold that we should turn first to Stalin. They believe that the future belongs to the Soviet Union and that we should look forward with the Communists to the dawn of the scientific age.

ELSE: Perhaps this is our last chance to make Europe decently human again. I'm a woman and I want a human world not a scientific age.

HOFACKER: I'm sure it's our last chance, if it is a chance at all. It's three o'clock already and we've heard nothing from Berlin. Stauffenberg's business is the first item on the conference agenda. His chair is next to Hitler's. He has the bomb in a brief case. He puts the case on the floor, at the foot of Hitler's chair. The fuse begins to work, he gets a telephone message and leaves for a moment. The bomb explodes.

ELSE: He can't fail.

HOFACKER: That's what I kept on saying to the General, and to Fink and Linstow. They seem to depend on me so much.

ELSE: I depend on you, Caisar.

HOFACKER: Else, we promised to tell each other the truth, come what may. The truth is, that he can fail. It's failed before. It may have failed already.

ELSE: If that's the case, why did you agree to this plan?

HOFACKER: I had no choice. It was the last chance to save the Reich from disaster. It had to be tried even if there was no hope of success.

ELSE: But there must be hope. You yourself must have some hope.

HOFACKER: But that's not why I'm doing this. One has to work on the assumption that hope is reasonable even up to the last moment.

ELSE: And the last moment, what will that be?

HOFACKER: Slow strangling in the Gestapo headquarters in Berlin, dying slowly after long torture.

ELSE: Why do you say this now? Do you want to kill me?

HOFACKER: Because you must be prepared, Else.

ELSE: I am prepared. I am ready. I've closed my eyes and seen the cord tightening round your neck . . . I have choked back every cry, suppressed every tear. I've even smiled politely at that beast Albrecht, with that picture of you in my mind. Is there anything else you want me to do?

HOFACKER: Yes, Else, there is. You must forget your love for me. You must smother your love and kill it. You must stop thinking of me.

ELSE: I don't think of you, you fool. You *are* my every thought.

HOFACKER: Else, you frighten me. If the worst happens, you're bound to betray yourself to the Gestapo.

ELSE: The Gestapo? When they are tearing my nails from my fingers to get me to betray your secret, the torture will help me to forget my pain.

HOFACKER: Else, I tell you now—and this is an order—if the worst happens and the Gestapo come for me, when you see the arrest, you must promise me you must behave as if you don't know me.

ELSE: No, Caisar. I refuse to believe that can happen. The men in the plot are unshakeable. They have all searched their consciences. To prevent the destruction of Germany and of Europe, because there is no other way they are determined to kill Hitler. They can't fail. There is no need to think of it.

HOFACKER: I must. I have some premonition that an evil force keeps watch over Hitler, guarding him, determined that he shall die only by his own hand. That is why you must promise me now . . .

ELSE: How can I promise such a thing? Ours was a difficult love from the start. Don't make its end unbearable.

HOFACKER: If not for your own sake, Else, then for mine . . .

ELSE: For your sake? Your appeal gets weaker, weaker.

HOFACKER: I know what goes on in the Gestapo's cells.

ELSE: I can imagine worse things than lying in a Gestapo cell.
(*Linstow is heard singing outside. Else and Hofacker stand listening and then move out to Countess's office.*)

Scene 6—The Staircase. Int. Studio. Day.
> (*Linstow runs upstairs, passes a greasy French black marketeer cowering on the stairs half afraid, half on his dignity, on the landing. Noise brings Hofacker to doorway to meet Linstow.*)

HOFACKER: Linstow!

Scene 7—The Countess's Office. Int. Studio. Day.
> (*Hofacker and Linstow enter Countess's office. Else meets them.*)

ELSE: Linstow.

HOFACKER: Linstow. What's up? What's the matter?

LINSTOW: Oh that Frenchman . . . that Frenchman . . .

HOFACKER: What Frenchman?

LINSTOW: That Frenchman with the black market stamped all over him. He passed and raised his arm with a 'Heil Hitler' just like Albrecht.

ELSE: But they all do that, Colonel Linstow.

LINSTOW: Yes, but now. Hitler. My God . . . (*continues to laugh while the others are astonished*) . . . What's the matter with you two?

ELSE: We don't understand . . .

LINSTOW: Can't understand? Why? Haven't you heard?

HOFACKER: Heard what?

ELSE: Is there something new?

LINSTOW: Hitler is dead. Hitler and Goering and Himmler, the three.

Scene 8—Military Governor's office. Int. Studio. Day.
> (*Linstow dances into Military Governor's office followed by Hofacker and Else.*)

HOFACKER: The bomb?

ELSE: Colonel, how did it happen, how did you hear?

LINSTOW: From Stauffenberg himself, from Berlin.

HOFACKER: Stauffenberg is alive?

ELSE: And successful?

HOFACKER: You heard from him himself?

LINSTOW: He had just got back to Berlin. He telephoned immediately after reporting to Beck.

ELSE: Then the bomb worked?

LINSTOW: It worked.

HOFACKER: Did he see Hitler dead?

LINSTOW: He saw the explosion. That was enough. It was terrific. The conference was not held in the underground bunker, but in a wooden hut belonging to the staff. Well, Claus planted the bomb and left as planned. The hut blew up before his very eyes. He didn't waste a moment. He went immediately by air back to Berlin to get the revolution under way.

HOFACKER: But he didn't see Hitler dead?

LINSTOW: My dear fellow. After that explosion? It will take three days to pick up the pieces.

ELSE: He must be right, Caisar.

HOFACKER: Did you recognise Stauffenberg's voice?

LINSTOW: Claus Stauffenberg? Nobody could imitate that voice. The news is quite authentic. Hitler and Goering and Himmler have finished with the Reich.

HOFACKER: I'm afraid to believe it. It's almost impossible to realise what it means.

LINSTOW: A revolt is like marriage—one sudden act and then a lifetime to grasp its meaning.

ELSE: That's right, Colonel. Realisation comes through action.

LINSTOW: Precisely Countess. You see, a woman's voice but a soldier's words.

HOFACKER: No, Linstow. Action now without certainty would be disastrous. We must be absolutely certain that Hitler is dead.

LINSTOW: My dear von Hofacker, those are a woman's words even if the voice is a soldier's. Hitler and Goering and Himmler have gone.
             (*The door opens and Stuelpnagel enters, his eyes alight, and his face showing clearly that he has heard the news. The Colonels stand to attention for a moment and the Countess goes towards him.*)

ELSE: Herr General, you've heard?

STUELPNAGEL: Yes, Countess, I heard.
                (Kisses her hand and turns to the Colonels to shake their hands.)
                Well, gentlemen . . . at last . . . the hour has struck
                . . . The beast has been destroyed . . . Germany is
                free.

HOFACKER: Is it a fact, sir?

STUELPNAGEL: Certainly, Caisar. The Devil's providence has failed
                this time.

LINSTOW: How did you hear, sir?

STUELPNAGEL: From Beck, from Beck himself, speaking from
                Berlin. He caught me in Fink's office.

HOFACKER: He knew for certain that Hitler was dead?

LINSTOW *(breaks out into peals of laughter again)*:
                You must pardon me, sir, but von Hofacker's like
                a man waking from a nightmare. He can't believe
                that the incubus has been thrown off.

STUELPNAGEL: Beck and Witzleben have taken command of the
                War Office and have called the Berlin garrison back
                into the City.

ELSE: There is a hope. Hope for Germany, for Europe, for
                us. At last, at long last.

STUELPNAGEL: Countess. Hold all incoming calls until I ring for you.
                (Else exits.)
                The reason given for the recall of the garrison is that
                the Gestapo has risen in revolt against the govern-
                ment. The first step, therefore, is to arrest every
                Gestapo official. The news of Hitler's death is being
                kept secret so far, but already Beck has heard that
                the Army in Holland and the South-East are with
                him.

LINSTOW: The revolt is under way.

HOFACKER: What about Field Marshal Kluge?

STUELPNAGEL: Beck tried to contact him at La Roche-Guyon but
                he wasn't there.

LINSTOW: The Field Marshal's conscience is a nuisance.

STUELPNAGEL: Blumentritt was there and told Beck to call again.
                Then it was arranged that we three should go there

tonight and put the new Government's plan before
Kluge.

HOFACKER: Beck is sure that Kluge is still with us?

STUELPNAGEL: He has no fear of that. The news of the bomb will
not be released until we are sure of every front. We
shall be sure before midnight.

LINSTOW: We must contact Kluge. With Rommel out of action
our hopes depend on him.

STUELPNAGEL: Tomorrow von Hofacker, you will become German
Ambassador to the French Government. Tonight
I shall call on you to explain Beck's strategy to
Field Marshal Kluge.

HOFACKER: Very well, sir. Field Marshal Kluge already knows
the plan.
(Stuelpnagel takes a letter from the safe.)

STUELPNAGEL: General Boineberg has placed a battalion of the
Paris garrison under the trees in the Bois de Boulogne.
At sunset they will move to the Boulevard Lannes
and arrest the entire Gestapo and imprison them at
Fresnes.

HOFACKER: Sir, to arrest and imprison the Gestapo is to start a
putsch, an act of revolution.

STUELPNAGEL: This is a revolution.

HOFACKER: Beck plans to keep Marshal Kluge in command. He
should be responsible for the revolution in France.

STUELPNAGEL: True enough.

HOFACKER: Then wouldn't it be wiser to wait? You will be seeing
Kluge tonight. You can send the command to
arrest the Gestapo from La Roche-Guyon after
getting his approval.

STUELPNAGEL *(considering the point)*:
I gave my word to Beck. I promised to take action
as soon as I heard of Hitler's death.

LINSTOW: Yes, but action with Rommel. The sad fact is that
now only Kluge can guarantee success in France.

STUELPNAGEL: Rommel is out of it now, so we must make sure of
Kluge.

HOFACKER: Kluge is cautious . . .

STUELPNAGEL: With the Gestapo imprisoned the revolution will be safe. There will be no other opposition. Then we can count on Kluge.

HOFACKER: Launch the boat with the captain on the bridge— and all without asking him.

LINSTOW: You're risking your life, sir.

STUELPNAGEL: I gave Beck my word. I shall keep my word. Kluge will keep his, I'll risk my life on that.
(*Else enters.*)
What is it, Countess?

ELSE: General Albrecht is back. He's waiting to see you— he's very impatient . . .

STUELPNAGEL: I haven't forgotten him, I've made arrangements for him. I want you to take this letter and deliver it to General Boineberg in person. The revolution begins here, now . . . Linstow . . . tomorrow you will be heading a court-martial which all the Gestapo leaders will face.

LINSTOW: At least the boulevards will be cleaner and fresher tomorrow.

STUELPNAGEL: Show him in, Countess.

ELSE: General Albrecht, will you go in now?
(*Albrecht enters and salutes.*)

ALBRECHT: Heil Hitler. Well, General, have you had Field Marshal Kluge's reply to Herr Himmler's order?

STUELPNAGEL: Not yet. But I have received important news from Berlin. Have you heard anything?

ALBRECHT: What news?

STUELPNAGEL: That the Gestapo has risen against the Government. I am therefore ordering the arrest of all members of the Gestapo, starting with yourself.

ALBRECHT: This is no time for practical jokes. What's the matter with you?

STUELPNAGEL: Put your revolver on the desk.
(*Albrecht throws revolver on desk.*)

ALBRECHT: You'll be sorry for this. I demand the right to telephone Herr Himmler.

STUELPNAGEL: I'm sure you shall speak to Herr Himmler tomorrow after your court martial. That is all.

Act II

Scene 1—Interior Château in La Roche-Guyon. Studio. Evening.
  (*The light is dimming, but not yet dark.*)

It is eight o'clock in the evening the same day, the sun about to set. We see a room in a château in La Roche-Guyon in Normandy, a big, handsome room on the ground floor. In the back is a french window opening out on a terrace with a lawn beyond. There are doors on each side, chairs here and there. A radio set, a jug and glasses stand on a small table in one corner. A heavy, round table stands in the centre back with General Blumentritt, Chief of Staff in the West, working at it.

A Private enters and puts some papers on the table before him. We hear aeroplanes—British planes—high above, and in the distance a warning siren sounds.

SOLDIER: Your afternoon's reports, sir, from the Seventh Army and the Panzer Divisions.

BLUMENTRITT: Any radio news?

SOLDIER: None since six o'clock, sir.
                  (*Marshal Kluge's car heard outside.*)

BLUMENTRITT: Isn't that Field Marshal Kluge's car?
                  (*Soldier and Blumentritt exit.*)

Terrace outside château. Evening.
                  (*Kluge walking slowly outside château.*)

Interior château. Evening.
                  (*Kluge enters château through french windows. Walks in slowly. Pours himself a drink and sits at table.*)
                  (*Blumentritt enters.*)

BLUMENTRITT: Ah, so it was you, Field Marshal. Had a long day?

KLUGE: Long and hard, Blumentritt.

BLUMENTRITT: How did the conference go?

KLUGE: Miserably.

BLUMENTRITT: Was everyone there?

KLUGE: Hausse, Eberbach, Dietrich, every general, every Chief of Staff.

BLUMENTRITT: Was there much talk about Rommel?

KLUGE: Of course. It was he who called the conference, I don't know why. Anyway Rommel's lucky—he's out of it.

BLUMENTRITT: Did the others think so too?

KLUGE: More or less. Nobody said anything; there was nothing much to be said.

BLUMENTRITT: Were they very dispirited, Field Marshal?

KLUGE: Every general, every Chief of Staff, just sat there, elbows on the table, eyes fixed on the maps—not a smile, not a joke. There we all were in the middle of a fine July day, the German High Command huddled together in a cellar, by candlelight, eating corned beef sandwiches and drinking stale cider out of broken cups with the drone of enemy aeroplanes in our ears.

BLUMENTRITT: Can the front hold, Field Marshal?

KLUGE: That's a very silly question, Blumentritt, a very silly question.

BLUMENTRITT: Let me put it another way: how long can we hold the present front?

KLUGE: If I had reasonable freedom—a general's normal freedom—from that corporal in Prussia, I could regroup, pull the fighting back from Normandy, call on the forces in Southern France, and prepare an orderly retreat. But Hitler insists on controlling every movement here in Normandy. This afternoon I read to the staff his latest order.

BLUMENTRITT: What was that?

KLUGE: "Attack with the Panzer Divisions at night and throw the English back to the sea."

BLUMENTRITT: The Panzer divisions, eh? What did Dietrich have to say to that?

KLUGE: Without raising his head he said: "He thinks they are the Gadarene swine—and I haven't enough tanks to drive them into the sea."

BLUMENTRITT: Field Marshal, the truth must be faced.

KLUGE: The truth everyone realises—the truth everyone is afraid to name.

BLUMENTRITT: Are you afraid to name it?

KLUGE: No, I am not afraid to name it; the truth is the war is lost.

BLUMENTRITT: Did the rest of the staff understand that?

KLUGE: Yes, they understood.

BLUMENTRITT: Did you discuss it with them?

KLUGE: Good God, no! Why do you ask?

BLUMENTRITT: Field Marshal, as soon as it is clear beyond a shadow of doubt that to continue fighting is useless, we have no right to go on losing German lives. That is the tradition, is it not?

KLUGE: Yes, that is the tradition, but I am not the man in command. It is not my responsibility. I gave an oath of loyalty to Adolf Hitler. He has taken into his own hands the direction of the fighting here in Normandy. The man is mad. But he's still the Commander in Chief. The responsibility is still his, not mine.

BLUMENTRITT: Have we the right to deny responsibility, betray it even?

KLUGE: Where there is no authority there cannot be responsibility. Therefore there is no betrayal involved. You know that as well as I do. The responsibility has been taken completely out of my hands.

BLUMENTRITT: At this very moment a battle is raging. The enemy is attacking in enormous strength. We know that. How can we deny responsibility.

KLUGE: I know. I know. We are throwing lives away because of some mad strategy. But if I accepted responsibility now, I would be false to my oath, false to the oath of a German Field Marshal in the service of his Fatherland.

BLUMENTRITT: Field Marshal, if the responsibility were to revert to you; what then?

KLUGE: Impossible. That is quite impossible as long as Hitler is alive.

BLUMENTRITT: Impossible? I'm not sure.

KLUGE: And why aren't you sure?

BLUMENTRITT: I have some news, sir.

KLUGE: From the front? From Caen?

BLUMENTRITT: No Field Marshal, from Berlin.

KLUGE: What is it?

BLUMENTRITT: A report that Hitler was killed at noon. Hitler and Goering and Himmler. It was a bomb.
(*Kluge struggles with the news.*)

KLUGE: What did you do?

BLUMENTRITT: I ordered the monitoring service to record all radio news from six o'clock onwards. To record foreign news, too.

KLUGE: Of course. Is the news true, do you think?

BLUMENTRITT: I have no proof.

KLUGE: Where did the news come from?

BLUMENTRITT: From Berlin.

KLUGE: Who spoke to you?

BLUMENTRITT: Marshal Beck, from the War Office.

KLUGE: From the War Office? Has Beck taken control of the War Office?

BLUMENTRITT: He was on the telephone asking for you, very urgently.

KLUGE: So, it's a *putsch*?

BLUMENTRITT: A *putsch*? Did you know of this plan? Did you expect this?

KLUGE: Know? Me? No, I knew nothing of the plan. It's you who said it.

BLUMENTRITT (*laughing*):
I didn't sir. I said nothing. But that is what's happened.

KLUGE: If Beck is in the War Office . . . He must have taken over the Government.

BLUMENTRITT (*chancing it*):
Field Marshal, my sympathies are with Beck.

KLUGE: What? (*Stirring out of a brown study.*) What did you say?

BLUMENTRITT: I knew nothing of a plan. We must continue to lead the fighting in Normandy knowing that this has happened behind us in Berlin. But believe me, there is no need for you to hesitate. I was pretty sure that Rommel expected something like this. He was here two days ago—and ready, ready for this. But he has been wounded and now—well—Rommel isn't here so—

KLUGE: Yes, I know. Rommel isn't a soldier but a Knight of the Round Table. He's a hero in a Wagnerian opera.

BLUMENTRITT: With things as they are, Rommel would have carried all the staff with him over to Beck—the Panzer army, too.

KLUGE: Perhaps. But I'm not a political crusader. I'm a soldier. An old soldier.

BLUMENTRITT: If you're with Beck, Field Marshal, if you are in his confidence.

KLUGE: I am not in his confidence. I promised him nothing. At least not while Hitler was alive. At least nothing contrary to my oath of loyalty.

BLUMENTRITT: But now? If Hitler is dead?

KLUGE: If? A new situation calls for new measures. If Hitler is dead, then the situation is different. Did you try to get the Wolf's Lair on the telephone?

BLUMENTRITT: Of course, several times. Without success.

KLUGE: No answer?

BLUMENTRITT: No. Then I tried asking for Keitel. I failed there, too. There was no one available.

KLUGE: No one available. Is the news true? Is it true? Everything depends on that now.

BLUMENTRITT: The news bulletin from Berlin is due any minute now.

KLUGE: If it's true we can act with Beck against the Nazis for the sake of Germany.

BLUMENTRITT: Beck is Germany's only hope. Without him there is none.

KLUGE: But we must be sure. We must know for certain before we commit ourselves.
(The telephone rings. Blumentritt lifts the receiver, listens, then gives it to Kluge.)

BLUMENTRITT: Von Blumentritt speaking . . . It's Marshal Beck. Will you speak to him? Will you speak to him?

KLUGE: I can't avoid it.
(He takes receiver.)

Kluge speaking. Yes, Beck . . . I see . . . Yes . . . (*To Blumentritt*) Beck's formed a new government. He's asking me to accept his authority.

(*A soldier has entered and handed a message to Blumentritt who in turn hands it to Kluge.*)

BLUMENTRITT: Ask him if this news bulletin from Berlin is true.

KLUGE: Field Marshal. I've just been handed a radio signal from Berlin. It states that an attempt on Hitler's life has failed . . . What? . . . Not true . . . Accept Stauffenberg's word? . . . Yes, but I can't . . .

BLUMENTRITT: Tell him that Stuelpnagel and his staff are on their way here from Paris. Say you'll call him back when you've heard from them.

KLUGE: Field Marshal. Stuelpnagel and Hofacker are on their way here. I'll speak to them and ring you back. Yes . . . Yes . . . I promise to listen to von Hofacker. I'll call you back. (*Replaces phone.*)

BLUMENTRITT: Yes, it's true. They are on their way and should be here any moment.

KLUGE: Thank you, Blumentritt. We must move very carefully.

BLUMENTRITT: Stuelpnagel is a rock, the quietest and the strongest of us all. We'll be able to depend on him.

KLUGE: O . . . Yes? (*Lifting the paper.*) What do you make of this signal?

BLUMENTRITT: If Hitler is dead, then Goebel's propaganda machine must deny it until a new Fuehrer is ready.

KLUGE: That's what Beck said.

BLUMENTRITT: But why—

KLUGE: Why what?

BLUMENTRITT: Why is Radio Berlin still in Goebbel's hands?

KLUGE: Exactly.

BLUMENTRITT: Do Beck and Witzleben understand the technique of revolution? Without capturing Radio Berlin the *putsch* cannot succeed. I'm not happy about Beck. He's a soldier without any experience of revolt.

KLUGE: Is Hitler dead or alive? We must know the truth. Everything turns on that. Nothing else is important now.

BLUMENTRITT: Nothing else is important to Germany.

KLUGE: Nothing else is important to us. If Hitler is dead, then the army can act—

BLUMENTRITT: Act with Beck?

KLUGE: That's what I promised.

BLUMENTRITT: Who knew of that promise?

KLUGE: Von Hofacker. He went between us.

BLUMENTRITT: And if Hitler is alive?

KLUGE: If he is alive. Then we have our hands full in Normandy. The battle will help us to forget.

BLUMENTRITT: Yes, the front will be our escape.
(A car is heard approaching. It stops.)
We can be so busy losing lives that we shall not have time to worry.
(A soldier stands at the door.)

SOLDIER: The Governor of France and his staff, sir.

KLUGE: Very well.
(Stuelpnagel, Linstow and Hofacker enter, stand to attention, and salute. Kluge shakes Stuelpnagel's hand. Blumentritt greets the others.)

KLUGE: How did you come? On Highway Three-One-Three?

STUELPNAGEL: Not likely. It was there that Rommel caught it. Their Air Force is practically blockading it.

KLUGE: It is a blockade. They are cutting us off from Caen now.

STUELPNAGEL: We came through Pointoise and chose roads that are hardly on the map.

KLUGE: Damn Goering and his Luftwaffe.

LINSTOW *(with a great guffaw)*:
De mortuis! Field Marshal.

KLUGE: *De mortuis?*

LINSTOW: Yes sir, the dead. It's a bit of Vergil. The dead, sir, sure enough.

KLUGE: What dead are you so sure about?

LINSTOW: Well, Hitler, Goering and Himmler. You must have heard, sir.

KLUGE: Yes. We heard. But hardly 'sure enough'.

BLUMENTRITT: We heard it denied, in fact.

LINSTOW (*quite cheerfully*):

Oh, but naturally, sir. What else do you expect from Goebbels?

KLUGE: Have you any proof that the Fuehrer is dead? Any positive proof—

LINSTOW: Yes, sir, indeed I have. Claus is my proof.

KLUGE: Do you mean Colonel Stauffenberg?

LINSTOW: Yes, he was a cadet in my year and has been my friend ever since. It was he who placed the bomb that killed them. He himself told me the news on the telephone. He saw it happen. He is in Berlin leading the revolt with Marshal Beck.

KLUGE: Be seated, gentlemen. I have received a radio signal from Berlin. It states that an attempt on Hitler's life has failed; that Hitler is well, that Goering and Himmler are safe, too.

LINSTOW: But that's only to be expected, sir. Give Goebbels some credit.

KLUGE: I am not convinced that Goebbel's announcement is false.

STUELPNAGEL: Sir, you and I have known Marshal Beck for a long time. We both served under him when he was Chief of Staff. You are one of his friends—you are privileged to be his friend. This afternoon he placed himself at the head of Germany in place of Hitler. Isn't that enough for you?

KLUGE: I have every respect for Beck; a great soldier, a great patriot. It seems that he has started a *putsch* and formed a new government . . .

STUELPNAGEL: "It seems," Field Marshal? Haven't you been speaking to Beck?

KLUGE: He telephoned me. Certainly he said that Hitler had been killed. And then he wanted me to acknowledge his government and his authority at once.

STUELPNAGEL: According to the plan, surely?

KLUGE: How can I acknowledge Beck's authority on Stauffenberg's word alone? We're in the middle of the battle of Normandy. Do you realise that if we lose this battle we shall not be able to hold our ground this side of Paris? No, gentlemen. Stauffenberg's word alone isn't enough. Why is Goebbels still in control of Radio Berlin?

(*The telephone rings and Blumentritt answers.*)

BLUMENTRITT: Colonel Linstow? Yes, he's here. Colonel Linstow, an urgent message for you from Colonel Stauffenberg.

LINSTOW (*goes to speak on telephone*):
Stauffenberg? Yes, Claus . . . Yes, it's Hans . . . What? . . . Claus, Claus . . .
(*Linstow drops the telephone and falls. Hofacker and Stuelpnagel rush to his side. Blumentritt replaces receiver. Soldier enters, hands paper to Blumentritt. Soldier exits.*)

BLUMENTRITT (*reading paper*):
'In a few minutes we shall be interrupting programmes on all stations to broadcast an important announcement concerning our Fuehrer Adolf Hitler.'
(*Kluge switches radio on and stands waiting.*)
(*Linstow leans on table, between Hofacker and Stuelpnagel. 'Tannhauser' overture.*)

RADIO
ANNOUNCER: Heil Hitler! Radio Berlin. Here is a special announcement. At noon today a murderous attempt was made on the life of Fuehrer Adolf Hitler. A bomb exploded in the hut in which he was in conference. Through the mercy of Providence the Fuehrer escaped unharmed. At the moment he and Marshal Goering are in conference with Signor Mussolini, Il Duce. Tonight the Fuehrer will speak to his people by radio and announce the vengeance that will fall on the small clique of army officers who plotted his death. Heil Hitler.
(*Kluge switches off the set.*)

KLUGE: At last the facts.

HOFACKER (*lifting Linstow*):
Come outside . . . you need some air.
(*Hofacker helps Linstow out on to terrace. Stuelpnagel and Blumentritt follow.*)

Scene 2—Exterior. Terrace. La Roche-Guyon. Studio. Evening.

BLUMENTRITT: Are you better, Linstow?

LINSTOW: The old trouble, sir, my heart.

BLUMENTRITT: Yes, I know. Take your time to recover before you tell us what you've heard . . . It's a fine night for the enemy bombers.

KLUGE: May we now hear your news from Berlin, Colonel Linstow?

LINSTOW: It's not very comforting, sir.

KLUGE: Comfort ye my people! Nobody does.

LINSTOW: While Stauffenberg was talking on the phone the Gestapo were breaking down the door to get at him. He barely had time for his message.

KLUGE: What did he say?

LINSTOW: He said: 'It's all over Hans.'

BLUMENTRITT: And Beck?

LINSTOW: Beck had just shot himself.

STUELPNAGEL: All over—the Devil's Providence.

BLUMENTRITT: Beck! . . . Beck! . . . Beck! . . . He was the conscience of the Corps. He was our inspiration.

LINSTOW: And Claus was like a son to him.

STUELPNAGEL: What about Stauffenberg?

LINSTOW: He was shot at the telephone. I heard them shoot. At the last moment he tried to warn us.

KLUGE: Well, now we know the truth. At least, the situation is clear now.

LINSTOW (*with an attempt at laughter*):
Well said, sir, well said. Beck is dead, Stauffenberg has been killed, but the professional viewpoint remains; the situation is clear.

KLUGE: Bunglers! They've bungled the *putsch*. It's unforgiveable.

BLUMENTRITT: The unforgiveable thing tonight is to be alive.

STUELPNAGEL: Beck has paid the price.

KLUGE: And left the rest of us to foot the bill. In the middle of the battle.

BLUMENTRITT: The battle will be our refuge.

KLUGE: The Gestapo will go through every staff at every front with a toothcomb. Hundreds of high-ranking officers will die. Hundreds will shoot themselves.

LINSTOW: The lucky ones.

KLUGE: Thank God that in spite of Beck I kept the High Command in France from burning their fingers. That's something . . . I hope that's something . . . (*Kluge goes back into château followed by Hofacker.*)

Scene 3—Interior château. Studio. Evening.

KLUGE: Well, we can do nothing now but get back to work, back to the battle in Normandy.

HOFACKER: On the assumption that everything is at an end?

KLUGE: Precisely. The words are Stauffenberg's own.

HOFACKER: But they were not true.

KLUGE: The bomb has failed. The *putsch* has failed. The whole thing has been bungled. That is the end.

HOFACKER: Sir, it is only the beginning. You yourself said that the Gestapo would be combing through every command on every front. They will come here, Field Marshal, here to La Roche-Guyon. They will come to this very room—unless you prevent them— and start asking questions about our meeting here tonight. They will want to know—and we all know how they will ask—what was the purpose of this meeting? What are we going to say?

KLUGE: The tradition of the corps will be defence enough.

HOFACKER: Thank you for the word. That tradition demands from you tonight action worthy of your rank. This is Germany's hour of destiny. The great German marshals of the past are with us in spirit. They, like Beck on the telephone, call for your help tonight.

KLUGE: Beck is dead. But he asked me to listen to you. Out of respect for his memory I am ready to listen.

HOFACKER: Thank you, sir. Four days ago, Field Marshal Rommel sent a formal report and a personal letter to Hitler. He was struck down before they were despatched. You read the report?

KLUGE: I did.

HOFACKER: And the letter? Have you sent them on?

KLUGE: They are ready to be sent.

HOFACKER: Rommel says in the letter that further fighting in France is useless, and appeals for an armistice in Normandy immediately.

KLUGE: Yes. That's in the letter.

HOFACKER: Did you say anything of this to the staff conference today?

KLUGE: Young man, what I say at a staff conference is my business.

HOFACKER: Forgive me, sir. It was Marshal Rommel who summoned today's conference. He called it so that he could read to the staff his letter to Hitler. He planned thus to win over all the army officers. He told you so in this very room. You then sent me to Beck with a message and a promise.

KLUGE: I gave no promise.

HOFACKER: But sir . . .

KLUGE: I gave no promise. I said that I agreed with Rommel's appraisal of the situation. I said I would work with Beck only if Hitler were dead. And now Beck is dead and Hitler is still alive.

HOFACKER: But Germany is dying. The Russians are thrusting through Poland. They are on the borders of Prussia, in reach of your own estate. Within a month Bulgaria and Rumania will have surrendered to Stalin. Then the road to Berlin and the road to Vienna will lie open to the Red Army. The Cossack and the Mongol will camp on Beck's grave.

KLUGE: All this has been a nightmare to me ever since Stalingrad.

HOFACKER: It is more than a nightmare. It is a fact. Once in Berlin, the Russians will stay, certainly for the rest of the twentieth century. Prussia will become part of Asia. West Germany will become a battlefield between Asia and America. And Hitler's atomic bomb—the bomb that was to stun the world and win victory for Germany at the last moment—that will fall into the hands of the Kremlin. German scientists will become their lackeys, and all Europe will become an insignificant corner of Communist Asia.

KLUGE: Yes, that is possible.

HOFACKER: Field Marshal, the tradition of the officer corps belongs to Europe. Our strength stems from Napoleon and Frederick. Germany—despite the Nazis—looks with Goethe to the Greeks. Luther's Reformation is part of Western civilisation. At this minute, and in this room, the destiny of Germany and the twentieth century of Europe, lies in your hands. The decision is yours.

KLUGE: No, I refuse to accept it.

HOFACKER: You may refuse, but you cannot escape. Destiny has trapped you. The future of Germany and of Europe depends on your answer now.

KLUGE: My answer? My answer to what?

HOFACKER: Will you accept Rommel's plan and set it in motion tonight? That plan which received your blessing when I took it to Beck?

KLUGE: Rommel's plan depended on the elimination of Hitler. The plan failed. It is now dead.

HOFACKER: The plan is alive, Field Marshal. From here to the Rhine there is no one who can hinder you tonight. Spend fifteen minutes on the telephone and you ensure the loyalty of every general. Then within two hours you can talk by radio with Montgomery or Eisenhower. In that way you can lay open the road to Berlin so that the British and the Americans get there before the Russians. In that way you can save Berlin. You can save Europe from Asia. Nothing in the plan need be changed.

KLUGE: But Hitler is alive.

HOFACKER: What does that matter? Tonight it is Germany and Europe that count, not Hitler.

KLUGE: While Hitler lives my oath stands, the oath of a German Field Marshal, an oath of loyalty and unquestioning obedience to the Fuehrer.

STUELPNAGEL: Field Marshal. What oath ever bound Hitler? He has broken his oath to the constitution. He has betrayed his oath to Germany. Therefore what does our oath count for now . . . Today our oath is nothing but a fiction—a breath of air.

KLUGE: A breath of air? Yes, I remember. Those were the words of Groener, the Chief of Staff, when he asked the Kaiser to abdicate . . . Let me remind you, gentlemen, the officer corps never forgave Groener.

STUELPNAGEL: It is Hitler, not the army, who has broken his oath.

KLUGE: 'Who sweareth to his hurt and changeth not'— isn't that the tradition of the Corps?

HOFACKER: Field Marshal, you know that Rommel had lost faith in Hitler and was willing to go through with the plan even though Hitler were alive?

KLUGE: Thousands of people in Germany and in the army have not lost their faith in Hitler. To operate the plan now would add a civil war to the war we are fighting already.

HOFACKER: Sir, there are occasions when Generals are called on to take heroic action. Why do I have to tell you? A hundred and fifty years ago on the journey through the snow from Moscow, General Yorck, on his own initiative, withdrew his forces from Napoleon's army. He opened the harbours of Prussia to the enemies of France in direct defiance of an order from the Emperor, Frederick William himself. That action created modern Germany. It was the most daring decision in the whole history of the German staff. Only Yorck's example can save Germany tonight. The situation is the same. The need is as great. Tonight Germany prays for a Yorck to save her again. And you, Gunther von Kluge, Field Marshal —are not you our Yorck?

KLUGE: The temptation is strong, von Hofacker, the romantic temptation—to be a hero in history books not a soldier in defeat . . . But I am a soldier, a Junker from Prussia. There is a tradition of loyalty and respect for command in the marrow of my bones. And now you ask me in wartime to betray my leader and my oath. Gentlemen, the name traitor horrifies me.

HOFACKER: To follow Hitler tonight is treason to Germany.

KLUGE: Hitler is alive. Do you want a civil war?

HOFACKER: On every front the army waits for its Yorck. There would be no civil war.

KLUGE: Even here in France the S.S. and S.D. and the Gestapo are all willing to die for Hitler.

STUELPNAGEL (*smiling*):
Not so ready as all that. By now every man of the Gestapo in France is locked up in Fresnes prison.

LINSTOW: Do you see, sir? All opposition is at an end. The *putsch* in France has already succeeded. Every officer is with you. The army awaits its Yorck.

KLUGE: What did you say?

STUELPNAGEL: The S.S. and S.D. are already in prison in accordance with Rommel's plan.

KLUGE: What did you say?

LINSTOW: Field Marshal, the situation is clear. France is free of the Gestapo.

KLUGE: Von Blumentritt, did you know of this?

BLUMENTRITT: I knew nothing of the Rommel plan, sir. Of course, General Stuelpnagel kept on trying to get you on the telephone without success . . .

KLUGE: General. On whose orders was this done?

STUELPNAGEL: In Paris, on my orders, sir.

KLUGE: And where did you get your authority?

STUELPNAGEL: From Marshal Beck. It was an important part of the Rommel plan and one to be carried out immediately when news of Hitler's death came. You knew that.

KLUGE: Let me ask you formally, who is in command in the West?

STUELPNAGEL: You, sir.

KLUGE: And you did this without consulting me, without my authority?

STUELPNAGEL: I couldn't get hold of you. I took the responsibility.

KLUGE: In the whole of my career—in the whole of my career—I have never known a General guilty of such disloyalty and such indiscipline.

STUELPNAGEL: Are you sure, sir? Are you quite sure? Did you never hear of a Field Marshal who agreed to a revolt and a new government under Beck? Who agreed without saying a word about it to his Fuehrer? Without warning him of his danger?

KLUGE: Are you threatening me, General?

STUELPNAGEL: I'm appealing to you, appealing to your common sense. I want to win you over, to get you to save Germany tonight. I am trying to show you that there is nothing in France to hinder you, that the army is anxious to follow you.

KLUGE: I'm beginning to understand. You need a Field Marshal to win over the army. But you will be leading the revolt. The Marshal is only a means to an end.

STUELPNAGEL: Sir, until I came here, I was sure that Hitler was dead. I believed that Beck had taken control, that he was leading the revolt and that you were with him. I was only a subordinate in the background.

KLUGE: And to force me to agree you started a *putsch* in Paris.

STUELPNAGEL: You gave your word to Beck.

KLUGE: I see your scheme clearly enough: it was to tie my hands. You started a *putsch* to force my hand.

HOFACKER: Field Marshal, for the sake of Germany, for the sake of the Germany that Beck died for tonight, will you please . . .

KLUGE: That was your intention, to force my hand.

STUELPNAGEL (*with light contempt*):
                I made a mistake. I realise that now. It was a mistake to expect you to keep your word.

KLUGE: General von Blumentritt, get on the telephone and order Boineberg to release the prisoners from Fresnes at once.

LINSTOW: You can't do that, sir. Boineberg is not in his office. All the garrison will be out on duty. You won't be able to get in touch with them until after midnight.

KLUGE: This has ruined everything. It's worse than a breach of discipline. No one in the whole of France will be safe any more. In Paris, in Normandy, in the hospital where Rommel lies—everywhere Himmler and the Gestapo will be hunting their prey.

STUELPNAGEL: How can they except through you?

KLUGE: You have betrayed your fellow officers to the gangsters.

STUELPNAGEL: But not if these gangsters are kept in prison.

KLUGE: Hitler is alive. The Gestapo must be released.

LINSTOW: You mean it's better to hunt with the hounds than run with the hare?

KLUGE: The Gestapo must be released. We can't afford a rebellion. They must be released.

LINSTOW: They must be released so that our fellow officers may be hanged.

HOFACKER: They must be released to complete the betrayal of Germany.

KLUGE: Gentlemen, this discussion is at an end.

STUELPNAGEL: The Field Marshal has chosen his path.

KLUGE: I choose the soldier's path—the path of duty.

STUELPNAGEL: Field Marshal, for your own self-respect, don't lurk behind a facade of morality.

KLUGE: It is my duty to remain faithful to my oath.
(*Linstow laughs. At a gesture from Stuelpnagel the three officers from Paris put on their hats and stand to attention before Kluge.*)

KLUGE: General, the orders I am about to give are very painful to me but they must be carried out. First, I order you to go forthwith to Paris and release General Albrecht and all the S.S. and S.D.

STUELPNAGEL: It shall be done, sir.

KLUGE: Second, I must relieve you of your command. From midnight you will cease to be Military Governor of France. I shall send my report to Hitler tomorrow. Goodnight, gentlemen.
(*The three salute and turn to leave. Linstow, Hofacker and Stuelpnagel exit slowly. Kluge goes after them and recalls Stuelpnagel.*)

KLUGE: Stuelpnagel.

STUELPNAGEL: Yes?

KLUGE: I'd like a word with you alone, please. Come out this way.
                (*Kluge and Stuelpnagel move out to terrace.*)

Scene 4—Exterior. Terrace. Studio. Night.

KLUGE: Stuelpnagel, if I were in your place . . .

STUELPNAGEL: I find that difficult to imagine . . .

KLUGE: If I were you I'd change into civilian clothes and disappear in Paris. The Americans will be there before the end of the month.

STUELPNAGEL: Gunther von Kluge, I pity you. I pity you with all my heart.
                (*Stuelpnagel exits. Kluge goes into château.*)

Interior, château. Studio. Night.
                (*Kluge enters from garden.*)

KLUGE: Blumentritt, have you ever been in debt?

BLUMENTRITT: In debt?

KLUGE: Yes.

BLUMENTRITT: No. At least I've never had a debt of any importance.

KLUGE: Two and a half years ago I was a good deal in debt.

BLUMENTRITT: How much?

KLUGE: A quarter of a million marks.

BLUMENTRITT: Yes?

KLUGE: I was in great trouble. I had to go to Hitler. He gave me a cheque to cover the whole amount.
                (*Silence.*)
                General, send a telegram to Hitler in my name congratulating him on his escape.

ACT III

Scene 1—Military Governor's Office.
We are back at the Military Governor's office in the Hotel Majestic in Paris.
It is 8.45 in the morning, Sunday, 23rd July. Countess Else von Dietlof
casts a last look at the contents of the steel cabinet, then locks it and puts

the key in her handbag on the table. At that moment General Albrecht comes in without knocking.

ELSE: General.

ALBRECHT: Good morning, Countess.

ELSE: What are you doing here?

ALBRECHT: Business, Countess, business.

ELSE: May I ask whom your business concerns?

ALBRECHT: The staff, Countess, the staff.

ELSE: They won't be here until nine o'clock.

ALBRECHT: What do you mean?

ELSE: The staff officers.

ALBRECHT: That's what I thought. But you're staff, aren't you?

ELSE: Why do you want to see me?
               (*Albrecht sits at desk.*)

ALBRECHT: For a few minutes. If you're not too busy. Yes, I'd like a few words—off the record—while we wait for the new Governor.

ELSE: What is it you want to talk about?

ALBRECHT: Several things. This office, for example.

ELSE: You mean you want to talk to me about my work?

ALBRECHT: Yes, and about your health and so forth. You got up very early this morning and you worked late last night.

ELSE: Yes, I work day and night. Isn't life hard?

ALBRECHT: Did you find it cold so early in the morning?

ELSE: Cold—in Paris in July?

ALBRECHT: Well, I just thought, passing through your office, that you must have found it cold: you've been burning a great deal of paper in the stove.

ELSE: Yes—but not because of the cold.

ALBRECHT: Then why?

ELSE: To save you trouble.

ALBRECHT: I don't follow.

ELSE: It's quite simple. If I don't burn them, then they get taken to Gestapo headquarters by the cleaning women.

ALBRECHT: Ooo! Were the papers you burnt as dangerous as all that?

ELSE: They were pretty dangerous.

ALBRECHT: Dangerous to whom? Not to General Stuelpnagel?

ELSE: You know well enough there were never any papers in this office in any way dangerous to General Stuelpnagel.

ALBRECHT: It really is a pleasure to cross swords with you. To whom, then, were the papers so dangerous?

ELSE: To you, sir.

ALBRECHT: To me?

ELSE: Yes, you see the papers I burnt were carbon copies of the report to Herr Himmler of what happened on Thursday night. They told how the S.S. and S.D. —officers and men—just surrendered, made no effort to resist arrest. It was all over in a few moments. Then how the army was overjoyed at the thought of destroying the Gestapo and only too disappointed that they had no excuse to shoot. And to crown it all, when the order for release came, every one of you refused to leave your cells ·in case you were treated by your own methods and 'shot while trying to escape'. You all had to be pushed out. There never was a more comic despatch. I burnt everything except the top copies to Himmler and the Fuehrer—I thought it would save the Gestapo embarrassment.

ALBRECHT: Well, I must admit your sarcasm shows spirit, Countess, and I admire that. But I didn't come here for jokes. I have questions to ask. An emergency enquiry begins today.

ELSE: An emergency enquiry?

ALBRECHT: Into what happened in Berlin and Paris. Have you heard about Stuelpnagel?

ELSE: What?

ALBRECHT: As you know he'd been recalled to Berlin, and on the way he tried to shoot himself but bungled it and shot out his eyes. But he will live.

ELSE: God, my poor General.

ALBRECHT: You were fond of him?

ELSE: 'Were'? I still am. I've been with him for three years. He's one of the finest men I've ever known.

ALBRECHT: Did you know he was involved in the plot to murder the Fuehrer?

ELSE: The General involved? Is that what you want to talk about? You don't know him, that's obvious. Assume for the moment that he was involved in the plot, do you imagine that he would dream of involving any woman who worked for him? He looked after me like a father.

ALBRECHT: When he was taken to the hospital at Verdun, the S.S. Hospital, he was operated on. As you may know, some men begin talking under anaesthetic, they start naming people . . .

ELSE: My God. Couldn't they let him die?

ALBRECHT: Dead men don't talk—which is a disadvantage. Not that it takes much to make a blind man talk.

ELSE: Herr Albrecht, don't be more disgusting than you can help.

ALBRECHT: Oh come, now, you really have got a lot to learn. I'm far more sentimental than most of the Gestapo.

ELSE: Have you any more questions to ask or have you finished?

ALBRECHT: Finished this conversation, you mean?

ELSE: I have work to do.

ALBRECHT: Oh, then we must stop . . . unless you feel like doing something to save Caisar von Hofacker.

ELSE (*catching her breath*):
What do you know?

ALBRECHT: I think everything there is to know.

ELSE: How?

ALBRECHT: That little French girl who's the maid in your hotel—you know, the one who makes the beds— she works for us, too.

ELSE: I love him, I love him with all my soul.

ALBRECHT: Soul is a mere metaphor. And as you know it's the body that counts.

ELSE: Yes, the body has its place—the body that's so
               vulnerable. Is he in danger?

ALBRECHT: You should know. Indeed, it's possible that you too
               will be invited to Berlin and persuaded to talk.

ELSE: Herr Albrecht, you won't frighten me that way.
               (*Else moves into Countess's office, followed by Albrecht.*)

Scene 2—Countess's Office. Int. Studio. Day.

ALBRECHT: Well, then, returning to this soul business. What
               would you do for von Hofacker if you had the
               chance?

ELSE: What's going on in your mind?

ALBRECHT: Have you heard the news from Normandy this
               morning?

ELSE: No. I haven't been able to think of the fighting.

ALBRECHT: The front has broken. The British and the Americans
               are pouring through.

ELSE: No.

ALBRECHT: They will be in Paris within the month. Nevertheless,
               the final defeat of Germany will not be an easy
               matter; the war can go on for months yet—long
               enough for Himmler to take care of the officers who
               have committed treason.

ELSE: They've counted the cost. They know the worst.

ALBRECHT: Know the worst? No one knows the worst that man
               is capable of.

ELSE: One can only die once.
               (*Else moves into Military Governor's office, followed by
               Albrecht.*)

Scene 3—Military Governor's office. Int. Studio. Day.

ALBRECHT: True, true, but when will the traitors be allowed to
               die, that is the question. By the time they are ready
               for the hangman, nobody will recognise them. They
               won't look like men—and their minds won't be
               human either.

ELSE: I think you're the devil.

ALBRECHT: Oh, Countess, you flatter me. Very well, then, let
               us strike a bargain.

ELSE: A bargain?

ALBRECHT: You know—Mephistopheles.

ELSE: What sort of bargain?

ALBRECHT: The emergency enquiry into the treason plot begins today. Himmler will conduct it in Berlin. I am in charge here; it's more than likely that the evidence in Berlin against Caisar von Hofacker is enough to have him arrested and taken there. So far there has been no such order but it can come any minute, and I have enough evidence here in Paris.

ELSE: I doubt that there can be any documentary evidence against him.

ALBRECHT: The record of his journeys is enough to condemn him.

ELSE: The record of his journeys? Is that all?

ALBRECHT: That, together with the people he visited. Beck, Witzleben, Goerdeler, Stauffenberg, Rommel.

ELSE: Why are you so interested in Colonel von Hofacker?

ALBRECHT: Did I say I was interested in him? Apart, that is, from a policeman's normal interest? No, I've no interest in him. My interest is in you. I'm proposing a bargain to you.

ELSE: And that means that you are prepared to sell the evidence you have against him?

ALBRECHT: Yes. In a few minutes General Blumentritt will be here to begin his work as Military Governor. I shall talk to him. Then, if you come down to the office there'll be a leave pass waiting for Colonel von Hofacker. He can use it to disappear. He can go to Switzerland. Isn't that a splendid offer?

ELSE: What if his arrest is ordered from Berlin?

ALBRECHT: Ah, if that order comes before he leaves here, then it's all over. I won't be able to lift a finger.

ELSE: Yes, I see. It's a strange offer coming from you, but of course it's not a gift, is it? What's the other half of the bargain?

ALBRECHT: I want a little pleasure before I leave Paris.

ELSE: Even though Adolf Hitler is finished?

ALBRECHT: Because Adolf Hitler is finished. What do you know about Hitler? You and your whole clique of officers and snobs and aristocrats who thought you could keep him under control? I was a child in the First World War, the son of a worker who was killed. I grew up through the long years of the blockade when German mothers were killing their unborn children and dying from hunger. Then came inflation and the failure of the mark, when five million marks in the morning and ten million marks in the afternoon couldn't buy a loaf of bread. And the whole of bloody Europe spending and guzzling while we young men tramped the streets without work, without hope, our bellies rumbling with hunger and aching with shame. And then came Hitler and National Socialism, the hope of the Reich. He gave work to everyone. He put food into starving mouths. He put boots on children's bare feet. And he made Europe tremble. We were revenged for the years we had spent in the dust. To me Hitler was a god. And now all that is ending. The saviour is facing defeat. His regime is ending.

ELSE: And because his regime is ending?

ALBRECHT: I want my own little revenge on all these blue-blooded bastards with 'von' in front of their names who stabbed him in the back. I want a night with a Countess of ancient German lineage. I'll sell you Caisar von Hofacker for that Else von Dietlof. The price of his freedom is that you come to me tonight.

ELSE: You must be mad.

ALBRECHT: I wouldn't say so. Well, is it a bargain?
(*She nods her head.*)
Ooo, that isn't enough. I want to hear you say 'I'll come to you tonight, Karl.'

ELSE: If he leaves Paris a free man.

ALBRECHT: That's fair enough. If he leaves Paris free. Well?

ELSE: I . . . I . . . I . . . will come to you . . . tonight, Karl.

ALBRECHT: Countess, I'll open your eyes tonight.
(*Else exits.*)

Scene 4—Countess's office. Int. Studio, Day.
          (*Else at desk. Blumentritt enters.*)

BLUMENTRITT: Good morning, Countess.

ELSE: Good morning, General.

BLUMENTRITT: I shall depend on you a good deal in my present job.

ELSE: I shall be in my office if you want me, General.

BLUMENTRITT: I'm expecting the staff officers soon. When they arrive, will you come in too?

ELSE: Here are the keys to General Stuelpnagel's files.
          (*As she takes the keys out of her handbag, Blumentritt sees that she has a revolver.*)

BLUMENTRITT: Thank you. I see you, too, carry a revolver.

ELSE (*putting the revolver back in her bag*):
          Just a small one, sir, in case of trouble . . . at night.
          (*Blumentritt goes into Military Governor's office.*)

Scene 5—Military Governor's office. Int. Studio. Day.

ALBRECHT: Good morning, General.

BLUMENTRITT: Ah, I see you're here before me, General Albrecht.

ALBRECHT: General Blumentritt, I would like to discuss things with you unofficially and on a friendly basis.

BLUMENTRITT: What is it you propose to discuss?

ALBRECHT: General Blumentritt, Himmler telephoned me last night. You heard that the Russians have broken through? Himmler is beginning to think that it's time to bring the war to an end.

BLUMENTRITT: Himmler? Are you surprised?

ALBRECHT: Surprise is not the word for it. Until last night I thought I was on dry land.

BLUMENTRITT: And then you felt it sink beneath you.

ALBRECHT: You and I must strike a bargain.

BLUMENTRITT: A bargain? What is it you propose?

ALBRECHT: This is what I propose. I'll play down any evidence against your staff here in Paris—on condition that you help the S.S. and the Gestapo get out of here with the garrison before the Americans and the British arrive.

BLUMENTRITT: I see. That's the bargain.

ALBRECHT: It's a fair one.

BLUMENTRITT: But Field Marshal Kluge has already ordered me to allow the Gestapo to question all the staff and to send their reports to Himmler. The Gestapo have their own way of asking questions, I'm told.

ALBRECHT: This questioning will be carried out in your office and not at Gestapo headquarters. You yourself can be present to prevent any unfair pressure.

BLUMENTRITT: But what about Field Marshal Kluge?

ALBRECHT: Between you and me, General, the Fuehrer has no faith in him. Hitler wants his blood. I'm happy to say, however, that there is no shred of evidence against him here in Paris. Unhappily I can't say the same for Stuelpnagel and his staff.

BLUMENTRITT: Poor Stuelpnagel.

ALBRECHT: I can do nothing for him.

BLUMENTRITT: Are there any others in immediate danger?

ALBRECHT: Of course there are. Beck's papers—and Goerdeler's too—have fallen intact into Himmler's hands. I must say, General, that it's typical of you regular army types to put everything down on paper—to write the battle-order, as it were—and then keep it. There is only one place—only one mark you— where there are no papers to be found.

BLUMENTRITT: Where?

ALBRECHT: Here in Paris. We searched high and low and found nothing. And I can tell you exactly why. A woman looked after them.

BLUMENTRITT: A woman with a revolver in her handbag. Is she under suspicion?

ALBRECHT: We shall see, but your greatest danger is Caisar von Hofacker. The papers in Berlin are enough for his life. He was the ringleader in the West . . .

BLUMENTRITT: But there's been no order—

ALBRECHT: It can come any minute.

BLUMENTRITT: You and he were hardly friends . . .

ALBRECHT: I said we should have to bridge the gulf between the Gestapo and the army, and von Hofacker is the key to everything. If he's arrested and made to talk, every single one of you will be implicated— every single one.

BLUMENTRITT: I see. You're being even more generous than I expected . . . How is it to be done?

ALBRECHT: He has leave due to him. You must give him a pass, he can disappear.

BLUMENTRITT: It shall be done immediately.
              (*Presses bell on desk.*)
              Yes, this is your day all right, yours and the Gestapo's.
              (*Else stands at the door.*)

ELSE: General, Colonel von Hofacker and Colonel von Linstow are here.

BLUMENTRITT: Thank you, Countess. Ask them to come in, and, Countess, I would like you to remain to hear what I have to say.

ELSE (*to the two Colonels*):
              Will you come in, please?
              (*The two Colonels enter and salute.*)

BLUMENTRITT: Please sit down, Countess. Colonel von Hofacker, Colonel von Linstow, this morning I intend to go to every office in the hotel and have a word with the staff individually. I have an order to give that will be bitter to you all. I asked you to meet me here because you were both on the personal staff of my friend Stuelpnagel. As a reprisal for the plot, and to prevent any further betrayal, Reichmarshal Himmler has been placed at the head of the German home forces. It is he, too, who is conducting the emergency enquiry into the plot. The enquiry in France will be conducted by General Albrecht.

ALBRECHT: General Blumentritt, when I spoke to Stuelpnagel yesterday, his mind was crystal clear. He admitted he knew of the plans made by the traitor Beck, but insisted that he had kept that knowledge to himself to avoid endangering any member of his staff. I know Stuelpnagel, and I am prepared to believe him. Therefore I hope that the enquiry in Paris can be formal and brief. But you understand, if orders come from Berlin to arrest anyone—the game will be up.

BLUMENTRITT: Any questions?
(*Throughout this the Colonels stand silently.*)
Very well.

ALBRECHT: General, there is one more order you have to give to your staff.

BLUMENTRITT: It's an order I find more than distasteful. Since 1933 the right to maintain the army salute has meant a great deal to us; it is part of our tradition. Now the army's independence is to cease. This is a bitter moment—but something far more bitter is about to descend on us; our united Germany is being faced with dissolution and defeat. In the face of this there is something more important to us than trying to hold on to a symbol, which is all our salute is. We must maintain to the end that most important discipline, obedience to command even at the moment of defeat. Gentlemen.
(*The men stand to attention.*)
I give you now the army's new salute: Heil Hitler! (*Albrecht first and then the two Colonels repeat quietly 'Heil Hitler'. Albrecht and Blumentritt turn to leave the room. Albrecht goes. Blumentritt stops at Colonel von Hofacker's side.*)

BLUMENTRITT: Colonel von Hofacker, I understand you have two weeks' leave due. I'm arranging for you to take it immediately . . . Countess, the pass for the Colonel will be in the office on the ground floor. My friend, Albrecht, suggests that you make haste. You can go immediately.
(*Exit Blumentritt.*)
(*The two Colonels look at each other.*)

HOFACKER: Heil Hitler—the final humiliation.

LINSTOW: Blumentritt has spirit. He was risking his life by saying what he did. He managed to invest even our shame with some dignity.

HOFACKER: I understand von Blumentritt. But what about Albrecht?

ELSE: Caisar, you heard what the Governor said. The sooner you leave here the better.

HOFACKER: I certainly don't understand him.

LINSTOW: He wants to save us—a short formal enquiry.

HOFACKER: But do you believe him?

LINSTOW: Blumentritt does.

HOFACKER: He must know something that we don't.

LINSTOW: Unless there's been a sudden conversion.

HOFACKER: I wonder what he has up his sleeve this time.

LINSTOW: Perhaps Thursday's events frightened him. You'd never have dreamt that the boys were so anxious to have a go at the Gestapo.

HOFACKER: There's more to it than that. He has some personal advantage in view.

LINSTOW: He gave you a pretty good hint to get out of here fast.

HOFACKER: Perhaps that's all a trap.

LINSTOW: But Blumentritt's working with him. They've struck some sort of bargain.

HOFACKER: Or he's playing some game without Blumentritt realising it.

LINSTOW: Anyway, you needn't worry—it's all right for you.

HOFACKER: What do you mean?

LINSTOW: You go on leave this morning.

ELSE: Hans, please . . .

HOFACKER: I haven't made up my mind to go.

ELSE: Are you out of your mind?

HOFACKER: To be arrested now would be some relief.

ELSE: Stop talking such romantic nonsense.

LINSTOW: Oh God, I'd give anything to be at the front.

HOFACKER: There is no front. It's broken, as Rommel said it would.

LINSTOW: Everything's breaking. The whole thing's a shambles.

ELSE: Caisar.

LINSTOW (*breaking out*): A shambles. We are not soldiers any more but a bundle of broken dolls.

ELSE: Caisar.

LINSTOW: Look at us. Claus Stauffenberg couldn't even wait
               to finish his job properly. Stuelpnagel can't even
               shoot straight, and three days ago I couldn't shoot
               Kluge because I hadn't got the guts. The officer
               corps is a shambles. We'll all go to our death
               chanting 'Mein Fuehrer, Adolf Hitler! Sieg Heil!
               Sieg Heil!'
               (*Else helps Linstow to window seat. Hofacker exits.
               Else exits.*)

Scene 6—Countess's office. Int. Studio. Day.

ELSE: Caisar, you heard what the Governor said. The
               sooner you leave here the better. I can bring the
               pass to the station if you go now to pack. There's
               a train from the Gare de l'Est at ten o'clock.

HOFACKER: I haven't made up my mind to go.

ELSE: The Governor has arranged everything.

HOFACKER: Leave is not obligatory.

ELSE: Don't be so foolish.

HOFACKER: I must have time to think.

ELSE: You have everything except time. No one has time
               any more except the Gestapo. Caisar, you heard
               the Governor's warning. Saving your life can be a
               matter of minutes now. And every second counts.

HOFACKER: I am responsible. I brought Stuelpnagel and his
               staff into this.

ELSE: Saying that won't help Stuelpnagel.

HOFACKER: He is blind and in the Gestapo's hands.

ELSE: Do you want to be arrested so that you can testify
               against him?

HOFACKER: It is my duty to take my share of the punishment
               along with the others.

ELSE: Don't you see that if they catch you, things will be
               far worse for the rest of the staff?

HOFACKER: Do you think I couldn't remain silent under torture?

ELSE: Are you so unsure of yourself that you have to
               prove it?

HOFACKER: No, no. It isn't that at all.

ELSE: Caisar, the minutes are passing. Our minds are confused.

HOFACKER: Yes. Everyone is in danger. That's why I can't run away to safety.

ELSE: Don't be so selfish and so cruel. Don't make things worse. Come with me now.

HOFACKER: Else, my dear, I have no right to go.

ELSE: No right?

HOFACKER: I have no right to safety, no right to flee from pain. I must stay to atone for some of Germany's shame.

ELSE: You have no right to throw away the lives of other people.

HOFACKER: I can't help that. I must go through torture to death, with Stuelpnagel and the rest. I've got to go through it all. I have no right to life.

ELSE: You have no right to kill yourself. Your life has cost too much. Too much has been promised, too much has been sacrificed.

HOFACKER: Else, what have you done? Are you responsible for Albrecht? Have you sold yourself to that swine? Answer me, answer me. Was that the price for my life?
(Hofacker catches hold of her and shakes her.)

ELSE: Caisar, this is no time for hysteria.

HOFACKER: So it's true, then? It's true? You can't deny it. God, it only needed this. We have betrayed everything, betrayed the Corps, betrayed Germany and Europe, and betrayed our honour, too, our personal loyalties. To be alive now is an act of treason.
(The air raid warnings sound high and long. Linstow enters hurriedly.)

LINSTOW: You still here? They're overhead. No one will be allowed out in the street.

HOFACKER: No one will be allowed to leave the building. There is plenty of time now. My choice stands.

ELSE: Hans, he's got to go.

LINSTOW: Don't be a fool. I'll try and get you some transport.
(Linstow exits.)

ELSE: I'll get your pass . . .
               (*Else exits. Hofacker goes into Military Governor's office.*)

Scene 7—Military Governor's office. Int. Studio. Day.
               (*Hofacker enters, stands facing window, turns and goes to
               map table, back to window. Albrecht enters Countess's office.
               Stands in doorway, Military Governor's office.*)

ALBRECHT: Colonel von Hofacker.

HOFACKER: General. (*He stands to attention.*)

ALBRECHT: I have just had orders by telephone to arrest you.

HOFACKER: Of course. I expected that.

ALBRECHT: You had plenty of time to get away.

HOFACKER: Too much. It's a pity you didn't come half an hour
               ago.

ALBRECHT: This is none of my doing. The order came from
               Berlin.

HOFACKER: Half an hour ago I had just one thing left that
               I could believe in. I have nothing to believe in now.

ALBRECHT: That's what we're all up against.

HOFACKER: I am the only one under arrest, I hope.

ALBRECHT: Linstow was arrested downstairs.

HOFACKER: Linstow, that must be a mistake.

ALBRECHT: We shall see. Have you a revolver?

HOFACKER: In my digs.

ALBRECHT: Poison?

HOFACKER: None.

ALBRECHT: False teeth?

HOFACKER: My teeth are my own.

ALBRECHT: I'm not fooling. Several have escaped by swallowing
               their false teeth.

HOFACKER: Escape is not part of my programme.

ALBRECHT: You romantic fool. Do you really believe there's any
               meaning to pain? Come on.

Scene 8—Staircase.
               *Countess Else von Dietlof enters as General Albrecht and
               Colonel von Hofacker come through the door.*

ELSE: Colonel von Hofacker, here is your pass to Berlin.

ALBRECHT: Countess, the Colonel is going to Berlin all right, but he doesn't need a pass.

(General Albrecht and Colonel von Hofacker pass her. Hofacker ignores her. They are joined by two S.S. men when they reach the top of the stairs. Countess Else von Dietlof leans over balcony.)

THE END

SELECTED BIBLIOGRAPHY OF THE WRITINGS OF SAUNDERS LEWIS

WITH REFERENCES TO ORIGINAL TITLES AND EDITIONS

PLAYS:

The Eve of St. John, The Welsh Outlook Press, Newtown, 1921.
Gwaed yr Uchelwyr (*Noble Blood*), Cardiff, 1922.
Buchedd Garmon (*The Life of Saint Germanus*), Aberystwyth, 1937.
Amlyn ac Amig (*Amlyn and Amig*), Aberystwyth, 1940.
Blodeuwedd, Gee, Denbigh, 1948.
Eisteddfod Bodran: Gan Bwyll (*The Bodran Eisteddfod: Take It Easy*), Gee, Denbigh, 1952.
Siwan a Cherddi Eraill (*Siwan and Other Poems*), Llyfrau'r Dryw, Llandybie, 1956.
'Gymerwch Chi Sigaret? (*Have a Cigarette?*), Llyfrau'r Dryw, Llandybie, 1956.
Brad (*Treason*), Llyfrau'r Dryw, Llandybie, 1958.
Esther: Serch yw'r Doctor (*Esther: Love's the Doctor*), Llyfrau'r Dryw, Llandybie, 1960.
Cymru Fydd (*The Wales to Be*), Llyfrau'r Dryw, Llandybie, 1967.
Problemau Prifysgol (*The Problems of a University*), Llyfrau'r Dryw, Llandybie, 1968.
Yn y Trên (*On the Train*), in the periodical *Barn*, August 1965, pp. 214–276 (first performed on the Welsh Home Service, 8th May 1965).

UNPUBLISHED PLAYS:

Excelsior, first performed on BBC Wales TV, 1st March 1962.
Y Cyrnol Chabert (*Colonel Chabert*), first performed on the Welsh Home Service, 17th December 1968.
Branwen, first performed on BBC Wales TV, 1st March 1971.

TRANSLATIONS:

Molière, *Le Médecin malgré lui* (*Doctor er ei Waethaf*), Wrexham, 1924.
Samuel Beckett's *En Attendant Godot* (*Wrth Aros Godot*), University of Wales Press, 1970.

CRITICAL WORKS:

A School of Welsh Augustans, Wrexham, 1924.
Williams Pantycelyn, London, 1927.
Ceiriog: Yr Artist yn Philistia, I (*Ceiriog: The Artist in Philistia, I*), Aberystwyth, 1929.
Ieuan Glan Geirionydd, University of Wales Press, 1931.

Braslun o Hanes Llenyddiaeth Gymraeg hyd 1535 (An Outline of the History of Welsh Literature to 1535), University of Wales Press, 1932.
Daniel Owen: Yr Artist yn Philistia, II (Daniel Owen: The Artist in Philistia, II), Aberystwyth, 1936.
Is There an Anglo-Welsh Literature? Guild of Graduates of the University of Wales, 1939. Pamphlet.
Ysgrifau Dydd Mercher (Wednesday Articles), Aberystwyth, 1945.
Gramadegau'r Penceirddiaid (The Grammars of the Traditional Poets), University of Wales Press, 1967.

NOVELS:

Monica, Aberystwyth, 1930.
Merch Gwern Hywel (The Daughter of 'Gwern Hywel'), Llyfrau'r Dryw, Llandybie, 1964.

POETRY:

Byd a Betws (The World and The Church), Aberystwyth, 1941.

POLITICS, ETC.:

The Case for a Welsh National Development Council, Caernarfon, 1933.
The Local Authorities and Welsh Industries, Caernarfon, 1934.
Y Frwydr dros Ryddid (The Battle for Freedom), Caernarfon, 1935.
Why We Burnt the Bombing School (Paham y Llosgasom yr Ysgol Fomio), Caernarfon, 1937.
Canlyn Arthur (In the Steps of Arthur), Aberystwyth, 1938.
Cymru Wedi'r Rhyfel (Wales after the War), Aberystwyth, 1942.
Plaid Cymru Gyfan (A Party for the Whole of Wales), Caernarfon, 1942.
Y Newyn yn Ewrop (The Famine in Europe), Gee, Denbigh, 1943.
Tynged yr Iaith (The Fate of the Language), BBC Publications, 1962.

EDITED:

Straeon Glasynys (The Stories of Glasynys), Aberystwyth, 1943.
Crefft y Stori Fer (The Craft of the Short Story), Aberystwyth, 1949.

SOME ENGLISH ARTICLES ON SAUNDERS LEWIS

'Welsh Profile, 4', Saunders Lewis, *The Welsh Review*, Vol. V, No. 4, Winter 1946, p. 258.
'Sketches for a Portrait', P. Mansell Jones; 'Saunders Lewis', R. O. F. Wynne, *Saunders Lewis, ei feddwl a'i waith (Saunders Lewis, his Thought and work)*, ed. Pennar Davies, Gwasg Gee, 1950, p. 18 and p. 28.
'Saunders Lewis', Idris Foster, *Dock Leaves*, Vol. III, No. 8, Summer 1952, p. 5.
'Profile—Saunders Lewis', *The Observer*, 8th August 1954.
'Saunders Lewis, the Dramatist', Emyr Edwards, *Wales*, No. 2, October 1958, p. 39.

'The Poetry of Saunders Lewis', Pennar Davies, *Poetry Wales*, Vol. V, No. 1, Summer 1969, p. 5.

'Saunders Lewis for a Nobel Prize?', *The London Times*, 17th September, 1970.

'Saunders Lewis', *The Welsh Extremist*, Ned Thomas, Gollancz, London 1971, p. 52.